POCKETBOOK POLITICS

POLITICS AND SOCIETY IN TWENTIETH-CENTURY AMERICA

Series Editors

WILLIAM CHAFE, GARY GERSTLE, LINDA GORDON, AND JULIAN ZELIZER

Meg Jacobs

POCKETBOOK POLITICS

ECONOMIC CITIZENSHIP IN TWENTIETH-CENTURY AMERICA

PRINCETON UNIVERSITY PRESS   PRINCETON AND OXFORD

Copyright © 2005 by Princeton University Press
Published by Princeton University Press, 41 William Street, Princeton, New Jersey
08540
In the United Kingdom: Princeton University Press, 3 Market Place, Woodstock,
Oxfordshire OX20 1SY

ISBN: 0-691-08664-8

Library of Congress Cataloging-in-Publication Data

Jacobs, Meg, 1969–
Pocketbook politics : economic citizenship in twentieth-century America / Meg Jacobs.
p. cm.—(Politics and society in twentieth-century America)
Includes bibliographical references and index.
ISBN 0-691-08664-8 (alk. paper)
1. Income distribution—United States—History—20th century. 2. Purchasing power—
United States—History—20th century. 3. United States—Politics and
government—20th century. 4. Consumption (Economics)—United States—
History—20th century. 5. United States—Economic conditions—20th century.
I. Title. II. Series.

HC110.I5J3 2004
339.4'2'09730904—dc22   2004043418

British Library Cataloging-in-Publication Data is available

This book has been composed in Baskerville Typeface
Printed on acid-free paper. ∞
pup.princeton.edu
Printed in the United States of America

10 9 8 7 6 5 4 3 2 1

To Eric

Contents

Illustrations

Acknowledgments _____

FINISHING A BOOK is a great feeling, especially when the final act consists of expressing gratitude to all those who have made this accomplishment possible. There are no thanks great enough for Nelson Lichtenstein. As a mentor and friend he has no equal. Since the beginning of graduate school, he has always inspired me to go further. Even when I went too far and announced that I was writing a whole new book from scratch, he stood by me. His willingness to read draft after draft and have endless conversations about history and life is a testament to his generous soul. Julian Zelizer has also been a source of unending support. Our daily, almost hourly, e-mails make my days a lot more fun than they would otherwise be. I thank him not only for his enormous help on this project but also for his friendship and good humor. In a solitary profession, he is a constant companion.

One of the most valuable and incredibly time-consuming things writers do is give each other comments on their work. I am thankful to know so many people who not only were willing to give their time but also had so many useful insights. Michael Bernstein, Lisa Cody, Colin Gordon, Howell Harris, Ira Katznelson, Tom Stapleford, Landon Storrs, and Olivier Zunz kindly read the whole manuscript. For commenting on earlier drafts, I thank Rawi Abdelal, Howard Brick, Judith Stein, Joseph Tohill, Frank Trentmann, and the LA study group. I am particularly grateful to Margaret Willard, who read the whole manuscript not once, but twice. As readers for Princeton University Press, Daniel Horowitz and Anthony Badger offered helpful suggestions at an early stage, while my series editors, Gary Gerstle and Julian Zelizer, provided invaluable advice toward the end. Throughout the whole process at Princeton, Brigitta van Rheinberg gave me tremendous support.

I am fortunate to work at good places with generous resources and smart colleagues. At MIT, my colleagues provide intellectual stimulation combined with good humor. Pauline Maier read every page closely and caught mistakes no else did. She and Bob Fogelson gave me sage advice on the framing of this project. MIT has also been particularly generous, and I thank the dean's office for support at crucial stages. I also am grateful for the time I spent at Harvard Business School as a Newcomen Fellow. At Claremont McKenna College, Lisa Cody was a model colleague in every way. As a graduate student, I received a one-year Smithsonian fellowship, and the administrators were kind enough to let me stay on for a second year with a fellowship from the Harry S. Truman Library. The

Franklin D. Roosevelt Library, the Hagley Museum and Library, and the Rockefeller Archives also provided helpful support. At the University of Virginia, Brian Balogh, Olivier Zunz, Stephen Schuker, and Martha Derthick all helped to nourish this project and have continued to offer guidance. I thank student researchers Chris Agee, Jennifer Conroy, Anna Kuperstein, and Julian Suchman. I owe special thanks to Shane Hamilton, who worked almost as hard as I did in the final months double-checking every quote and footnote.

While it is important to be understood in a book, it is more important to be understood in life. For that great gift, I thank Anna Aizer, Alison Clarke, Jenny Eisenpresser, Cary Federman, Joanne Freeman, Walter Friedman, and Shelley Nickles. I am especially grateful to Lisa Cody and Steve Pincus, who have helped me in life, in this book, and the whole world that lies in between. I also want to thank my in-laws, Roger, Gerda, Jane, and Eve, who remind me that life is more important than books.

I come from a family of shoppers and businessmen. My mother, Eleanore, and my three sisters, Deborah, Lynne, and Katie, have made me see as clearly as anyone I write about in these pages exactly what a powerful woman at the marketplace and elsewhere looks like. I thank them for their hard-nosed, no-compromise attitude as well as for their general support of me from beginning to end. This book would not have been possible were it not for the inspiration from my father, Arthur, and his father, Sam, who each built successful businesses from nothing. My father, who died too young, and my grandfather, who lived to be very old, are testaments to what can be achieved with hard work, vision, and love from one's family. I hope that in some small way the effort that went into this book honors their memory.

Finally, there is Eric Goldberg, to whom this book is dedicated. Eric is my husband and my best friend. No one knows better than he what went into writing this book, and no one helped me more than he did. I am forever grateful for his line-by-line edits, his unending patience, and his never flagging confidence in me. And of course for his gift of Abigail. Spending time with them is the greatest joy of all.

POCKETBOOK POLITICS

Introduction _____

Economic Citizenship in the Twentieth Century

WAL-MART is the biggest retailer in the world. Its trademark slogan,
"Everyday Low Prices," draws shoppers in search of good deals on everything from diapers and dishes to DVDs. With more sales than its top five
competitors, Wal-Mart is hugely successful, but Sam Walton's low-price
strategy is hardly new. For over a century, mass retailers have used price
appeal to win customers and steal market shares. In 1909, when Edward
Filene's famous Boston Bargain Basement opened, immigrant Jewish,
Irish, and Italian women lined up around the block to buy a knockoff
dress for seventy-five cents or a stylish hat for fifty cents. Volume sales and
low profit margins allowed Filene's to charge the cheap prices that lured
tens of thousands of bargain hunters into the store. Rather than cater to
upper-class Boston matrons, Filene's was the first store to sell machine-
made dresses at prices that middle- and working-class women could afford.[1]

But, for all their low-price appeal, Filene's and Wal-Mart are worlds
apart. Wal-Mart has achieved its success by ruthlessly cutting costs and
paying rock-bottom wages, justifying those measures by the low prices it
offers. In contrast, Edward Filene and other reformers of the early twentieth century knew that bargains were not enough in an era defined by
inflation, limited budgets, and expanding consumer desires. For the
next half-century hundreds of strikes, demonstrations, and boycotts
were, in effect, protests against rising prices and inadequate income.
From the immigrant wage-earning shopgirls to the native-born white-
collar clerks, urban Americans flocked to Filene's and other department stores to get the best prices while they also fought for better wages
and workplace conditions. And when they were unable to afford the
abundant lifestyle they desired, they turned to the government to solve
their pocketbook problems.

Since Filene's era the question "How much does it cost?" has attracted attention not only from the nation's shoppers but also from
its statesmen. The twentieth-century American polity developed in response to that very consumer concern. From Woodrow Wilson to
Franklin Roosevelt to Richard Nixon, national politics turned on public
anger over the high cost of living. This book asks why these consumer
issues led to what this study calls "pocketbook politics," how these politics transformed modern government, and why they declined. It begins

with the explosion of prices at the turn of the century and ends with the arrival of the Great Inflation of the 1970s. Throughout this long era, the political dynamic between consumers' search for the best buy and reformers' efforts to redistribute wealth and power drove domestic politics and constituted a central strand of American liberalism.

Indeed, the twentieth-century ideology of economic citizenship, based on participation in the mass consumer economy, would become essential to the definition of modern liberalism itself. This was a departure from the reigning political ideology of the nineteenth century, which placed a premium on self-sufficiency and the virtues inherent in an America composed of millions of small producers. Farmers and artisans epitomized this producer ideology, but even wage earners cherished their sense of economic independence, as with those craft unions and mechanical societies that fostered pride in manual skill and autonomy in the world of shop-floor production. In the twentieth century, as the economy and society became increasingly organized around a new national mass consumer market, the means to consume became important not only for securing three square meals a day but more broadly as a marker of economic citizenship and full membership in the American polity. Consumption was replacing production as the foundation of American civic identity.

Yet the struggle to make ends meet, let alone purchase all the fancy goods on display in department stores, was an inescapable reality of the twentieth-century consumer economy. Its failure to generate what progressives called consumer "purchasing power" aggravated the manifest inequalities of modern industrial capitalism. Beginning with the great labor strikes of 1877, contemporaries feared that growing disparities of income and the rise of a new wage-earning class were subverting American notions of egalitarianism, civic involvement, and political liberty that had prevailed throughout the nineteenth century. So too did they come to fear that the purchasing-power problem emergent early in twentieth century was threatening a stable American social order and enduring democracy. Thus the question of how to provide Americans—from the shopgirls at Filene's to the skilled mechanics at Ford to the filing clerks, secretaries, and service workers of modern corporations—with the purchasing power to become full economic citizens would dominate much of the century's politics.

Pocketbook Politics

The fulfillment of twentieth-century economic citizenship would not be achieved without conflict. When Henry Ford introduced the moving assembly line in 1913, he revolutionized modern production. Within a few years, Ford squeezed two-thirds of the cost out of a Model T, vastly increased output, and managed to pay most male workers double the going rate.[2] But few other firms could easily adopt Ford's five-dollar day and low-price, high-volume strategy. While accelerating American economic productivity, the technological and business advances of the early twentieth century did not automatically lead to the cheaper prices and higher wages that would enable the masses to participate in the new consumer economy. Even the shopgirls who worked at Filene's and earned more than salesclerks at other stores found it hard to survive on eight dollars a week, let alone buy the goods they were selling. The gap between an ability to mass-produce an array of items and the ability of people to afford them was an inherent tension of the new consumer economy that would transform modern American politics.

This book aims to reperiodize reform in twentieth-century America. Rather than see the twentieth century as divided by distinct eras of political reform, we need to appreciate the continuities of a certain kind of American liberalism that transcends the chronological divisions of traditional political history. From the inflationary years of the early twentieth century through the inflation of the early 1970s, the "purchasing-power question" of what people could afford remained on the political agenda, regardless of the state of the economy or the policies pursued by Congress or the president. There were always competing social and economic issues vying for political attention, but for most of the twentieth century the purchasing power of the public was never far from the center of American politics.

"Purchasing power" was shorthand for redistributive economic policies designed to enable the working and middle classes to buy basic necessities and still have enough left over to shop at Filene's and even drive a Model T. This agenda, with its goal of redistributing wealth and income through government wage and price policies, resulted in a radical restructuring of American capitalism. In spite of the nation's deep commitment to a free market, the fact that so many people were unable to purchase the goods it offered made pocketbook policies popular across income, class, ethnicity, and region. Americans continued to define themselves by a number of other categories such as profession, gender, ethnic background, or residence. But the fact that every person was also a shopper made a consumer interest potentially powerful. In contrast to the narrow appeal to social solidarity mounted by the relatively small numbers of white male native-born trade unionists, a consumer ideology quickly spread among the immigrant masses, especially women, and attracted a broad spectrum of the middle and working classes.

The prominence of pocketbook politics casts doubt on the traditional view of twentieth-century American consumer society as profoundly depoliticizing. According to this point of view, the desire for material goods

led to a popular quest for individual material advancement, but only at
the cost of an oppositional consciousness and a turn away from a collective struggle for power. As early as 1906 the German sociologist Werner
Sombart declared that all American socialisms "have come to grief on the
shoals of roast beef and apple pie." If not everyone could obtain a high
standard of living, there was enough evidence of social mobility and economic advance to make those goals, and by extension the system of American capitalism, seem worthy. "As the material condition of the wage
worker has improved—and the increasing comfort of his way of life has
enabled him to savor the corrupting effects of material wealth," explained
Sombart, "so has he been impelled to love the economic system which has
shaped his fate." As late as the 1960s, New Left scholars similarly saw mass
consumption as the coffin of class consciousness. More recently, feminist,
labor, and cultural historians have examined how consumption has served
as a terrain for class and gender struggles. Yet New Left assumptions about
participation in the mass market bringing anomie, fragmentation, and the
decline of democracy endure. Writing almost one hundred years after
Sombart, historian William Leach laments that in the twentieth century,
the "democratizing [of] individual desire" displaced the democratizing of
"wealth or political or economic power." Selfish individualism and materialism, the argument has gone, undercut public mindedness, diluted class
solidarity, and insulated American society from radical politics.[3]

Yet for much of the twentieth century, a preoccupation with how much
things cost had a deeply politicizing effect on Americans as consumers.
While prices are ubiquitous and not inherently political, they became so
in response to the rising cost consciousness and state-building efforts of
the twentieth century. Early in the century, a confluence of historical de-
velopments made inflationary prices the subject of political debate.
Between 1870 and 1920, the percentage of Americans living in cities doubled to over fifty percent. By 1920, more people worked in factories than
on farms, and less than one-quarter of the workforce was self-employed.
At the same time, people were now purchasing basic necessities in the
market rather than producing them at home. These multiple forces of industrialization, urbanization, and the commercialization of daily life coincided with the rise of inflation as the new and defining characteristic of
the economy.[4] In this context, prices were a dominant index of living
standards. Over the next half century, prices then became a central political problem during the course of two world wars, when the rate of inflation reached double digits, and even during the Depression, when prices
fell slower than wages. These national crises enabled and necessitated a
radical expansion of government involvement in the economy through a
set of public policies and institutions to combat what contemporaries
throughout this decades-long era called the high cost of living.

Pocketbook politics, which began with housewives protesting inflation at the grass roots and continued with workers demanding more at the bargaining table and on picket lines, led to a powerful alliance of middle-class consumers and organized labor. That alliance supported the creation of a new mass-consumption political economy that challenged the traditional prerogative of businessmen to set wages and prices. For much of the century, Americans made demands as consumers with rights in the marketplace. A consumer was no longer someone who just purchased items for sale. Now he, or more likely she, shopped around, looked for bargains, and substituted cheaper products in an effort to stretch family dollars. At times she even took to the streets to protect her pocketbook. From the turn of the century through midcentury, precipitous price hikes often led to food riots, consumer boycotts, and rent strikes. Organized labor also embraced a consumer identity and insisted on a "living wage." Demands for higher pay were not new, but twentieth-century wage earners justified them on the basis of their right to an "American standard of living." Walter Lippmann, perhaps the most astute political writer of the Progressive Era, described what he saw as a rapidly spreading "consumer consciousness." In 1914 he wrote, "The real power emerging today in democratic politics is just the mass of people who are crying out against the 'high cost of living.' That is a consumer's cry." When shoppers started to question whether prices were reasonable or unreasonable, they began a line of inquiry that, according to Lippmann, "runs counter to the whole fabric of the old commercialism." "To talk about 'reasonable returns' is to begin an attack on industrialism which will lead far beyond the present imaginations of the people who talk about it. . . . Just where those words lead nobody knows."[5]

State-Building from the Bottom Up

Pocketbook politics were so powerful because they relied on a mutually reinforcing dynamic between the public and the government. Today, as over one hundred years ago, we are told that the consumer is the standard-bearer of the free market. But throughout much of the twentieth century, policymakers acted on behalf of the "consuming public" to regulate the nation's markets in the interests of ordinary citizens. Americans have experimented with many ways to regulate the economy, from nationalizing industry to setting up regulatory commissions to breaking up monopolies. In contrast, a community of purchasing-power progressives, whose story is told in these pages, supported giving ordinary people the necessary authority and institutional tools to monitor prices and set wages. The rise of economic citizenship in the twentieth century depended both on political elites who made policy and on ordinary men and women who took their votes and their protest to the streets, markets, and factories.

This book encourages a new way of studying state power by integrating popular politics and elite policymaking. The functioning of large administrative states can be understood only by exploring the ways that they legitimize their authority, which can include delegating power to citizens. Conversely, popular movements have succeeded in effecting change only to the extent that they win support at elite levels. Unlike most social historians who focus exclusively on consumers at the grass roots, *Pocketbook Politics* breaks new methodological ground by insisting on the centrality of national politics and the state in the nearly century-long fight to fulfill the American Dream of abundance.[6] We know a good deal about the business and culture of the mass market. We also know about the rise of the modern welfare state and postwar Keynesian tax-and-spend fiscal policies, which sought to smooth the rough edges of modern capitalism.[7] But we know less about the intersection of what consumer advocate Caroline Ware called "concrete daily economic experience" and economic policy-making. It was this powerful dialectic that Ware understood by her use of the phrase "economic citizenship."[8] Thus, this book combines political and social history, drawing on government documents and presidential records as well as on grassroots sources and popular periodicals, in order to show the dynamic interplay between the state and its citizenry over marketplace issues during the twentieth century.

The vision of economic citizenship that resulted was at once radical and conservative, full of reordering possibility and inherently limited. Americans did not develop the kind of welfare state that became common in many industrialized countries. Measured by European standards, the American welfare state comes up short, most obviously in its lack of national health insurance. Americans' commitment to private enterprise helps to explain this comparative weakness. But pocketbook politics led to regulation of the market by a variety of laws and institutions that promoted militant unionism, government price controls, and a Keynesian program of full employment. Through its support of a strong union movement and its ability to empower consumers to monitor prices during times of war and depression, the federal government intervened directly in the American economy, thereby undermining a nineteenth-century belief in limited government. Efforts to reform wages and prices had their own radical thrust that went to the heart of capitalism and sparked fierce debate. On one side, a reform coalition of ordinary Americans, mass retailers, and national politicians fought for laws and policies that promoted mass purchasing power. Opposing them were the millions of small businessmen and manufacturers who fiercely resisted this low-price, high-wage agenda that threatened to bankrupt them. Those policies gained acceptance because they were built on grassroots participation—what contemporaries termed democracy in action and I call state-building from the bottom up.

Precisely because they relied on popular mobilizations at factories and markets, these policies penetrated deep into society and the economy. A new political elite concerned about promoting mass purchasing power allied itself with a new industrial union movement, each providing the other with legitimacy and strength. By midcentury, massive unions represented one out of every three workers and created a set of powerful collective-bargaining institutions industrywide. Framing its demands in the language of purchasing power, the labor movement justified itself as the engine that would drive redistribution for the entire consuming public. The purchasing-power rhetoric also mobilized many organized consumer groups nationwide who supported the higher wages of workers and joined them in the fight for fair labor standards and for fair prices. Women of all classes and political leanings participated in a wide range of consumer movements, from Jewish mothers protesting beef prices on the Lower East Side, to Eleanor Roosevelt and other upper-class women wearing only union-made dresses, to hundreds of thousands of middle-class women in both world wars marching into neighborhood stores to enforce compliance with popular notions of fair prices. That widespread, popular mobilization represented a pervasive, and therefore threatening, regime to the nation's capitalists.

Mobilizing citizens was a necessity of modern statecraft and yet a potential source of instability; citizens, once empowered, could not always be controlled, and thus state-building from the bottom up was a double-edged sword. The fact that all Americans acted as consumers gave purchasing-power rhetoric its wide appeal. For politicians, the language of consumerism was a way to stitch together various groups with other interests, promising each sector a higher income. But Americans never saw themselves only or even primarily as consumers. And the inability to stop inflation made a diverse coalition of supporters difficult to sustain: in particular, consumers' desire for cheap prices ran up against labor's demands for higher wages. Since inflationary pressures from war to government spending to collective bargaining were endemic to the midcentury economy, those who were unorganized came to feel squeezed. Once labor's higher wages began to drive up the cost of living, mass unions started to lose their middle-class allies and even to alienate the skilled working-class elite who deeply resented the gains made by their less-skilled counterparts. When purchasing-power policies failed to deliver higher standards of living, apathy, resentment, and disenchantment were the result. This book explores the pocketbook politics—filled with hopes, fear, and tensions—and the new kind of American state that resulted.

From Department Stores to Departments of Government

Part 1, "The High Cost of Living and the Rise of Pocketbook Politics, 1900–1930," begins with the inflation of the early twentieth century that put these pocketbook politics powerfully on the agenda. It starts when millions of immigrants and middle-class Americans moved to the cities and confronted a new era of inflation that exploded during World War I. Inflation, as much as the lure of advertising or the desire for new consumer products, shaped Americans' experiences in the marketplace and made them feel uneasy and powerless. This generation saw monopolies and wasteful middlemen as the villains responsible for more than doubling the cost of daily living between 1900 and 1920. That impulse to point a finger was characteristic of the Progressive Era, when problems of modern life tended to be identified not as natural phenomena but rather as social problems that could be solved through rational, or at least political, means. Contemporary economists explained that inflation resulted from an expansion of the gold supply, but the public, seeking to politicize seemingly impersonal economic forces, blamed trusts and middlemen. The high cost of living resonated precisely because it was not just a problem of the urban poor, the unemployed, or the tenement dwellers; it affected everyone, especially the new white-collar middle classes living on fixed salaries. Walter Lippmann commented: "We hear a great deal about the class-consciousness of labor. My own observation is that in America today consumers' consciousness is growing very much faster." Lippmann understood that as the new mass market promised Americans a better life, they would begin to demand low prices, high wages, and better-quality products as a basic right.[9]

The massive inflation of World War I and the unprecedented decade of productivity that followed made mass purchasing power a pressing political issue. During the war, runaway prices threatened to erode living standards of millions of urban Americans, including wage earners upon whom production for national defense now depended. In that context, President Wilson legitimized the notion that Americans had basic rights as consumers and put the expanded wartime governmental authority behind what was popularly called "fair prices" and "living wages." Liberal policymakers shared with ordinary Americans the fear that rising prices were dangerously outstripping wages, threatening economic and political instability. The prosperity of the interwar years only intensified progressives' commitment to a purchasing-power agenda of high wages and low prices. As national production nearly doubled in the 1920s, labor leaders began to emphasize the pitfalls of underconsumption. According to this theory, low wages, or what Edward Filene called "counterfeit wages," presented just as big an obstacle to economic citizenship as high prices. Modern technology was accelerating production exponentially, but the failure to distribute these enormous numbers of goods remained an intractable issue, stubbornly defying the conventional wisdom that supply automatically creates its own demand. Without enough people able to purchase these goods, this group argued, the economy would collapse.

Part 2, "Purchasing Power to the People, 1930–1940," examines how this community of progressives transformed their agenda of mass purchasing power into a program of national recovery and reform during the Great Depression of the 1930s, pushing it from the margins to the center of political debate. As New Deal policymakers, they sponsored a distinctly American kind of statecraft to increase purchasing power through a set of state institutions, strong unions, and organized consumers. Since the budget of the federal government was so small, Keynesian spending was not available as a remedy, and thus reformers looked to other means to stimulate demand. In the early 1930s, they created a new government regime of institutions that mobilized workers and consumers to secure a low-price, high-wage economy. The salient success of their campaign came with the passage of the National Labor Relations Act in 1935, which gave workers the right to organize and engage in collective bargaining. The purchasing-power argument helped organized labor win middle-class support for this radical reform, aligning the interests of a strong union movement that insisted on higher wages and cheap prices with those of the rest of society.

As expansive and transforming as it was, the purchasing-power agenda contained inherent tensions. Three internal strains plagued the New Deal coalition of farmers, labor, and the middle class and made it politically vulnerable. The first stemmed from a conflict between urban residents' need for affordable food and farmers' need to earn a living. Like other citizens, farmers had imbibed the promises of the new marketplace. But for them fair prices meant high commodity prices. Though their numbers had dwindled since the nineteenth century, they retained a strong hold on political imagination, they had disproportionate representation in Congress, and their interests were promoted by a powerful lobbying organization. That was a particular problem for the New Deal Democratic Party, as its leaders understood that electoral success depended on winning the votes of both farmers and labor. Legislation and public policies that benefited certain groups of consumers therefore could work against the interests of other groups.

The second major tension existed between organized labor and the unorganized middle classes. The more success labor had in achieving high wages, the more consumers would have to pay for these gains in the form of higher prices. Moreover, the rising power of labor meant more than just higher wages for the blue-collar worker: unionization generated strikes, shortages, and challenges, in the factory and out, to traditional hierarchies of race, gender, ethnicity, and skill. Thus, the emerging clout of the semiskilled, multiethnic masses created the third major tension as the skilled native-born working-class elite recoiled at the advances being made at their expense. By the 1940s, the idea of a unified consumer interest, if it had ever existed, was ready to come apart at the seams.

Part 3, "The Evils of Inflation in War and Peace, 1940–1960," examines how wartime inflation enabled President Roosevelt to unite his coalition behind the drive for fair prices, reinforcing it with calls for patriotism. As Wilson had during World War I, FDR targeted runaway inflation as a threat to not only the production effort but also the preservation of democracy. Roosevelt, however, resorted to an even more sweeping program, the creation of a nationwide system of price controls and rationing. The policy of mandatory wartime controls, run by the Office of Price Administration (OPA), mobilized millions of housewives to enforce compliance in local communities. What made OPA so powerful was the support it received from unions, whose membership had grown by nearly 50 percent. Because patriotism demanded acquiescence and because unions had faith in the New Deal state, organized labor agreed to a wage freeze for the duration of the war. As they had also signed no-strike pledges, union leaders had little choice but to throw their weight behind price controls to protect their members' living standards. The politicization of wages and prices during the war, actively supported by a mobilized consuming public, represented the high point of the purchasing-power agenda. Though controls were only a wartime emergency measure, they emboldened Americans to insist on stable prices. For the next three decades, the public repeatedly demanded price controls as a remedy to inflation.

The inability to control inflation would prove the downfall of labor liberalism in the postwar years. After the war, the nation's businessmen, from the large industrialists to the small producers and shopkeepers, sought to dismantle the OPA and sever middle-class support for organized labor. They did so in part by blaming the industrial union movement for the explosive rise in consumer prices, thus exploiting a central tension of the purchasing-power program. With the end of controls, prices skyrocketed and unions staged massive strikes to protect their wartime gains. Although the consumer price index fluctuated comparatively less after 1948, it took middle-class consumers more than a decade to forget the fearful, explosive burst of wage-price inflation that had threatened their living standards in the immediate postwar years.

The booming economy of the 1950s, far from establishing the foundations for the "golden age" of American capitalism, unleashed antagonisms and anxiety over inflation. Cold War spending and the full-employment, high-wage economy of this era sustained healthy rates of economic growth. But they also led to creeping prices that exacerbated persistent middle-class fears of economic instability, uncertainty, and change. Moreover, now that many Americans were buying luxury goods like cars and televisions for the first time, they believed that the cost of living was spiraling upward, despite the fact that the overall price level remained relatively stable. The concern with inflation undercut middle-class political solidarity with organized labor, dissipating and weakening, as early as the 1950s, the alliance created during the New Deal and World War II years.

But all that was in the future. This story begins with the turn-of-the-century bargain hunters.

Part I

THE HIGH COST OF LIVING AND THE RISE
OF POCKETBOOK POLITICS, 1900–1930

From the Bargain Basement to the
Bargaining Table, 1900–1917

ON JANUARY 4, 1909, William Filene's Sons and Company opened its Bargain Basement. Almost instantly, swarming crowds descended upon this underground discount store. On some mornings, before the store opened at nine o'clock, customers formed long lines around the corner in anticipation of particularly good sales. On a typical busy Saturday, seventy-six thousand shoppers passed through its doors. Once inside, people grabbed, pushed, and shoved. Amid this frenzy there was no time for dressing rooms. The basement sold all classes of goods, with well-to-do women buying two-hundred-dollar cloth coats alongside working girls paying five dollars for a frock. Within two years, the Bargain Basement turned a profit.[1]

Heralded as a "new kind of store," Filene's Basement captured a key aspect of the twentieth-century American mass market—good quality for less money. Daily newspaper advertisements promised the latest fashions, but their emphasis was on the low prices. This simultaneous sales pitch was nicely summed up by the store's motto, "Style and Economy." Early ads in the *Boston Globe* boasted that the basement "[brings] down the cost of clothes ready to wear to a point where it is cheaper to buy than to make them, [thereby reducing] the cost of living in thousands of fami- lies." And thus it provides a "genuine service to thousands of people in and around Boston to whom saving is important or necessary."[2]

Filene's knew its customers. In Boston, as in many other cities early in the twentieth century, Americans were plagued by what contemporaries termed the "high cost of living." The promise of better living standards drew millions of wage seekers to America's cities from the faraway farm- lands of southern Italy and the market metropolises of eastern Europe as well as from the American countryside. But their dream of economic abundance and greater financial security was not so easily attainable, es- pecially as the deflation of the late nineteenth century gave way to a new era of inflation. Between 1897 and 1916, the cost of living went up roughly 31 percent, and then it skyrocketed during World War I.[3] For immigrant wage earners, the high cost of living, including rent, com- bined with the seasonal nature of many jobs, frustrated their dreams of wealth. Native-born workers in skilled organized trades earned higher wages, but rising prices threatened to subvert any income gains. For white-collar workers on fixed salaries, inflation undermined the security of their new middle-class status.[4] With millions of Americans caught in a vise between their expenditures and their income, a marketing strategy based on cutting prices made good business sense.

What made good sense for some could hurt others. The comparatively cheaper prices of mass retailers combined with consumers' demands for better buys posed a serious threat to many manufacturers and small merchants, who had been accustomed to setting their prices with little interference. Now they resented the competition from the cut-price retailer and disdained the bargain hunters, women in particular, whom they considered the worst kind of consumer. Rather than recognizing her as efficient and frugal, they saw her as a shopper who easily fell prey to fake deals, bought discounted merchandise in a state of near delirium, and presented a danger to herself and to society. The female bargain hunter was at once too weak to withstand the bait of cut prices and too headstrong in her search for the best buy. At the same time, many businessmen felt squeezed by the demands of newly organized workers. From bargain basements to company bargaining tables, the evolving mass-consumption economy brought with it a new price-consciousness and a different kind of social politics in which citizens made demands as consumers. Together, the bargain hunter, organized labor, and the mass retailer challenged the authority of the producers and merchants who had dominated the nineteenth-century economy.[5]

The Bargain Revolution

When the Bargain Basement opened its doors, Filene's was already one of a handful of well-known urban department stores. This Boston store typified what its founder and president, Edward Filene, would describe as a historic leap "from shopkeeping to mass distribution." In 1891, Edward Filene and his younger brother, Lincoln, took over ownership of their father's small retail stores in and around Boston. William Filene, a German Jewish immigrant, had come to the United States after the failed German Revolution in 1848. After several false starts, he established a successful dry-goods store and a men's shop in Lynn, Massachusetts. With the help of his sons, he stayed open until midnight to accommodate the long hours of Lynn's factory workers. The Filenes also operated two more small shops: a glove store and a lace store, on Winter Street in Boston. As the city grew and became more affluent between 1870 and 1900, the brothers saw their opportunity. In 1901, they incorporated the business into William Filene's Sons Company and consolidated their smaller operations into a larger Boston store. There

FIGURE 1.1. Edward A. Filene, president of William Filene's Sons and Company, became one of the premier mass retailers by selling machine-made women's clothing. He was a leading spokesman for mass consumption by the working and middle classes.

they sold women's clothing and accessories. Within a year, they saw annual sales double to just over one million dollars. Soon the brothers would look for a new location in order to expand.[6]

As early as the 1860s, retail merchants had opened department stores in Boston, New York, Chicago, Philadelphia, and dozens of other cities to cater to a new urban clientele. In the last quarter of the nineteenth century, dramatic improvements in productivity led manufacturers to worry about how to distribute all their wares. Department stores developed as one response to this so-called crisis of distribution. These stores sold huge volumes of a variety of goods, from silverware to silk stockings, all under one roof. Cities with large populations and concentrations of capital had the greatest number of stores. As urbanization spread, their numbers grew. By 1915, four thousand department stores existed in cities throughout the country, from Detroit to Des Moines to Denver. By 1920, these stores accounted for 16 percent of all retail sales, an impressive figure, given that the total number of retail stores had neared one million. Even though they laid claim to only a minority of sales, these modern emporiums represented the vanguard of new retailing methods and captured the public imagination.[7]

A century ago, department stores were socially, culturally, and economically revolutionary. As huge modern structures, they transformed urban landscapes. In 1846, A. T. Stewart's Marble Palace in lower Manhattan was the largest building in New York. A half-century later, in 1902, Macy's in New York and Marshall Field in Chicago opened new stores, each occupying more than one million square feet of floor space. Four of Henry Ford's Highland Park factories would have fit inside each building. New forms of public transportation made these stores accessible to large urban crowds and to growing suburban ones as well. During busy seasons, Field's had as many as 250,000 shoppers each day. Employees of major department stores alone numbered in the thousands.[8]

Between 1900 and 1906, Filene's business expanded at more than twice the rate of Macy's and Field's. To accommodate a fivefold increase in sales, the Filene brothers opened a bigger store in 1912, whose eight floors aboveground and two below street level occupied a full city block. Designed by the famous architect Daniel Burnham, it combined classic motifs with elaborately ornate detail. Thirteen elevators ferried on average 10,000 shoppers from floor to floor every hour. On September 3, 1912, the store's opening day, 235,000 visited the new emporium. Headlines read, "All Boston Out to See New Store." They were not far off. By the end of the week, three-quarters of a million people had come, a number slightly greater than the metropolitan population. Filene's soon had the highest dollar sales per square foot of any American store.[9]

When shoppers came to a modern department store, they entered a carefully constructed consumer paradise. More than mere goods were on offer; these palaces of consumption sold lifestyles. A well-dressed mannequin, posed in the act of taking her dog for a walk or strolling through a faux park, helped customers visualize the life of leisure that her costume seemed to reflect. On the first day of the new Filene's, models paraded around the store, giving a preview of winter fashions.

The appeal to fashion found a receptive audience in a recently urbanized population. As one person moving among anonymous crowds of strangers, the shopper made an impression based on appearance rather than on family background and personal character. A new advertising industry understood and played on the importance of what economist Thorstein Veblen, in *The Theory of the Leisure Class* (1899), famously called "conspicuous consumption." In 1870, companies spent thirty million dollars on advertising; by 1910, this dollar amount had reached six hundred million, or 4 percent of the national income. Inside department stores, the clerks supplemented the buyers' selections with expert advice on fashion and style.[10]

The physical structure of the stores also cultivated desire. New window displays drew shoppers and encouraged public loitering. By 1915, Americans were consuming half of all the plate glass in the world. Inside, consumers gazed all around as they walked amid the grand aisles and lofty atriums. Electric lighting, shimmering glass, and coordinated color schemes presented a full sensory experience for shoppers, some of whom had never seen such well-lit interiors. In 1901, Filene's painted its walls and all surfaces shades of green. Whereas previously shoppers had to request a specific item hidden inside solid wood cases, glass counters put all merchandise attractively on display. Mirrors heightened the sense of choice, as reflections appeared to double or even treble the number of items for sale. The American writer Theodore Dreiser captured the desire to possess fashionable goods in his novel *Sister Carrie* (1900). Dreiser described Carrie standing in a department store, awed by "the remarkable displays of trinkets, dress goods, stationery, and jewelry. Each separate counter was a showplace of dazzling interest and attraction. She could not help feeling the claim of each trinket and valuable upon her personally."[11]

Although they looked palatial, these new institutions were in fact a democratic departure from the past. Welcoming in passersby, they abandoned the nineteenth-century practice of charging a fee or insisting on a purchase as conditions for entrance. The economics of high fixed costs and the need for rapid turnover of merchandise meant that stores depended on impulse purchasing. Their free entry policy, along with their grand physical construction and accessible layout of goods, promoted shopping as a leisurely activity. Shoppers touched and tried on hats, gloves, and dresses free from merchants' scrutiny and under no obligation to buy. As one contemporary, Edgar Goodspeed, described it, "A vast throng of happy people, mostly women, streams continually through the broad aisles of these great houses, which, wonderful to tell, stand wide open to the public from morning till evening, so that any may come in or go out whether he have money or no."[12]

To secure as many sales as possible, the stores implored all potential shoppers to enter, regardless of class or color, and invited them to browse up and down the aisles. For immigrant newcomers, purchasing clothes, food, and furniture was an easier and faster path to Americanization than learning English. When Mary Antin, a Jewish immigrant from Russia, came to Boston in the 1880s, she went with her family almost immediately to a department store to purchase new clothes. As she recalled three decades later in her autobiography, "In a dazzlingly beautiful palace called a 'department store,' we exchanged our hateful homemade European costumes, which pointed us out as 'greenhorns' . . . for real American machine-made garments, and issued forth glorified in each other's eyes." Large chain stores provided access to consumer goods for many urban black Americans who faced discrimination at local stores. Mamie Garvin Fields, a black South Carolina teacher who moved to Boston in 1913 and worked as a seamstress, recalled in her memoirs how she made regular shopping trips to Filene's, even if only to imitate the styles she could not afford.[13]

To facilitate shopping, department stores proclaimed a new policy: "satisfaction guaranteed or your money back." Store managers in fact complained that returned goods were becoming a big problem. Between 1900 and 1930, customers returned 15 to 28 percent of their total charge purchases. By taking goods home, trying them on, even using and then returning them promptly, or not so promptly, shoppers signaled their determination to try on new lifestyles, revealing a sense of entitlement to play the part of, if not actually to become, the new American consumer. To make shopping even easier, department stores arranged for free delivery, and, most important, they extended credit. The extra services, which added to the aura of magnanimity and beneficence, helped diffuse attacks on department stores as economic predators gobbling up smaller businesses, and they also stimulated sales.[14]

Who did all the shopping? Women, of course. But these new commercial sites fostered a new public woman. Breaking from the ideology of separate spheres that confined them to private arenas, women now moved freely in many commercial public spaces. A variety of cheap amusements provided access for a nickel. Unaccompanied by men, they traveled to dance halls, movie theaters, and amusement parks, though, as contemporary diaries record, shopping remained their predominant activity. Contemporaries designated the New York area from Fourteenth to Twenty-third Streets between Broadway and Sixth Avenue as the Ladies' Mile. Edward Filene described the atmosphere inside his department store as an "Adamless Eden." Retail expert Paul Nystrom explained, "Under the guise of service, the modern department store has come to be a sort of club house and amusement place for women." In 1899,

Marshall Field opened the first large tearoom, seating five hundred for afternoon tea. Many stores provided a wide range of community functions, from lending books to mounting art exhibits to serving as headquarters for women suffragists.[15]

The participation of women in the marketplace accelerated in the decades after the Civil War. By 1880, many goods formerly produced in the home had become items sold in stores. Homes now depended on prepared foods, ready-to-wear clothing, and store-bought tools and furnishings. As late as 1890, communities had customarily designated one day a week as baking day, but within a generation families were eating store-bought bread almost exclusively. Between 1910 and 1915, the annual per capita consumption of canned fruits increased by over 50 percent and canned vegetables by 25 percent. In this economy, women became key actors and acquired a public role as shoppers. As early as 1915, women were credited with making up to 85 percent of consumer purchases.[16]

Women went to the market as family provisioners, a role facilitated by the tradition of family members handing over their sealed pay envelopes to the female head of the house. Diaries from the late nineteenth century reveal endless shopping trips that produced detailed notes on the cost and quality of goods for sale. On her downtown outings, the poet and playwright Josephine Preston Peabody reveled in what she called the "songful isolation of the crowd." She wrote in March 1914, "To Boston I go this day as much to keep continuity of thought as to search for certain bargains." Even in working-class communities, women included leisurely shopping as part of their daily domestic routines. In 1913, on New York's Lower East Side, the fifty-seven blocks of this Jewish immigrant neighborhood contained 3 large department stores, at least 50 dry-goods stores, 112 candy and ice-cream stores, 93 butcher shops, and 43 bakeries.[17]

To be sure, consumers had to be convinced that the products sold by these new commercial institutions were desirable. The campaign for women's ready-to-wear clothes is instructive. Before the twentieth century, most people, with the exception of the very rich and the very poor, made their clothes at home. When Alexander Hamilton wrote his *Report on Manufactures* in 1791, 80 percent of American households sewed their own clothes. Until the demand for uniforms in the Civil War, only slaves and sailors wore ready-made garments. With the manufacture and spread of the sewing machine in the last half of the nineteenth century, mass-produced clothes became readily available and affordable. In 1860, the sewing machine made its first appearance in Boston dress shops, and, within a decade, nearly all the city's shops had adopted it. Still, the virtues of this new machine-made clothing had to be sold to an

American public, especially to women, for whom the possession of domestic skills, such as knitting and sewing, was a valued trait. In their newspaper ads, retailers denigrated home production and self-sufficiency as
an outdated ascetic ethos. They portrayed women who sewed as old-
fashioned and those who wore ready-made garments as modern. By 1914,
the annual revenues of the machine-made women's clothing industry
totaled nearly half a billion dollars. Filene's was the first large store to sell
machine-made dresses, and it soon became the biggest seller of ready-
to-wear women's clothes in the country. Ads for the Bargain Basement
promised that these manufactured goods would endow individuals with a
larger wardrobe that required less work at half the cost of hand-sewn
garments with no sacrifice in quality.[18]

As much as department stores aroused desire, they made price a selling
point, thereby transforming the very nature of economic exchange. Before the implementation of price tags and a set-price policy, independent
negotiation determined each market transaction. Local knowledge and
conventions might have governed neighborhood markets, but each exchange was subject to individual bargaining. The seller judged the social
position of the buyer in order to arrive at the highest price possible. The
advent of department stores' huge sales forces and modern systems of
inventory required centralizing and standardizing prices; thus, each item
displayed a single, fixed price. Store tags and newspaper ads boldly
announced prices that clerks had to honor. Consumers often brought advertisements with them to assure compliance. And these prices were likely
to be cheaper than those at local neighborhood shops. In order to amor-
tize their high fixed costs, the department stores required rapid turnover
of stock. Higher sales volume allowed them to charge a smaller markup
for each item. The stores worked hard to educate consumers about
economies of scale, an extraordinary development that made even luxury
items like furs more affordable. Filene's ran ads that instructed shoppers
on this policy: "The store policy of selling high-grade merchandise at a
low margin of profit is applied to Furs as to all other departments." "Because we are unusually large dealers in furs, we sell on the basis of a small
profit on a large volume—rather than a large profit on a small volume."[19]

Price tags also made clear what one could not afford. The notion that
everyone, regardless of background or class, could purchase a better life
was a powerful and radical idea. But what if you came up short? Getting
rung up at the register was a reality from which consumers could not
escape.[20] Americans, especially urban wage earners and salaried workers, now could judge their own worth by what their paychecks could
buy. They needed money to be consumers, and, when they did not have
it, they knew by exactly how much they were short. Price tags dangling
their dollar signs led to a new cost consciousness. Dreiser's entire novel

hinges on Carrie's desperate drive to get money for "the kind of clothes she liked." Fresh off a midwestern farm, an excited Carrie craved a jacket, shoes, stockings, and a skirt until "she had got beyond, in her desires, twice the purchasing power of her bills." Millions of other urban dwellers found themselves without sufficient funds for luxuries or necessities. In an environment where money was needed for most things, contemporary writings capture a climate of endless cost calculations and penny-pinching. William Leiserson, a Russian Jewish immigrant who would later become a leading advocate of collective bargaining, for example, recorded every penny he spent in the summer of 1906. With his money running short and desperation setting in, he finally landed a job working at Sears, Roebuck and Company, where he earned twelve dollars a week as a billing clerk.[21]

Mass retailers like Sears understood the dilemma posed by this modern money trap and offered a way out through its cheaper prices. By purchasing directly from the manufacturer and selling straight to consumers, Sears and its main competitor, Montgomery Ward, promised a savings of 40 percent over the prices of local merchants. These mail-order giants found a ready clientele among rural Americans who also had begun to purchase manufactured consumer goods and appreciated the lower prices. Aaron Montgomery Ward started his catalogue in 1872; by 1884, the catalogue had 240 pages and listed nearly ten thousand items. Through its high quality and low prices, the company largely succeeded in establishing trust with its faraway consumers. Sears was even more successful. In 1893, in the middle of a severe depression, Richard Sears started his business from his post as a Minnesota railroad station agent by selling watches to other station agents. Premised on low margins and high volumes, the Sears mail-order catalogue that he launched soon became known in rural areas as the "farmer's bible." The company sent the 1904 catalogue to more than one million people; the 1927 catalogue went out to seventy-five million people.

The mail-order industry's low prices disrupted local markets. The 1899 Sears catalogue, for example, which was mailed to thousands of potential customers across the country, communicated a pointed message: "This book tells you just what your storekeeper at home pays for everything he buys—and will prevent him from overcharging you on anything you buy from him." The implication was that merchants were themselves stocking through Sears, and, if not, they ought to be. Like the department stores, the catalogues schooled Americans about the new mass economy. In advertising a particular hardware tool, the 1902 Sears catalogue bluntly explained that the country merchant "is compelled to pay more for this article than we would pay, for we buy in very large quantities direct from the manufacturers."[22]

Retailers everywhere offered good deals. Between 1912 and 1915, the Great Atlantic and Pacific Company opened a new "economy" A & P grocery store every three days. By the time of his death in 1919, Frank W. Woolworth was operating 1,081 five-and-dime stores across the country. Department-store managers set up "comparison offices," from which they sent out "spotters" to pose as buyers in other stores to check out the competition's costs and quality. With the need to clear their stock and move yesterday's fashions, department-store managers constantly reduced prices. Sales and downwardly spiraling price wars were a regular feature. As its stark full-page newspaper ads made clear, Macy's prided itself on underselling its competition. This New York landmark was famous for its price wars, especially with its next-door neighbor, Hearn's. In 1902, Macy's and Hearn's competed over silk, a legendary battle that drove prices down from forty-one cents for a yard to eleven yards for a penny. By making bargains routine and engaging in notorious price battles, department stores, chain stores, and mail-order catalogues put price into the competitive equation.[23]

The idea of the bargain became most prominently institutionalized when Filene's opened its Bargain Basement in 1909. Marshall Field had introduced the first bargain basement as early as 1879. But Filene's made its basement famous. It got its start as a temporary Christmas store in December 1908, selling gifts that ranged in price from twenty-five cents to five dollars. To make it a permanent attraction, the brothers had to dispel the image of a basement as a cramped, disease-ridden, poorly ventilated sweatshop. The Filenes made their tunnel entrance into a "brilliant spectacle of light, glass, color, and merchandise." The main attraction was the illuminated glass floor stained with peacock colors. An observer reported, "It is as if some one had taken a gorgeous Tiffany stained glass lamp shade and flattened it out, stretched it to huge proportions and used it for a floor." A ceiling of mirrors overhead made this innovation even more striking. Newspaper publicity told shoppers that they could board a train in San Francisco and come to Filene's new subway shop "all the way under shelter." Such protection made shopping comfortable in the freezing cold and sweltering heat. The basement was the first large area in a department store to be fully air-conditioned.[24]

Posted prominently throughout were plaques announcing the "basement rules." Each item had a price tag with the date of its first appearance on the floor. Through a schedule of automatic markdowns, managers systematically reduced the price of unsold items by 25 percent after twelve days, by 50 percent after eighteen days, and by 75 percent after twenty-four days. After one month on the selling floor, all unsold merchandise was given away. If a pair of gloves or silk neckties remained,

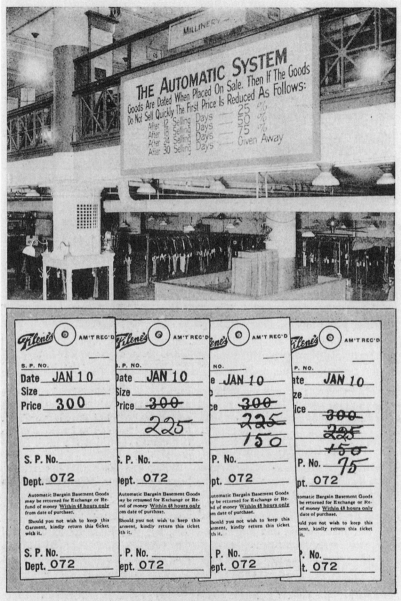

"IT INSURES BARGAIN PRICES"

"The buyer cannot forget that he has to sell the merchandise as well as buy it." The price tags and the large sign in the photograph above show why. If a buyer gets too much merchandise that must be marked down, he is unprofitable to the store.

FIGURE 1.2. Filene's Bargain Basement attracted thousands of bargain hunters daily in search of great deals on everything from fur coats to men's suits to wool socks. Prominently displayed in large signs and price tags, the basement rules explained the system of automatic markdowns.

the store shipped them off to charity. It was more important to keep merchandise moving than to worry about the profit on any one sale. The key to the plan was what Filene called its "automaticity," hence the name Automatic Bargain Basement. Markdowns happened at regular intervals in fixed increments. Any consumer who spotted a ticket inaccurately marked received a prize of five dollars. Critics denounced the basement as "Filene's Folly," predicting that people would wait out the deadlines on discounted merchandise, if they bought at all. But the pessimists were confounded when customers snatched up 90 percent of new items within twelve days; less than one tenth of 1 percent went to charity.[25]

Contrary to popular perception, few of the goods came from upstairs. Instead, the basement had its own buying staff, who hunted out wares to sell at bargain prices. They looked for manufacturers' surplus stock, seconds, factory clearances, discontinued styles, other retailers' overstock, or closeout merchandise. Ever-changing tastes and fashions inevitably led to inefficient distribution and imperfect markets, or what Edward Filene called "the lawlessness of production." He considered these remaindered goods as "frozen capital" that was clogging the economy. Purchasing and reselling these items, the basement made a profit by "clearing the market." Filene believed that a market existed for all goods at adjusted prices. As he put it, "The success of the ABB depends upon extraordinary prices to force quick selling." To other retailers, he boasted that "7,067 pieces of men's winter wool underwear were sold in two days in July when the thermometer registered 93 degrees."[26]

These sales were the stuff of legend. Everyone knew that the basement could sell sixty-two thousand bars of soap in three hours or eight thousand suits in a single day. Historical Trolley Rides made a stop at Filene's Basement. And every year Filene's drew more tourists than Faneuil Hall or the Old State House. In 1921 the store served as the location for the movie *One Flight Down*, the first feature-length film shot inside a store. Just as fashion trickled down from the floors above, so did the notion of the best buy, value, and economy trickle up.[27]

Across the country, bargain seekers could go to one of many discount stores. By 1913, a decade after opening his first store in a Wyoming mining town, J. C. Penney operated forty-eight dry-goods and clothing stores and spread the idea of good quality at cheap fixed prices throughout the West.[28] Shoppers could also visit entire discount neighborhoods, of which New York's Lower East Side was only the most well known. In the decades after 1881, hundreds of thousands of Jewish immigrants moved to or passed through this neighborhood. The street names—Grand Street, Hester Street, Rivington Street—became synonymous with good deals. Covering just a short distance, a shopper could go to one of 129 shoe stores, 94 hat stores, 84 furniture stores, or 22 furriers. Pushcart peddlers set up permanent markets along the same commercial thoroughfares. Because they could procure bargains at nearby wholesale markets and factories, they sold quality goods at cheap prices. Aware of the competition from department stores, including nearby Lord and Taylor's on Grand Street, they mimicked display strategies of the department stores, utilizing mannequins and mirrors. Selling to a wider pool of customers beyond their Jewish neighbors, they even decorated their carts for Christmas.[29]

A new inflationary economic culture encouraged the spread of a bargain-hunting ethos as shoppers searched for good deals. Whereas bargaining had previously revolved around "clever talking," bargain hunting now was based on shrewd comparison shopping and close scrutiny of prices. Observers noted that bargain hunting had become "the great American indoor sport." According to journalist Clara Belle Thompson, American women were "confirmed bargain hunters," and all belonged to the "League of Amalgamated Bargainers." Reports of spectacular sales, such as the following in *Outlook* magazine, sounded like accounts of riots: "The store opened at eight o'clock. An hour earlier street-car traffic past our corners began to suffer from cramps and congestion. Plate-glass windows were broken in—our neighbors' as well as ours. Crowds howled at the doors." Once inside, "bargain-hunting women wedged into the cars so tightly that it was impossible to close the elevator doors. . . . The crowds rushed in. Tables overturned. Cash registers smashed."[30] This invasion of shoppers was hardly as dramatic as the great labor conflicts of the late nineteenth century like the Haymarket bombing of 1886 or the Homestead strike of 1892, but the mob scenes inside stores suggested another side to the struggle over daily economic life.

Consumers wanted new products, often items that they had learned about through advertisements. But now they could shop. For the average working-class American, the ability to shop signaled a departure from the endless cycles of debt and dependency at company-town stores or local county shops. These new downtown stores stood open and permitted touching, sampling, and comparing. Smart shoppers navigated and negotiated their way through brand-name sales pitches, often obtaining similar merchandise at cheaper prices. The catalogues, as well as the mass-circulation magazines, educated the consumer in the privacy of her own home, a service that was particularly liberating for African Americans in the South, whose access to consumer goods was restricted. The creation of new spaces for mass consumption expanded the possibilities of the marketplace, rather than simply commodifying many aspects of daily life.[31]

After browsing through the aisles free of charge, shoppers could go home and make their own imitations of the goods they had seen and tried on. Lower East Side factory girls used scraps from the hats they were sending uptown to style their own millinery concoctions. Mary Wood of the General Federation of Women's Clubs reported a similar phenomenon in rural areas. "The farmer's wife studies by lamplight the catalogues sent out by the large department stores to her door, and through them she supplies many necessities in the home at bargain prices and copies the styles portrayed in hats and gowns." In a world premised on commodified superficiality, culture could easily be improvised and appropriated. A Russian immigrant garment worker, Ida Richter, explained, "We used to love the American people, to copy them. . . . I saw people who looked better and dressed better and I wanted to be like that." As one social commentator put it, "buying happiness" was easier than inheriting it. And yet that could cause tensions. "Nothing is more entertaining than the horror of the rich at the extravagance of the poor. Having exhausted ingenuity and sacrificed health to get what they call a market for their goods, they are shocked to find common people wearing them."[32]

Critics saw department stores, with their atmosphere of arousal, temptation, and envy, particularly among working-class and middle-class women, as dangerous sites of moral transgression. Thorstein Veblen condemned conspicuous consumption as symbolizing the abandonment of hard work, respectability, and self-restraint in favor of profligacy and instant gratification. Many moralists, including the liberal Protestant minister Washington Gladden, worried that economic abundance signaled the decay of Christian virtue and piety. The indulgence in material pleasures suggested a departure from the long nineteenth century of Victorian morality. In its promotion of the new art of window dressing, the *Dry Goods Reporter* candidly explained, "Goods should be so displayed as to force people to feel that they really wish to possess them." And turn-of-the-century newspapers reported a high incidence of shoplifting. Physicians invented the term "kleptomania" in an effort to diagnose theft by respectable middle-class housewives as a medical condition that resulted from the infirmity of women's nature. Explaining illegal actions as a physiological disorder rather than a calculated response to marketing strategies reflected a discomfort with a consumer culture premised on temptation. The trap for working-class women was even worse: prostitution. Department-store clerks who worked amid so much luxury were particularly at risk. According to a 1911 report by the Vice Commission of Chicago, "Some of the girls who are most tempted, and enter the lives of prostitution, work in the big department stores, surrounded by luxuries, which all of them crave." Mrs. Doubleday, wife of the publisher, did not want her husband to publish *Sister Carrie*, because she objected to Dreiser's representation of this young, attractive, penniless woman, whose only recourse for satisfying her desires was to let herself be "treated" by well-to-do successful men. That was understood at the time as a form of prostitution.[33]

The mass retailers sparked hatred not just from moralists but also from their competitors. Local merchants vigorously opposed mail-order firms and department stores. They were surrounded by an economic landscape undergoing rapid and radical change, a transformation that called into question their traditional economic power. They could not survive the one-two punch of glittering store windows and shiny catalogues that undercut their prices and undermined their cultural authority. These small merchants accused the department stores of causing the economic hardships of the 1890s. An exasperated Kansas City merchant fumed, "I am being victimized by three department store houses, and street peddlers." To thwart the mail-order giant, rumors circulated that Richard Sears was African American, and much was made of the fact that Sears's partner, Julius Rosenwald, was Jewish. Local merchants encouraged burning catalogues in big town bonfires. Some paid ten cents for every catalogue offered to the blaze, while others swapped children's movie tickets in exchange for the hated books. Local communities cast the catalogue companies as predators. "Did they ever do your home town any good?" In such a hostile climate, Sears resorted to sending merchandise in unmarked packages.[34]

Alongside countless instances of local protests, opponents also led an organized campaign against mass retailers. Commercial associations throughout the Midwest formed the Home Trade League of America in 1906 to resist the mail-order houses. Thomas J. Sullivan, an ardent opponent, circulated scripted articles for editors to run in local papers. Organized opposition culminated in an attempt to thwart Congress's efforts to create parcel post. Before the implementation of rural free delivery in 1896 and parcel post in 1913, farmers and small-town residents had to travel to the nearest post office to collect their goods. Only four privately owned express companies delivered packages heavier than four pounds. Such restrictions placed obvious limitations on a national distribution network. Many local merchants as well as jobbers, traveling salesmen, and other middlemen did not welcome efforts to open up market networks to outside influences. They must have been galled by the campaign for parcel post that well-known department store owner John Wanamaker led from his position as U.S. postmaster general between 1889 and 1893. Farmers and organized labor, backed by the mail-order-catalogue houses and urban retailers with mail departments, successfully pressed for expansion of the mail services, but only in the face of serious sustained opposition. The more the mass market spread, the greater the resistance it encountered.[35]

The Campaign for Fair Trade

The fear of mass retailers reflected more than the atavistic longings of small-town America. These protests were not simply sentimental "last hurrahs" before an inevitable triumph of a nationally integrated mass-consumption economy. Even name-brand manufacturers of products distributed across the country were wary of the new processes of provisioning that at once disrupted and challenged older economic arrangements and local networks. A broad coalition of manufacturers, small businessmen, and local shopkeepers understood that the proliferation of goods and a democratization of services undermined old power relations and social hierarchies. Although they did not have identical interests or ideologies, they were unanimous in their contempt for the price-chiseling retailer and the bargain-hunting consumer. Price-cutting suggested an alternative sensibility, in which producers no longer determined the value of their goods. Though certainly their influence over markets had never been complete, the institutionalization of price-cutting came as a direct affront to producers' sense of control. An opponent of mass retailers exhorted, "The price cutter is not a philanthropist, he is a robber, stealing the advertising and filching the good will of another's product; and like all thieves he does not share his booty with the public."[36] Price-cutting department stores were considered as no better than parasites. Through marketing strategies, legislation, and court battles, this coalition sought to enforce manufacturers' right to fix the resale prices of their products. The "campaign for fair trade," as its advocates called it, captured the depth of ambivalence, perhaps even hatred, toward the volatility of the new consumer marketplace.

Attempts to control consumer markets began with the invention of brand names in the late nineteenth century. The advent of a reliable nationwide railroad system had brought with it the potential for new and distant markets. But capturing them required a change in the existing distribution system. Throughout much of the nineteenth century, wholesalers and drummers traveled the country to peddle nondifferentiated goods to local merchants. Manufacturers could circumvent the power of these middlemen to push particular products, but only if they could forge a direct relationship with the consumer. Brand names became the means to create a stable and predictable consumer demand. In the best-case scenario, manufacturers would advertise their goods in mass-circulation magazines, and consumers in turn would demand that local merchants stock these products. In some cases, consumers had to be convinced that mass-produced goods offered advantages over generic equivalents. Often the smaller the distinction between competing brands, as with cigarettes, toothpaste, and food products, the more a company would invest in advertising to build consumer loyalty. The turn of the century witnessed the spread of new, nationally advertised brands, such as Kellogg's, Ivory, Nabisco, Coca-Cola, Kodak, Beech-Nut, Gillette, Victor Talking Machine, and Ingersoll.[37]

Once they had created brands, manufacturers worked to eliminate price competition, a goal they were not willing to leave to chance. They worried that if some retailers sold their product at a cut rate, consumers would not believe that the item was actually worth more. Fair-trade advocate William Hard put it succinctly: "Demoralize the price and you demoralize the product."[38] Beginning in 1912, in a practice that was becoming common, Kellogg's printed the price of ten cents on each box of Corn Flakes, accompanied by a warning to retailers and wholesalers to adhere to this price.[39] Publishers too sought to regulate their markets. On the inside cover of their books, Bobbs-Merrill announced to customers, "The price of this book at retail is one dollar net. No dealer is licensed to sell it at a less price, and a sale at a less price will be treated as an infringement of the copyright." Other producers tied price to the marketing strategy, as occurred when the Ingersoll Company introduced its Dollar Watch and Nabisco advertisements announced that only five cents would buy a package of Uneeda biscuits.[40]

The manufacturers came up with good prices, but department stores, mail-order catalogues, and chain stores did them one better. As Filene's explained to its customers, it bought in large quantities and thereby got discounts, establishing its high-volume business on smaller margins. Macy's, the best-known cut-rate department store, sold many items at reduced prices. The New York store regularly offered Ingersoll Dollar Watches for eighty-nine cents and the Victor Talking Machine for eighty-nine dollars instead of one hundred. Macy's cut prices on books too. In one instance precipitating a lawsuit that the publisher pursued all the way to the Supreme Court, Macy's sold Bobbs-Merrill's *The Castaway* for eleven cents below the asking price of one dollar. Grocery chains also routinely cut prices. The A & P economy stores sold Cream of Wheat for twelve cents instead of fourteen, an action that resulted in Cream of Wheat cutting off the chain's supply, a gesture made at considerable sacrifice, given the fact that the A & P operated fifteen thousand stores.[41]

Manufacturers feared what they ominously called "the substitution evil." As advertising campaigns moved beyond simply introducing a new product like packaged crackers, they promised intangible benefits— matrimonial bliss, youth, social acceptance—that they could not actually deliver. Since all toothpastes would freshen breath, it seemed unlikely that one was more likely to find its user a husband—or a wife—than another. So why not buy a cheaper brand? Price-cutting would only impel shopping around for cheaper substitutes. The fear was especially real for specialty manufacturers in new consumer industries, such as fashion textiles, furniture, and jewelry, which accounted for half the value of all manufactured products. Manufacturers in this sector faced great instability and uncertainty, because rapidly changing tastes made their markets particularly unpredictable. Specialty firms sought to create unique goods, in order to gain high profit margins. But, as these producers well understood, stylized products presented great opportunities for cheaper knockoffs and imitations.[42]

Companies acted vigilantly to prevent substitution by intensifying advertising campaigns. Many ads appealed directly to consumers. Pabst Extract, a tonic to help "the nervous wreck—to prepare for happy, healthy motherhood," counseled consumers to "refuse to accept a substitute. No 'cheaper' extract can equal Pabst in purity, strength, and quality." In an even bolder strategy, the company offered monetary incentives for customers to serve as enforcers. Pabst promised customers a thousand-dollar reward for reporting druggists who suggested an alternative product. Another advertisement for Cascarets Cathartic Candy warned, "Now and then, dealers try to substitute 'something just as good.' It's a lie! Don't let them do it, and if they try, write us confidentially at once. . . . Beware of Imitations!" The country's national drink urged, "Do more than ask for 'Grape Juice'—say Welch's—and GET IT!"[43]

Manufacturers, both small and large, went to great lengths to prevent price-cutting. In the depression of the mid-1890s, when they found themselves with extra stock, D. Appleton and Company destroyed three hundred thousand books rather than risk depressing the market. Various trade associations, such as the New England Manufacturing Jewelers' Association or the American Publishers' Association, emerged at the turn of the twentieth century as a mechanism to limit price competition among similar products. But such agreements failed as often as they succeeded. In many consumer industries, each product was in fact different, distribution was diffuse, and the temptation to chisel great. Mass producers likewise turned to collective action and had better success in setting prices. Higher outputs and economies of scale promised greater returns, but because large capital investments brought increased risks, these producers did not instantly pass on savings in cost to consumers. All sorts of firms joined together to control production and prices. Between 1897 and 1904, American companies consolidated in the great merger movement: just over 4,000 firms combined into roughly 250.[44]

The merger movement did not stop manufacturers from championing the small merchant against the evil "distribution trusts." This made good business sense. In small stores, where a culture of deference still predominated, merchants retained the power to push one brand in favor of another or in place of a generic substitute. And thus they could be key allies in the fight to win and retain customers. Manufacturers feared that the self-service ethos of discount stores would encourage consumers to select competing brands, especially on the basis of price. Indeed, the "price appeal" of chains led to their proliferation. As early as 1916, Philadelphia's 1.5 million residents were buying nearly 70 percent of their groceries from chain stores. By 1929, chains sold one-third of all groceries nationwide and accounted for 20 percent of retail sales in all lines of business.[45]

The threat of mass retailers and chain stores was palpable, especially for small merchants. Neighborhood druggists now sold brand-name toothpaste, elixirs, tonics, disinfectants, soaps, and razors, while local grocers retailed boxed cereal, packaged crackers, and canned soup. These items presented simultaneous opportunities and risks. The life of many independent merchants was always precarious. The large number of stores created fierce competition. The credit that many extended to customers made it more difficult to operate a successful business. On basic staples they usually saw little profit. Brand-name goods yielded larger margins. But the fact that consumers could buy branded goods elsewhere posed the possibility of a diminishing clientele, especially if chain stores offered better deals.

Small merchants joined with manufacturers to form the American Fair Trade League (AFTL) as a lobbying organization. The AFTL drew support from druggists, booksellers, grocers, hardware stores, tobacco merchants, and other specialty retailers who feared for their survival and from large manufacturers, such as Ford, Packard, B.V.D., and Colgate, which were eager to exert control over the resale price of their products. To counter the Supreme Court's repeated rulings against price-fixing schemes, this group introduced legislation in Congress. With President Wilson's support, Representative Raymond Stevens and Senator Henry Hollis, both Democrats of New Hampshire, proposed the Stevens Bill as an amendment to the Clayton Antitrust Act. Under the guise of eliminating unfair cutthroat competition, the bill would have legalized resale price maintenance and banned quantity discounts for large retailers. The U.S. Chamber of Commerce wanted the amendment to stipulate that "no merchant, firm, or corporation shall offer such articles for sale at a price other than stipulated by the producer." It defended its position as an effort to "uphold producer's rights." As of 1914, nineteen states— Louisiana, North Carolina, South Carolina, Arkansas, Oklahoma,

Missouri, Kansas, Iowa, Wisconsin, Michigan, Nebraska, Idaho, North Dakota, Montana, Wyoming, California, Utah, New Jersey, and Massachusetts—had passed legislation prohibiting price-cutting. Only in the Great Depression, amid massive deflation, did price-fixing schemes gain enough national political support to succeed through the passage of the Miller-Tydings Act of 1937. Until then, supporters introduced a new price-fixing bill nearly every year, but, given the fragmented nature of federal policymaking and Congress's limited legal capacity to interfere in commerce, these efforts met with no success.[46]

Supporters of resale price maintenance (RPM) appropriated the language of President Wilson's New Freedom program. Conceptualizing it essentially as a backward-looking program, New Freedom advocates argued that the government needed to protect the small independent businessmen by thwarting the development of large monopolistic corporations that threatened to eliminate economic competition. By extension, manufacturers claimed that price-fixing was essential to defend the small retailers from the distribution trust. Kellogg's, Eastman Kodak, Waterman Fountain Pen, and Hamilton Watch reported that over 90 percent of their retailers favored RPM. American Fair Trade lawyer Charles Miller argued, "It is a healthy sign to see the large manufacturers of standard brands fighting the battle of the small retailers for their very existence." The U.S. Chamber of Commerce canvassed its members, who overwhelmingly supported price maintenance. In a report, it claimed that there were "social advantages of such distribution conveniences as are represented by neighborhood stores and by small but skillful merchants." Congressman M. Clyde Kelly of Pennsylvania declared, "I stand with Littlefellow & Company, against the Soak-em-good mail order houses. I consider the neighborhood store a necessity and I want it to have a fair chance, no more and no less, to grow greater and finer."[47]

The assault against the price chiseler created strange bedfellows. None other than Louis Brandeis, the "People's Lawyer," championed manufacturers' rights. A spokesman for the small shopkeeper and the petite bourgeoisie as the bulwark of American society, Brandeis was one of the leaders in the campaign for fair trade. He argued that the price-cutting of large department stores, mail-order catalogues, and chain stores undermined the economic, and thereby the political, authority of the independent merchant. With the decline of the small shopkeeper, he claimed, "The social loss is great; and there is no economic gain." Brandeis served as counsel for Kellogg's in its defense against the Justice Department's accusations of illegal price-fixing. In 1914, American Fair Trade League president Charles Ingersoll asked Brandeis to draft the Stevens Bill. Fair-trade legislation, Brandeis explained at a dinner for the National

Association of Advertising Managers, "seeks to protect the small man against the powerful trust, against the capitalistic combination." He chose to ignore the fact that the advertisers in his audience represented some of the larger corporations. Indeed, many prominent mass-circulation magazines that depended on national advertising came out in favor of RPM. *Publishers Weekly, Printer's Ink*, and the Curtis Publishing Company, which published the *Ladies' Home Journal*, all lent their pages to the cause.[48]

Female shoppers, according to the fair-trade champions, needed protection from the predatory practices of price-cutters. Retailers sold well-known brands at cut-rate prices as bait to draw consumers. Reporter James Collins explained, "The bargain price was made on something she knew, so that she would come to the store and be fooled by all sorts of things that she didn't understand at all."[49] As C. E. LaVigne of the American Fair Trade League explained, department stores preyed on ignorant women by offering well-known brand-name goods at cut prices "as a decoy to reach the purse of the consumer." He feared that price-cutting merchants would use B.V.D. underwear, for example, marked down to "create a market for that mass of unknown articles around it." In the presence of such prices, women would lose their heads and grab inflated, overpriced goods on counters near the underwear. LaVigne hoped that, with price-fixing legislation, "it would then be impossible to advertise a dollar article at 69 cents and put it in the center of all such nondescript merchandise, and thus lure the public."[50] Christine Frederick, consulting household editor of *Ladies' Home Journal* and wife of J. George Frederick of *Printer's Ink*, agreed that modern women needed the protection and guidance that only branded goods with their national reputation provided. Frederick favored the manufacturer's right to fix one price, believing that it would prevent a chaotic world in which "every customer who by 'haggling' or 'bargaining' hopes to 'jew' the dealer down." "If we do not have standards of quality with a mark so that we can recognize them, and a price that doesn't fluctuate, we women buyers for the family are helpless and confused." H. C. Brown of Victor Talking Machine asserted that "maintaining the price is a protection to the public against exploitation."[51]

Manufacturers walked a fine line between appealing to consumers and mistrusting them. Supporters of price maintenance presented themselves as defenders of the consumer while simultaneously evincing contempt for the comparison shopper. According to a Blackman Talking Machine spokesman, the "bargain hunter" was not to be trusted. Manufacturers encouraged consumer desires while discouraging shopping around. Consumers were supposed to buy on impulse rather than compare prices. Edward Rogers, a lawyer for RPM, explained, "The effect of an advertisement of a particular article is not lasting. It creates an immediate impulse to buy or it is of little use. . . . The potential purchaser must be able to obey the impulse while he has it. It must not be permitted to wear off. . . . While he is in the notion he must be able to buy the thing at the time he wants it at the first shop he sees. He must be made to feel that he can get it at one place as cheaply as another, otherwise he will shop around for a bargain and in the meantime he forgets; the impulse to buy that particular item has evaporated."[52]

Behind this fight over price maintenance stood two clashing views of American life. The companies advocating fixed prices made money by creating and selling to new consumer markets. But they were not eager to relinquish any of their authority to determine the worth of their goods. To abandon a fixed price would lead to chaos and the destruction of economic value in an increasingly destabilized world where women were asserting their independence in the market. At just the time that women were beginning to demand the vote and organize into social clubs to reform public life, the female shopper represented yet another instance of challenges to entrenched nineteenth-century customs governing female public behavior. Even progressive intellectuals who defended the rights of the working classes to higher living standards were wary of this new culture of temptation and spending. In his denunciation of cut-rate prices, Brandeis primarily attacked the distribution trust, but he also pointed an accusing finger at the complicit consumer and her "search for the cut-throat bargains." Brandeis championed the rights of many underdogs, but not consumers. For them, he had the greatest disdain. "Thoughtless or weak, [the consumer] yields to the temptation of trifling immediate gain; and selling his birthright for a mess of pottage, becomes himself an instrument of monopoly."[53] For Brandeis and his allies, the defense of price was as much a moral as an economic imperative. Precisely because of its ability to reorder economic and social relations, the mass market was not foreordained and did not automatically prevail.

Mass retailers, on the other hand, announced that they were the consumer's true defender and lobbied against passage of price maintenance legislation. These retailers claimed that women had too much sense to fall for price gimmicks. At RPM hearings in 1917, Macy's Edmond Wise mocked the bill's supporters: "Of course, the people of the United States, and especially the women, are such hopeless ignoramuses that they need the intervention of this committee to come in and protect them." He continued, "The shoppers of the United States are such fools that, when they come in and see a Gillette razor advertised below $5, they will go and buy their household supplies at a very much higher figure at that place." He made fun of Charles Ingersoll's advocacy of RPM "when he sought—tearfully sought—to protect the poor women shoppers of New York from their own ignorance." In a statement that was both good politics and good business, F. Colburn Pinkham, the secretary of the National Retail Dry Goods Association (NRDGA), a trade association of large retailers, explained, "I have too much respect for the intelligence of the average woman shopper today." Marshall Field's J. M. Barnes denounced the price-fixing supporters' pretense to protect the consumer from herself as "paternalism." Several years later, a report of the NRDGA asserted, "The majority of women know values. You cannot fool them and get away with it."[54]

Economists and other opponents of RPM argued that consumers were not easily duped. Harvard economist Frank Taussig asserted, "Let the retailer retail as he sees fit and continue to trust . . . in the good sense of the purchasing public." "I suspect we shall have to content ourselves with the conclusion (or assumption?) that the ordinary purchaser is not endlessly gullible, that the predatory dealer is likely to overreach himself in the end, that honest business pays as a whole." Economist H. R. Tosdal, a leading authority on price maintenance, agreed that consumers themselves, rather than manufacturers, were the best protectors of the consumers' interests. "The saving of time claimed for consumers under fixed resale prices by making it unnecessary to 'shop' in order to secure the cut prices is a matter which concerns the consumer's right to dispose of his time as he sees fit."[55]

Consumers had no organized presence in these debates, though many who claimed to represent them opposed RPM. The American Federation of Labor (AFL) and the General Federation of Women's Clubs (GFWC) testified against price-fixing on behalf of working-class women who needed to maximize their household incomes. GFWC representative Mary Wood explained, "The woman, who is the home-keeper, this wife of the ordinary wage earner, has no time to sew. . . . Why should she be deprived of the benefit of those 'cut rates'?" As she explained, "It is in the interest of her family to look out for 'bargain sales,' and she scans the evening paper for advertisements of reductions in food and clothing." Though it was indeed self-serving to defend bargains, Edward Filene, too, sympathized with efforts to stretch income. As he put it in his testimony, "Every reduction in price . . . makes for the real freedom of the wage earners." Wood explained that wage earners benefited by traveling downtown to get three bars of Ivory soap for ten cents rather than paying five cents for one bar at the local store. Though it would cost money to get there, shoppers could then take advantage of other bargains as well. As to taking the bait of a "loss leader," Wood refuted the notion of the ignorant housewife. Female shoppers were smart and did not require the producer to protect them from themselves. "The average purchasing woman has sense enough to know an inferior article when she handles it or sees it." If RPM became law, Wood concluded, "the consuming public would be forced to pay inflexible prices and in the majority of cases suffer."[56]

Resale price maintenance was never an easy sell to consumers, ever in search of a good deal, and inflation further undermined its appeal. Throughout much of the nineteenth century, Americans had experienced steady or declining prices. After the Civil War, prices dropped and reached their lowest point during the depression of the 1890s. But as prices started to climb at the beginning of the twentieth century, the economic reality of inflation weakened producers' push for price maintenance and opened the way to a consumer agenda.

A New Consumer Consciousness

The early twentieth century marked a significant departure in how Americans understood, and therefore tried to improve, their standard of living. Throughout much of the nineteenth century, many Americans earned their income as farmers or small craft artisans. Amid the agricultural hardships and declining commodity prices of the late nineteenth century, farmers supported inflationary policies as a way of easing their debt and increasing the value of their land. These agrarian producers understood purchasing power in terms of the quantity of money, an issue determined in large part by the gold supply and the metallic basis of the currency. That way of thinking about the so-called money question reached a crescendo with William Jennings Bryan's 1896 presidential campaign for free coinage of silver. As new sources of gold were discovered, as inflation replaced deflation, and as large segments of the population moved to the cities to earn wages and salaries, Americans' mind-set shifted.

When twentieth-century Americans thought about purchasing power, they focused less on the money supply and more on wages and prices. Just as representatives of labor organized and lobbied for higher wages and better working conditions, so too did reformers and the urban masses push for better prices. Between 1896 and 1914, the annual rate of inflation hovered between one and two percent annually.[57] For those living on limited incomes, a jump in prices, even if small, could mean the difference between affording an item or going without. Employers routinely utilized a workforce of low-wage, seasonal workers, which exacerbated the ability of the working classes to make ends meet. Once people had to shop for items required in daily life, they became more cost conscious, especially if the prices they paid were constantly inching upward. Contemporary economists were likely to attribute this inflationary trend to impersonal forces, such as the expansion in the money supply. But many Americans saw conspiracy. Immigrant mothers, middle-class housewives, and organized labor utilized the consumer label in their battles for better living standards. These consumer politics did not instantly assume programmatic or institutional forms or map neatly onto partisan divisions, but daily contests at the marketplace did lead to an inchoate pocketbook politics.

Politicians began to appeal to voters as consumers in partisan fights over tariffs, the defining issue of nineteenth-century political economy debates. As free-trade representatives of a largely agrarian constituency, Democrats opposed Republican protectionist tariff policies that benefited manufacturers and led to higher prices. In his 1888 unsuccessful presidential bid, Grover Cleveland pointed to the protectionist tariffs of the Republican Party as the chief culprit threatening to raise the cost of living. Two years later, Democrats forcefully denounced the McKinley Tariff of 1890 for foisting artificially high prices of manufactured goods onto the public. When Democrats achieved substantial midterm electoral victories in 1890, they gave partial credit to the influence of "shopping women" on their voting husbands. In the Midwest, where partisan competition was most fierce, Democrats went so far as to pay peddlers to increase the price of pie tins and then blamed the Republican tariff. Though imaginative, their simultaneous push for higher farm prices and cheaper prices for manufactured goods would remain a source of contradiction for the Democratic Party as it sought to move beyond its base among southern farmers and appeal to urban working-class voters. These partisan appeals were only the beginnings of a rhetorical strategy to appeal to voters as consumers. Indeed, in response to consumer critiques of the Payne-Aldrich Tariff of 1909, Republican senator Henry Cabot Lodge of Massachusetts denigrated what he called "this myth of a consuming public." "Where is this separate and isolated public of consumers? . . . This is a Nation of Producers."[58]

Fights over the price of meat brought the interests of urban consumers front and center. In the 1880s, Gustavus Swift's introduction of refrigerated railroad cars and warehouses enabled the expansion and consolidation of the country's meatpacking industry. While consumers benefited from the ready availability of processed and fresh meat, any price increases made them increasingly suspicious of the so-called Beef Trust. A Federal Trade Commission investigation conducted during World War I later revealed that the "Big Five" packers, including Swift and Armour, had established pooling agreements to parcel out the market and set prices. By the war's outbreak, the Big Five were processing 50 percent of all red meat and distributing two-thirds of fresh meat. In some markets, their dominance was virtually unchallenged.

In New York City, for example, they controlled 97.7 percent of fresh beef distribution. That concentration prompted allegations of a "Beef Trust," akin to the more well-known Progressive Era attacks on railroads and Standard Oil. Agitation for the Sherman Antitrust Act of 1890 derived, in part, from opposition to the meat industry's consolidation and control over prices. Concerns over high prices made concrete the loftier debates over the structure of modern capitalism. In 1902, when meat prices spiraled up, U.S. Attorney General Philander C. Knox brought proceedings against the big packers, charging them with conspiracy in restraint of trade.[59]

Consumers, too, launched protests against rising prices. In Edward Filene's hometown of Lynn, Massachusetts, a city with a vigorous labor sensibility, 1,700 General Electric employees vowed not to eat meat. From Portland, Maine, to Topeka, Kansas, unionized workers joined in support. For these laborers, the ability to afford meat was a significant marker of their status, as revealed in the 1906 anti-Asian pamphlet of AFL leader Samuel Gompers, *Meat vs. Rice: American Manhood and Chinese Coolieism.* Communities formed anti-beef-eating leagues, promising to go without meat for one month in an effort to bring prices down. In the beef heartland of Missouri and Nebraska, consumers switched to fish. Protesters appropriated antitrust language to explain their actions. Playing their part as a Goliath, Swift, Armour, and Morris formed the National Packing Company, a vertically integrated organization stretching from the stockyards to the butcher shops. Muckraker Charles Edward Russell confirmed popular suspicions in his investigation into the "Greatest Trust in the World." In *Everybody's Magazine,* Russell warned the public, "Day and night this monstrous thing grows and strengthens until its grip is at the nation's throat." The publication of Upton Sinclair's *The Jungle* (1906), which portrayed the gritty and gruesome conditions of the packinghouses, further fueled the popular animus and spurred government action. Passage of both the Pure Food and Drug Act and the Meat Inspection Act in 1906 gave recognition to the political importance of this consumers' interest. Their passage also demonstrated the ability of mass sentiment to overcome the constraints imposed on Congress by the commerce clause, which limited federal interference in economic affairs. Though these measures were silent on the question of prices, the perception of exorbitant profits and price gouging helped to make the packers politically vulnerable.[60]

White-collar workers on fixed salaries felt particularly victimized by price increases. Between 1880 and 1930, the number of salaried employees increased eightfold in response to the growing demands from new corporations and government bureaucracies. These jobs gave real opportunities to the sons and daughters of immigrants and farmers for advancement into a rapidly expanding new middle class. But inflation imposed limitations in a world where few were self-sufficient. According to Paul Douglas, author of *Real Wages*, salaried workers, especially teachers, saw a decline in their actual income. Rising prices were all the more jarring for the generation of older middle-class professionals and elites who grew up during the deflation of the nineteenth century. In a further departure from the past, prices continued to climb even after the recession of 1907. Price increases exacerbated people's lack of leverage and control over daily market transactions. From August 1906 to September 1907, *Harper's Bazar* ran a regular feature, "The Increase in Household Expenses," that captured a new set of market anxieties.[61]

As corporate trusts increased in number and influence, many white-collar workers came to believe that prices were unnaturally high. Newspaper accounts of trusts fueled suspicions that businesses were engaging in a conspiracy to impose higher prices. Writing in 1908, muckraking journalist Ray Stannard Baker captured this sense of shared injury: "The unorganized public, where will it come in? The professional man, the lecturer, the writer, the artist, the farmer, the salaried government employee, and all the host of men who are not engaged in actual production or delivery of necessary material things, how will they fare? . . . Is there any doubt that the income of organized labor and the profits of organized capital have gone up enormously, while the man-on-a-salary and most of the great middle class, paying much more for the necessaries of life, have had no adequate increase in earnings?" Frustration easily turned into acrimony, especially when muckrakers revealed a vast network of interlocking trusts that seemed to set the terms of trade arbitrarily. "The high cost of living," President Woodrow Wilson declared, "is arranged by private understanding." The progressive journalist Walter Weyl, author of *The New Democracy* (1914), wrote, "The universality of the rise of prices has begun to affect the consumer as though he were attacked by a million gnats. The chief offense of the trust becomes its ability to injure the consumer."[62]

Striking workers gained white-collar support when they included lower prices as part of their demands. To be sure, Americans have a long history of hostility to organized labor. The potential conflict between the high wages that labor has sought and the low prices consumers have desired is real. But in this era, where there were only pockets of union and consumer strength, such tensions were largely latent. A mutual antipathy toward the overweening power of trusts provided a basis for a broader alliance. Soon after the government announced its investigation into meat price increases, Chicago's Union Stockyard teamsters went on strike, and they received support from the community. According to the *Chicago Evening Post* on June 4, 1902, "Arm to arm with teamsters . . .

were young women in summer gowns and well-dressed clerks and business-men." Municipal strikes also revealed urban residents' sympathy for workers, both of whom felt gouged by public franchise corporations. In Saint Louis, when the Street Railway Employee Union struck in 1900, the workers did so to prevent "the great organized power of tyrannical trusts . . . from crushing down wages and pauperizing the great masses of people, thereby destroying the purchasing power of our customers and injuring our business." Sympathizing with the workers, other citizens refused to ride.[63]

From streetcars to storefronts, new sites of consumption could easily become transformed into places of protest. Once basic goods and services became commodified, changes in prices wreaked havoc. In 1901, the average wage-earning or clerical family spent 40 percent of its annual income on food. That percentage remained as high as 35 percent in 1940. Rent amounted to roughly 25 percent and clothes about 15 percent, leaving little for discretionary income, out of which also came medical expenses. Given those economic realities, making ends meet was no easy accomplishment. As the main provisioners, women found price increases particularly challenging. One commentator, Dr. Henry Leffmann, explained in 1910, "The cry against the high prices of the necessaries of life is heard all over the land. The housekeeper does not need to consult statistics nor to read the discussions of Congress. She finds out the condition whenever she visits the grocery store or market."[64] Daily trips to the grocer allowed for regular price comparisons. Fancy packaging could obscure the value of many mass-produced goods, but basic necessities presented fewer obstacles to buyers' judgment. Women could discern if bread was stale and loaves smaller. They spent much of their time and family budget buying bread, milk, and meat. Because these basic, nondurable items required immediate purchase to prevent spoiling, they made effective targets for consumer action. And now urban markets provided consumers a collective site for protest. With slight fluctuations in price, necessities became politicized.

In May 1902, when local meat prices increased by 50 percent, from twelve cents a pound to eighteen, New York's Lower East Side house-wives reacted swiftly. These Jewish women transformed the shopping streets into meeting halls and planned a neighborhood boycott of kosher butchers designed to put pressure on the packers. Their actions assumed violent proportions when they marched into local butcher shops and destroyed high-priced meat. "Armed with sticks, vocabularies, and well sharpened nails," the *New York Daily Tribune* reported, these women "made life miserable for the policemen." On the first day, the police arrested seventy women and fifteen men for disorderly conduct, and one hundred more the next day. Mass meetings drew crowds as large as twenty thousand, and the boycott quickly spread to Harlem, Brooklyn, and the Bronx. Five hundred leaders formed the Ladies' Anti-Beef Trust Association. They appealed to the mayor for the right to assemble, they went door-to-door to gain sympathizers, and they distributed flyers declaring, "Eat no meat while the Trust is taking meat from the bones of your women and children." In Brooklyn, four hundred women stood patrol outside butcher shops to assure compliance. As the boycott grew, it succeeded in winning the support of the Retail Butchers Association, which helped to turn the tide against the Beef Trust. Three weeks later, the result was a decline in wholesale prices to nine cents and retail prices to fourteen cents.[65]

The same scene played itself out in other cities, including Boston. Not far from Filene's, Jewish communities came together in pursuit of what their New York counterparts labeled "the great struggle for cheap meat."[66] In Boston, retail butchers took it upon themselves to lead the boycott against wholesalers for two months. In Boston's West End, a crowd of two hundred mobilized to prevent a wholesaler from operating his own shop. Newspaper accounts noted that women took "a prominent part in the demonstrations." When a customer came out with his purchases, a woman named Sarah Goldstein grabbed the meat and hit him in the face with it. She slapped an officer who attempted to restrain her. According to reports in the *Boston Globe*, "She was more like an insane person than one in her own senses." Boycotters broke the plate-glass windows of two wholesale shops. In the nearby North End, striking butchers distributed Hebrew circulars declaring "Down with the Trust." "We strike already for nearly two months that we should be able to sell meat cheaper to the poor working people, so they can have meat every day for their children." They appealed to their community not to patronize the handful of open wholesale stores. Local neighbors obliged by attacking customers and denouncing them as "scabs." They assaulted women "who were on their way home with packages of meat, took away the bundles, threw the meat to the ground and trampled on it."[67]

Housewives' actions extended to rent, another major cost that grew as the influx of immigrants placed pressure on available housing. In immigrant ghettos, moving was frequent, often occurring when tenants could not come up with the next month's rent. But in New York that strategy became increasingly difficult as the 1901 Tenement Housing Act slowed the rate of new building and the construction of the Williamsburg Bridge eliminated approximately seventeen thousand homes. When landlords proposed a 20 to 30 percent increase for May 1, 1904, women organized a rent strike of two thousand tenants. As with the butcher boycott, their actions yielded a short-term success. But it was not long before hard times exacerbated housing costs. In the

summer of 1907, roughly one hundred thousand people found themselves out of work. Those conditions set the stage for an even larger rent
strike than the one three years earlier. Pauline Newman, then a sixteen-
year-old garment worker at the Triangle Shirtwaist Factory and dubbed
the "eastside Joan of Arc" by the *New York Times,* organized a rent strike
with the backing of the Socialist Party and troops of Lower East Side
housewives. Six hundred women went door to door to build support.
On December 26, 1907, they appealed to one hundred thousand Lower
East Side renters to strike. In a dramatic gesture, they demanded a rent
decrease of one or two dollars per month, or roughly the amount that
rents had advanced over the previous five years. Within days this fer-
ment spread to Brooklyn and other parts of Manhattan, including non-
Jewish communities. Fifty thousand residents, representing ten thousand families, agreed not to pay. Though the strike ended quickly once
landlords secured eviction orders, two thousand families got their rents
reduced. Sympathetic to their plight, settlement-house leaders Lillian
Wald and Mary Simkovitch launched a campaign for rent controls fixed
at 30 percent of a family's monthly income.[68]

These female protesters lived in a world of politics—the socialist politics
of the factory and the daily politics of the marketplace. Housewives understood that their purchasing power was set not just by their husbands'
higher wages and successful union campaigns but also by their own skill
and agency in the marketplace. In New York, at least five times between
1902 and 1908, immigrant mothers organized mass protests against price
increases. These Lower East Side women drew on their shared Jewish faith
and socialist ideas. But to a certain extent, their actions reveal the economic and political expectations of their adoptive homeland. At the time
of the 1902 butcher boycott, the striking New York housewives had lived in
the United States for an average of eleven years and had become accustomed to higher standards. As one striker put it, "In the old home I never
had enough meat. . . . Now fat meat was mine for the asking." By the turn
of the century, an American consumed on average 140 pounds of meat annually. Not only did these women expect a higher standard of living in this
land of plenty; they also took public action. Appropriating the right to free
speech, the New York women asserted, "We will not be silent; we will over-
turn the world." For Pauline Newman, one of the rent strike's organizers,
this event launched a career in union organizing and electoral politics.
One year after the rent strike, the Socialist Party nominated her to run for
the post of secretary of New York State.[69]

These consumer protests were at the vanguard of a new twentieth-
century politics. At first glance, they appeared to be just the angry
outbursts of an almost premodern mob. The Socialist Party, in spite
of its interest in Newman, largely ignored these women, and its paper,

The Worker, trivialized the butcher boycotts. "We cannot oppose the aggression of twentieth century capitalism with weapons fitted to the petty conflicts of eighteenth century small producers." Beginning with German socialist Werner Sombart, theorists have seen American high standards of living as depoliticizing. In 1906, in answer to his question "why no socialism in the United States?" Sombart explained, "The American worker lives in comfortable circumstances. . . . He dresses like a gentleman, and the working woman like a lady, so that his outward appearance tends to make him unaware of the distance which separates him from the ruling class." But limitations of purchasing power in fact politicized working- and middle-class Americans. The push for better prices and higher living standards—what journalist Walter Lippmann grasped as "a young social power"—was a unifying, radicalizing, and politicizing power that helped to give rise to the reform politics of the Progressive–New Deal era.[70]

Throughout this pre–World War I period, incomes often did not keep pace with mounting consumer expectations and rising prices. Whether buying food or frocks, women faced that pocketbook reality at the market every day. Lippmann predicted that consumer complaints were likely to increase as women's political power expanded. "The mass of women do not look at the world as workers; in America, at least their prime interest is as consumers. It is they who go to the market and do the shopping; it is they who have to make the family budget go around; it is they who feel the shabbiness and fraud and high prices most directly." Upon what did Lippmann base his observations? As an upper-class assimilated New York Jew who moved in the world of the indomitable Theodore Roosevelt and the Harvard philosopher William James, Lippmann did not suffer any economic difficulties. But he was obviously aware of the working-class unassimilated Jewish women on the Lower East Side who took to dumping peddlers' carts at the first sign of higher prices, a concern that was shared by middle-class housewives.[71]

The consumer impulse toward emulation and acquisition could have a mobilizing impact not only in the marketplace but also at the bargaining table. If high prices constituted one obstacle to an improved standard of living, then so too did low wages. Consumer protesters understood that the market basket and the pay envelope were two sides of the same cost-of-living coin. Pauline Newman, veteran of the rent strike, helped to organize the "uprising of 20,000" in New York's garment industry in November 1909, when tens of thousands of teenage girls stopped their sewing machines. Newman led the workers out at the Triangle Shirtwaist Factory. At the same time, fifteen-year-old Clara Lemlich, who later became a prominent community activist, rallied workers at the Leiserson Factory to walk off the job. Both were modern factories, but still these women felt

FIGURE 1.3. In 1909, New York teenage garment workers staged a massive uprising against low wages and poor factory conditions. On the picket lines, strikers
wore their fine hats and fancy clothes, demonstrating their dual roles as consumers and producers.

that they and their sisters in sweatshops deserved better. When the *New
York Evening Journal* interviewed Lemlich, she explained, "Sometimes a
girl has a new hat. It is never much to look at because it never costs more
than fifty cents, but it's pretty sure to be spoiled after it's been at the
shop." She went on, "We're human, all of us girls, and we're young. We
like new hats as well as any other young women. Why shouldn't we?" She
and her peers had made daily sacrifices to purchase their hats. "Even if it
hasn't cost more than fifty cents, that means that we have gone for weeks
on two cent lunches—dry cake and nothing else." Her rhetoric resonated
with striking teenagers, who donned their best clothes on the picket lines.
Sombart was only half right: they were ladies, but that did not deaden
their political impulses.[72]

    Between 1909 and 1915, women garment workers erupted in strikes
at factories across the country, from New York to Boston to Philadelphia
and from Cleveland to Kalamazoo. Those actions, and countless other
stoppages, ultimately led one-half of these workers to join a union,

a density of unionization higher than in any other industry. Whereas Sister Carrie sold herself to a man to solve her purchasing-power problems, these teenagers joined together to protest long hours, hard work, and difficult working conditions. They took collective action not only for higher pay but also for a better life. Labor organizer Rose Schneiderman, who began working in a department store at the age of thirteen before taking a higher-paying job as a cap maker, captured this sentiment. "The woman worker wants bread, but she wants roses too." Two years later, Pauline Newman explained, "Let us not think of a piece of bread. Let us think of the working woman as a human being who has her desires to which she is entitled."[73] The quest for the feather in the hat, far from trivial, imagined and was predicated on a fundamental transformation of group consciousness, industry, and law.

Fresh from her victories on the shop floor, Newman went to Boston to urge middle-class women to shop at department stores that sold only union-made goods.[74] Newman's union-label campaigns on behalf of the International Ladies' Garment Workers Union duplicated the efforts of the National Consumers' League (NCL). The NCL appealed to middle-class housewives as consumers and sought to transform their purchasing power into a political force for labor reform. NCL general secretary Florence Kelley explained, "Since the exodus of manufacture from the home, the one great function of women has been that of purchaser." Kelley came from a family of reformers. Her father, William Pig Iron Kelley, served as a Radical Republican from Philadelphia from 1860 to 1890 who supported Reconstruction in the South. Her aunt, Sarah Pugh, was an abolitionist who would not wear cotton, because it was a slave product. Kelley herself was a committed socialist, dedicated to political and economic reform. In Illinois, while living at Jane Addams's Hull House, Kelley lobbied for state oversight of factory conditions and then served as the first chief factory inspector of Illinois from 1893 to 1896. As secretary of the Consumers' League, Kelley beseeched middle-class women to shop only at retail stores that treated their employees fairly and to buy only those goods made under fair factory conditions.

Kelley worked hard to make shoppers aware of the reciprocal relation between mass consumption and poor labor conditions. The rise of the ready-to-wear industry created fast-changing fashions that spawned the sprouting of sweatshops to meet new demands. To move goods quickly, department-store clerks worked long hours with little rest, particularly during the busy holiday season. These "Christmas cruelties" were well known. Because the stores made labor visible in a way that coal mines, for example, did not, Kelley thought that shoppers would be sympathetic. To jolt the middle class into a more immediate sense of personal connection with the plight of garment workers, she also explained that sweatshop conditions could affect consumers through the airborne travel of germs. As she put it, women were "in great danger as ever of buying smallpox measles, scarlet fever, infectious sore eyes, and a dozen other forms of diseases of the skin." Thus she called upon the consuming class to buy only items that had received the NCL white label of approval. That label banned sweatshop production, overtime, and child labor. For every day Kelley spent at her New York desk, she spent another traveling the country to build grassroots support. By 1905, NCL had established sixty-four local leagues. Membership levels reached their highest point of fifteen thousand in 1916.[75]

Raising children and keeping a clean and healthy home increasingly became public affairs. Communitywide issues, such as the water supply and public health, impinged on private duties. Moreover, as diseases spread and public understanding of germ theory increased, the domestic world became linked to the workplace. In the early twentieth century, new grassroots voluntary associations, such as the National Consumers' League, the General Federation of Women's Clubs, the American Home Economics Association, the Women's Trade Union League, the Women's Christian Temperance Union, and hundreds of other mothers' societies and clubs, relied upon their members' moral authority as mothers and housewives to demand new regulations of the market. Considered unfit to participate in electoral politics, women found they could enter the public stage in defense of their families and homes. The General Federation of Women's Clubs, founded in New York in 1890, had chapters in all forty-eight states, and it achieved a membership of one million by 1911. Though more socially conservative than the National Consumers' League, its members too defended better working conditions. In Kentucky, for example, the NCL was the local chapter of GFWC. This movement toward what was called municipal housekeeping signaled the extension of the women's sphere into a generalized reform impulse. The women in such groups did not simply represent their own interests as middle-class consumers but had a larger vision that extended to improving the living standards of the working classes.[76]

One horrific event galvanized this reform community. In 1911 the Triangle Shirtwaist Factory, where Newman had worked, went up in flames. With doors locked shut, 146 young girls lost their lives, with dozens hopelessly jumping to their death. Their burnt bodies lined the New York sidewalk. That tragedy underscored the importance of legislative reform to improve factory conditions. In its aftermath, Frances Perkins of the National Consumers' League and future secretary of labor in the New Deal forged a long friendship and working relationship with Pauline Newman of the International Ladies' Garment Workers Union (ILGWU) and Rose Schneiderman of the Women's Trade Union

League (WTUL). The horror of the fire attracted the attention of reform politicians from Theodore Roosevelt to Al Smith and Robert F. Wagner, who, years later as New York's senator, called upon these women reformers to help draft New Deal legislation.[77]

The Triangle fire made clear that simple moral suasion, even when backed with the threat of consumer boycotts, could not transform the world of industrial work. The NCL, along with the WTUL, believed that protective wage and hour legislation was essential, especially for working-class women. By 1900, 5 million women were earning wages, with 1.25 million working in manufacturing jobs, mostly in cotton mills, garment shops, commercial laundries, and canning plants. Although the textile industry was the third-largest industry after steel and oil, male trade unionists routinely dismissed female workers as unreliable, seeing them as transient and willing to accept low wages. The ILGWU, as an affiliate of the AFL, showed only lukewarm support for the 500,000 unskilled immigrant women and children earning low wages in fifteen thousand garment shops.[78] In light of such a weak commitment from its allies, the NCL turned to the regulatory powers of the government. In 1908, the NCL recruited Louis Brandeis to argue for the Supreme Court to uphold maximum-hour legislation for female workers in *Muller v. Oregon*. In what became known as the Brandeis brief, proponents presented sociological evidence to prove that long hours were a problem for women as potential mothers. Appealing to a moral imperative to protect women under the state's police powers, Brandeis won an important victory, which was nullified when the Court overturned the ruling in 1923. In contrast to Brandeis, the WTUL and the NCL did not consider that women needed to be physically or morally shielded from workplace demands. They endorsed this sex-based approach as necessary, given women's exclusion from many AFL unions and the denial of their right to vote in national elections. With grassroots support and a reliance on social-science expertise, the NCL lobbied successfully for the passage of the first minimum-wage legislation for female workers in Massachusetts in 1912.

Edward Filene lent the full weight of his authority to this effort. As the biggest retailer of women's ready-to-wear clothes, Filene's played both a symbolic and a real role in structuring Boston's female labor market. Filene supported the NCL's minimum-wage efforts and also complied with the union label. Within his store, Filene paid a comparatively high wage of eight dollars a week. He also encouraged the creation of the Filene's Cooperative Association (FCA) in 1902 to represent the store's 2,700 employees. The FCA set store hours and closings as well as other workplace policies. In its 1908 ads, just as it was introducing the Bargain Basement, Filene's appealed to its customers to help eliminate Christmas cruelties. The ads asked customers to begin shopping earlier "to make the work easier and the holidays happier for the people in the stores." While they were perhaps a thinly veiled attempt to draw shoppers into the store sooner, the ads also made clear that the store was "not open evenings." Nor would it be open for business on Saturday, December 26, one of the busiest shopping days of the season, because the FCA had voted to close the store.[79] In part Filene believed that his generous labor policies would appeal to an increasingly sympathetic consuming public. But he was also genuinely committed to meaningful labor reform and working-class consumption, two goals that he saw as inextricably linked. Though separated by culture and class from his employees, Filene found himself drawn into a widening circle of reformers.

Filene was among the earliest and most articulate members of an emerging group of reformers who thought that mass consumption was the twentieth-century version of socialism. Mass consumption meant just that to him—widespread consumption by the masses. Their enjoyment of higher living standards did not require government ownership of private industry. But Filene understood that the redistribution inherent in mass consumption—the high wages and low prices—would not happen automatically. Instead, capitalists had to allow workers to play a meaningful role in industrial affairs. For his part, Filene intended to transform his workers into share owners, and he even rewrote the store's constitution to provide for the future transfer of his and his brother's stock to the employees. Filene developed an intimate lifelong friendship with the journalist Lincoln Steffens, which began when Filene invited this muckraker to Boston to expose the city's corruption. When Filene visited the Soviet Union years later and reported favorably on what he saw, Steffens responded that Filene had become more of a communist than he was.[80]

To many liberals, the bounty of the new American marketplace enabled, and indeed required, the fulfillment of the American dream. Progressive reformer Herbert Croly, in his classic treatise *The Promise of American Life* (1909), claimed that "the American democracy . . . has promised to Americans a substantial satisfaction of their economic needs; and it has made that promise an essential part of the American national idea. . . . What the wage-earner needs, and what it is to the interest of a democratic state he should obtain, is a constantly higher standard of living."[81] The idea of an American standard of living as a right galvanized the AFL. In the battle for the eight-hour day, AFL leader Samuel Gompers explained, "Continual improvement, by opening up new vistas, creates new desires and develops legitimate aspirations. It makes men more dissatisfied with unjust conditions and readier to battle for the right." In part because of these efforts, the workweek declined from sixty-six hours in 1850 to sixty hours in 1890 to fifty-five hours in 1914. As wage labor increased in the late nineteenth century, organized labor began to articulate demands as much on the basis of workers' needs as consumers as on their value as producers, and the unionized workers insisted on receiving what their leaders called a living wage. No longer self-employed, workers saw high wages that provided a comfortable lifestyle as one route to economic freedom. And high wages were a politicizing force. The more workers had, the more they wanted. Demands based on needs could be infinite, as evidenced early on, in 1898, when United Mine Workers leader John Mitchell expressed the opinion that the American standard of living should include a six-room house with indoor plumbing, a separate parlor and dining room, multiple bedrooms, and a library! In 1906, Father John Ryan published *A Living Wage*, which justified labor's demands on America for decent pay as the moral cost of doing business.[82]

The AFL's campaign for a living wage fell halfway between its understanding of union members as producers and as consumers. AFL members were among the most highly skilled workers, and they took pride in their craft. As technology and scientific management gradually encroached upon their skills, their embrace of a living-wage argument was in part a sincere attempt to preserve a sense of autonomy, but as consumers rather than producers. And in part it was a public-relations ploy. Amid the depression of the 1890s, the AFL made rhetorical gestures about the importance of working-class purchasing power to the national economy. Gompers lamented that "the workmen have created, create, and will continue to create, in excess of their ability to consume." He argued that "in the end the toilers must be the great body of consumers."[83] But the AFL, for its part, had committed itself to nativist exclusionary policies. Between 1881 and 1914, twenty-five million immigrants came to the United States from southern and eastern Europe, including two million Jews, and most entered the industrial workforce. The majority found themselves excluded from AFL unions eager to maintain a privileged position in a rapidly changing industrial economy. That practice of exclusion cast doubt on AFL claims to act on behalf of the great body of consumers. Only unions that represented the masses could make such a case with legitimacy.

A new twentieth-century industrial unionism of the unskilled immigrant masses put working-class purchasing power at the center of its program. In 1914, Sidney Hillman, a Jewish refugee from the Russian Revolution, led the semiskilled garment workers in forming their own union, the Amalgamated Clothing Workers (ACW). The bolt from the AFL's conservative United Garment Workers represented a significant break with the older forms of craft unionism that dominated the AFL. In Russia, Hillman had been a member of a family of rabbinical scholars, and he moved as comfortably in elite intellectual circles as he did among his immigrant brethren on the shop floor. When he came to Chicago, he got a job at Sears in the infant-clothing department for eight dollars a week and then went to work at Hart, Schaffner and Marx, a modern manufacturing firm of better-quality men's clothing that employed ten thousand Jewish and Italian immigrant workers. Hillman and his Progressive Party allies had this unskilled, uneducated constituency in mind when they envisioned a new unionism of the masses. In the next few years, the ACW organized roughly ninety thousand garment workers and won such long-sought improvements as the eight-hour day and abolishment of the sweatshop. The ACW argued that its workers deserved higher wages not just as Americans—indeed, many were not—but as consumers. Like Filene, they asserted that, in a consumer economy, workers' purchasing power was vital for national prosperity and economic growth.[84]

This idea that workers were also consumers was not unique to the labor movement. Just as Hillman formed the ACW, Henry Ford announced his famous "five-dollar day." Ford was motivated in part by the need to secure a more reliable workforce. In 1913, when Ford introduced the moving assembly line, he had to hire over fifty-two thousand workers to fill only thirteen thousand positions. Such a high rate of turnover undermined the efficiency of the assembly line. Thus the five-dollar day, which amounted to double the average industrial wage, went a long way toward stabilizing this semiskilled immigrant workforce. At the same time, Ford also invoked a broader vision of workers earning enough to buy the cars they were producing. Indeed, as both Ford and Filene understood, the logic of mass production pointed in that direction. The five-dollar day popularized the purchasing-power argument for higher wages.

Mass production made the high wages and low prices of Fordism possible but not inevitable. Though American manufacturers turned out more consumer goods at better prices and paid higher wages than their counterparts in other industrialized nations, a new group of reformers believed that these corporations had not gone far enough. Indeed, the very existence of the bargain basement stood as a visual reminder of the consumers who could not afford to shop upstairs. As the debate over resale price maintenance revealed, low prices sparked pitched battles. And higher wages would come only with protracted conflict. In response to the rising prices of the early twentieth century, consumers mobilized at the storefront and on the shop floor. The rapid inflation that came with the outbreak of World War I intensified struggles over the high cost of living and transformed what had been isolated episodic protests in defense of mass purchasing power into pressing national problems.

Chapter Two

Business without a Buyer, 1917–1930

PROTESTS AGAINST the high cost of living came to a head during World War I. In February 1917, the progressive Republican senator William Borah of Idaho warned about the dangers of escalating costs and blamed monopolies for driving up food prices. From the floor of the Senate he cautioned, "The price of those things which enter into daily living, of everything which we wear and which we eat, has reached a point where it presents a national crisis." Thousands of housewives from the Lower East Side had erupted in a mass demonstration against the high cost of food the same day. Leaders called for half a million mothers to march against the preeminent New York bank J. P. Morgan, which was helping to coordinate and finance American sales to France and England. It was not so much that these women opposed war as that they felt aggrieved by its inflationary consequences. Ida Harris, president of the Mothers' Vigilance Committee, explained their position in presenting their appeal to provide relief first to the mayor of New York and then to President Wilson. "We do not want to make trouble. . . . We want to soften the hearts of the millionaires who are getting richer because of the high prices. . . . We haven't got any politics. We are just mothers, and we want food for our children."[1]

The cost of living more than doubled in the five years after the outbreak of European hostilities in 1914, reaching a high in the immediate postwar years. The precipitous rise in living costs contributed to a near revolutionary combustibility that characterized the war years. The wartime labor shortage combined with the urgent need for industrial production presented organized labor with an unusual opportunity to assert its power on the shop floor and in the corridors of Washington. The wartime rhetoric of democracy and self-determination further emboldened and inspired organized labor to conflate unionization with patriotism. To be sure, labor could go too far, especially when the Bolshevik Revolution of 1917 made labor activity, particularly that led by American socialists, increasingly suspect and subject to state surveillance. But, overall, wartime conditions favored what contemporaries called "industrial democracy" as evidenced by a doubling of union membership as well as the creation of the National War Labor Board, which oversaw the institutionalization of experiments with unionization, government arbitration, and work councils.

What made labor even more insistent in its demands and potentially more powerful was the price problem. The collapse of Russian czardom began with a February 1917 women's protest over the cost of bread and cabbage. Such revolutionary upheavals were not about to engulf the United States. But most thoughtful Americans also knew that the social tensions, as well as the democratic aspirations, unleashed by the Great War were thoroughly entwined with the clamorous increase of working-class protests in all large urban centers over the inflationary danger and the social inequalities it generated. Framing its agenda around issues of dwindling purchasing power and protection of living standards, labor struck a sympathetic chord as inflation indiscriminately affected all of the working and middle classes. Popular demands to combat inflation, much like strikes over shop-floor control, were a political hot potato that required attention at the highest levels.

The War Creed of the Kitchen, 1917–1918

World War I dramatically accelerated inflationary trends that had been under way since the turn of the century. When Woodrow Wilson ran for president in 1912, he pledged to fight the tariff in order to bring down the cost of living. In spite of that promise, prices increased and then soared with the outbreak of war. Between June 1915 and July 1917, the general price level increased by 85 percent. In just three months after America entered the war, clothing costs skyrocketed by 30 percent. According to the National Industrial Conference Board, over the course of the war wage earners' cost of living increased by 65 percent. Clothing went up by 93 percent, and food, which accounted for 43 percent of a working-class family's budget, rose by 83 percent. Housing increased by 20 percent. Inflation posed a crisis not only for wage earners but also for middle-class professionals and white-collar workers on fixed salaries who saw little wartime gains in their income.[2]

The rise of food prices presented serious problems. Although America remained neutral until 1917, the food it sent to the Allies was a central component of American foreign policy. Shipping losses from German U-boats intensified the Allies' food needs, leading America to triple its wheat and meat exports. The combination of increased demand and a poor grain crop in 1916 produced a severe food shortage. Wages went up, but prices, especially of food, rose higher. In New York, for example, a dozen eggs went from thirty-two cents to eighty cents in a year.[3]

The strain of this situation was dramatized in the housewives' protests of February 1917. Angered by the soaring prices of potatoes, chickens, and onions, thousands of Jewish women took out their immediate frustrations on peddlers, overturning carts on Rivington Street and enforcing a boycott of these items. The demonstrators were not the most destitute women but rather women who had come to expect a decent standard of living. One housewife explained, "I could buy butter once on my husband's wages—I don't see why I shouldn't have the same to-day." They marched on the mayor's office demanding food. Abraham Cahan, editor of the *Jewish Daily Forward*, allowed a mass meeting at Forward Hall, the Socialist Party headquarters, where thousands of women formed the Mothers' Anti–High Price League. They sent a letter to President Wilson proclaiming, "We, housewives of the City of New York, mothers and wives of workmen, desire to call your attention, Mr. President, to the fact that, in the midst of plenty, we and our families are facing starvation. . . . [T]he American standard of living cannot [be] maintained." Several days of protest culminated in a mass rally at Madison Square Garden.[4]

These New York demonstrations had national implications as protests erupted in Chicago, Philadelphia, Boston, Saint Louis, and Baltimore.[5] Unlike earlier periods of unrest, this time women moved on from street protests to organize consumer groups as a way to push for permanent reform. In that effort, working-class radicals were joined by middle-class housewives active in women's clubs. In the Progressive Era, women's clubs had largely focused on improving social conditions or on domestic science; now they became acutely sensitive to the problem that inflation presented to their middle-class members and to the working classes. In New York, leaders representing four hundred organizations demanded the creation of municipal markets where the city would buy food and distribute it at regulated prices, a proposal that received support from the governor and the state senate minority leader Robert F. Wagner. Wilson, feeling pressure, authorized the Federal Trade Commission to launch an investigation into food prices.[6] Even as protests ceased, the threat of working-class agitation loomed large, especially when America's entry into the war sent prices sky-high and made the middle classes sympathetic to a reform agenda.

How, though, to stop the upward price spiral? Throughout the period of inflation, the Wilson administration condemned high prices that helped to breed instability, from New York's Lower East Side to Seattle's shipyards. Wilson largely relied on moral exhortations, and once Congress declared war on April 6, 1917, the president launched a sustained campaign against inflation. Immediately he called on the nation's businessmen to adhere to "fair and just market prices," and his administration attacked profiteering as part of its war program. But that rhetoric was undermined by the realities of wartime demands. Alleviating inflation required a rapid increase in supply, which meant countenancing prices high enough to motivate maximum output, even the inflated prices of inefficient or monopolistic producers.[7] Thus Wilson's anti-inflation campaign, while tinged with a radical flavor, was not enough to fix the purchasing-power squeeze as prices rapidly outstripped wages. The trick then became to create new government agencies that had authority over both prices and wages without centralizing all economic activity. Compelling higher wages and lower prices yet leaving those decisions in private hands required a delicate balancing act.

To achieve that goal, the Wilson administration established new state agencies designed to mobilize groups of citizens who would enforce its will democratically. On the price side, the president set up the Food Administration under Herbert Hoover. Hoover had made his fortune as a successful mining engineer. At age forty, he retired and turned his energies and skills to public affairs. His successful organization of relief in war-torn Belgium had made him a household name. In May 1917, Hoover responded to Wilson's request to return home and address the food situation. Without any official powers or congressional authority, Hoover set up headquarters in a suite of Washington hotel rooms with a staff of volunteers. To free up food for the Allies, he quickly initiated a nationwide propaganda campaign for "meatless Tuesdays" and "wheatless Wednesdays."[8]

In communities across the country, prominent women lent their names and organizational talents to enlist housewives in the anti-inflation crusade. The first step was to reduce demand through a conservation movement. Hoover urged the nation's schools and leading women to offer instruction in home economy. After taking a home-economy course, women would become captains of Food Saving Teams and train other women to live frugally. Eleanor Roosevelt, the wife of Assistant Secretary of the Navy Franklin Roosevelt, organized a Food Saving Team in Oyster Bay, Long Island. Mrs. Roosevelt held daily conferences with her staff on conservation methods. "Making the ten servants help me do my saving has not only been possible, but highly profitable," the future first lady reported. After one month's effort, the Food Administration selected her household as a model for other large homes. On April 12, 1917, the General Federation of Women's Clubs (GFWC) launched a nationwide conservation pledge campaign among its membership of over one million women. Such grassroots efforts worked in tandem with Wilson's appeals to the nation's housewives to plant and can their own vegetables.[9]

The administration recognized the need not only to conserve food but also to rein in rapidly escalating prices. The president could ask Americans to consume less only if he also asked the nation's producers

"COUNTY FAIR" IN BRYANT PARK

Photo, New York Herald.

An exhibition of canned products was held in the war garden on Forty-second street, New York, and eleven of the Commission's National Capitol Prize Certificates were awarded to prize-winners in the various subdivisions of Manhattan. These were presented by President Charles Lathrop Pack, the blue ribbon going to Mrs. I. C. Kahn, at left of table decoration.

FIGURE 2.1. The nation's housewives, including many prominent women, supported the U.S. Food Administration's wartime campaign for food conservation. In addition to the patriotic act of canning, a conservation technique demonstrated here by women in Bryant Park, New York, housewives joined the government in condemning profiteering at the market.

and businessmen to make sacrifices. In addition, the press on resources threatened to continue propelling costs skyward, a situation that had already proved volatile and was driving up the cost of war. To solidify the conservation effort and clamp down on prices, President Wilson urged passage of the Lever Food Control Bill, which would formally establish the Food Administration as a government agency, with Herbert Hoover at its head. Wilson's willingness to push legislation that would restrict the prices of farmers, a key Democratic constituency, reflected the exigencies of war as well as the president's increasing friendliness to labor. Yet the urgings of a wartime president did not translate into action. The Lever Bill stalled in Congress for months.[10]

In spite of congressional delays, Hoover lost no time in organizing the nation's housewives and recruiting them into voluntary government service. In this war economy, women's social roles became thoroughly politicized. The War Department's Council for National Defense created a Women's Committee to oversee voluntary efforts. With the help of the GFWC, the 9,790 local units of the Women's Committee sought to register the nation's women as lay members of the Food Administration and urged housewives to "Get Behind Hoover." In July 1917,

Hoover led his own consumer pledge campaign to deputize these women into his agency. "I accept membership in the United States Food Administration, and pledge myself to carry out the suggestions of the Food Administrator, so far as I am able." In exchange for signing a pledge, each housewife received an official membership card to put up in a window. She also received "The War Creed of the Kitchen," urging patriotic conservation and elimination of waste. Newspapers printed pledge forms daily while members of the GFWC and other women's groups, including the Woman's Suffrage Party and the Young Women's Christian Association, went door-to-door to register housewives.[11]

This mobilization signaled a new kind of federal power, one in which the state legitimized its authority and cried out its policies by delegating a measure of power to its citizens. The Food Administration concentrated authority over prices in a one-man administrative agency, and it also relied upon a dense web of volunteers who acted on the government's behalf to enforce its mandate. By suggesting that certain profits were "unfair or unreasonable," the Food Administration replaced a market standard for prices, whereby business decided what to charge its customers free from government interference, with a patriotic political yardstick. Though Hoover would gain authority to intervene directly in setting prices and supply, his agency largely functioned by institutionalizing the notion of a "fair price" and relying on consumers to require business compliance.[12] As Hoover explained, "The Food Administration is a volunteer organization to be endowed with powers by the Government." Responding to critics, he asserted, "There is no dictatorship in volunteer effort. It is by voluntary mobilization that we can answer autocracy with democracy." Hoover employed the language of democracy in an attempt to reconcile this broad new administrative power with deep-seated fears—fears that he himself shared—of government intervention and economic regulation. He therefore characterized the Food Administration as simply "the organization of democracy."[13] Rhetoric aside, his agency's reliance on a large network of volunteers with an extensive reach over market transactions made it a pervasive and potent regulatory force. While much new power accrued to the state, Hoover also depended on the volunteer efforts of ordinary Americans, over whom he had limited control.

Hoover's agency built on and fostered the public activism of preexisting women's groups. Whereas industrial mobilization drew the business elite to Washington to participate in the newly created War Industries Board (WIB) and stimulated the formation of trade associations with which government agencies could work, consumer mobilization appealed to all the nation's housewives in their localities.[14] In the process, the Food Administration reinforced the emergence of a popular consumer culture predicated on getting more for one's money. Though asking for consumer sacrifice, its program helped to justify and spread popular notions of antagonism toward profiteering and unreasonable prices similar to those that had animated earlier sporadic protests.

Throughout the summer of 1917, the Lever Bill encountered fierce resistance. For over two months opponents, who feared the precedent of government intervention in the economy, tried to prevent its passage. The debate also revealed unavoidable tensions between farmers who demanded high prices and urban consumers who opposed them. Bread was a key item, given its centrality to the Allied war effort and to working-class households. To stimulate production without dramatically raising prices, the bill specified a price for wheat to enable a "reasonable profit guaranteed by the government." Since commodity prices had peaked at a considerably higher level in the spring than the bill now specified, wheat farmers and their representatives staged a serious protest. In the Senate, Agricultural Committee chairman Thomas Gore from Oklahoma, a large wheat-producing state, strongly opposed the bill. What Hoover called "speculation" others called "the legitimate pursuit of farming and of business."[15]

Government restrictions on wheat prices unleashed widespread fears of intrusive government policies. The National Council of Farmers' Cooperative Associations, representing four hundred thousand grain growers, offered to support the bill but demanded restrictions on other products. Representative Gilbert Haugen from Iowa called for price controls on shoes and clothing. Inevitably this suggestion provoked fierce opposition from southern Democrats, who as Wilson's core supporters were politically safeguarded from restrictions on cotton prices. Still, calls for controls triggered alarm among southerners and representatives from manufacturing areas. Senator Lawrence Sherman of Illinois denounced the bill as "foolish, autocratic, confiscatory, unconstitutional, and idiotic." "We don't want to put a food dictator in who is merely going to ship cargoes over to Great Britain." Along with other leading Republicans such as Senator Henry Cabot Lodge of Massachusetts and Senator James A. Reed of Missouri, Sherman railed against the specter of a "food dictatorship." In general, they resented Wilson's presidential encroachment on what they deemed to be congressional affairs. Opponents launched several failed efforts to curb Hoover's sole authority, including an attempt to create a congressional war board to oversee war expenditures. The insertion of an amendment to ban the manufacture of intoxicating beverages further delayed the bill's passage. Only the need to regulate prices for the 1917 harvest and strong support from southern Democrats, who won their exemptions for cotton, led to its enactment.[16]

Once the Lever Act finally passed on August 10, 1917, Hoover's agency spun out across the nation. On his forty-third birthday, Hoover assumed the official post of U.S. food administrator. In its final form, the Lever Act forbade hoarding, speculating on, monopolizing, or manipulating the nation's food and fuel supply. According to the *New York Times*, Hoover "immediately served notice on speculators and profiteers that the time of reckoning had come for those who would not cooperate in the efforts of the Government to obtain lower prices for the consumer." In the fall of 1917, Hoover initiated a second round of the pledge campaign under the slogan "Food Will Win the War." Each state had its own food administration with a campaign committee to sign up housewives. These state and local committees in turn relied upon GFWC women to chair local headquarters in each district. In New York, for example, Chairman Arthur Williams turned to the president of the local federation chapter to recruit sixteen thousand women to mobilize the district's 1.2 million housewives. The U.S. Food Administration announced that "half a million canvassers are ready for the campaign to induce at least 13,000,000 of the country's 22,000,000 housewives to sign the pledge to conserve food during the war." Within weeks, one in three families had signed a pledge. In an organizational form that would recur in the next world war, the Food Administration employed three thousand people on its Washington staff and recruited eight hundred thousand volunteers.[17]

Hoover's campaign elevated ordinary household concerns into a vital national cause and imbued it with patriotic fervor. In New York's inaugural ceremony, soldiers' mothers signed the first pledge cards. More than a public show of patriotism, this ceremony enlisted women as voluntary agents in a branch of the federal government. Each housewife who signed a pledge received the shield of the Food Administration to wear on her sleeve in the kitchen. Hoover told them, "Every pound of fat is as sure of service as every bullet, and every hog is of greater value for the winning of this war than a shell." O. H. Van Norden, chairman of the Speakers' Bureau of the Food Administration, told a New York audience, "The war is going to be won by the kitchens of America." New York's Food Supply Committee distributed a 112-page pamphlet, *Hints to Housewives*, with suggestions for meat substitutes and economizing recipes. In response, women prepared "Hooverized" menus.[18]

The Food Administration enlisted the support of all kinds of organizations to reach Americans. Churches throughout the country implemented a system of weekly report cards, on which each family detailed its conservation efforts as stipulated in the Food Administration's guidelines for seven meatless meals, seven wheatless meals, and seven meals of leftovers. Chain stores and department stores enrolled in the effort to get housewives' signatures and distribute information. Because the government's administrative capacity was limited, it accepted the help of New York insurance companies to process pledge cards.[19]

Like Wilson, Hoover denounced profiteering. To ask Americans to conserve without challenging price hikes was politically untenable and economically unsound. In his "campaign for lower prices," Hoover relied on more than moral suasion and mass mobilization. The Lever Act created the United States Grain Corporation and the Sugar Equalization Board to influence market prices. Hoover controlled Allied purchases and could even negotiate the price of hogs. He also invoked the Lever Act's powers of licensing to eliminate "unreasonable" spreads between wholesale and retail prices. As the *New York Times* reported, "The middlemen and others will be forced at all times to open their books to the agents of the Food Administration." That prospect of opening the books and scrutinizing company profits would remain a potent political tool through the New Deal and into the post–World War II decades. By threatening to revoke licenses if prices were substantially higher than costs, the government had at its disposal a "complete check on the operations of all who would seek to profit at the expense of the consumer." The threat extended to all meat packers, cold-storage warehousemen, millers, canners, grain dealers, wholesale distributors, and retailers doing an annual business greater than $100,000 who, in Hoover's estimation, "exact[ed] exorbitant prices." By December 1917, Wilson gave Hoover the authority to limit profit margins on foodstuffs to prewar levels.[20]

The Lever Act empowered the Food Administration to regulate large retailers who earned more than $100,000 annually, but it took aim at smaller merchants. At the time, there were 400,000 food retailers in the country; of these, only 1,200 were regulated under the Lever Act. Many of these prominent mass retailers collaborated with Hoover and assisted in the conservation movement. Michael Friedsam, president of the B. Altman department store, assisted in the New York State food-saving campaign by coordinating the distribution of twenty-five thousand posters to merchants to use in window displays. He served as New York's quartermaster general and retail merchant representative in the Food Administration. In Boston, Edward Filene played a leading role in organizing retailers behind Hoover. Filene's manager, Louis Kirstein, and Julius Rosenwald of Sears aided the U.S. quartermaster in requisitioning food, clothing, and shoes. William Lutey, operator of Montana's largest retail, wholesale, and mail-order grocery chain, served as that state's food administrator. Mass retailers supported Hoover's philosophy of eliminating waste and increasing efficiency, because they saw themselves as the vanguard of modern distribution. These businessmen

FIGURE 2.2. Compliance with the U.S. Food Administration "fair prices" rested largely on public pressure. The government issued suggested prices printed bi-weekly in local newspapers for merchants to display and consumers to take along on shopping trips.

regarded the mom-and-pop stores as the extortionists who cheated the consuming public. The Food Administration reinforced this perception of local shops as bastions of higher prices. In October, Hoover began to publish wholesale prices so consumers could evaluate the markup at retail, and the administration asked newspapers to publish "official fair price" lists for twenty-one basic food items daily.[21]

Hoover faced real limitations, as the example of meat demonstrates. Exhortations to limit its consumption yielded mixed results. In one beefless day, the Waldorf Astoria Hotel conserved 2,000 pounds of meat. Massachusetts hotels and restaurants saved 640 tons of meat in one month. Yet annual meat consumption declined by a mere 4 percent, from 140 to 135 pounds per person. Allied demand and grain policies that raised production costs caused meat prices to double. To deter speculation, Hoover suspended trading in red-meat futures. He also set limits on packers' profits and earnings. To obtain their compliance with production quotas, however, Hoover was compelled to allow packers a generous rate of return. *New Republic* editor George Soule explained, "Just because their monopoly is so nearly complete their machinery must be utilized and their help secured." Under pressure from such criticism, the administration authorized the Federal Trade Commission (FTC) to unleash "a force of accountants" to search through the books of the large Chicago meat packers and "determine whether the price of meats to the consumer could be brought down." To head the investigation the FTC recruited Stuart Chase, an accountant who, by decade's end, would found a consumer movement for lower prices and better quality.[22]

Hoover had little interest in overthrowing deeply entrenched market practices, but his morally charged rhetoric stimulated popular expectations and demands for him to do so. That became clear in the developing crisis over milk. By 1914, almost half of the milk in major metropolitan areas was coming from just a few national distributors. Beginning in 1915, demands of well-organized dairy farmers led to a rapid increase in milk prices. Faced with higher feed costs, they grew restless in the fall of 1917 and threatened to strike for even higher prices. Hoover tried to appeal to them without much success. In Boston, the Chamber of Commerce and the presidents of the Massachusetts Institute of Technology, Amherst College, and Williams College formed the Milk Consumers' Association to investigate prices. The attorney general of Illinois charged milk producers with a nationwide plot to raise milk prices. By December, a growing crisis forced the Food Administration to hold federal hearings in New York, Boston, Chicago, and San Francisco. Responding to "discontent among consumers over increasing prices," these regional milk tribunals empowered local bodies "to determine . . . the reasonable prices of milk to be paid."[23]

Socialists and progressive reformers had always wanted to regulate milk and meat, and they now had their chance. Frederic Howe, a well-known urban reformer and the commissioner of immigration of the New York Ports, popularized plans to establish distribution of food direct from producers to consumers. In his book *The High Cost of Living* (1917), Howe argued that the near-monopolistic control of distribution increased the cost of food. Ignoring the international causes of inflation, Howe instead castigated villainous middlemen and nefarious trusts. Only abolishing them, creating public markets, and nationalizing the packinghouses would end "monopoly prices." Those sentiments were widespread, and consumers and government authorities took action. In New York, for example, the state commissioner of food and markets, John Dillon, met with labor leaders from the AFL, the United Hebrew Trades, and the Women's Trade Union League (WTUL) to organize a plan for distributing milk directly from the farmers to the city's three hundred thousand wage-earning families. To deal with the emerging crisis, particularly in milk and bread, the city gained the right to purchase food and sell it at cost.[24]

These consumer politics at the marketplace were matched by even more radical changes on the shop floor. Between April and October 1917, the greatest strike wave to date caused the loss of six million workdays involving over one million workers. As demand for employees increased and labor markets tightened, organized workers saw their opportunity to reassert control over job processes that had been lost to the twin forces of technology and employers' efforts to improve efficiency. This crescendo of strike activity also was a response to rising prices that were eroding wage gains. In this politicized economy, government officials felt compelled to provide a role for labor in national planning. In early 1918, Wilson established the National War Labor Board (NWLB). Staffed by a team of sympathetic reformers, the NWLB mediated more than one thousand strikes, institutionalized a system of collective bargaining, and gave new legitimacy to the organized labor movement. Between 1914 and 1920, the number of unionized workers doubled to five million, exceeding enrollment in the American Expeditionary Force in Europe. The war led to union gains in the mines, in the garment trades, and in mass-production industries previously ignored by the AFL, such as meatpacking and steel. In factories across the country, workers appropriated the language of America's war to "make the world safe for democracy" and applied it to the shop floor. The effect was electrifying, as work, and even unionizing, became patriotic acts.[25]

To quell the threat of strikes, the Wilson administration sought to reach an alliance with patriotic workers and to put in place many Progressive Era reforms. The NWLB prohibited strikes and lockouts in exchange for union recognition, the eight-hour day, and equal pay for equal work. The Department of Labor created the U.S. Employment Service and the Women in Industrial Service Division under WTUL's Mary Van Kleeck. In the District of Columbia, the National Consumers' League succeeded in obtaining a minimum-wage law for women. At Florence Kelley's request, Edward Filene testified on the bill's behalf. With the help of Amalgamated Clothing Workers' Sidney Hillman and Filene's Louis Kirstein, the army implemented labor standards for the production of uniforms.[26]

Wartime inflation put consumer purchasing power at the top of the nation's political agenda and moved to the fore a policy network of labor-oriented intellectuals and policy planners. In yet another wartime victory for organized labor, a group of policymakers helped to institutionalize wages based on the cost of living. The NWLB relied on well-organized workers to boost their income and linked democracy in the workplace to the maintenance of living wages for the masses of industrial employees. As director of the U.S. Shipping Board's Emergency Fleet Corporation, Filene was part of this group. He worked with journalist Walter Lippmann, now assistant to the secretary of war, and Assistant Secretary of the Navy Franklin Roosevelt to establish living-wage scales for workers in government plants. To adjust wages throughout the economy, the Bureau of Labor Statistics recruited University of Chicago sociologist William Ogburn to conduct the first national cost-of-living study. From his post as secretary of the National War Labor Board, W. Jett Lauck made the living wage the basis of public policy.[27]

These state-supported institutional reforms represented a substantial break from the prewar antiunion political economy. But a rising price level threatened to blow apart any labor accommodation. Wilson had appointed Frank Taussig, a well-respected economist, and Robert Brookings, a wealthy businessman and founder of the Brookings Institution, to head a price-fixing committee. It did not bode well for price stability that Taussig described the wartime economy as dominated by "soaring prices, speculative advances, manipulations by middlemen, a runaway market." By the spring of 1918, Brookings warned Wilson, "The labor wage and cost of living are inseparable. It is probably our most important economic problem." "[There is] no greater stimulus to strikes for advanced wages than the constantly advancing price of shoes and clothing." In a visionary plan that went nowhere, Brookings appealed to manufacturers to mass-produce affordable "Liberty" items for "working people." In particular he tried to sell his idea of a "Liberty shoe," one that was high quality with few frills at an affordable price. While rejecting such schemes, the business mobilizers of the War Industries Board recognized the need for conciliatory action. WIB member George Peek warned shoe executives about the risks of high prices: "It would mean an intolerable situation which would force . . . Government ownership or control of practically all the basic goods of the country—and that is no theory." WIB chairman Bernard Baruch feared that the only way to forestall more drastic alternatives would be to "stabilize the price of shoes and standardize the styles."[28]

In sum, wartime inflation set in motion a new politics predicated on the problem of working-class purchasing power. The war brought inflationary concerns to the fore and influenced political and economic debate for a generation. Fearful of massive unrest as prices outpaced wages and salaries, the wartime government ratified an incipient consumer consciousness and facilitated the growth of organized labor. The administration's denunciations of manufacturers, middlemen, and merchants as war profiteers and its creation of a state oversight apparatus to monitor wages and prices validated and encouraged grassroots activism at the market and on the shop floor. That mobilization, made possible by war, was an end run around direct controls that policymakers worried would inhibit production at a moment of great national need. American participation in the war lasted for less than two years, but the experience had an enduring impact. As prices shot up, the campaign against the high cost of living prompted local activism that often went beyond the government's appeals and developed its own powerful political momentum.

Make Way for the Consumer, 1919–1925

The end of the war in 1918 brought no respite from what the *New Republic* called the "realities of the price problem." By the beginning of 1919, the situation had reached a boiling point. With the prospect of falling markets, manufacturers were reluctant to cut prices. In a program even more ambitious than resale price maintenance, WIB's George Peek and other industry representatives pushed for the creation of a peacetime industrial board to suspend antitrust laws and maintain prices. Even without an explicit program, prices went up, fueled by an influx of gold and an expansion of credit to facilitate wartime government borrowing. From the armistice in November 1918 until June 1920, prices increased by over 30 percent. Buoyed by the acceptance of the living-wage idea and the achievement of other real gains, AFL president Samuel Gompers vowed that labor would not let wages fall. The great strike wave that besieged the nation in 1919 resulted not just from intense class antagonisms and the quest for industrial democracy but also from wages that were out of kilter with rapidly rising prices. As conservative economist Irving Fisher put it, "Radicalism rides on the wave of high prices." With workers' real wages declining, "there is, now, and long has been, a real basis for labor discontent."[29]

President Wilson now found himself between opposing camps. Organized business representatives sought to fix prices just as organized labor and a consuming public mobilized to defend itself against the high cost of living. Upon his return from the Paris Peace Conference, the president launched a forceful attack against profiteering, hoping to appease the public and forestall labor unrest. The Food Control Act's antiprofiteering provisions had empowered the Department of Justice to go after profiteers, and now federal agents mounted an assault. Attorney General A. Mitchell Palmer, who would soon become known for his prosecution of radicals in the Red Scare of 1919, led the charge and singled out the meat packers. The Federal Trade Commission investigation had found the packers guilty. Palmer promised to unleash "the wrath of the American people" on them and considered appointing women as special agents to detect profiteering.[30]

The administration's call to arms encouraged grassroots activism. Women were mobilized. Having helped to secure the passage of the Nineteenth Amendment, which gave them the vote, elite clubwomen all across the nation continued their drift to political activism and joined the fight against the "high cost of living." President Rita Yawger of the New York GFWC chapter condemned the high price of fish and suggested malfeasance. "Is it not strange that fresh fish from the Atlantic Ocean is cheaper in Pittsburgh than it is in the Port of New York?" She questioned why "people residing at the ocean's edge are forced to pay a higher price for their living than those living hundreds of miles distant from the source of supply." Upper-class privileged women announced their loyalty to their working-class sisters and declared their commitment, as Helen Varrick Boswell put it, to "bringing down sugar and eggs and milk to the purchasing power of Mrs. Murphy, of the Bowery, and Mrs. Horowitz, of Rivington Street."[31]

In this campaign against high prices, Mary Rumsey, the daughter of railroad financier Edward Henry Harriman, played a leading role. Rumsey had long used her social standing for community service, as she would later when she assumed national prominence in the New Deal as the country's official consumer advocate. In 1901, at age twenty, the young Mary Harriman organized the Junior League for the Promotion of Settlement Movements. During the war, she served as president of the Community Councils of National Defense. Along with Rose Schneiderman, president of the New York Women's Trade Union League, Rumsey sat on the Industrial Relations Sub-Committee of the Community Councils, consulting with President Wilson on labor issues. With Rumsey as a leading voice, that body endorsed the principles of collective bargaining, profit sharing, industrial democracy, unemployment insurance, and workmen's compensation. Sympathetic to the squeeze on people's pocketbooks, the committee argued that the high cost of living was a major cause of industrial unrest. A graduate of Barnard and member of its board of trustees, Rumsey led a drive to boost teachers' salaries. After the war, she pushed for the maintenance of community councils as the basis of local cooperative groups. Rumsey had developed an interest in agricultural cooperatives and dairy farming on her family's large estate on Long Island, and she had helped organize the Eastern Livestock Cooperative Marketing Association. In the fall of 1919, she fought rising costs as chair of the New York Fair Price Committee on field activities.[32]

With the support of the Food Administration, prominent women organized fair-price committees to police prices of basic commodities such as milk, bread, and butter. Harriet Elliott of the Women's Committee of

"KEEP YOUR HANDS OFF THE SCALES!"

—Chapin in the St. Louis *Republic.*

FIGURE 2.3. The St. Louis *Republic* 1919 cartoon captures popular sentiment blaming postwar inflation on merchants who gouged the consuming public. In this particular case, the butcher rests his hands on the scale to inflate the price of meat artificially.

the Council of National Defense recruited eighty thousand members nationally from community councils, many of whom came from the seventeen thousand local chapters of the GFWC. Elliott would later build on this experience when she became a leader in price control during World War II. In August 1919, the *New York Times* reported that "a small army of women is being mobilized to co-operate with the Federal Food Administrator." Women received a blank report card to record "excessive prices charged by their neighborhood grocers" and were instructed to send them to the Food Administration. They also investigated specific complaints brought to their attention and reported those charging "excessive" prices to state district attorneys.[33]

Under Rumsey's command, fifty thousand New York women fought high prices through a store-to-store canvass. Reaching into all New York neighborhoods, Rumsey's troops "spread fair price propaganda through every home in the five boroughs." According to the *New York Times*, women now "think themselves entitled to a say-so about the establishment of food prices." Rumsey understood the threat these policing activities posed. "We are not going to set off any bombs under retailers, but we do want to learn if they are justified in charging the present prices."[34] In the context of recent anarchist bombings that terrified the nation, her words were not received as idle rhetoric.

Fair-price committees gathered local market knowledge to construct fair-price lists for publication in the country's newspapers. A typical headline read, "Fair Price Committee's List of What Groceries Should Cost New York Consumers." Captions under the price of products like beans, flour, sugar, bread, and milk stated, "It is suggested by the Fair Price Committee that the reader cut out these prices and keep them for reference when making purchases." Arthur Williams, the New York food administrator, asserted, "Housewives are being educated in buying. They know what certain foods ought to be purchased for and where the prices are inflated, they file a complaint with us." A Brooklyn woman wrote in appreciation after encountering what she believed to be an inflated price for a three-and-a-half-pound bag of flour: "Thanks to your list I knew the price was excessive, so I went to another dealer." Studies by the U.S. Statistical Division suggested that such public pressure was effective. Meat packers complained that these so-called fair prices would force them out of business.[35]

The fair-price committees extended their reach to cover other basic necessities, such as shoes and clothing. In 1920, shoes cost three times their 1913 level. At a mass rally at New York's Cooper Union, Francis J. Heney, chief counsel for the FTC, aroused the crowd with warnings that the big packers' "tentacles are reaching far and wide." Through their influence over by-products such as leather, they had "a death grip on the clothing industry now in addition to the food monopoly." Michael Friedsam, head of the Fair Price Committee on Clothing and Shoes, announced that he would investigate every phase of production and distribution "to compute a fair margin of profit." He called for the production of a line of low-priced items, the very thing that the shoe manufacturers had resisted.[36] In the campaign for resale price maintenance, proponents had tried to appropriate the language of fairness.

But it was clear that fair prices had come to mean lower prices, determined not by businessmen but by consumers and their government supporters.

Shopping around for the best buy had become a national imperative. The Bureau of Labor Statistics reported that retail food prices in December 1919 had almost doubled since 1914. When army surplus shops sold food and other basic staples at cut-rate prices, thousands lined up. Edward Filene encouraged members of Boston's Federation of Women's Clubs to "Go back to the shopping-around habit. Many prices are no longer competitive because the storekeeper thinks he has a permanent clientele and can charge them whatever he wishes. Make him realize that you will not buy from him if you can buy as good or better articles at a less price elsewhere." Though no longer the nation's food administrator, Herbert Hoover concurred: "The relief [to profiteering] may be found in the public's shopping around. If the public will go from one store to another comparing prices before purchasing, the small amount of profiteering that exists will quickly be wiped out."[37]

In a sense, the fair-price campaign was not particularly radical. Most attacked small businessmen rather than large structural forces of the modern economy. As the *New Republic* noted, and Hoover's comment hinted, the causes of inflation transcended "the personal greed of particular individuals." Royal Meeker, the U.S. commissioner of labor statistics, explained the situation in early 1920 in even bolder terms: "If all the profiteers in the world could be apprehended and thrown into jail or lined up and shot, it would have no appreciable influence on prices." Irving Fisher, president of the American Economic Association, explained that charges of profiteering were simply political and missed the true cause of inflation. According to this Yale economist, the influx of gold from Europe, combined with the Federal Reserve's expansion of credit, were the true forces behind a monetary inflation. Less than one-third of war financing had been based on taxation; the rest had come from borrowing.[38]

Yet the antiprofiteering campaign lent validity to more radical protests. Though skeptical of the campaign's effectiveness, the *New Republic* noted, "The profiteer hunt will help to destroy the illusion, if it persists anywhere, that great private wealth is in itself tangible evidence of great public service, or even of great natural ability."[39] The shared language of workers and consumers in asserting their demands for fairness and the right to a high living standard gave each group a more radical cast and carried the threat of a widespread challenge to corporate power and local businessmen. A Minnesota merchant bemoaned the fact that "the Attorney Generals and the radical newspapers" led consumers "to believe that every time they made a purchase at a retail store they were being held up and robbed."[40]

In the summer of 1919, the New York Consumers' League, the Socialist Consumers' League, and the Progressive Women of the Bronx unleashed strikes against butchers and bakers. Amid wartime housing shortages, rents escalated and agitators staged massive demonstrations against landlords. The Socialist Party organized rent strikes between 1917 and 1920, forming tenant groups from the Lower East Side to East Harlem to Brooklyn and the Bronx. Clara Lemlich, a veteran of the 1909 garment strike, led her Brownsville building on strike.[41] Jewish women paraded with banners that proclaimed in Yiddish, "We are striking!" Two thousand Brooklyn renters went on strike, declaring "Down with profiteering landlords!" A crowd of two hundred women tenants turned on their landlord's son, Abraham Ernstedoff. Ernstedoff's mother came to his aid, wielding a rolling pin. Esther Yerkowitz, one of the striking tenants, grabbed the pin and struck back, hitting the landlord's son. To quell unrest, Mayor Mike Hylan established the Committee on Rent Profiteering. Volatile and intense, these rent wars spurred the state legislature to enact rent controls in 1920.[42] Popular protests over the cost of living could therefore yield real results.

Pocketbook issues found support from the clubwomen in the nation's heartland to Socialists on the Lower East Side. Upon her return from the Paris Peace Conference, where she represented women wage earners, Rose Schneiderman ran for the U.S. Senate in New York as the newly formed Farmer-Labor Party candidate. Schneiderman campaigned against the high cost of living, calling for publicly owned terminal markets, municipal sales of bread, milk, and coal, state-owned packinghouses and mills, more affordable housing, and social insurance. At their 1920 annual convention in Iowa, the General Federation of Women's Clubs voted support for the Department of Justice's attack on profiteering and for government branding of textiles and clothes. They also affirmed their support of minimum-wage legislation for women. Journalist John Spargo, describing the rise of a new "consciousness of the consumers, as consumers," noted that it "tends to unite by ties of common interests the overwhelming majority of the people. The controlling interest of the consumer is efficient and economical service. . . . They all want to be able to secure shelter and fuel, food and clothing for themselves and their families at prices which they can pay." He concluded optimistically, "Any real socialization of the economic life of modern nations will have to be based upon the interests of the consumer and governed by the service ideal." He titled his article, "Make Way for the Consumer!"[43]

The power of this "high cost of living crusade" was not lost on its opponents. Together, consumer and labor movements triggered a wave of repression of radical political activity. The elections of 1918 had yielded substantial Republican victories and returned Congress to that party's control. Wilson's wheat policies had cost Democrats over twenty House seats in major wheat states, and conservatives everywhere chafed to eliminate wartime regulations and reverse this wartime popular mobilization.[44] In contrast to the fair-price campaigns, a more conservative line of attack blamed consumers themselves as "profiteers' accomplices." Even the administration played both sides of this issue, initiating a national thrift campaign against extravagance in the fall of 1919.[45] The director of the Savings Division of the Treasury Department, W. M. Lewis, announced, "A veritable orgy of extravagant buying is going on, . . . nothing else can be expected than high prices." Orrin Lester, also in the Treasury Department, advocated "judicious buying." "Let 'Refuse to Buy' become a national slogan. Let the people start a movement to police their own pocketbooks." That would end the "mad wave of extravagance" that he blamed for the "H.C.L." Joining in the reproof of consumer profligacy, a reporter for *Literary Digest* stated, "We shall always have the problem of the high cost of living so long as we have an extravagant and thoughtless consuming public." The idea that consumers were extravagant suggested a lingering nineteenth-century moralism. *Ladies' Home Journal* contributor Christine Frederick explained, "We have all been participants in a wild, bacchanalian orgy wherein we cast aside our usual sense and caution and flung our money insanely to the winds, gorging ourselves on every delicacy and indulging our desire of licentious spending until we finally achieved an economic debauch."[46]

Returned to power, Republican leaders reined in any lingering constraints on corporate interests. They dismantled the Railroad Administration, which had controlled the country's transportation during the war, and rebuffed proposals to nationalize the nation's coal mines. Senator James Watson, a Republican from Indiana, demanded an investigation into the FTC, declaring it to be "permeated with red flag socialism and anarchism." Senator Lawrence Sherman echoed that sentiment, charging the FTC with treason and conspiracy. Both represented meatpacking interests and sought to discredit the FTC's profiteering charges. Senator Watson indicted FTC's meat investigator Stuart Chase. Among the activities that made Chase suspect was the fact that he and his new bride had spent their honeymoon in Rochester, New York, investigating life among the poor. Under Chase's charge, his critics claimed, the FTC's Chicago office had become "the center of Socialistic activities." Chase associated with well-known radicals such as Victor Berger and Lincoln Steffens, and he called for recognition of the Soviet government.[47]

The fall of 1919 brought an ideological and structural shift in the American political economy in response to the fear of radicalism sweeping the world. The Bolshevik victories during the Russian Revolution seemed to augur the beginning of worldwide socialist upheavals, a specter made real by the wave of terrifying strikes that gripped the country in 1919, when a stunning four million workers struck to retain their wartime gains amid a postwar inflationary surge. The Amalgamated Clothing Workers' Sidney Hillman wrote to his daughter, "One can hear the footsteps of the Deliverer. . . . Labor will rule and the World will be free for ever." The strike wave began in early 1919 in the Seattle shipyards when workers protested wage cuts. Their action soon escalated into a citywide general strike. Throughout the year, 20 percent of the nonagricultural workforce went on strike in the steel, coal, railroad, textile, meat, and countless other industries. In the fall, 350,000 steelworkers and 425,000 coal workers walked out, as did the Boston police force and New England telephone operators. Attorney General Palmer warned Wilson about the political costs of continuing Democratic support of labor. In September, Wilson forcefully broke the steel strike and intimidated the miners.[48]

Conservative antilabor elites won a new audience in what became known as the Red Scare. The problem of high prices persisted, but the social energy they ignited soon dissipated as all radical behavior became suspect. Attorney General Palmer, who had previously attacked meat packers, now went after labor and its allies. He initiated raids on radicals throughout the country, issuing arrest warrants and deportation orders. Frederic Howe, author of *The High Cost of Living* and a close friend of the president, found himself under attack for having delayed deportation of radicals detained on Ellis Island in his capacity as commissioner of immigration. The federal crackdown played out locally. In Mount Vernon, New York, a crowd of two thousand citizens, including members of the American Legion, chased a campaigning Rose Schneiderman out of town. The New York Assembly refused to seat five elected Socialists. The most celebrated case of political repression came when two Italian-born anarchists, Nichola Sacco and Bartolomeo Vanzetti, were arrested on murder charges. When they received the death sentence, thousands throughout the world condemned what they perceived to be an unfair trial. In a small gesture of sympathy, Filene's manager, Louis Kirstein, hired Sacco's son as his driver.[49]

Anxious to flex their muscles, the U.S. Chamber of Commerce and the National Association of Manufacturers coordinated a nationwide attack on unions. In 240 cities, the business community led an open-shop drive, dubbed the American Plan, against union workers. These businessmen appropriated a wartime patriotic language of democracy, dulled its radical edge, and used it to clampdown on labor. In addition to the specter of Bolshevism, conservatives redirected blame for the high cost of living from business to labor. If workers won their wage demands, higher costs would be the result. During the coal strike, for example, Palmer insisted that any wage gains "will insure unreasonably high prices in all commodities for at least three years to come."[50]

Workers and their allies defended themselves to little effect. W. Jett Lauck, the former secretary of the War Labor Board, charged capitalists and financiers with a "deliberate campaign of propaganda and misrepresentation to fasten upon labor the responsibility for high prices; in other words to play off the two sets of victims, the public and the workers, against each other." "Where profiteering is rampant, it can be proved conclusively that the guilt is ascribable to price gouging and not to wage awards." Lauck captured national headlines for weeks, arguing that the inflated prices and excessive profits of packers, steel and copper companies, flour millers, and cotton and wool interests bilked the American public.[51] At the annual convention of the United Shoe Workers of America in 1919, Stephen Walsh of Lynn, Massachusetts, insisted, "We are not responsible for the prices, but on the contrary, we feel that we are not receiving a fair share of the profits of production." Edward Filene agreed with this labor leader from his hometown and denounced what he called "counterfeit wages." "It is not a question of 'how much wages,' but 'what wages will buy.'" Given the rise in living costs, "no one can blame the wage earner if he is discontented and keeps demanding higher pay."[52]

The economy took a nosedive in 1921, undercutting labor and consumers' new-found strength. The drastic decline undermined labor's wage demands and led to major union setbacks. With four million workers unemployed by 1921, labor had little leverage, and union membership rapidly dwindled. Amid a precipitous fall in prices, manufacturers turned the logic of living wages on its head and initiated a massive wage cut. The recession of 1920–1921 wiped out labor's wartime gains. Labor expert Evans Clark concluded, "The cost of living argument, which had been so convincing when prices were going up, was turned against labor with deadly effect." Devastating wage cuts revealed the limitations of the living-wage argument, prompting, as Clark explained, "wise heads in the labor movement [to] cast about for some sword to wield in wage disputes that was not double-edged."[53]

In the wake of such rapid economic reversal, liberal reformers in and around the labor movement explained the decline by asserting that high prices had exceeded what consumers could afford. Though marginal politically, in the 1920s, a group of "purchasing-power progressives" formalized a critique of high prices and low wages into an economic theory of underconsumption. In a momentous shift, these critics supplemented claims about the right to an American standard of living as morally correct and politically essential with an economic argument about the need for mass purchasing as the key to national prosperity. As the nation slid deeper into depression, liberals sympathetic to the interests of organized labor denounced the "folly of wage cutting." Lauck argued that failing to pay a living wage "saps the strength of the nation itself."[54] As products accumulated on shelves, the National Association of Manufacturers and the U.S. Chamber of Commerce urged consumers to "Buy now and put the money back to work." "Your purchase keeps America employed." But labor leaders claimed that the nation's consumers, from white-collar employees on fixed salaries to skilled tradesmen to unskilled factory workers, lacked the necessary purchasing power to sustain demand. Massive cuts in wages would only hasten decline.[55]

The idea of mass purchasing power was put on the agenda by a network of labor progressives and liberal thinkers in response to the unresolved questions of the war. They now justified their demands for living wages based on workers' status as one of the nation's largest groups of consumers. They aimed to discredit and marginalize a nineteenth-century moral sensibility in which individual and family prosperity stemmed from virtuous personal character, hard work, and thrifty behavior. In a modern capitalist economy, they argued, individuals had little control over the larger structural forces that shaped their economic destiny. Not only were prices too high, they claimed, but also wages were too low. Linking the politics of inflation with the politics of income distribution, they developed their critique into a theory of underconsumption and argued that workers had to be able to consume for the economy to prosper.

At a time when many Americans lived at or below the subsistence level, these purchasing-power progressives saw mass consumption as a great liberating force that would preserve democracy, enhance the quality of life, and forestall destabilizing economic cycles. After the Supreme Court repealed minimum-wage legislation in 1923, Rose Schneiderman urged a new law for women, one that would "permit her to live in a decent neighborhood, eat wholesome food and dress in an attractive way."[56] But labor advocates now argued that increasing income was no longer only a matter of social justice and economic fairness. Workers, especially the unskilled masses of immigrants, would have to receive higher wages to soak up the avalanche of new products. The Labor Bureau, Inc., which was founded in May 1920 by Evans Clark, George Soule, and David Saposs and developed into a key institution of this purchasing-power advocacy network, chided the businessman who mistakenly "thinks of the wage-earner merely as a factor in production costs and forgets that he also makes up one of the most numerous classes of consumers."[57]

The Labor Bureau, which assisted hundreds of unions in their negotiations, demonstrated the links between purchasing-power progressives and the left wing of American politics.[58] From 1913 to 1917, Clark had taught government at Princeton University, where he was involved in pacifist politics. In 1915, he married Freda Kirchwey, editor of the *Nation*. In 1917, he became the research director for the Socialist members of the New York City Board of Aldermen, and two years later he began to work for a Soviet trading bureau in New York, arranging the sale of 135,000 pairs of surplus army shoes to the Soviets. George Soule cowrote with J. M. Budish *The New Unionism in the Clothing Industry* (1920), a largely heroic account of the rise of the Amalgamated Clothing Workers, a union made up predominately of immigrants. David Saposs, himself a Jewish immigrant, worked briefly as the education director of the Amalgamated and shared Soule's commitment to this new unionism among immigrant workers. During the war, Soule had consulted with Secretary of War Newton Baker on labor policy, served as a committeeman of the Farmer-Labor Party, and contributed to the *Nation* and the *New Republic*. Both Soule and Clark had been branded radicals during the Red Scare. At the Labor Bureau, they consulted not only on wages, hours, and shop conditions—the bread-and-butter issues of traditional AFL craft unions—but also on "broad questions of industrial policy." They hired Stuart Chase as their in-house accountant to examine company books and evaluate earnings, and they retained progressive reformer Otto Beyer as a consulting engineer.[59]

These purchasing-power progressives envisioned a socialized capitalism in which the industrial union movement played a crucial role. In part, they took their inspiration from Herbert Hoover, who served as secretary of commerce from 1921 to 1928. From that post, Hoover championed the need for greater efficiency and improved productivity in American industry. As a former engineer, he believed in devising technocratic solutions to seemingly intractable problems, like the business cycle and industrial strife. Coauthored with the Federated American Engineering Societies in 1921, Herbert Hoover's study *Waste in Industry* faulted inefficient management practices more than organized labor for wasteful production practices that unnecessarily raised costs. Throughout his tenure, Hoover worked closely with trade associations to improve and stabilize production through voluntary cooperation among business leaders. To curb the worst excesses of the market, he supported unemployment insurance, countercyclical public-works spending, wage arbitration in rail and coal, and an end to the twelve-hour day in steel mills. The last goal he succeeded in achieving. His technocratic solutions came fundamentally from a production point of view, as he believed in improving production and eliminating waste, figuring that higher wages would naturally follow.[60]

Labor progressives embraced Hoover's war on waste and advanced their own laborite version. Stuart Chase wrote *The Tragedy of Waste* (1925) with the help of George Soule and the Labor Bureau staff. Whereas

Hoover looked to voluntarism and business self-government, Chase asserted that only a vibrant union movement and national industrial planning, like the system that had existed during the war, could result in a doubling of productive power. In just a few wartime years, thirty million workers did the job of forty million, and production increased. Chase wrote, "War control lifted the economic system of the country, stupefied by decades of profit seeking, and hammered it and pounded it into an intelligent mechanism for delivering goods and services." In the absence of a national-planning state, unions could help regularize employment, improve production, eliminate waste, and, most crucially, insist on the redistribution of productivity gains from profits to wages. The Labor Bureau urged a "steadily rising wage level, to increase the buying power of the industrial consumer" as the way to maintain prosperity.[61]

The argument's commonsense appeal only thinly disguised its radical agenda. On the face of it, the authors' claims seemed reasonable and hard to refute: if workers had more disposable income, they could consume more products. Regardless of the size of wage earner's income as a percentage of the population's, it could always be bigger. As long as businesses turned out a greater number of goods, they would need larger markets. In addition, that line of reasoning did not put the interests of wage earners immediately at odds with those of other employees, since the claim was that a larger income for workers would help to sustain economic growth, thereby enlarging the economic pie for all. The argument was made radical, however, by these advocates' insistence not simply on higher wages but also on wage gains as great as productivity gains. In 1923, Soule, speaking for the Labor Bureau, called for an increase in average real wages, "at least in direct relation to increases in productivity." High levels of productivity enabled an American style of redistribution. Soule explained, "The increase in productivity alone has been rapid enough to furnish substantial increase in income to every one, without robbing Peter to pay Paul."[62] That rhetoric was meant to disguise what was indeed a redistributive agenda. Since productivity would nearly double in the 1920s, the Labor Bureau's linking of pay to productivity meant that wage increases would be substantial.

The promotion of consumption by the immigrant masses, in and of itself, gave this program a radical edge amid the culture wars that raged in the 1920s. The strong antagonism to the spread of consumer society in the 1920s echoed the moralists' disdain of department stores at the turn of the century. The flapper—a liberated, sexually free, young woman—emerged as the iconic image of the 1920s that spread through the rapidly expanding mass media of advertising, radio, and movies. Many small-town and rural Americans, including those who migrated to the cities, found in the flapper all that was worrisome about a culture

that was becoming increasingly urban, secular, and centered on pleasure seeking and self-fulfillment through material possessions. The
most extreme form of resistance to consumption came with the ratifica-
tion of the Eighteenth Amendment in 1919, which began the era of
Prohibition. Drinking was seen not only as an abandonment of thrift,
sobriety, and hard work; it was also associated with the looser morals of
the city, especially among the immigrant populations. This deep ambivalence over modernity made a program premised on greater consumption by the immigrant masses suspect.[63]

The purchasing-power labor agenda not only challenged cultural
norms but also came up against existing partisan divisions. Its labor-
centered vision in which mass unions boosted real wages stood in contrast to the reigning Republican political economy of tax cuts and high
tariffs that found widespread support among industrialists, middle-class
professionals, small businessmen, and native skilled workers. The labor
platform also found little support from the Democratic Party still dominated by southern farmers, whose lobbying for agricultural price supports threatened to raise the cost of living. For urban residents the
rhetoric of fair prices meant cheap food, but for farmers fair prices
meant government subsidies. Having expanded their production dramatically from 1914 to 1920 in large part by borrowing, farmers found
themselves in a terrible bind when commodity prices collapsed between
1920 and 1921. Although they could not overcome a presidential veto,
representatives of southern cotton producers joined those of midwestern grain growers to pass the McNary-Haugen Bill to create a system of
price supports. Without a home in either major party, labor leaders and
consumer-minded reformers supported Robert La Follette of Wisconsin
as the 1924 presidential candidate of the Progressive Party. La Follette's
failure to capture much support signaled that an urban liberal agenda
promoting labor and consumer rights would have to wait.[64]

Although marginal politically, throughout the 1920s these purchasing-
power progressives began to solidify a network and articulate a consumer
argument premised on high wages, mass consumption, and industrial
unionism among the millions of unorganized unskilled immigrant
workers. The Amalgamated Clothing Workers (ACW) more than any
other union embraced this vision of consumer utopia. The ACW's Sidney
Hillman explained: "The question of a high living standard for the
American workers is a matter of vital importance to the entire nation. . . .
Any attempt to lower the living standards is certain to bring with it industrial depression." The Amalgamated and the International Ladies'
Garment Workers Union (ILGWU), made up mostly of Russian Jews and
Italians with smaller numbers of Poles and Lithuanians, represented 57
percent of garment workers. With a higher percentage of union members

than existed in any other industry, these unions stood as evidence of the ability to spread unionism among the masses. In 1922, the ACW demonstrated the potential of workers' collective purchasing power by opening its own bank. Within three months deposits totaled nearly one million dollars.[65]

Purchasing-power progressives often gathered to exchange ideas at Brookwood, a resident labor college for union organizers. After her electoral defeat, Rose Schneiderman joined Fannia Cohn of the ILGWU and other union activists to set up Brookwood on a sprawling forty-two acres in Katonah, New York. Its leaders envisioned Brookwood as a training ground for a more expansive industrial labor movement. David Saposs of the Labor Bureau played a prominent role as director of education, and his book *Left Wing Unionism* was required reading. John Brophy of the United Mine Workers and William Z. Foster of the steelworkers' union lent support to the school. Pacifist minister A. J. Muste of the Amalgamated Textile Workers became its first director. The garment, hosiery, and electrical unions funded scholarships for their organizers. Stuart Chase and Otto Beyer gave lectures. Cohn and Schneiderman taught classes on winning the following of the "flapper" generation and organizing wives and mothers of workers into women's auxiliaries. Jett Lauck, now a consultant to the United Mine Workers, also regularly participated. He decried the current state of union affairs in *Political and Industrial Democracy, 1776–1926*, a book that Edward Filene offered to help promote. In the 1930s, Brookwood graduates would provide a cadre of organizers for mass industrial unionism.[66]

Filene emerged as a leading spokesman for industrial unionism and mass purchasing power. In 1919, Filene created the Twentieth Century Fund and endowed it with nearly half a million dollars of company stock. He asked Newton Baker, of the National Consumers' League executive board, and Henry Dennison, another liberal businessman, to serve as board members. He also invited the chairman of General Electric, Owen Young, who agreed with Filene that "the 'producing consumer' is so often the missing link in the economic evolution."[67] Initial grants went to the Women's Trade Union League, the National Consumers' League, the League of Women Voters, and the Bryn Mawr Summer School for Industrial Workers. In 1923, the fund also gave money to the AFL's Matthew Woll for a biography of Samuel Gompers and to striking railroad workers. The bulk of money went toward the establishment of a credit union movement to give wage earners access to affordable loans.[68] To run the fund, Filene, in 1928, would recruit the Labor Bureau's Evans Clark, whom he had met when they were both mediating a strike in the garment trades.

Filene promoted a purchasing-power program in hundreds of public addresses and publications. At the Taylor Society, an organization of

like-minded labor reformers and engineers, Filene insisted, "Mass production can live only through mass distribution, and mass distribution
means a mass of people who have buying power."[69] At the 1924 U.S.
Chamber of Commerce convention, a far less sympathetic audience,
Filene told his colleagues, "The reduction in price should come out of the
elimination of middlemen and the present wastefulness of production
and distribution—not out of wages and salaries."[70] "Production cannot be
profitable," he claimed, "unless it produces, first of all, consumers."[71]
There was no better example of the success of high wages than Henry
Ford, who "has proved beyond question that it is possible to reduce prices,
raise wages, shorten hours, and increase total profits at the same time."
"The one weak spot in the Ford system," Filene was quick to point out in
an article in the *Nation*, was "its undemocratic organization."[72]

Filene publicly supported industrial unionism to solve both labor and
macroeconomic problems. In August 1920, labor economist John
R. Commons explained to the readers of the *Independent* "Why Mary Smith
Wants to Work at Filene's." The short answer was the Filene Cooperative
Association (FCA), whose power exceeded that of many federated labor
unions. It had its own credit union and food cooperative and published its
own newspaper, the *Echo*, available for two cents every Friday. It had a
board of arbitration, made up solely of employees with complete authority
to decide cases of dispute. Employees also were allocated four of nine positions on the store's board of directors.[73] In the 1920s, other leading capitalists sponsored similar welfare measures among their employees as a way
of forestalling unionization. Filene, however, supported the FCA as part of
a broader reform agenda that included workmen's compensation, the
eight-hour day, unionization, collective bargaining, and minimum wages
for women.[74] Filene popularized these ideas in his simply titled book *The
Way Out* (1924). No longer did businessmen have to choose between social justice and profits. "Good social policies are the surest recipe for big
and continuous profits."[75] Filene's commitment to giving workers a measure of democratic control in his store ran deep. So deep, in fact, that it
cost him his job when, in 1928, his brother and other stockholders, all liberals themselves, forced him out.

Purchasing-power progressives saw a campaign for low prices as intimately connected to their support of high wages and labor reform. In
Brooklyn, Clara Lemlich joined forces with Kate Gitlow to form the
United Council of Working Class Housewives. Though they had ties to
the Communist Party, they appealed to all mothers interested in fighting
for a better "quality of life." Their efforts paralleled those of the
National Consumers' League and labor unions, which staged rent boycotts and protested high food costs.[76] In 1925, George Soule and Stuart
Chase of the Labor Bureau joined Wesley Mitchell of the National

Bureau of Economic Resources and E.R.A. Seligman, another prominent economist, on the Producers and Consumers' Organizing Committee to create a public milk monopoly.[77] Mary Rumsey allied with other prominent women in the Consumers' Committee of Women to oppose the Fordney-McCumber Tariff of 1922 and later the Hawley-Smoot Tariff of 1930 as unduly raising the cost of living. This group had the support of the middle-class General Federation of Women's Clubs and the Women's Joint Legislative Committee. The latter body was formed to support wage and hour legislation for women, and it included Eleanor Roosevelt and future secretary of labor Frances Perkins among its members.[78]

Thus an array of activists with different interests, from communist agitators to labor intellectuals to middle-class reformers, embraced the consumer label as a way of pushing for liberal economic reform. In one of the first textbooks on consumer behavior, University of Chicago economist Hazel Kyrk described the consumer as extorted, threatened with adulterated goods, and, in general, "the helpless victim of powerful interests." "The very word 'consumer' is coming to connote the man with a grievance, the one whom the profit system operates to despoil rather than to benefit."[79] Wartime inflation had legitimized the notion of a consumer interest, made clear that the public's inability to keep up with rising prices was a problem national in scope, and suggested the need for large institutional mechanisms to influence the wage-price relationship. The community protests, economic treatises, and labor ideas that grew out of the war rested on the premise that a successful resolution to the purchasing-power question required a program of not only industrial productivity but also consumer activism and unionization. In a bold effort to reinvent itself, the American Federation of Labor would now tackle the problem.

Purchasing Power to the Workers (I), 1925–1930

At its 1925 annual convention, the AFL leaders jettisoned a half-century of tradition when they embraced consumer purchasing power as the basis of wage demands. Samuel Gompers's recent death afforded the opportunity for this historic break. From the AFL's founding in 1886 through World War I, the core idea of unions had been a "Fair Day's Wage for a Fair Day's Work." That idea reflected a producer sensibility and a Christian moralism that prevailed among brotherhoods of skilled workers. But the slogan was no longer enough. It did not take into account the wage-price problem. The living-wage idea that supplemented notions of fairness was also powerful and effective, particularly in a period of rapid inflation and in the presence of a government willing to support organized labor in its collective bargaining. But in the absence of those conditions, a living wage often amounted to no more than what William Ogburn called "a dying wage." In 1925, the AFL leaders traded its outmoded rhetoric for a rationale that justified high wages as essential to sustaining macroeconomic demand. Adopting the rhetoric of his more progressive union brothers, AFL vice president Matthew Woll argued that only higher wages could expand the nation's consuming power.[80]

What led to this historic shift in direction? The immediate impetus came in response to wage cuts in the textile industry. A strike in the anthracite mines also provided a backdrop. The 1920s were "the lean years" for organized labor. Unions claimed 20 percent of the American workforce (compared to 40 percent in England and Germany) and had lost one million members since 1920. Management enforced yellow-dog contracts, which prohibited workers from joining unions, and relied on courts to issue antiunion injunctions. Large manufacturing firms created hundreds of company unions to forestall independent unionization. Outside of the garment industry, unions were strong in the building, printing, and transportation trades but had made few inroads in mass-production industries.

To survive, the AFL needed to expand its base or, at the least, recast its appeal. Woll now pushed the federation to take a formal stand against all wage reductions. John Frey, president of the Ohio State Federation, insisted that "labor has not shared the benefits nor have the masses of people had sufficient buying power to keep production steadily expanding. . . . [T]he time has come when we must restate our philosophy of wages and the principles upon which it rests." What became known as the Frey Resolution captured the expansiveness of the AFL's thinking. "Social inequality, industrial instability and injustice must increase unless the real wage and purchasing power of workers be advanced in proportion to man's increasing power of production."[81] Frey had served in the Hooverite National Bureau of Economic Resources and had contributed to its productivity studies. Now he pushed for the wage hikes that he claimed had failed to accompany production advances.

The purchasing-power argument deliberately aligned the interests of the worker with those of the rest of society. AFL president William Green explained, "Both justice to the individual worker and the economic health of the nation at large demand that labor share the benefits of capital." Green prefigured the Keynesian thinking that would dominate postwar liberal economics, but he emphasized the redistribution of wages through a strong union movement rather than the fiscal powers of the state. "If America's prosperity is to be maintained, it must be possible for the masses of workmen to buy and use the things they have produced."[82] Woll and Frey, who had both grown up in the union movement as skilled craftsmen, consciously adopted this new, expansive rhetoric of the consuming masses as an antidote to waning union power. By the 1930s, they would become staunch labor conservatives, defending the AFL's skilled craft unions against encroachment by unskilled mass industrial unions. But in the mid-1920s, their embrace of an argument for enhancing the masses' ability to purchase goods and services represented a streak of radicalism. That switch conceded a further loss of labor's control over production, but it also signaled the beginning of a powerful new argument that would push labor to the center of national political economic debates for the next several decades.

The idea of underconsumption gained a following not only in labor halls but also at academic conferences, in mass-circulation magazines, and in corporate boardrooms. Two months after the 1925 AFL convention, Frey attended the joint meeting of the American Economic Association and the American Association for Labor Legislation. The meeting was notable for its open and fluid exchange between the world of ideas and the world of business. Frey sat on a panel with investment banker Waddill Catchings on "the consuming power of labor and business fluctuations." Frey asked the audience, "Why is it that with this tremendous power to produce there should be idleness and that manufacturing plants should be operated but part of the time?" "Is it not," he answered, "because the capacity of modern industry to produce exceeds the power of the mass of the people to consume and to use?" To avoid depression, "The workers' real wages—the purchasing power of their wages—must increase in proportion to man's increasing power of production." Catchings affirmed the AFL's analysis. "An increase in the amount received by labor as a whole without a corresponding increase in price is what we seek." This investment-bank president called for discussing "how we may reduce the relative amount going to profit makers, and increase the share of wage-earners."[83]

In the 1920s, Catchings and William Trufant Foster coauthored a series of popular books with titles such as *Money* and *Profits* that endorsed labor's demands for higher real wages. They argued that "the chief cause of the trouble should be called 'underconsumption.' " "Since underconsumption is the chief cause of our troubles," they concluded, "adequate consumer income is the chief remedy."[84] In their widely read 1927 book, *Business without a Buyer*, written amid the flush decade of the 1920s, they warned against this hidden consumption problem. Years before the Great Depression descended upon the country, Catchings and Foster ominously predicted, "The failure of consumer demand to keep pace with the output of consumers' goods is the chief reason why prosperity ends in depression."[85]

The two had met as students at Harvard, and both had connections to liberal businessmen and progressive intellectuals. At the brokerage firm of Goldman, Sachs, Catchings specialized in consumer-sector mergers, facilitating, for example, the expansion of Warner Brothers into a big entertainment conglomerate. Given their reliance on mass markets, some leaders in consumer-goods and mass-retailing industries became increasingly receptive to purchasing-power arguments. Although such attitudes did not always translate into corporate policy, even some capital-intensive producers with relatively low labor costs also saw the macroeconomic value of boosting their workers' income.[86] While Catchings made a fortune on Wall Street, Foster had been appointed the first president of Reed College in 1910; during his tenure there he was influenced by the ideas on working-class purchasing power put forth by two economists on his faculty, Paul H. Douglas and William Ogburn. He returned to the Boston area in 1920 and became associated with leading business reformers, including Filene, whom he regarded as a "comrade in the quest."[87]

The idea of lagging wages became a staple of this progressive crowd. During the 1920s, Foster ran the Pollak Foundation for Economic Research in Newton, Massachusetts. At that time, the foundation funded Paul Douglas's research on real wages that compared wage rates to the cost of living. Following his brief stint at Reed, Douglas had become a well-respected economist at the University of Chicago. A convert to the Quaker faith, Douglas developed a deep commitment to social service. He would later become a leading liberal senator from Illinois. During the war he had worked with Filene as a navy labor arbitrator. He belonged to the Intercollegiate Socialist Society and helped form the League for Industrial Democracy. Like Stuart Chase and Evans Clark, Douglas supported recognition of the Soviet Union. In 1925, he led a movement within the American Economic Association to elect the iconoclast economist Thorstein Veblen as president. Influenced by his World War I experience, Douglas embarked on a decade-long investigation into workers' real wages, confirming through this research that workers had gained in real wages by 27 percent since 1890. While businessmen and politicians embraced Douglas's finding as evidence of American progress, Douglas was quick to point out that those gains were not evenly distributed. White-collar workers, for example, had lost by 5 percent. He also noted that his numbers did not consider the impact of unemployment, which substantially mitigated advances in wage rates, especially in seasonal industries. Also, the gain in real wages lagged far behind the gain of 52 percent in national productivity.[88]

The unprecedented increase of American industrial production raised an urgent question. Could Americans actually consume the output that American business was capable of producing? The improvement in productivity during the 1920s, facilitated in part by another great wave of corporate mergers, heightened postwar concern over markets that had begun with the depression of 1920–1921. Between 1914 and 1926, Ford doubled production while the population increased by only 15 percent.[89] Who would buy all these new cars? Journalist Samuel Strauss captured this historic challenge: "The economic emphasis is changing; it is shifting from how to make things to how to dispose of the things that are made so that the machine can be kept in constant operation. The problem before us today is not how to produce the goods, but how to produce the customers."[90] This distribution question represented a significant departure from an age of scarcity and was the context in which labor advanced its demands for more wages and income redistribution as the key to perpetuating American prosperity.

In contrast, many American businessmen looked to creative new marketing techniques, rather than higher wages or lower prices, to ensure consumer demand. The 1920s witnessed the rise of a sophisticated advertising industry. Clever marketing enhanced desire by appealing to the insecurities of a newly mobile white-collar urban mass. Before Listerine launched its new ad campaign, Americans had never heard of halitosis. Once they came to fear bad breath, profits rose from $100,000 in 1920 to $4 million in 1927. Manufacturers also realized the potential for expanding sales by stylizing their products. Murray French of the Fontius Shoe Company in Denver, Colorado, explained, "Desires do not happen; they are created." He described the shoe industry's efforts to promote "shoe consciousness" among men. The industry initiated a $4 million national campaign with the slogan "Shoes Mark the Man," whose purpose was to show that if men did not pay attention to their shoes, they would "lower their social standing, degrade their business prestige, crucify their self respect." Through this campaign, shoe executives hoped to encourage men to purchase more than their customary annual two pairs. "Style is laying golden eggs for us."[91] With new styles, old products quickly grew obsolete even before they were ready for the trash.

General Motors revolutionized the search for new markets through its adoption of style and mass credit. Ford had lowered the price of his Model T as much as possible by establishing a profit margin of just two dollars per car. Rather than look farther down the income slope, GM's Alfred Sloan looked up, making style as much a selling point as price. Sloan introduced annual model changes and pioneered GM's "ladder of consumption," which ranged from Chevrolets at the low end to Cadillacs at the top. He created a trade-in market that conflated aspirations of social mobility with bigger, fancier cars. Every night General Motors set the New York sky ablaze with its one-hundred-foot-wide electric sign at the top of its Fifth Avenue building. Underneath its logo, lights flashed the motto "A Car for Every Purse and Purpose," while in neon the names of Chevrolet, Oldsmobile, Buick, and Cadillac were lit up in sequence. To enable more consumers to purchase cars, GM also created the General Motors Acceptance Corporation in 1919 to facilitate buying on credit. By 1926, consumers were purchasing "on time" at least two-thirds of all cars, as well as radios, vacuum cleaners, and other appliances. Consumer debt more than doubled to $7.6 billion from 1920 to 1929, making consumer lending the tenth-largest industry.[92]

Purchasing-power progressives saw these business tactics as masking more fundamental problems of nominal wages, monopoly prices, and consumer powerlessness. Filene illustrated the problem with the example of a debt-ridden printer who earned sixty dollars a week but had committed himself to weekly payments of seventy-two dollars for his house, car, radio, and furniture. Stuart Chase decried installment sales as a "lien on purchasing power of the future." And the Labor Bureau warned, "The increase in installment buying . . . is no substitute for higher real wages." Catchings and Foster also criticized this new form of debt. All worried that, in the absence of savings and personal loan banks, debt would drive wage earners into the grip of loan sharks. Indeed, in the 1920s loan-sharking operations grew rather than receded as consumers found themselves overextended. In 1909, Filene had helped enact the first credit-union legislation in Massachusetts after observing how credit unions in India, Europe, and Canada enabled communities to provide their members with low-interest loans. In the 1920s, the Twentieth Century Fund and Leon Henderson of the Russell Sage Foundation worked actively to reform credit laws to make small loans available to the working classes at reasonable rates. Henderson would draw on this experience in the 1930s as a New Dealer and later as head of the World War II Office of Price Administration. With the help of the Credit Union National Extension Bureau financed by Filene, thirty-one states had credit-union laws by 1929. Massachusetts alone had three hunderd credit unions with one hundred thousand members and assets of thirteen million dollars.[93]

Business executives, too, found that installment selling and slick new advertisements could not expand their markets indefinitely. Auto companies feared the problem of saturation as the rate of car registrations slowed considerably. In 1927, Chevrolet paid dealers twenty-five dollars to destroy used cars. Businessmen knew that anywhere from 30 to 65 percent of the public did not have much disposable income. J. Walter Thompson Company, a leading advertising agency, sponsored an essay contest in 1925 on the "purchasing power of the consumer" as a way to discover more about the market. The winner, William Berridge, who that same year had joined Catchings and Frey on the American Economic Association panel discussion of labor's consuming power, concluded that the nation's ten million wage earners and their families constituted the nation's largest "untapped market."[94] Chester Bowles, who would become famous in World War II as Henderson's successor at the Office of Price Administration, made a name for himself as a maverick in the advertising industry by convincing General Foods and Maxwell House to make unheard-of price cuts to attract more customers.

Many businessmen in mass-production industries came to appreciate the importance of widespread purchasing power, especially as employment slowed in 1927. As president of Bethlehem Steel Company, Eugene Grace remarked, "Unemployed textile workers cannot buy automobiles." Grace articulated a new understanding of the connection between workers' income and national prosperity. "In the old days we looked on the annual pay roll with horror, as something subtracted from the profit and surplus accounts. More recently we have learned that the national pay roll is the source of profit and surplus, and the only source." Grace explained that living wages were not enough; they had to be consuming wages. "If the ruling wage rate is only a living wage, the consumer can buy nothing more than the necessities of life. As wages rise the market rises for comforts and luxuries." On the eve of the stock-market crash, Charles Abbott, the executive director of the American Institute of Steel Construction, expressed an increasingly common view. "We must take on the responsibility of providing a larger income . . . in order to increase consumption." "The principal difficulty will never be over-production. The trouble is under-consumption."[95]

The motivation to pay high wages came as much from the desire to forestall unionization as from a concern about mass markets. Nevertheless, the fact that business made these arguments drove a stake through older ways of thinking and gave a measure of legitimacy to left-wing calls for redistribution. In 1926, the *New York Times* editorial staff announced, "It is today widely recognized that the purchasing power of the masses is one of the prime determinants of general business prosperity." Evans Clark claimed, "Henry Ford has probably done more to liberalize the world's employers than all the labor leaders put together, by the simple device of proving that wages can go up and hours down without reducing profits—even increasing them, in fact." Here was demonstrable proof that higher wages were good business. "Capitalism," Clark concluded, "seems to be staging a social revolution of its own."[96]

Yet labor reformers argued that business remedies would still fall short, and they attributed a lack of purchasing power to the failures of unionization. Amid the fantastic wealth of the 1920s, John Frey cautioned, "There is another side to this talk of prosperity." In 1927, at least 1 million workers were without jobs and another 3.5 million, especially in coal, textiles, garments, and glass, worked part-time. In addition, only well-organized skilled building, print, and transportation workers received high wages, leaving behind government employees, clerical workers, and the majority of unskilled and semiskilled laborers. The National Consumers' League used the occasion of its thirtieth anniversary to call attention to the low wages that prevailed in the South, where the textile mills, representing the region's largest and still growing industrial employer, paid their workers at a rate that was 25 percent lower than what northern businesses typically paid. Future New Deal agricultural experts Louis Bean, Mordecai Ezekiel, and Rexford Tugwell worried about farmers who, as a class, were heavily mortgaged and had little purchasing power.[97] Throughout the economy, average wage rates had lagged behind gains in productivity by nearly 40 percent since 1899. The Labor Bureau warned, "Labor's gain . . . has not been sufficient to increase its purchasing power as much as production has grown." They predicted that an industrial recession would result from "a failure of the real incomes of farmers, wage earners and salaried employees to keep up with a rapidly increasing productivity." AFL president William Green cautioned American management against shortsighted policies. He admonished, "The Nation cannot destroy its purchasing power through the creation of an army of unemployed and expect to maintain increased commodity production. . . . Buying power [is] at stake."[98]

The threat to purchasing power came not only from low wages but also from high prices and poor quality. Prices remained stable throughout the decade, but that did not prevent critics from claiming that they should have come down as department stores, mail-order catalogues, and especially chain stores increased their percentage of sales. Turning against his peers as well as his partners, Filene emerged as a leading critic of current distribution practices, claiming that high-pressure sales drove up costs unnecessarily. To an audience of 250 leading retailers, Filene insisted, "Retail distribution has a great many flaws. The difference in cost between producer and consumer is about double. That should not exist. The job of a big store is to develop methods to sell goods to its customers as cheaply as possible." Filene promoted his "model stock plan," a system by which retailers could simplify their selections, reduce costs, and increase turnover. The goal was to offer "the best buy," an item of good quality at an affordable price. While advocating the chain store, he opposed the merger of Filene's into Federated Department Stores on the grounds that the move would expand operations without cutting costs. The Commerce Department, under Hoover, initiated a distribution census in eleven cities to discover why, in fact, prices were increasing substantially from the time a product left the manufacturer until it reached the consumer.[99]

For their part, consumers faced serious obstacles in their search for the best buy. In a 1912 essay, "The Backward Art of Spending Money," economist Wesley Clair Mitchell had laid out the problems that the modern consumer faced. She no longer had enough information to evaluate the "prices of milk and shoes, furniture and meat, magazines and fuel, hats and underwear, bedding and disinfectants, medical services and toys, rugs and candy." In the 1920s, the number of brand-name goods exploded, products became more technologically complicated, and advertisements obscured as much as they explained, all of which made comparison shopping more difficult. Faith Williams, an economist with the Department of Agriculture, sympathized with the "American housewife" in her attempts at "stretching the household dollar" and was hopeful that "many housewives already are seeking some more adequate basis for purchases than beautiful pictures, appealing slogans, and the endorsement of movie actresses."[100]

In a series for the *New Republic,* the Labor Bureau's Stuart Chase teamed up with F. J. Schlink of the Department of Commerce's Bureau of Standards to show exactly "how defenseless the consumer is." "He buys blindly, chaotically, as the sluice gates of 'distributive pressure' open and close." Prices often did not reflect quality, and advertisements and labels misinformed and misrepresented. Without standardization of sizes, weights, and materials, consumers could not make adequate judgments of value. Even with simple products like bread, consumers faced such a range of sizes and weights that it was hard to compare the value of one loaf to another. They conceded that the "wonderland" of the new consumer market brought pleasure, but they concluded that "all of us it irks occasionally—particularly when we contemplate what it costs us."[101]

In 1927, Chase and Schlink's book *Your Money's Worth* became a best seller and was a selection of the Book-of-the-Month Club. The phrase used for its title was picked up and repeated so often that it entered popular discourse. The authors claimed that the Bureau of Standards saved the government one hundred million dollars a year by publishing product information for government purchasers. And they demanded that consumers have access to such information. Since the late nineteenth century, a growing community of domestic scientists had recommended that the Bureau of Agricultural Economics and the Bureau of Home Economics should grade and test consumer products. Now those proposals garnered popular support.[102]

The success of *Your Money's Worth* suggested the appeal of greater product information, especially among middle-class consumers with disposable income. It was a great irony that as modern conveniences, from cold creams to vacuum cleaners, improved living standards, they also made life, or at least shopping, more complicated.[103] As consumer advocate Helen Sorenson explained, Chase and Schlink's book "crystallized a vaguely felt, but widespread, discontent." Sociologist Robert Lynd later referred to their book as the "*Uncle Tom's Cabin*" of the consumer movement. In response to popular demand, the authors formed Consumers' Research two years later, a private organization that conducted tests on branded goods and published the results. A list of sponsors included Wesley Mitchell, George Soule, Rexford Tugwell, and Morris Cooke. Adolph Berle served as counsel. Though it was a technocratic testing agency, its founders believed that the ultimate solution would come from the creation of a "militant organization of consumers." "He can get his money's worth if he is willing to organize to get it. The market always responds to organized pressure."[104]

When Hoover ran for president in 1928, he based his campaign on the prosperity of America's "Wonderland." Gross national product went from $74 billion in 1922 to $103 billion in 1929. Auto production led the way and had a ripple effect on other industries like steel, petroleum, chemicals, rubber, and glass. Mass-production industries, from appliances to aircraft to movies, also grew rapidly. In the single year of 1928, stock prices nearly doubled in value, fueled by large profits, the easy-money policy of the Federal Reserve, and the practice of buying on margin. Though wary of the speculative boom, Hoover seized on these optimistic trends when he accepted his party's nomination for Republican candidate, declaring, on August 11, 1928, "We in America today are nearer to the final triumph over poverty than ever before in the history of any land." In building his electoral base, Hoover capitalized on the relations with business trade associations he had forged as commerce secretary. He also built on his past connections with the nation's housewives and called upon women's clubs across the country to conduct a Hoover pledge campaign. Native-born Republican women supported Hoover, but many Catholic and immigrant women voted for the Democratic candidate, New York governor Al Smith.[105]

Smith's Catholicism and his attack on Prohibition determined his fate. But the support he did win revealed the growing Democratic appeal among the urban masses. Mary Rumsey, who had worked so fervently for Hoover's Food Administration, now campaigned for Smith. In breaking with her family's Republican tradition, she explained that her father's "period was a building age, when competition was the order of the day. Today the need is not for a competitive but for a cooperative economic system." Filene dubbed Smith "the true prosperity candidate," because "with Governor Smith prosperity will be more widely dispersed than it is now. He is the happy champion of the masses." The industrialized states of Massachusetts and Rhode Island went to Smith, as did the nation's twelve largest cities. In 1926, New York union leaders had helped elect Robert F. Wagner as U.S. senator, and he would soon emerge as the nation's leading urban liberal. In 1928, those same groups supported Franklin Roosevelt's campaign for governor. Upon winning, Roosevelt announced his intention to carry out a labor program that would include anti-injunction legislation, an old-age pension system, workmen's compensation, and protective legislation for women. His labor agenda was shaped more by his wife Eleanor's connection to female reformers and trade unionists than by any innate commitment to labor. The fate of urban liberalism, promoted energetically by labor and middle-class female reformers, and the Democratic Party would become increasingly intertwined.[106]

Hoover was not unmindful of the problems of what he dubbed "the new era." As secretary of commerce, he convened a Conference on Unemployment in 1928 and endorsed the "Foster-Catchings theory" of countercyclical spending on public works to offset industrial depression. With Hoover's support, Foster drew up plans for a Planned Prosperity League, which he conceived as a nationwide organization for every community to create a reserve of public-works projects in the event of a depression. Foster and Catchings popularized those ideas in *The Road to Plenty*, a book that Senator Wagner distributed to his colleagues. Hoover sympathized with purchasing-power theorists, but he read the evidence differently, a rift that became apparent with the publication in May 1929 of a study he had initiated, *Recent Economic Changes*. Many of its nine hundred pages of expert studies affirmed Hoover's optimistic outlook by heralding prosperity and declaring that production was indeed balanced by consumption.[107]

The stock-market crash on Black Thursday in October 1929 began a three-week slide, during which an astonishing one-third of the market's value disappeared. Few thought it spelled the beginning of a depression. Contrary to fable, most Americans did not own stocks. Since less than 3 percent were stockholders, the vast majority of the population felt no immediate effect from the events on Wall Street. By April, the market had regained 20 percent of its losses. For months there were widespread predictions of recovery—the American Economic Association thought the market would bounce back by June 1930. Even critics did not think the crash would in and of itself lead to decline. "In a week the colossal sum of $50,000,000,000 was squeezed out of the Wall Street figures, but does this mean the end of prosperity?" asked Stuart Chase. "Frankly I do not think so."[108]

Purchasing-power progressives thought the problems lay elsewhere. In August 1929, Foster announced a new study by Paul Douglas documenting that, between 1923 and 1927, real wages did not advance. Moreover, total employment in 1928 lagged 13 percent behind that of 1923, even as production reached a high. The employment prospects for 1929 did not look any better. New mass-production industries were expanding, but not fast enough to absorb workers from declining industries such as coal, lumber, and textiles.[109] In 1928, Senator Wagner had warned, "With bread lines and idleness come diminution in purchasing power, a gradual slackening of business and industry and great unemployment. Behind this curtain stalk misery, want, hunger, and discontent in all our cities." Even those with jobs faced structural poverty, irregular employment, and low wages. Amid the prosperity of the 1920s, the bottom 40 percent of the population earned an average annual income of $725, of which over 80 percent went toward food, housing, and clothing. Labor expert William Leiserson admonished, "Consumers do not have enough purchasing power to buy all that is produced."[110]

As the economy began its decade-long descent into the Great Depression of the 1930s, the lack of purchasing power was a ready-made explanation for labor and consumer reformers. After a decade of similar utterances, Filene's statement that "mass production can live only if there is mass consumption—that is, only if the masses are able to buy all the goods produced" gained new resonance. The Labor Bureau asserted, "What America needs now is higher wages without higher prices. . . . [A]ny slackening of production recently felt in American manufacture is due to inadequate purchasing power of the consuming public for the greatly enlarged quantities of goods which industry is capable of turning out." Over the next year, employment declined rapidly, as did wages in the nonunionized industries like textiles, iron, and steel. The Labor Bureau gloomily predicted, "We are in for a great deal of trouble."[111]

The purchasing-power progressives believed that the cure for underconsumption could come only through major institutional reform. Checking the power of corporations to set prices and wages required a vast and powerful mobilization of industrial laborers with the middle classes as their allies. The Labor Bureau concluded, "The task of increasing the purchasing power of the consumer as rapidly as industry can produce more goods is not one merely for vision and good will, it is a gigantic job of industrial and social organization, in which many forces must play a part."[112] Such thinking would come to center stage during the New Deal, when these very same reformers assumed power.

Part II

PURCHASING POWER TO
THE PEOPLE,1930–1940

The New Deal and the Problem of Prices, 1930–1935

THE GREAT DEPRESSION thrust the question of consumer purchasing power to the center of American politics and New Deal state-building. With millions unemployed and millions more working at reduced wages, newspapers, magazines, and political speeches were filled with reports of starvation, Hoovervilles, and misery. Liberal thinkers singled out "underconsumption" as a leading cause of the downward economic spiral. While thousands of factories stood idle, one-fifth of families did not have kitchen sinks, two-fifths did not have electric lights, and one-third did not own cars. Edward Filene expounded his view of how the country had fallen into its state of distress: As the rich got richer, he said, "millions of the masses were trampled in the process and lost their buying power, the machinery of production choked with its own product, unemployment spread like a pestilence, and the world starved in the midst of plenty." The halt in business investment posed a bigger problem for the economy, but the general public, unschooled in economics, preferred the explanation of inadequate consumer spending. As sociologist Robert Lynd put it, "The consumer has become a 'problem.' "[1]

Yet diverting more money into Americans' wallets was no simple matter. There were few government agencies and no precedents for massive federal spending on relief or jobs. And no federal framework existed for raising wages. Moreover, dwindling consumption was only one factor contributing to the Depression. With factories running at half capacity and investment basically nonexistent, politicians and policymakers understood the importance of reviving business production and stanching the deflationary slide. In three years, prices had fallen precipitously, and the banking system stood in shambles. In a series of miscalculations, the Federal Reserve raised interest rates and reduced the amount of money in circulation. Farmers felt the collapse of prices and the closing of banks most severely as they saw their income take a nosedive and watched their land being repossessed. Adding to these domestic pressures on the American economy were the declining markets and monetary instability abroad. Tackling any one of these problems would have been difficult. Overcoming all of them must have seemed almost impossible.

The central challenge for policymakers was the need to lift wages and prices at the same time. On the one hand, many of the New Dealers

who came to power under Franklin Roosevelt were committed to promoting policies that would increase industrial wages and farmers' incomes. On the other hand, they understood that pushing up wages
meant allowing businessmen to collude in price-fixing so they could
cover their increased costs and still make a profit. Likewise, to help the
farmer, commodity prices would have to go up. Such inflationary measures, while potentially restoring business confidence and agricultural
prosperity, acted directly counter to the purchasing-power agenda of
low prices and did little to put a floor under industrial wages. Throughout the early years of the New Deal, policymakers were torn between
raising prices or boosting buying power. Divided in its economic analysis and political calculations, the New Deal would try to do both.[2]

Buy Now—If You Can, 1930–1933

Before the Depression was a year old, business leaders and politicians
launched a "Buy Now" campaign. As inventories piled up and factories
grew desperate for orders, persuading consumers to buy goods took on
greater urgency. "Spend twenty dollars and start the return of prosperity," urged Boston's Mayor James Curley. The *Raleigh News and Observer*
implored its readers, "Let's buy something. . . . What you buy, people
will have to make—it will put them to work, and they will have money to
spend for what you have to sell. Start now—buy to-day, to-morrow, and
the next day." The Edison company of New Jersey gave each of its three
thousand employees five dollars and told them to spend it.[3]

But these volunteerist remedies did not work. The *Journal of Commerce*
reported, "The consumer is being asked to buy more of everything at a
time when he is often unable to pay for pressing immediate necessities."
"Slogans," they concluded, "can not bring about revival." As the *New
Republic* pointed out, "Consumers could not at will enlarge their purchases." To make matters worse, by the spring of 1931, many large firms
began to cut wages. "While wages are slashed and earnings shrink a
sustained buying advance is not possible and employment conditions
cannot improve," concluded the Labor Bureau. "Without a stable consumer demand, most manufacturers cannot increase their output and
their very failure to do so is responsible for the tragedy of unemployment and all the attendant evils of idleness." At the 1931 U.S. Chamber
of Commerce convention, *Business Week* reported, "The 'Buy Now' idea
seems to have faded out. . . . There appears to be increasing doubt as to
what buyers should use for money."[4]

To prevent further erosion of consumer demand, President Hoover
urged the nation's businessmen to hold fast to existing wage levels.
Unlike earlier recessions, leaders now recognized the worker's crucial

That's for Use, but Not as a Wall Ornament
—Hanny in the Philadelphia "Inquirer."

FIGURE 3.1. Popular thought of the 1930s supported the idea that Americans could spend their way out of the Depression in spite of rising unemployment, wage cuts, and bank failures. The idea of underconsumption helped to justify New Deal reform.

role as consumer in bringing about recovery. At the 1931 American Economic Association meeting, John Frey of the American Federation of Labor (AFL) acknowledged the impact of the purchasing-power ideology: "For a long time a majority of our economists and our production engineers as well have considered the laborer almost solely from the standpoint of a producer. It is only recently that they have begun to realize that his function in society as a consumer is of equal importance." Frey emphasized, "It is the wage earner and his dependents who constitute the bulk of the American market, and it is on the American market that our industries must depend for the sale of over 90 percent of all that the nation produces."*Business Week* wrote that since 1921 businessmen have begun "to look upon labor more as a consumer of mass production than as an item of production cost." The editors urged their readers to "maintain a salary and wage scale that permits a high standard of living and thus of purchasing power." They were advised to cut costs by improving management and reducing sales expenses, instead of resorting to wage cuts. In words that echoed labor's position, they stated, "There still has appeared no rational explanation of how 'starvation in the midst of plenty' because of lack of purchasing power can be cured by still further reducing purchasing power."[5]

Amid falling prices and profits, however, these admonishments often fell on deaf ears. The absence of easy credit or effective trade associations to counter deflation made wage cuts inevitable. Employers "still regard wage maintenance as a sound national policy," *Business Week* explained, "but many are wondering if they are justified in supporting much longer a national policy which, mistakenly or no, they feel is hurting their own business." Even at Filene's, management cut wages as a cost-saving measure. After months of staunchly maintaining its pay scale, U.S. Steel announced a 10 percent wage cut in September 1931. Its action opened the floodgates. Within ten days, over one million additional workers saw a reduction in their paychecks. By this time, nearly 25 percent of the workforce was standing in unemployment lines.[6]

As another winter of depression approached, the nation faced a crisis. Hoover's plea to the professional class to give voluntarily to the unemployed was an insufficient remedy. Charity funds reached depletion, as did state and local resources. The number of strikes increased. The rise of totalitarian regimes in Europe heightened concerns about the dangers of economic chaos, motivating business leaders to advocate some form of nationwide planning to bring about recovery. In September 1931, Gerard Swope of General Electric called for a suspension of antitrust laws to enable trade associations to institute industrywide planning. The goal would be to limit production, stabilize prices, and thus reverse a massive deflation. The Swope Plan, as it became known, also stressed the importance of implementing pensions and unemployment insurance. By the end of 1931, the U.S. Chamber of Commerce supported the idea of self-government for business.[7]

Many social reformers, labor leaders, and liberal economists, while favoring some sort of industrywide planning, looked to the government rather than to business for leadership. They sought to implement programs such as federal relief, federal public works, federal insurance, lower tariff rates, bank reform, and public ownership of utilities. In April 1932, Senator Wagner sponsored a billion-dollar public-works program. The Socialist platform recommended what it grandly called the social control of business. Although liberal groups did not adopt this premise for their campaigns, they nevertheless began to propose policies that had once seemed politically implausible. Even while endorsing Socialist Party candidate Norman Thomas, Paul Douglas served as an adviser to Governor Roosevelt's Unemployment Committee. Soon many liberal reformers would attain positions of power within the New Deal government.[8]

From left to right, a consensus emerged that purchasing power had dropped by 30 percent as a result of unemployment, the increase in part-time jobs, and wage reductions. Even those who had jobs saw their income fall faster than prices. Rents fell nearly 20 percent by 1933, but evictions became commonplace. The United Council of Working Class Women asked New York City to repeal its eviction law, while communist-led Unemployed Councils rallied neighbors to block evictions. Writer Alfred Kazin, who grew up in Brownsville, remembered "those first terrible winters of the depression, when we stood around each newly evicted family to give them comfort and the young Communists raged up and down the street calling for volunteers to put the furniture back." At the same time, a decline in the quality of goods so inflated prices that they no longer reflected the numbers stamped on the tags. According to retail expert Paul Nystrom, "This new form of exploitation [reached] menacing proportions." Workers' difficulties in making ends meet was validated by the National Industrial Conference Board's report announcing that the industrial population had lost more than half of its buying power since 1929.[9]

Who was to blame? For at least a decade, purchasing-power progressives had pointed to the growing concentration of corporate control over the American economy. They viewed the decrease in purchasing power as symptomatic of and connected to the disorganized condition of consumers and workers. They supported labor's denunciation of income maldistribution, and they also worried about the ability of corporations to fix prices and deceive consumers. Liberal social scientists, such as Rexford Tugwell, Paul Douglas, Gardiner Means, Adolph Berle, Robert Lynd, Walton Hamilton, Leon Henderson, and Isador Lubin, were as much concerned with the exploitation of consumers as they were with labor reform. Paul Douglas's "real purchasing power" linked consumers in the marketplace to workers on the job. As he explained, "These common interests of consumers and citizens tend frequently to be ignored by radicals because of their preoccupation with the struggle in the workshop. . . . But they tend in the main to be different facets of a common issue, namely, that of how society can collectively plan and control its economic and social life so that the interests of its members may best be furthered."[10]

For this group of scholarly activists, the Depression offered incontrovertible evidence that the modern consumer was powerless in the face of manipulative advertising, mass technology, and a maldistribution of income. Purchasing-power progressives believed that monopolies not only paid insufficient wages but also subverted flexible price adjustments. "Perhaps reasonable prices will result from the sheer generosity of business men in a land of Fords and Frigidaires. Or perhaps the competition of industrial giants, monopolistic in their respective fields but with fierce inter-industrial competition for the consumer's dollar, will have the same result," wrote Dexter Keezer and Stacy May in *The Public Control of Business* (1930). More likely, though, would be the need "to have a drastic overhauling of the system of government control of business."[11] Although sensitive to the dehumanizing nature of modern industrial work, these reformers appreciated that mass production brought about greater efficiency and enabled higher living standards. But the Depression seemed to confirm that few business leaders voluntarily passed on the savings achieved through mass production by lowering prices or raising wages. Rather than break up corporations, this community of reformers saw organized consumers and a strong labor movement as necessary antidotes to corporate power. They had made these arguments in the 1920s, but now they reiterated them with the conviction that they had been proved right.

To these reformers, the antisocial behavior of large corporations helped to explain the Depression. They advanced a structural argument that located the problem not just in the wrongdoings of malevolent merchants and manufacturers but also in the rise of monopolistic forces unchecked by any counterbalancing organized pressure groups. In 1932 Adolph Berle and Gardiner Means published *The Modern Corporation and Private Property*, a treatise that became one of the intellectual underpinnings of the New Deal. Berle taught law at Columbia University and had met Means when they served in the army in Plattsburgh, New York. Both were the sons of Congregational ministers. Berle's father was part of the Social Gospel movement, and the young Adolph had worked at the Henry Street Settlement in his youth. As an undergraduate and then a law student at Harvard in 1915–1916, Berle studied institutional economics and sociological jurisprudence. By the time he started his own law firm in New York in 1919, Berle had come to believe that the modern corporation had to develop a sense of social responsibility. Means, too, combined an institutionalist training with real-world experience. After operating a textile mill in Lowell, Massachusetts, he went to Harvard to study economics, where he rejected the neoclassical view promulgated there that consumers and their demands regulated the market and drove competition. His views on the marketplace were strongly influenced by Caroline Ware, whom he married in 1927. Ware, a historian of textile mill workers and former teacher at the Bryn Mawr School for female industrial laborers, affirmed his conviction that, in a modern economy of large monopolistic forces, individuals had little power to bargain or negotiate.[12]

Published in the depths of the Depression, Berle and Means's critique of corporations captured public attention. In spite of antitrust laws, they argued, the two hundred largest nonbanking corporations controlled about half of corporate wealth and nearly one-quarter of the nation's wealth. The separation of management from ownership constituted the distinguishing feature of modern corporations and resulted in passive stockholders and the concentration of decision making in even fewer hands. Corporate managers could set prices and production levels without fear of competition. Berle's colleague at Columbia, the economist Rexford Tugwell, shared their reservations about managerial behavior. Tugwell argued that "those individuals who insist upon the right to make profits fail to accept the responsibility of stabilizing private investment and of maintaining the continuity of society's producing, selling and consuming operations."[13] In essence, large corporations set prices beyond the reach of the consuming masses while paying wages insufficient to sustain demand.

Berle and Means believed that corporate power required social responsibility to justify it as legitimate. "The passive property rights of today must yield before the larger interests of society." Those included fair wages, security, service, and stability, all of which they acknowledged "would divert a portion of profits." The " 'control' of the great corporations should develop into a purely neutral technocracy, balancing a variety of claims by various groups in the community and assigning to each a portion of the income stream on the basis of public policy rather than private cupidity." This seemingly flat rhetoric bespoke a radical vision of how to reorder American political economy. It suggested a public policy based on redistributing profits and premised on the needs of labor and consumers as essential to national prosperity and political harmony. "The allotment of purchasing power is a social function of the first importance and should be restored to the federal government," wrote Stuart Chase. After Roosevelt's nomination as presidential candidate, both Berle and Tugwell became important advisers in his famous Brain Trust, which Roosevelt established during his campaign and continued after his election.[14]

According to these reformers, particularly Means, the concentration of economic power could have potentially disastrous consequences. When faced with a declining market, corporate managers elected to cut production, employment, and wages rather than reduce prices. From their point of view, cutting prices could prompt unpredictable cutthroat competition without a guarantee of sales; in contrast, maintaining prices coupled with reducing production at least trimmed costs. Means called that type of restrictive behavior "administrative competition," and he labeled the result "administered prices." Manufacturers were no longer setting prices "by higgling and bargaining in the market place [a reference to Adam Smith], but by the administrative action of a small body of officials. This means that prices . . . are not determined in the market place but are fixed by administrative action." In the auto industry, for example, "each of the big three companies drastically restricted its own production so as to maintain its own prices" during the Depression. In this world of administered competition, the consumer had little leverage. As Means summed up, "The shift from economic activity coordinated by the market to administered coordination has steadily reduced the consumer to a mere appendage of the production system." The consumer is "forced to take what is offered at the price at which it is offered, or go without."[15] Means's theory of "administered prices," too heterodox to submit as his Ph.D. thesis, would frame liberal politics for the next generation as reformers sought to balance corporate interests against those of labor and consumers.

The problem of powerless consumers became a topic that drew prominent liberals as an important adjunct to the labor problem. Organized labor had declined in influence in the 1920s, and the 1930s made its weakness ever more apparent. Degradation in the factories and the inability of unions to protect their members' interests was hard to ignore as work conditions deteriorated and violence erupted in cities across the country. While sympathetic to the inequalities on the shop floor, many reformers in and out of the labor movement also stressed the ways in which a lack of power at the market further eroded the security of working-class Americans, as consumers everywhere found themselves increasingly exploited. Robert Lynd, author of the classic study *Middletown: A Study in American Culture* (1929) and a leading authority on consumption, explained, "All ideas of automatic balance [between consumers and producers] are permanently relegated to the museum of the past." Based on his observations in Muncie, Indiana, Lynd concluded that the modern consumer "has been taken for granted in the role of a noiseless servant named Demand and, like a servant, bled white of all personality and urgency and reduced to the convenient position of one who can always be counted on to be unostentatiously but infallibly there when needed."[16] According to Lynd, the oligopolistic structure of American industry subverted the operations of the free market. No longer did consumer wants call production into being; rather, an interlocking network of large corporations, national advertisers, and large retail merchants manipulated consumer desires.

Consumers not only paid higher prices; they also had insufficient information on which to base decisions about their purchases. First articulated by Stuart Chase and F. J. Schlink during the 1920s, this idea was absorbed by housewives as they struggled to stretch meager incomes. The packaging and increasing technical complexity of mass-produced goods presented shoppers with what Rexford Tugwell called "the problem of choosing." Trying to decipher the mechanical virtues of an ice maker or a vacuum cleaner could prove impossible. Without any standardization or enforcement, labels on manufactured goods were virtually meaningless. Lynd suggested, "It is an open question whether such tendencies—the need to buy more things, the wider range of choices coupled with the growing complexity in the fabrication of commodities and the adroitness of the exploitation of the consumer at many points, are not rendering us less literate as consumers than any recent generation of Americans." Consumer expert Persia Campbell described "the housewives of the nation" with "little money in their pocket-books and very little training in how to spend it wisely."[17]

Consumers, however, were more resourceful than these observers thought. Smart shopping became a necessity across class lines, and department stores reported that "the uncanny instinct of the consumer for true bargains" was "growing steadily more acute." In March 1933, Chase and Schlink's newest investigation, *100,000,000 Guinea Pigs*, joined *The Modern Corporation and Private Property* on the best-seller list. By that time, Consumers' Research had a membership of over fifty thousand. Its bulletins reported the results of the product testing it performed. The establishment of Consumers' Research and the spate of "guinea pig" books suggested the growing appeal of advice about getting the most for one's money. At a minimum, these publications supplied a language for discussing consumer problems. In the 1930s, the nation's organized women's clubs added government regulation of consumer products to their agendas. Smarter buying and better quality, though, were limited solutions to larger economic problems.[18]

On the campaign trail, Franklin Roosevelt appropriated consumer language, most famously in his speech at the Commonwealth Club in San Francisco on September 23, 1932. If not yet organized into an effective interest group, the consumer was emerging as a prominent figure as politicians sought to combat the economic decline. The Commonwealth speech revealed the influence of the Brain Trust. Berle wrote the speech

one month after the release of *The Modern Corporation.* Unusually for
Roosevelt, who took an active part in his speechwriting, the candidate delivered this address to two thousand prominent West Coast businessmen
without having read it ahead of time. Radical and sweeping, the speech
formulated ideas that would come to constitute core New Deal beliefs.
The speechwriter's viewpoint became apparent as Roosevelt talked of the
inordinate economic power of a few hundred corporations and forecast a
future of "all American industry controlled by a dozen corporations, and
run perhaps by a hundred men." In the nineteenth century, Roosevelt explained, Americans had benefited from economic concentration, but
that was no longer the case. "A mere builder of more industrial plants, a
creator of more railroad systems, an organizer of more corporations, is as
likely to be a danger as a help. . . . Our task now is not discovery or exploitation of natural resources, or necessarily producing more goods. It is
the soberer, less dramatic business . . . of meeting the problem of underconsumption, of adjusting production to consumption, of distributing
wealth and products more equitably, of adapting existing economic organizations to the service of the people." For the sake of national prosperity,
the government would have to assume the task of assuring that "purchasing power is well distributed throughout every group in the Nation." "We
must build toward the time when a major depression cannot occur again;
and if this means sacrificing the easy profits of inflationist booms, then let
them go; and good riddance."[19]

Once FDR became president, he would weave different constituents
into a new governing coalition, and to do so, he embraced the language of
the consumer as pliable and politically useful. Regardless of his economic
beliefs, which included a commitment to balancing budgets, he found
consumerist language helpful in selling different, even contradictory, New
Deal programs. On the campaign trail, for example, he defended policies
that would ensure both high wages for organized labor and higher prices
for farmers. Rather than justifying these measures as the perquisites of special interests, he cast workers and farmers in the more palatable role of
consumers. FDR's use of consumerist language reflected his masterly political skills, but his rhetoric was also inspired by the theories of purchasing-
power progressives and by three decades of public expectations that the
nation's high standard of living would continue to improve.

Buy Now under the Blue Eagle, 1933

Roosevelt's consumer rhetoric made great politics, but it did not readily
translate into a plan for economic recovery or meet with universal approval. Urban liberals supported proposals for public-works and relief

spending, share-the-work schemes, and institutionalizing labor standards. The AFL lobbied successfully for a thirty-hour-week bill, which would distribute available work and wages among its members, thereby stimulating demand. Business planners, though, saw overproduction as a bigger threat than underconsumption, and they advocated the suspension of antitrust laws. From their perspective, restraining competition was essential to ending the debilitating downward cycle of decreasing wages and cuts in prices. Farmers too suffered from overproduction, and their representatives lobbied for inflationary measures, including the purchase of silver, to increase their incomes. All these schemes were too radical for more conservative advisers, who insisted on a balanced budget and a commitment to the gold standard as steps to renew business confidence. Roosevelt, himself a fiscal conservative, announced a 15 percent pay cut for federal employees.[20]

The new president faced challenges from the moment he took office. During the winter of 1933, the banking system almost collapsed. Nine million Americans had lost their savings since 1929, and thirty-eight states had shut down their banks. After calling Congress into an emergency session, Roosevelt pushed forward two banking bills that rescued the financial system. In his first fireside chat, delivered to an audience of sixty million radio listeners, FDR convinced the public that the banks were again safe. At the same time, Roosevelt came under sustained pressure to inflate the currency, especially from farmers eager to ease their debt and raise commodity prices. To the horror of the business community, FDR announced the United States's departure from the gold standard in April 1933. To provide immediate relief to the millions of unemployed, FDR also succeeded in creating the Federal Emergency Relief Administration (FERA). In his first two hours in office, the FERA director Harry Hopkins spent five million dollars.[21]

Once in session, a Democratic Congress embarked on a far-reaching recovery program, starting with the agricultural sector. In his final campaign speech, delivered in Boston, Roosevelt had stressed the need to increase farmers' income in order to create a market for industrial goods. Paying farmers higher prices "will give them the buying power to start your mills and mines to work, to supply their needs. They cannot buy your goods because they cannot get a fair price for their product. You are poor because they are poor." According to Rexford Tugwell, now undersecretary of agriculture, the Great Depression had been precipitated by a massive decline in agricultural purchasing power. During the 1920s, farmers had been caught in a downward cycle of debt and overproduction that led to declining commodity prices. Since 1929, farmers' prices had plunged by half, whereas manufacturers' prices had declined by only 25 percent. Passed in May 1933, the Agricultural

Adjustment Act created the Agricultural Adjustment Administration (AAA) to restore "parity," a more favorable relation between farm prices and industrial prices, such as had existed immediately before World War I. The government would accomplish this end by creating an allotment system, whereby the AAA paid farmers to reduce production. A tax on canners, millers, packers, and other agricultural processors financed these payments.[22]

The AAA was, by design, inflationary. The hope, at least of its left-leaning supporters under the influence of Tugwell and AAA general counsel Jerome Frank, was to exert public pressure on processors to absorb the tax rather than pass the program's cost on to consumers in higher food prices. In addition to increasing the purchasing power of farmers, the act simultaneously committed the AAA "to protect[ing] the consumers' interest." These reformers also wanted to force processors to "open their books," allowing government scrutiny of their profits to prevent them from charging excessive prices. At a minimum, they sought to prevent processors from raising prices higher than their tax incidence. But that goal was hard to attain, especially given the fact that the leadership of the AAA was committed to raising commodity prices, regardless of the impact on the cost of food. From the beginning, urban consumers regarded the AAA with skepticism and resentment, an outlook that was reinforced by national headlines reporting farmers plowing under ten million of acres of cotton and slaughtering six million baby pigs to comply with production restrictions.[23]

Now the question of industrial recovery took center stage. The thirty-hour-week bill had passed in the Senate, in spite of FDR's opposition. Roosevelt doubted its economic logic and worried about the political consequences. To derail it, he asked New York senator Robert F. Wagner to draft an alternate measure. For years, they had known and worked with each other in the New York senate. As a state senator, Wagner had led the fight for workmen's compensation, protective legislation for women and children, and prohibition of child labor. He had also fought for women's suffrage, popular election of senators, and direct primaries. As a judge, he had upheld rent laws and the right to strike.[24] Wagner was part of a new urban liberal coalition that was becoming more important within the Democratic Party. In 1920, the twelve largest cities voted Republican. By 1928, Democratic candidate Al Smith won these urban areas with a small plurality of 21,000 votes. By 1932, Roosevelt's margin in these cities neared 1.8 million and would grow with each subsequent victory. In Congress, the new urban bloc helped to set the New Deal agenda, particularly regarding industrial policy. Never powerful enough on its own to enact legislation, it won support for the New Deal from Democrats of the South and progressives of the

West, eager for infrastructure development, as well as from farmers who looked to the government for a return to prosperity. Though not a stable coalition, the Democratic alliance of urban and rural constituents was willing to work together during the early days of the New Deal.[25]

Under FDR's orders, Wagner brought together leaders who differed sharply about how to restore employment. He consulted with national planners like Rexford Tugwell and Jerome Frank of the AAA, labor leaders like Sidney Hillman of the Amalgamated Clothing Workers and Jett Lauck of the United Mine Workers, and reform-minded members of the business elite. After intense negotiation, Congress passed the final National Industrial Recovery Act in May 1933 and created the National Recovery Administration (NRA) to oversee what were called codes of fair competition and was to last for two years. Over the summer, each industry would submit a code setting maximum hours and minimum wages to improve working conditions and increase labor's income. The act included a collective-bargaining clause, Section 7a, guaranteeing workers the right to organize and participate in establishing codes. In exchange for that historic shift in federal labor policy, the act suspended nearly half a century of antitrust laws, thus enabling producers to plan collectively for stable production and prices. This recovery measure also created the Public Works Administration (PWA) with funds of $3.3 billion to provide jobs and immediate stimulus through government spending, largely on construction projects that would revive heavy industry.[26]

The NRA, like the AAA, tried to strike a bargain between raising producers' prices and enhancing mass purchasing power. As the *New York Times* explained, the plan intended for "prices high enough to cover increased labor costs and to leave in addition a 'reasonable' profit for the employer, but low enough to encourage the consumption of goods and to protect the public against gouging." There was no provision for fixing prices, but it soon became clear that the NRA would tolerate price agreements, thereby extending the "administered prices" criticized by Means to all industries. Industries, such as coal and textiles, that were plagued by cutthroat competition welcomed the opportunity to collude. The trick for the NRA would be to allow business to set prices only high enough to enable bigger wages.[27]

Many NRA supporters hoped Section 7a would bring about the ability of labor to enforce business compliance with the minimum-wage policy. Moreover, if all businesses had to comply with these basic pay standards, wages would effectively be removed from competition. According to Paul Douglas, the idea behind the NRA codes was "to induce all businesses to do collectively what they could not do individually, namely, to increase their total wages bill and to restore more workers to employment." The act, explained Douglas, aimed "to squeeze purchasing power in at the bottom in the form of an increased wages bill." Even Adolph Berle, who was not as far to the left as Douglas was, explained, "When people talk of 'creating purchasing power' what they really mean is that the national income goes not into stagnant pools of unneeded investment but into the hands of people who need goods." In an NRA drafting session, a former student of Tugwell's, Leon Keyserling, who had been at the AAA for only a couple of weeks, voiced the group's thinking: "I think the act has got to do something about improving wages, about improving labor conditions, about protecting collective bargaining so that it will be in better balance, and so we will have a stimulation of consumer interest and consumer buying, or otherwise we're not going to get recovery." Wagner shared that perspective, and several days later he hired Keyserling as his chief legislative aide.[28]

The commitment to redistribution through higher wages revealed the limitations of New Deal thinking about a modern welfare state. The public works of the NRA, like the farm subsidy program, were financed by regressive taxes, in this instance from excise taxes on consumer products. These inflationary, regressive measures that taxed the poor more heavily than the rich contradicted a purchasing-power agenda by acting as a redistribution program in reverse. Congress financed the new federal relief and employment programs this way because there was no politically acceptable alternative of raising revenue. At this point, less than 5 percent of the population paid taxes. Moreover, most New Dealers, from budget director Lewis Douglas on the right to Senator Wagner on the left, were committed to a balanced budget. Thus even progressives like Wagner accepted a regressive financing system, in which the percentage of income and corporate taxes in relation to other sources of revenue actually declined in the 1930s. Their vision for the New Deal was at once conservative and radical. Their fiscal conservatism imposed serious restrictions on redistributive public spending. In all the New Deal years, the government would never spend enough to end the Depression. Congress spent six times more on defense during World War II than all New Deal expenditure combined. But that fact was not just the result of fiscal constraints. New Dealers committed to redistribution never wanted to build a permanent welfare state but rather hoped to reform the institutions of capitalism through a system of collective bargaining. A powerful organized industrial labor movement would redistribute income through higher wages, but only if the NRA could moderate the power of business to restrict production and set prices.[29]

New Dealers were also powerfully aware that these new measures stood on shaky constitutional ground. The legal, structural, and historical weaknesses of the American state, encapsulated in the restrictive commerce clause, substantially hindered the federal government's ability to recalibrate wages and prices. Much as President Wilson had done earlier, the Roosevelt administration appealed to and relied on popular groups to enforce wage and price policy. Given the doubtful constitutional basis for federal intervention in those matters, the legislative draftsmen hoped that a new union movement would compel compliance with higher wages and shorter hours while mobilized consumers would act as a brake on the price hikes built into these new regulatory measures. Their expectation was that strong executive leadership combined with grassroots mobilization would mitigate the enhanced power of producers to regulate the market in their own interests. Their hope reflected not only political pragmatism but also a commitment to economic citizenship.

Roosevelt wasted no time mobilizing public opinion to overcome the contradictions between reflation and raising purchasing power that were built into the NRA. Aware of the government's limited authority over wages and prices, he turned to exhortation and public pressure. He implored the nation's managers to raise wages without substantially increasing prices, "even at the expense of full initial profits." Roosevelt asked merchants not to increase prices beyond those charged on July 1, 1933. He warned, "If we now inflate prices as fast and as far as we increase wages, the whole project will be set at naught." Putting people back to work and paying minimum wages would help resuscitate the economy. The hope was to add three or four million workers to the payrolls in the next few months. The expectation was that, with "the rising purchasing power of the public," merchants could expect increased sales. The president appealed to businessmen to "refrain from taking profiteering advantage of the consuming public." He explained, "The aim of this whole effort is to restore our rich domestic market by raising its vast consuming capacity."[30]

The NRA launched a massive publicity campaign under the direction of General Hugh Johnson. Johnson had proved his talent when he led the Selective Service Administration in World War I. Now the general used his publicity skills to whip the nation into an NRA frenzy. All who complied by rehiring workers at minimum wages would place a Blue Eagle on their products and places of business. As Johnson later explained, "To make it possible for such a public opinion to support those who were cooperating to create employment and purchasing power . . . we designed the Blue Eagle." Perched on a cogwheel with a thunderbolt in one talon, the eagle summoned industry, labor, and consumers with the motto, "We Do Our Part."[31] The Blue Eagle appeared almost overnight on window placards, sales receipts, labels, advertisements, mastheads, and on virtually all forms of printed business materials. As it had done with the Food Administration, the government sought to arouse public opinion to carry out its wage and price policies.

FIGURE 3.2. The National Recovery Administration issued consumer placards in exchange for pledging to shop only at stores that complied with minimum wages and maximum hours. FDR hoped that public pressure would induce businessmen to raise workers' purchasing power and moderate price increases as the path to economic recovery.

In his campaign, Johnson adopted the purchasing-power explanation for the cause and cure of the Depression. "Prices have risen faster than wages and consuming power. That must end." He appealed to the nation's businessmen to "get people back to work at reasonable wages and increase their buying power." Johnson's argument about the importance of high wages had mass appeal in an era when so many were barely subsisting. Two million spectators turned out for New York City's NRA parade. At a rally in Boston, Johnson cautioned, "Never for one moment forget that 80 per cent of the buying in this country is done by people who earn less than $1,800 a year, and that is the overwhelming majority of the population. Whether we come out of this depression depends on whether we can put this great army of buyers back to work and to buying, by giving them wages high enough to permit them to buy and start business going." A year after the New Deal went into effect, the *New York Times* remarked, "For the past year we have viewed what is doubtless the greatest effort . . . in history to increase . . . the purchasing power of its people."[32]

Central to the NRA's success was its recruitment of the nation's thirty-five million female shoppers. President Roosevelt called upon housewives to moderate necessary price increases by patronizing only stores that displayed a Blue Eagle. At a mass meeting in Saint Louis, Johnson declared, "It is women in homes and not soldiers in uniform who will this time save our country from misery and discord. . . . It is zero hour for housewives. Their battle cry is 'Buy Now under the Blue Eagle.'" Johnson appointed Democratic supporter Mary Hughes to head the NRA Women's Division. With the help of 1.5 million volunteers, Hughes led a nationwide consumer pledge campaign. In exchange for signing, consumers received a Blue Eagle sticker for their front doors. The White House proudly exhibited one. Hughes adopted "Every Woman A Consumer-Signer" as her motto. Johnson warned, "When every American housewife understands that the Blue Eagle on everything she permits to come into her home is a symbol of its restoration to security, may God have mercy on the man or group of men to attempt to trifle with this bird."[33]

Across the country, the NRA initiated local consumer drives, calling upon the volunteer experience and networks of middle- and upper-class women. Hughes instructed her staff: "Remind groups such as women's clubs, church and school gatherings . . . that the success of the N.R.A. largely depends upon their adherence to their pledges." In small-town Pajaro Valley, California, volunteers planned a drive to get "100 percent Signup By Consumers," explaining that "the real power of the recovery campaign lies with the consumers." The local NRA women's committees came from women's clubs and American Legion Auxiliaries. They went house to house canvassing for consumer pledges and warned merchants who did not display a Blue Eagle that they "will be asked to give an accounting." Within weeks, millions of housewives nationwide had signed the pledge. The NRA announced, "Women of the country have been mobilized . . . in their communities to place the enormous purchasing power of women solidly behind the NRA."[34]

FIGURE 3.3. General Hugh Johnson, head of the NRA, launched a nationwide publicity campaign to win support for this New Deal recovery program. From knitting NRA quilts to marching in mass parades to dressing up in NRA costumes, American women demonstrated their initial enthusiasm for this program.

In October 1933, the NRA launched a "Buy Now" campaign, touting it as an essential part of recovery. "The housewives of this country, the purchasing agents who spend 85 percent of the family income, will realize that now is the time to buy," announced Johnson. "Every dollar spent now is helping to keep the wage earner in her family on a payroll." Hughes wrote to her supporting officers: "Urge the 'Buy Now' campaign all you can. It is really the next logical step, for if the merchants have taken on new help and are paying higher wages, they must of course have our support." Eleanor Roosevelt too implored the nation's women to spend. In Massachusetts, Filene led the "Buy Now" campaign as NRA's state chairman. Throughout the country, nearly one million Boy Scouts participated in promoting this spending campaign.[35]

In spite of the appeal to buy now, if anything, consumers had a harder time at the market than before the New Deal. Public exhortation did not prevent many businesses from using the NRA codes to fix prices, nor did it stop food processors from passing on higher costs of the AAA tax. Rapid increases in the price of bread, milk, and meat, as well as many other manufactured goods, surpassed most wage increases. As employment expanded, the overall wage bill grew. But cost-of-living increases meant a lower real income for individual workers. In July, food prices alone went up nearly 10 percent. The *New Republic* predicted that, like earlier, similar, drives, the "Buy Now" campaign would fail because the public lacked purchasing power. Isador Lubin, the new commissioner of the Bureau of Labor Statistics (BLS), thought the situation did not look good. During World War I, Lubin had worked at the Food Administration. Now, at the BLS, he gathered monthly data on food costs in fifty-one cities, leading him to predict that prices were just beginning an upward spiral. "Soon, no doubt, our radios and movies will reverberate with a new version of that classic . . . 'The high cost of living.' "[36]

The New Deal precipitated a massive showdown over prices. On one side, the NRA codes ratified price-fixing, which manufacturers, advertisers, and small retailers had long sought. Macy's, a staunch opponent of price maintenance, led mass retailers in denouncing the code's price-fixing provisions. But merchants and manufacturers were well organized, and they prevailed. Codes for goods as diverse as underwear, ice, farm equipment, fertilizer, and oil burners included price-fixing agreements. Of the 700 codes, 568 contained minimum-price provisions. Food processors also took advantage of the suspension of antitrust laws to fix prices. In spite of their antiprofiteering rhetoric, both Johnson and AAA director George Peek were more committed to restoring farmers' stability than to protecting urban purchasing power. Both were veterans of the War Industries Board's postwar battle to maintain prices. After the war, they went into the farm-implement tool business. They coauthored *Equality for Agriculture* (1922), a treatise for farm parity. Now Peek saw his job in simple terms: "It's just to put up farm prices." As long as farmers got a fair return, Peek did not try to limit food manufacturers' profits.[37] On the other side, working- and middle-class Americans resisted price hikes they thought unreasonable. The invocation of consumer concerns and the use of a purchasing-power rationale created its own dynamic, arousing public expectations that intensified the tensions built into and exacerbated by the New Deal and made them even more difficult to manage.

To deflect criticism arising from the inflationary aspects of the New Deal programs, New Dealers blamed high prices on monopolistic corporations and price-gouging merchants. And the public largely accepted that explanation. The early New Deal was plagued with a range of problems: recovery and jobs remained elusive, business forcefully resisted giving labor a voice in setting NRA codes, and social tensions approached a boiling point. In that context, the price problem further pinched Americans' pocketbooks and added fuel to the antibusiness sentiment. With business's reputation plummeting, wartime accusations of profiteering resurfaced, and consumers once again regarded the government as the proper authority to assess what constituted a fair price.[38] It would not be long before Americans in their capacity as consumers became more demanding. In their protests, they received aid and encouragement from the same reformers who had fought for fair prices during the inflationary years of World War I.

Consumer-minded members of the administration understood that high prices could undercut public support for the New Deal. Purchasing-power progressives in the AAA prodded consumers to apply pressure to food processors and distributors. The AAA appointed Frederic Howe as the consumers' counsel. Howe, a municipal reformer, had blamed monopoly interests for rising food costs during World War I. His job now was to ensure that manufacturers and distributors did not add more than the cost of the processing tax to agricultural products, such as bread and cotton goods. He also had authority to investigate complaints and launch formal investigations. He used this post as a platform to attack the middlemen he had long sought to regulate.[39]

At the same time, General Johnson announced the creation of an NRA Consumer Advisory Board (CAB) as a way to co-opt and blunt criticism. At the textile hearings, the first industry to submit codes of fair trade, Johnson appointed Mary Rumsey to head the CAB. Like Howe, Rumsey was another prominent veteran of the fight against high prices during World War I. The CAB's mission was "to see that the codes do not contain clauses which may either boost prices unfairly, subsidize monopolies or lower the quality standards of consumer goods." As Rumsey summed up the board's aim, "Prices must not rise beyond purchasing power." "To inflict an excessive burden upon the consumer would be to defeat the very object of the administration's entire project—the increase of purchasing." She would work with the Bureau of Labor Statistics and the Bureau of Home Economics to publicize information on prices and the cost of living. She appointed Dexter Keezer, a leading theorist of business regulation, as CAB's executive director. As the daughter of E. H. Harriman and sister of Averell Harriman, Rumsey used her connections in elite circles to win an audience. In the early years of the Depression, Rumsey had organized voluntary efforts financed by local communities to find emergency work for the unemployed.[40] Now, as head of the CAB, she led a national campaign to protect Americans' interests as consumers.

Neither the CAB nor the consumers' counsel exerted much, if any, leverage in drafting or administering recovery codes. Both bodies faced serious institutional obstacles. The CAB, for example, could not compete with the well-organized and well-financed industrial representatives it encountered. Unlike trade associations representing one industry, the CAB had to be a jack-of-all-trades. Keezer explained that, in any given week, the CAB had to advise in the drafting of over fifty codes. The codes applied to markets as diverse as chewing-gum manufacturing, the powder-puff industry, automotive maintenance, and building and loan associations. More problematic, the president proved unwilling to condemn price agreements at a moment when the constitutionality of the AAA and the NRA hung in doubt, fearing that such a stance would only fuel legal challenges from New Deal opponents. The best his appointees could do was channel and foment public opinion.

In spite of their weaknesses, the existence of these New Deal consumer bodies gave reformers a position of authority and legitimized their activism. From their government posts, they articulated critiques of New Deal policies that resonated with and animated popular protests. Drawing on at least a decade of social thought, they donned the consumer mantle to organize working- and middle-class support behind reforming and democratizing American capital. An early CAB memo explained, "The consumers' interest is not to be regarded as limited to the retail market for consumers' goods. . . . An adequate safeguarding of the consumers' interest . . . calls for a complete check upon industrial processes from the raw material to the finished good and its distribution to the ultimate consumer." As CAB's Thomas Blaisdell explained, they were fighting to bring about the "socialization of monopoly and the civilization of competition."[41]

Since the fair-price campaigns in 1919, Mary Rumsey understood that the price problem was connected to inadequate labor standards and the absence of effective labor and consumer organizations. Rumsey received her CAB appointment at the suggestion of her Washington roommate and close friend Secretary of Labor Frances Perkins. Rumsey regularly had the ear of Eleanor Roosevelt. Both would be at Rumsey's bedside when she died the next year from a horseback-riding accident. All three had long supported the abolition of child labor and elimination of sweatshop conditions, and the Blue Eagle sanctioned those goals. The first lady sewed the first NRA label of the coat-and-suit code authority into her winter coat as a symbol of her solidarity; Perkins stitched the first NRA dress label into one of her gowns. Rumsey appointed friends such as Rose Schneiderman of the Women's Trade Union League, Mary Dewson of the National Consumers' League, Frances Zuill of the American Home Economics Association, Belle

Sherwin of the National League of Women Voters, and Grace Morrison Poole of the General Federation of Women's Clubs to serve on the CAB. In addition to representatives of the female reform network, Rumsey recruited popular economist William Trufant Foster, president of the Cooperative League James Warbasse, and living-wage advocate William Ogburn. Consulting members included Gardiner Means, Paul Douglas, Robert Lynd, and Sidney Hillman, as well as historian Charles Beard, family-budget expert Jessica Peixotto, and corporate liberal Owen Young. This group conceived of consumer and labor issues as intimately linked. In praising the textile code, Rumsey announced that it would "increase the purchasing power and leisure of 500,000 worker-consumers."[42]

From the beginning, Rumsey targeted rising prices as a key issue that beleaguered the nation's families. The CAB's main function, she explained, was to answer the question, "Is the bill presented to the American family for the fair-practice codes a fair bill?" Rumsey sought powers to prevent runaway prices and echoed the president's call for restraint. She called on Secretary of the Interior Harold Ickes to check excessive oil prices, and she likewise protested against hikes in coal prices. She expressed particular concern for white-collar workers, "hard hit" by rising prices, and urged them to report complaints. Within the CAB, Rumsey established a complaint committee chaired by General Johnson's wife, Helen. The committee intended to expose those who displayed the NRA Blue Eagle while failing to comply with its provisions. Emily Newell Blair, a major Democratic Party worker and Rumsey's eventual successor, became head of the Consumers Protective Bureau, which was charged with disclosing cases of profiteering. The first lady too condemned high prices. "Consumers," she declared at a press conference, "must learn to defend themselves against too sudden and too high a rise in prices of the things they buy." She urged women to report gougers.[43]

In the summer of 1933, rising bread prices became a battleground issue when urban consumers blamed farm relief. Their complaints motivated Secretary of Agriculture Henry Wallace to talk tough against increases. With the advice of Gardiner Means, who had moved to Washington to become Wallace's economic assistant, the secretary warned bakers and wheat processors against coordinating an industrywide price hike. He threatened to label every loaf with a notice that the processing tax on wheat added only one cent to the cost. In spite of his sympathy for food processors, the AAA's George Peek recognized the political dangers of inflation. "Pledg[ing] protection of the consumer" and threatening antitrust action, he announced, "We are prepared to use every power at our command to prevent the unreasonable increasing of bread prices."[44]

Wallace and the bakers went to war. The secretary told forty-nine mayors across the country that the attorney general would investigate complaints of profiteering in their cities. The U.S. Bureau of Agricultural Economics, long a seedbed of progressive reform, released a report asserting that any increase of more than one and a half cents was unjustified. The New York commissioner of markets, Jere Ryan, ordered bakers to print the weight of a loaf on its wrapper to prevent them from charging the same price for a lighter loaf. Rising prices now had a dynamic of their own, and, in spite of Wallace's warnings, bakers began to charge eight cents for the usual five-cent, one-pound loaf. Bread prices rose everywhere, from Saint Paul to Indianapolis, from Syracuse to Bismark, and from Norfolk to Boston and Philadelphia.[45]

These price increases were front-page news, and they generated a genuine popular backlash. As soon as the AAA processing tax went into effect, Secretary Wallace publicly urged consumers to resist "price racketeering." When bakers raised their prices above what the public deemed fair, consumers from every state across the country mailed bread wrappers to their new allies in Washington to demonstrate what they perceived to be unfair price increases. Along with these waxed wrappers, citizens sent letters that revealed the degree to which New Deal rhetoric had penetrated the popular consciousness. "We are glad to see you [are] after the profiteers," wrote an Ohio man. An Ohio woman who signed off as "A Consumer" asked, "Are we getting a square deal? . . . A pound loaf sells for 10¢." A distraught citizen from York, Pennsylvania, who sent in a newspaper clipping announcing an end to the nickel loaf, inquired, "Is it justifiable or is it profiteering?" A California housewife bemoaned "the increased price on milk and bread." "Is it justifiable?" she too asked. Reporting an increase in local wheat prices, an Ohio woman demanded to know, "Is this a fair increase? . . . It appears that improved machinery and mass production have made things worse for the consumer."[46]

These letters reflect the pervasive influence of the New Deal's most progressive antibusiness rhetoric. Complaints came from housewives and husbands, from working-class and middle-class citizens, and from urban as well as rural residents. Most Americans now relied on store-bought bread, and thus even consumers in the wheat-producing states of Kansas, Illinois, Iowa, Nebraska, Montana, and Minnesota sent in complaints. From Pedro Moya, president of the Local Independent Union of the Cigar Industry of Tampa, to Harry Gockel, president of Ozark Junior College, Missouri, Americans complained to the government about the rise in bread prices. The letters sometimes represented a collective act, as in the case of the appeal by John Murphy, mayor of New Haven, Connecticut, on behalf of his city. For others, sending a letter was an

FIGURE 3.4. When bakers raised their prices beyond the one-cent AAA processing tax in the summer of 1933, Secretary of Agriculture Henry Wallace urged
consumers to resist this "profiteering." In response, consumers from across the
country sent bread wrappers to Washington demonstrating local increases they
felt unjustified and asked for redress. An Indiana consumer sent in the wrapper
shown here, with a recent three-cent increase indicated by an eight-cent band
over the old five-cent price.

individual plea to take action. Charles White from Delaware urged Wallace to "get busy and have these profiteers prosecuted." The desire to have the New Dealers investigate prices could even transcend party lines. Stanley McGilligan, a dentist who owned a small farm outside Urbana, Illinois, explained that he "ha[s] been a Republican but I'm saying 'Amen' to many things being done by the President."[47]

Consumers' Counsel Howe and other left-leaning New Deal supporters launched a crusade against unjustified monopoly price increases. It was Howe's job "to see that no unfair profits were taken by unscrupulous people." "We are going . . . to see . . . that consumers are protected," announced Howe. He initiated investigations into bread prices all the way from San Francisco and Seattle to Savannah, Georgia, and Scranton, Pennsylvania. "Every extra cent charged the public means thousands of dollars less in consumers' pockets."[48] In New York, Mayor Fiorello LaGuardia led a campaign against racketeering at the city's markets. He recruited members of the General Federation of Women's Clubs to appear on the city's daily radio program to tell consumers what foods they could purchase in abundance and at low prices. Deputy Commissioner Frances Gannon explained, "The housewife must be able to . . . judge what are the best values on the market for the day." The mayor was aided by ninety Civil Works Administration employees, who conducted a citywide survey on food costs.[49]

In August, the office of the consumers' counsel began publishing *Consumers' Guide*. Utilizing local price information, each bimonthly issue of the government newsletter listed prices for bread, milk, meat, cotton goods, and other necessities from fifty-one representative cities. It reported the spread between manufacturers' costs and the prices charged to consumers. As *Business Week* explained, "The idea is simple enough—to awaken public sentiment and put its power behind the drive to get more money for the farmer without gouging the consumer." The *Consumers' Guide* findings ran in newspapers and aired on radio broadcasts. Howe sent thousands of copies to women's clubs and consumers' leagues. He encouraged housewives to compare the listed prices to those in their local stores. "Where local prices are far out of line . . . consumers should ask an explanation."[50]

Bread was just the beginning of the consumers' counsel's campaign. NRA codes administered by business had worked too well. Recent price increases more than doubled the cost of ladies' hosiery, men's socks, cheap shirts, and union suits. Howe accused cotton-goods manufacturers of gouging the public. He also worked to expose the high price of milk, which he linked to inadequate consumption among the working classes, especially children. In August 1933, 120 Jewish women from Philadelphia wrote to Wallace, "We wish to voice our protest against the

unwarranted rise of prices in all foods, particularly MILK." In response
to such popular agitation, the AAA held public hearings on milk prices
in Philadelphia, Boston, Baltimore, and Chicago.[51]

By the fall, the initial enthusiasm for the NRA waned. The early New
Deal had brought no end to the Depression. Continuing hardships inevitably produced social chaos and labor unrest, especially as big business
dominated the administration of the NRA and stifled the participation of
organized labor and consumers. Clarence Darrow, the nation's most
celebrated progressive lawyer, offered a scathing report: "The choice is
between monopoly sustained by the government, which is clearly the
trend in the NRA; and a planned economy, which demands socialized
ownership and control." Big business, critics charged, exploited the
consuming public through refusing wage advances, restricting production, and imposing artificially high prices. New Deal supporter and
popular economist David Cushman Coyle summed up the opinion of
average Americans: "There is a growing recognition that inadequate
buying power is resulting from the fact that prices have risen faster
than wages."[52]

At a moment of massive deflation, why did prices gain so much political attention? And by extension, why did consumers rise to prominence
in political debates? They had no organized presence in Washington,
they benefited directly from few policies, and, if anything, they seemed
to bear the brunt of New Deal experimentation in the form of higher
food and industrial prices. Yet New Dealers from Roosevelt on down
constantly claimed to act on their behalf. That strategy reflected the
success of purchasing-power progressives to conflate their laborite
agenda with the nation's economic goals and add a moral dimension to
its purpose. What made the New Deal so expansive and thus so threatening was not simply its success in igniting a mass union movement and
challenging business prerogatives. Equally critical was that it also legitimized, fostered, and institutionalized a broadly conceived consumer's
interest both on the shop floor and at the market. Americans had never
fully asserted their interests as consumers. And, as was becoming increasingly clear, achieving success in this area required empowering
unions through new labor legislation. But by using the language of purchasing power to justify its policies, the New Deal won popular support
for the redistributive agenda of low prices and high wages. That view,
whether correct or not, was supported by both a progressive core of the
New Deal elite and large segments of the public. James Martin, a white-
collar worker who saw his income drop by 40 percent in four years, reflected on the difficulties he faced as a middle-class consumer. "I have
nothing with which to buy the clothing, furniture, rugs, automobiles,
books, lamps, and other merchandise whose production would keep

our factories busy and restore employment to millions. That is why the factories are largely idle. . . . We have even cut down on food." "The burden of having to pay 1929 prices for so many necessities is crushing us—and making it impossible for us to 'Buy Now' "[53]

The corporate-dominated NRA codes came under sustained attack as the cause of restricted output, higher prices, degraded standards, and reduced purchasing power. William Ogburn resigned from the CAB, declaring that current NRA policies jeopardized Americans' safety through higher prices. "The real issue is price. If prices go up too fast and too high, they will get out of range of wages, salaries, and industrial purchasing agents, and a setback to recovery will occur." "This," he asserted, "is a delicate problem—how to get prices high enough to lure industry but not too high for consumers. Consideration of price is, I think, the greatest need in the NRA today." Ogburn's resignation prompted the *New York Times* to conclude that Americans in their capacity as consumers "are the real forgotten men. They are remembered only when it comes time to settle accounts. . . . [T]he consumer, with or without larger purchasing power in his pocket, will be, as so often before, the man who pays."[54]

Victimization bred resentment and put pressure on the administration to live up to its promise of mass purchasing power. In his letter of resignation, Ogburn warned that as prices increased and quality of goods declined, "the voices of the consumers will undoubtedly be loud." Chicago residents, for example, protested when the NRA milk code eliminated the three-cent savings for shopping at cash-and-carry stores rather than getting home delivery. Stuart Chase predicted the consumer's growing strength: "Far from being puny, she is an Amazon towering, portentous, blocking the whole economic horizon of the years before us." *Business Week* reported that retailers faced "balky consumers." "The women cheered Blue eagle parades—but they don't like the higher prices in the stores." Across the country, local NRA compliance boards received hundreds of thousands of complaints. In response to growing agitation, the NRA announced that industries would be required to submit information justifying recent price hikes. The administration also appointed Gardiner Means and Isador Lubin to a newly created Federal Price Board. At the same time, Means formally joined the CAB to consult on price increases.[55]

NRA critics seized the moment. Embracing the consumer label, purchasing-power progressives staged a widely publicized confrontation with the administration in December 1933. In response to price increases, fifty citizen groups formed the Emergency Conference of Consumer Organizations. The conference comprised middle-class reform and labor groups sympathetic to the problems wage-earning and white-collar families faced at the market. "Consumer purchasing power is declining," they warned. These reformers used the consumer rhetoric that the president himself had employed to demand more radical government intervention. They asked Roosevelt to strengthen the CAB to protect the interests of lower-income citizens. "It is time that the millions of helpless consumers developed a champion for their interests," they insisted. "The logical one is the government itself." At the urging of Mary Rumsey and Frederic Howe, Eleanor Roosevelt arranged a meeting at the White House between the Emergency Conference and General Johnson. The Conference delegates deplored the absence of consumer representatives on NRA code authorities. They denounced the treatment of CAB members as window dressing and insisted, "Only through the adequate representation of consumer interests can any degree of industrial recovery be had." They called for the creation of a Department of the Consumer, with "effective power to safeguard the consumer against price-gouging and against shoddy standards of manufacturing." Johnson temporarily diffused these attacks by offering jobs to two of the Emergency Conference leaders, Leon Henderson of the Russell Sage Foundation and F. J. Schlink of Consumers' Research, as his special assistants. Henderson accepted and would become the most important voice for the New Deal's purchasing-power program over the next decade.[56]

Creating a Consumer Movement, 1934–1935

Left-leaning New Dealers looked to the creation of a powerful consumer movement as a way to enforce redistributive policies. The agitation over prices reflected public frustration but was not effectively channeled into political action. The *Nation* regretted that "the NRA program must depend for its enforcement principally upon the cooperation and assistance of the most helpless and unorganized workers, the habitually unprotesting American consumer, and the distressed housewife." Assistant Secretary of Agriculture Rexford Tugwell described the CAB bluntly as "a spearhead without a shaft." To save the New Deal, CAB executive director Dexter Keezer insisted, "There must be activity at the grass roots." The NRA field agents, too, felt a "vital need for a vigorous consumers' campaign." Even technocratic economists like Gardiner Means did not underestimate the significance of popular mobilization. Means claimed, "Basic to the protection of the interest of people as consumers and the maintenance of balance in our economy is the need for consumer organization."[57] These policymakers sought to supplement labor's forceful push at the factories with a show of consumer strength at the shopping counters.

By mobilizing this consuming public, the CAB sought to transform underconsumption from an abstract theory critical of high prices into the ideological basis of a social movement and sustained political activism. Drawing on her wartime experience in community organization, Mary Rumsey argued that Americans had a special role to play as consumers in thwarting excessive prices. The CAB announced plans to organize consumer county councils. "We are appealing to the consumer to become the watchdog of the nation, not the hangdog." In his State of the Union address in January 1934, President Roosevelt "encourage[d] the slowly growing impulse among consumers to enter the industrial market place with sufficient organization to insist upon fair prices and honest sales." He and others in his administration embraced the involvement of consumer groups partly because they recognized that the NRA, which was on shaky legal ground, needed grassroots support. Code enforcement by a battalion of housewives was preferable to direct involvement by government administrators, which might result in a test case of NRA's constitutionality. Thus, the administration granted approval to set up two hundred county councils on an experimental basis.[58]

The drive to organize consumers combined administrative pragmatism with left-wing economics and political mobilization. Chairman Rumsey appointed economists Paul Douglas, then serving as chief of the CAB's Bureau of Consumers Economic Education, and William T. Foster to oversee the establishment of the consumer councils. A year earlier, Douglas had been a leading voice of the Left and a strong proponent of consumer cooperatives, which he hoped would serve as "vital cells in a truly self-governing and democratic America." Like Tugwell, Berle, Means, and Henderson, he was now an official New Dealer. Douglas conceived of his assignment as part of "building a Consumers' movement" staffed by "energized liberals." At the White House Consumer Conference, Douglas announced that each consumer council would consist of a representative from a woman's organization, a county agricultural agent, a home demonstration agent or a home economist, a "dirt" farmer, a moderate- or low-income housewife, an employed manual worker, and a cooperative or credit-union member.[59]

Indeed, these councils reflected the boldness of the consumer vision. According to Douglas, representatives were to have ties to labor and cooperative movements as well as to women's social clubs and teachers' organizations. In theory, these grassroots organizations would serve as local enforcement agencies by adjudicating "consumers' complaints against undue price increases." The CAB encouraged them to study the distribution and costs of food items to prevent "unreasonable prices and lowered quality of goods." If local bodies lacked the clout to monitor market transactions adequately, the complaints would be forwarded to the NRA Fair Price Section. The Department of Justice and the Federal Trade Commission would then investigate suspicions of monopolistic practices.[60]

These councils never lived up to their audacious plans, and even at their most potent they paled in comparison to the threat of ten million organized union members. But in their conception, and at times their operation, they demonstrated how the purchasing-power problem could mobilize citizens at the market.

This fair-price movement aroused much local enthusiasm. In March 1934, Tillie Kaplan of the Bronx wrote NRA consumer representatives that the housewives of her neighborhood were launching "a severe strike movement . . . against the price of bread." They insisted that local bakers reduce the price from ten to six cents a pound. Kaplan linked these "strike meetings" to creating a New York county consumer council. Once established, the council demanded a cut in milk prices. In December, it began distributing shopping lists to housewives and running weekly radio shows to advise on good buys. Throughout the country, local councils became repositories for the AAA's *Consumers' Guide*, the NRA's *Consumer Notes*, and the Bureau of Home Economics' *Market Basket*.[61]

These New Deal programs legitimized consumer activity and raised what Robert Lynd identified as a growing "consumer consciousness." As a result of the New Deal, Lynd found, the "word 'consumer' has got into popular language." From the chronically poor to the newly down-and-out white-collar workers, Americans sent thousands of letters each day to the White House, making requests for everything from groceries and eyeglasses to Eleanor Roosevelt's used dresses. Those requests reflected a new sense that the government would provide for them as consumers. *Scribner's* ran a feature written by an "everyday housewife," who claimed that "for the first time in my history I am making a point of reading everything which the President of the United States writes, and of listening to his broadcast speeches." In "a message which seemed to be directed straight to me" she responded to the president's decree that "consumers should organize." What did she want? "I want a good quality of peas, at a fair price, and as purchasing agent for my family of consumers it is my duty to see that I get value for our money." She urged "the housewives of this country" to take political action.[62]

New Dealers argued that individual consumers could gain power through a government-enforced system of quality standards and grade labeling. Massive unemployment and rising prices made such a system imperative to prevent further erosion of purchasing power. Within the AAA, Rexford Tugwell and Jerome Frank pushed for compliance with tougher food regulations and labeling. To thwart their efforts, Peek transferred food industry codes out of AAA jurisdiction to the NRA, where industrial representatives would resist any reforms. To counter business dominance, CAB members Robert Lynd and Caroline Ware, a longtime consumer advocate, composed the "Lynd Report," which recommended government-issued quality standards on consumer products for use in NRA codes. Ware explained, "If the modern consumer is to be as good a bargainer as was his grandfather among his cronies at the village store, he must be told what he is buying." "Without accurate information," she insisted, "the buyer is not an equal party to the bargain."[63]

Demands for government standards came to a head at the canning-industry code hearings in February 1934, when consumer representatives went on the offensive. "The industry is yours, but the money that supports the industry is ours," threatened Lena Phillips, president of the National Council of Women. Appropriating the language of Schlink and Chase's best-selling book, Mrs. John Boyle of the Washington, D.C., Consumers' Council declared, "When I buy canned vegetables I want to get my money's worth. When I go to the grocery store, I see some cans that say 'fancy,' others say 'selected.' . . . The label of none of them tells me what grade I am buying, I do not know until I get home and open the can just what grade I have bought." She insisted, "I want a guarantee that I am buying exactly what I pay for." Karl Hauck from the CAB agreed that the nation's housewives "are entitled to know just what they are buying." As Lynd's committee reported, "A low price, *per se*, is obviously of no benefit to the consumer if the quality is equally low."[64]

For the next four years, these purchasing-power advocates pushed for the Tugwell Food and Drug Bill to regulate the industries that had gained notoriety for fraudulent advertising and adulterated goods. The American Home Economics Association, the General Federation of Women's Clubs, the American Association of University Women, the League of Women Voters, and the Women's Trade Union League lobbied in Washington for this measure and mobilized their constituencies. The protracted fight for the Tugwell Bill brought coherence to a burgeoning consumer movement spreading among national women's organizations of all political persuasions. Mass retailers like Macy's also supported the bill on behalf of the consumer, who is "entitled to know what she is purchasing." Business lobbyists found this groundswell of support terrifying and put up great resistance, fearing that this measure "would make the Secretary of Agriculture dictator of their industries." The president of *Printers' Ink*, Roy Dickinson, warned that such regulations took aim not just at advertising and labeling but at the entire profit system.[65]

Fights over labeling canned peaches may seem petty, but they reflected an emerging consumer consciousness with organizational force and friends in high places. The nation's newspapers and magazines, dependent on advertisements of brand-name goods for revenue, were reluctant to report on the Tugwell Bill and the growing consumer movement that supported it. And yet, the degree to which consumer consciousness had spread was revealed in a parody, published in the

Saturday Evening Post, that took the form of a love letter from a consumer to her congressman, confessing that she had betrayed him by falling in love with Rexford Tugwell: "I want to tell you, Con[gressman] about Rex Tugwell.... It is the finer things about me, the little things, that he cares about—things you could not imagine politicians like Washington and Jefferson and Lincoln caring about—I mean my teeth and hair and cuticle and things like that, that mean so little to most statesmen, and yet, to us, mean so much.... You have never cared for me, really, as these men are caring today.... If any man could break me of my bad buying habits, Rex is that man, Con."[66]

From his new government post as General Johnson's consumer adviser, Leon Henderson gained prominence as the administration's chief critic of corporate practices. Henderson had served in the Taylorite Ordnance Department in World War I. He taught industrial management at the University of Pennsylvania and economics at the Carnegie Institute of Technology. He worked for the progressive Pennsylvania governor Gifford Pinchot and then for the New York Russell Sage Foundation as the head of its Remedial Loans Department. As a crusader against loan sharks, Henderson knew firsthand the difficulties faced by wage earners with few economic resources. To Henderson, the NRA only exacerbated economic problems through "the erection of an artificial price structure." "The fact that the fixing of high prices and control of production can result only in an ever-narrowing circle of possible consumers is ignored by industry." "The average citizen," he argued, "is being penalized by price-fixing arrangements."[67]

The louder Henderson complained, the more power he gained. He went on the warpath by accusing the woolen-goods industry of gouging the public with extortionist clothing prices set by the NRA code. Days later, General Johnson appointed Henderson as head of the NRA Research and Planning Division. That agency investigated the impact of codes on employment and purchasing power. His predecessors included Stephen DuBrul of General Motors and Alexander Sachs of Lehman Brothers. Henderson, an outspoken opponent of monopolistic practices and a strong supporter of the consumer and organized labor, promised to shift the division leftward. It was no secret that Henderson believed, as the *Baltimore Sun* put it, that "price trends resulting from the NRA code policies to date threaten to destroy the whole recovery program by freezing prices beyond the reach of the consumer." Henderson charged that high prices were not necessary, that they swelled corporate profits. "For the first time in the history of the Government, we're going to have a detailed statistical check-up in industry." "We're certainly going to raise the question of profits and net earnings of industry." If price-fixing "persists, a lower standard of living is inevitable."[68]

General Johnson knew he could not ignore the price problem, as it was only one of a series of crises threatening the NRA. In February 1934, Johnson invited all NRA critics to Washington to air their grievances at what he publicly called a "Field Day of Criticism."[69] Workers were now in open rebellion, business was complaining loudly, the NRA had legal challenges pending, and other strategies and explanations for ending the Depression competed for attention. In this mess, consumers were just one voice among many. But what made theirs so powerful was the way in which they framed the price problem as part of a larger structural critique of modern capitalism. These consumer advocates saw rising prices, inadequate wages, and a maldistribution of income as the inevitable result of the concentration of economic control. That argument gave ideological cover to the labor movement, which began to advance its claims on purchasing-power grounds. It was the reciprocity and seeming harmony of labor and consumer interests that made their critique of the New Deal at once appealing to a broad audience and therefore radical.

On the eve of the Field Day, the CAB captured national headlines and helped set the agenda by taking aim at the open-price agreements included in two-thirds of the codes. Such provisions, they claimed, were necessary only where the "sick," highly competitive natural-resource industries suffered from cutthroat competition. In others, they unnecessarily drove up prices and blocked recovery. The CAB insisted, "The consumer's interest requires that goods be turned out in large and increasing volume . . . [with] prices kept low." Walton Hamilton, a leading authority on the subject, also argued that consumers were hurt by corporate collusion on prices under the NRA. If price-fixing was necessary, he said, then the government should do it: "The consumer should pay this much; the producer is entitled to no more." The same consumer groups that had testified on behalf of the Tugwell Bill along with labor leaders like Sidney Hillman of the Amalgamated Clothing Workers spoke out loudly against price-fixing.[70]

Mass retailers were alive to a growing crisis, and they sided with consumers. Fearing protests against higher prices, the National Retail Dry Goods Association, representing 5,200 retailers, adamantly opposed price-fixing agreements.[71] Edward Filene made front-page news by telling his fellow businessmen that they "were making a mistake" in maintaining prices. The nation's twenty-three thousand chain grocery stores pledged to "continue to give to the consuming public the benefit of economical mass distribution." President R. E. Wood of Sears announced that the mail-order giant would cut 1935 prices by 16 percent, outdoing Montgomery Ward's 6 percent cut. Retail expert Paul Nystrom cautioned, "If prices go too high, if consumers have neither the purchasing power nor the faith in the fairness of such prices, then they will not buy." He predicted a "period of severe consumer resistance" in the months to follow. Q. Forrest Walker, Macy's economist, warily agreed. Meyer Parodneck of the Emergency Conference of Consumer Organizations reported, "The buyer's strike is on. Government figures prove it. Only the transfer of power from big business, which throttles recovery, to the people will stop it."[72]

Six months after the NRA's inception, the euphoria that had surrounded it in its early days was gone. Employment and purchasing power had increased, but not enough. Although the Recovery Act had provided three billion dollars for public works, administrators had spent little of that sum, and the capital-goods industry remained stalled. Industry had not made anywhere near a full recovery, and in some instances NRA codes actually lowered wages. Since most workers, except the lowest paid, received more than the required forty-cents minimum, employers threatened to fire workers and rehire them at a reduced wage. Women workers too, in tobacco, textiles, and food processing, feared worsening conditions under the codes. Lucy Randolph Mason of the National Consumers' League and Maud Schwartz of the Women's Trade Union League condemned sex differentials in wage rates that institutionalized lower wages for women.[73]

If the price problem led to simmering resentment, business refusal to recognize NRA-sanctioned unions proved red-hot. By the end of 1933, two-thirds of the largest manufacturers had established company unions, often run by corporate officials, to counteract the spread of independent trade unionism. After a tour of the nation's major cities, Edward Filene observed, "Employers generally, and especially the large national corporations with branches throughout the country, do not intend to allow labor to successfully organize." A steelworker wrote to Senator Wagner to protest Bethlehem Steel's subversion of labor's right to organize as granted by Section 7a. Scribbling across a piece of company-union propaganda, he urged Wagner to call the "rats to Washington . . . to prove the company unions are a farce." Eugene Grace, president of Bethlehem Steel, served as head of the company union. "Let us have a Senate investigation," the steelworker demanded. Under the "company union, we are driven to slavery . . . slavery for the workers, millions for the officials, we only want justice." Workers soon labeled the NRA the National Run Around.[74]

FDR hesitated amid this crisis precisely because he understood how high the stakes were. Shortly after the Field Day, the president threw his moral weight behind the purchasing-power program before four thousand NRA code members assembled in Washington. Roosevelt told them that their task was "to create consuming power." He reiterated that the aim of the New Deal "was to increase the buying power of wage earners and farmers." "I asked that management give first consideration to increasing the purchasing power of the public." "With millions still unemployed the power of our people to purchase and use the products of industry is still greatly curtailed." He endorsed labor's program of higher wages, telling the nation's business leaders "to reemploy more people at purchasing wages and to do it now." His message was clear. "As between profits first and humanity afterwards and humanity first and profit afterwards we have no room for hesitation." He asserted, "Never again will we permit the social conditions that permitted . . . a maldistribution of wealth and power." Those conditions he labeled "un-American." These were powerful words that gave enormous legitimacy to unions and had broad popular appeal. But fearful of precipitating a constitutional showdown over NRA, the president did not back them up with meaningful action. Neither General Johnson nor the president took active steps to check the growth of company unions.[75]

As conditions deteriorated, a group of over two hundred prominent liberals sent a public letter to the president in May 1934 asking for a powerful NRA to fulfill its original promise. The list included Paul Douglas, Adolph Berle, and Robert Lynd, as well as leaders of many women's groups now associated with the consumer movement. These activists saw the price problem and the labor problem as intimately connected. One passage of the letter read, "With wages lagging behind profits, and production already beginning to grow beyond the power of the wage-earning market to consume, the weakness of the NRA set-up (with its code authorities dominated by industrial interests) is registered in price practices which jeopardize the whole recovery program." "Our whole wage structure has been undermined by the rapid increase in prices," it concluded. The writers worried that "the failure to develop an effective enforcement machinery is so grave" that the NRA would trigger the same resistance as Prohibition. To increase purchasing power and counter the price-fixing tendencies of the NRA, they recommended unionization, collective bargaining, consumer organization, a federal consumer agency, a national system of unemployment insurance, and a revision of home mortgage policy. These were far-reaching demands with radical implications, as the *New Republic* made clear in this statement: "Collective labor action is the police force on which the government must rely." "Far from interfering with recovery, the use of strikes to date has, for the most part increased the chance for it. There probably ought to be more strikes and bigger ones rather than less."[76]

FDR was unwilling to support tougher action on the labor front, anxious that measures of support for workers would only further alienate the business community at a time when restoring production was the number

one goal. While unions might boost purchasing power, they also were disruptive to the shop floor. That would become clear during an explosive
outburst of strikes in the summer of 1934. Instead of fueling this fire, the
administration now intensified its attack on monopoly prices, if for no
other reason than to deflect growing criticism of the NRA and the AAA.
Within the administration, Henderson's stature grew. Roosevelt later remarked to John Maynard Keynes, "Just look at Leon. When I got him he
was only an economist." When Johnson resigned from the NRA at the
White House's suggestion, Henderson and Walton Hamilton became two
of a new five-member National Industrial Recovery Board. To be sure,
corporate leaders counterbalanced their votes. But Henderson reiterated
his commitment to "reduce all industrial prices radically" as "the only way
to bring about consumer demand." "Government should see to it that
monopolistic groups do not write the codes."[77]

The early New Deal had been a mixture of successes and failures. The
NRA did put two million people back to work and, under the AAA,
farmers' income grew. The Home Owners' Loan Corporation helped
one in five Americans refinance their mortgages. And a string of alphabet
agencies—the Public Works Administration, the Civilian Conservation
Corps, the Federal Emergency Relief Administration—provided the
most down-and-out with new sources of income. These tangible benefits
paid off for the Democrats in the midterm elections of 1934. Although
the Democrats expected to lose seats as part of a regular pattern of
midterm elections, in fact their party scored impressive gains in both
the House and Senate that helped to ease the way for further New Deal
reforms. But exactly what actions to take remained far from clear.[78]

The idea of artificially rigged prices now entered political debate as a
way to explain the longevity of the Depression. In early 1935, just as
Congress began deliberating whether to renew the NRA, scheduled to
expire in the summer, Senator William Borah introduced Gardiner
Means's report *Industrial Prices and Their Relative Inflexibility*. Written
with help from Leon Henderson and Isador Lubin of the Bureau of
Labor Statistics, the report explained that the NRA codes only exacerbated and sanctioned a preexisting tendency toward "rigid prices." In a
sweeping condemnation of industrial practices, Means wrote, "Modern
industrial organization . . . has . . . destroyed the free market." Individual businessmen maintained prices and reduced production in hopes of
getting profits. But "the drop in production throws workers out of employment, reduces their income and so further reduces their demand."
In the iron and steel industry, for example, prices fell 20 percent while
production fell 83 percent; car prices dropped 16 percent while production declined 80 percent; and cement and agricultural implements
fell at the same rate as automobiles.[79]

These critiques of corporate practices were politically popular, even if they ignored the economic realities of many firms. "What was formerly termed a conspiracy in restraint of trade is now known as a code authority," explained the city purchasing agent for Milwaukee at congressional hearings. Business engaged in "widespread racketeering" through "artificial, arbitrary and capricious price controls." The CAB echoed that sentiment. "In so far as [the codes] boost prices they operate to reduce output and impair living standards. They are anti-consumer both in intent and effect." These officials blamed businessmen for acting selfishly. "In attempting to guarantee themselves a profit margin, they have tried to shift to other groups in the community those risks which it was their own function to assume." Underscoring their point, they concluded, "the effort to stabilize profits comes perilously near to stabilizing poverty." One hundred and fifty consumer councils publicly announced their opposition to price-fixing. "The consumer's option of refusal to buy when prices are not right is not adequate protection, and when exercised, it defeats the purpose of the act to get consumers to buy more." At an American Home Economics Association convention, Paul Douglas criticized the NRA's creation of "a system of capitalistic syndicalism." Expressing a view shared by other purchasing-power New Dealers, he said, "[The] consumer is forced to suffer." [80]

The problem of prices was about to get worse. In August 1934, Secretary Wallace had announced that the terrible drought throughout western farming regions would result in the smallest grain crop in three decades. That reduction threatened to bring shortages of food products, including meat, pork, and eggs, and made higher prices likely. To head off exorbitant price increases, Wallace coupled his announcement with a warning to would-be food gougers. At a press conference, Roosevelt promised to direct the administration's efforts to "combat excessive rises in prices." His first step was to drop tariffs on imported feed for livestock. Rexford Tugwell and other AAA New Dealers advocated a federal licensing system for food retailers. "To prevent profiteering under the guise of alleged local food shortages," Frederic Howe called for "100,000,000 price skeptics." "Consumers must beware of being stampeded by false rumors," Howe cautioned, and he advised consulting AAA price reports in newspapers and on the radio, in order "to spot unwarranted price increases." [81]

The drive of New Dealers to energize an informed consuming public reaped a response beyond their expectations. Meat prices went sky-high in the spring of 1935, and once again women took to the streets. In New York, Minneapolis, Chicago, Detroit, and cities in Pennsylvania, housewives formed City Action Committees against the High Cost of Living. Members consisted of a broad coalition of women's social clubs, settlement-house workers, black churches, mutual-benefit societies, and left-leaning activists. In New York, Clara Lemlich Shavelson of the United Council of Working Class Women became a leader of this alliance. In a repeat of the World War I–era boycotts, the High Cost of Living Committee organized strikes against retail butchers, demanded a 30 percent reduction in prices, and succeeded in closing hundreds of butcher shops across the city. Protesters policed the stores, proclaiming that "women who [had] the temerity to try to buy meat quickly found themselves pulled from the shops by outraged non-purchasers." The boycott drew its strength from Jewish neighborhoods, where housewives closed 3,000 of the 4,500 kosher butcher shops, and from Harlem, where protesters closed another 65 stores. Housewives marched in front of packers' warehouses, accusing a "profiteering packers monopoly" of fleecing the consuming public. On several occasions, the picketers became violent, and several were arrested.[82]

In Detroit, strike leaders won widespread compliance from consumers who signed pledges not to buy meat. Mary Zuk, the wife of an unemployed factory worker and the group's leader, insisted, "We aren't going to pay such high prices for meat and that's all there is to it." In Hamtramck, a Detroit neighborhood, five hundred Polish housewives picketed butcher shops, carrying placards that read "Strike Against High Meat Prices. Don't Buy," and assaulting patrons. "We are not going to be satisfied with investigating meat prices alone," Zuk warned. Within a week, the committee threatened a "general strike against the high cost of living." That rhetoric reflected Zuk's Communist Party affiliation. But the *New York Times* reported that, in spite of some Communist participants, "the prime movers do seem to be bona fide housewives, solely interested in keeping the budget within speaking distance of the pay envelope." Zuk led a delegation of "meat-strikers" to Washington, where they demanded action. Challenging the packers' claim that processing taxes had driven up the cost of cattle, spokesman Dinah Ginsberg asserted, with fists clenched, that "the meat packers are hiding behind the Government skirts. . . . It's the packers, not the Government, that are to blame." Under pressure, the Federal Trade Commission dispatched investigators to Detroit to assess the spread between the packers' costs and consumer prices.[83]

No sooner had the meat crisis subsided than the new consumers' counsel, Donald Montgomery, went on a campaign against bakers, asserting that they were cheapening the quality of their bread while charging more. Montgomery fit the profile of the purchasing-power progressive. Trained in economics at the University of Wisconsin, he investigated the packing industry for that state's Department of Markets. He moved to Washington in 1928 to work for the Federal Trade Commission in its securities division. In 1934, he got a job as an examiner at the

Securities and Exchange Commission. By the time he came to the AAA, he had considerable experience in investigating the books of American corporations. Montgomery routinely pressed for "open books and record clauses" in all AAA marketing agreements. Such clauses would reveal the extent to which any price markups were warranted. If the federal government helped to subsidize agricultural prices, then the consuming public was entitled to see the books. Montgomery announced an investigation into bread prices in Los Angeles, Dallas, Toledo, Milwaukee, Pittsburgh, Allentown, Philadelphia, New York, Buffalo, and Washington.[84]

The potency of consumer activism drew its strength from a dynamic relationship between consumers and their New Deal advocates. After Mary Rumsey suffered an untimely death, Montgomery provided vigorous leadership for consumer issues. He continued a program of active involvement with local councils and supplied them regularly with copies of *Consumers' Guide*. His field agent, Iris Walker, traveled across the nation to help sustain close relations with far-flung communities. Consumers came to regard the government as the proper authority on "fair prices." This two-way relationship signified a new, potent political culture, in which government officials supplied consumers with the ammunition of product and pricing information that they then used for their local activism. The High Cost of Living Committees had relied upon the AAA's *Consumers' Guide* in shaping their demands. Consumer actions were no longer just community affairs but were connected to a New Deal state. In exchange for New Deal assistance, these urban voters became loyal Democratic supporters.[85]

By the mid-1930s, many middle-class women's groups were making the protection of consumer pocketbooks a top priority. As Burr Blackburn of the Household Finance Corporation explained, "Upper middle class women ... are taking hold of this consumer movement in the same spirit that women leaders fought for Woman Suffrage and Prohibition. If business refuses to cooperate with them they will enjoy a fight." The American Home Economics Association, which had pushed for the Tugwell Bill, now called for nationwide consumer education classes in the country's schools. The American Association of University Women issued a regular consumer study guide, called *Scientific Consumer Purchasing*, to its 880 branches. The National Congress of Parents and Teachers and the League of Women Voters lobbied for consumer legislation. The more politically conservative and socially prominent General Federation of Women's Clubs also became engaged in consumer affairs. It counted over two million members in fifteen thousand clubs and cosponsored a weekly discussion of consumer problems on national radio with Donald Montgomery. All these groups came out strongly against price-fixing, alive to the very real pocketbook problem of prices exceeding family

income. Collectively, their membership totaled five million.[86] Though
hardly calling for the overthrow of capitalism, their experiences of the
Depression and in New Deal Washington made them broadly sympathetic to a purchasing-power agenda of low prices and high wages.

As part of their political awakening and New Deal sympathies, these
women also supported labor demands for more effective organization.
During the Depression, when organized labor was still institutionally
weak, middle-class consumer groups understood the centrality of unionization as a key lever in protecting mass purchasing power. An important
politicizing moment came when employees of Consumers' Research, the
testing agency set up by Chase and Schlink in 1929, went on strike in
1935. All these women's groups relied on Consumers' Research for their
product information. Therefore, a strike by its workers brought the
labor issue front and center for middle-class clubwomen and sparked
a controversy that rippled throughout the labor liberal community.
F. J. Schlink disavowed the unionization and wage demands of his
employees, and he would soon become a staunch conservative. But
prominent consumer liberals, including Robert Lynd and Stuart Chase,
one of the organization's founders, supported the strikers. Reinhold
Niehbur of the Union Theological Seminary chaired an impartial investigation that ruled favorably for the workers. The League of Women
Shoppers, a left-leaning organization of prominent women, lent its
name to the cause and joined the picket lines. So too did middle-class
women's groups. After weeks of bitter acrimony, the strikers formed
the Consumers Union, a group that consciously sought to merge consumer and labor groups in support of better prices and products. The
Consumers Union hired only union workers, established a labor advisory
board that included A. Philip Randolph of the Brotherhood of Sleeping
Car Porters and Homer Martin of the United Automobile Workers, and
charged a lower subscription fee for its reports than Consumers'
Research had.[87] This conflict and its resolution symbolized the degree to
which consumer and labor issues had become intertwined.

The NRA had failed to restore prosperity by the time the Supreme
Court declared it unconstitutional in the summer of 1935. This agency's
abrupt end meant the demise of the Consumer Advisory Board, but
Roosevelt created a new Consumer Division, located in the Labor
Department. He appointed Walton Hamilton as chairman, with instructions to find "ways and means for the consuming public to get more for
its money." Hamilton had consulted with the CAB and was a leading authority on price-fixing. This Yale economist now applied theory to practice in an investigation of milk prices. Hamilton worked with consumers'
county councils and with women's groups to investigate prices and standards. The Bureau of Labor Statistics and the AAA consumers' counsel

also continued their price investigations. Roosevelt appointed Leon Henderson, Robert Lynd, and Emily Newell Blair, Rumsey's successor as CAB chairman, to the Consumer Division. These policymakers fought to establish a permanent Department of the Consumer to ensure that "prices will be kept fair."[88]

By 1935, the New Deal had not cured the Depression, but it had identified purchasing power as a major problem, one that linked debates over prices and product standards to the fight for higher wages and stronger unions. In June 1935, Emily Newell Blair told two thousand of the nation's leading advertising executives that the Depression had made consumers less receptive to marketing and more concerned with price and quality. The consumer today, she told them, "fears poverty more than pyorrhea." "Tastes have given way to needs, vanity and pride to use-value. The gas-per-mile car is more important than a streamline. The shrinkage of a dress counts more than the latest style. The amount of peaches in a can counts more than the size of the peach, the quality of a cold cream in a jar more than a delicate aroma—and price above all."[89] The Depression had made Americans more cost-conscious. The New Deal had made them believe that more purchasing power at the market was both their right and a matter of national necessity. With the NRA dead and the consumer movement just coming to life, the trick would be to bolster labor's power as a political solution and an organizational force to combat high prices and low wages.

The New Deal and the Problem of Wages, 1935–1940

LIBERAL NEW DEALERS believed that labor was pivotal to the success of their consumer-oriented public policy. According to Senator Wagner, the purpose of the National Recovery Administration (NRA) had been to "spread adequate purchasing power among the masses of consumers and thus prime the pump of business." Jobs and the total wage bill had risen since 1933. But profits had increased much more. With the NRA in shambles, the government had no mechanism or labor law to compel higher wages. Wagner warned that "failure to maintain a balance between wages and industrial returns" had short-circuited the recovery that started in the initial New Deal months. As the New York senator put it, "The rise of business activity . . . collapsed in short order because no adequate purchasing power had been built up to sustain it." The key to national prosperity, then, was to strengthen labor's ability to take home more pay.[1]

The 1935 National Labor Relations Act transformed the American political economy by marshaling the power of the federal government squarely behind organized labor. Labor won the legal right to organize and engage in collective bargaining without fear of discrimination or intimidation by employers not just as a matter of industrial justice but also as a measure of economic recovery. The purchasing-power logic, readily embraced by the bill's labor supporters, made this measure palatable to other members of the New Deal coalition and to top government officials. After the Supreme Court declared the NRA unconstitutional, the administration, casting about for another way to achieve industrial recovery, threw its support behind this labor bill. As the Depression stretched out, labor's insistence on the economic necessity of higher wages gained widespread appeal and was backed by New Deal rhetoric, laws, and policy.

Yet this historic shift in labor rights, precisely because of its boldness, raised a fundamental question for the Democratic Party. How could the administration hold together a diverse New Deal coalition of labor, farmers, and middle-class consumers? Indeed, the advance of the New Deal–labor alliance in the mid-1930s generated a political backlash when it became clear that, in the hands of a militant trade-union movement, the purchasing-power program entailed far more than a general wage hike. Strikes, challenges to management prerogatives, and a disruptive social upheaval disturbed the industrial status quo. Roosevelt's 1937 court-packing scheme to ensure that the Supreme Court upheld the Wagner Act as well as other New Deal measures and his 1938 electioneering efforts to purge anti–New Deal southerners from the Democratic Party were other divisive consequences of labor's newly won rights. A new recession in 1937 made Roosevelt and the New Deal even more politically vulnerable.

To deflect responsibility for the new economic downturn and unite his constituents, FDR continued his shift to the left. He explained the recession by trumpeting the purchasing-power critique: wages were still too low, prices too high, and production too limited. Rather than blame the inflationary policies of the Agricultural Adjustment Administration (AAA) or the interruption of production caused by strikes, FDR held business politically and morally accountable for the recession of 1937–1938. That logic inspired New Dealers, in the late 1930s, to construct vigorous policies to regulate American capitalism, including a federal minimum-wage law, the creation of a committee to investigate monopolies, and, in an unprecedented move, support for deficit spending as a measure of recovery, not just of relief. Of all these, an intensified attack on monopoly prices proved particularly useful in unifying organized labor and an increasingly coherent consumer movement behind the New Deal. Despite intensifying hostility to it, the purchasing-power agenda, with its emphasis on high wages, low prices, and energetic government, would be deployed again in World War II for the purpose of restructuring American capitalism.

Purchasing Power to the Workers (II), 1935

Senator Wagner insisted that wage increases through unionization were necessary to correct the "failures of consumer demand." When Roosevelt took office, only 10 percent of the industrial workforce was organized. The NRA's Section 7a galvanized the labor movement. In a typical pamphlet, the American Federation of Labor (AFL) announced to workers, "The struggle for your rights is not won when the law is passed. It will not be won until you have a strong union, recognized by your employer as the agency to represent you, and an agreement to set standards for wages and hours." "WIN YOUR RIGHTS AS A WORKER! JOIN YOUR UNION!" By the end of 1933, organized labor had made considerable headway in coal, men's clothing, and ladies' garments. The United Mine Workers' (UMW) John L. Lewis told his union, "The President wants you to join a union." This new government labor policy spurred unionization not only among the unorganized mass-production sectors of auto, rubber, electrical goods, and petroleum but also in less likely sectors, such as journalism, the movie business, retail trade, and even among agricultural workers, who had been explicitly excluded from Section 7a.[2]

Fearful of its destabilizing impact, FDR took only tentative steps to aid organized labor. In August 1933, he created a temporary National Labor Board (NLB) to mediate disputes and appointed to that new body Walter Teagle of Standard Oil, Gerard Swope of General Electric, Louis Kirstein of Filene's, William Green of the AFL, John Lewis of the UMW, and labor economist Leo Wolman. Wagner and William Leiserson, chairman of the Petroleum Labor Policy Board, were also members. In spite of this impressive roster of sympathetic appointees, the NLB had little power to enforce business compliance. The NLB lawyer, Phil Levy, regularly sent Senator Wagner's aide, Leon Keyserling, cases "demonstrating particularly shocking violations that nothing in particular can be done about." National headlines captured the chaos and unrest unleashed by Section 7a. Without a stronger labor bill, Leiserson stated, "We have not only danger of monopoly prices and production but also monopolistic practices with respect to labor."[3]

Section 7a inspired hope and frustration, as revealed in letters sent by oil workers to Leiserson when he was chairman of the Petroleum Labor Policy Board. George Knox from Tulsa, Oklahoma, signed his letter, "[From] an admirer who believe[s] in the NRA. And one so help me God is trying to make it so. Please let me hear from you. You don't realize how much pleasure it would give me. Keep this secret as it would cost me my job." A Texas oil worker wrote, "I never would have written this, but was forced to do it, as I don't think we are getting justice, and hope there won't be any mention of my name for they might lay me off." Senator Wagner warned the National Association of Manufacturers, "Increasing unrest is inevitable if the hopes inspired by the Recovery Act are frustrated."[4] In February 1934, Wagner introduced the National Labor Disputes Bill to create a permanent labor board.

In the spring of 1934, the country erupted in violence. Corporate hostility to the new independent unions precipitated the greatest strike wave since the end of World War I. The city of Toledo, Ohio, for example, descended into violent disorder when workers at Auto-Lite, an automotive parts supplier, staged a strike for union recognition in April. Other local unions threatened a general strike, and soon the governor called in the Ohio National Guard to restore peace. Citywide civil strife also broke out in Minneapolis, San Francisco, and in textile mill towns scattered throughout the South and the East. In San Francisco, an action on the docks became a general strike that necessitated federal intervention. Roosevelt dispatched Labor Secretary Frances Perkins, who awarded the longshoremen a decisive victory. In June 1934, the president established the National Labor Relations Board (NLRB) as an independent body.

Securing union gains required a change in federal labor policy. That became clear during the great textile strike in the fall of 1934. On September 1, hundreds of thousands of textile workers from Maine to Alabama walked off the job, demanding a reduction from forty to thirty hours a week without a cut in pay. Mill owners had accommodated what little wage increases the NRA forced on them by stretching out the work week, an unintended consequence of New Dealers' obsession with achieving high wages. In protest, workers in mill towns scattered up and down the eastern seaboard coordinated a walkout. That was an impressive feat. But with an oversupply of cotton, conditions favored employers, and the union lost. Volatile and disruptive, the strikes of 1934 were, in some instances, successful. But a widespread industrial labor movement seemed unlikely without a tougher labor law and strict enforcement.[5]

The automobile industry exemplified the need for stronger labor legislation. In late 1934, the administration ordered an investigation into the auto industry by Leon Henderson of the NRA and the commissioner of the Bureau of Labor Statistics (BLS), Isador Lubin. They had full authority to investigate profits, dividends, wages, and all other economic aspects of the industry. Three weeks later, Henderson and Lubin held several hearings in Detroit. As neighbors, the two were fast friends as well as political allies, and they shared a purchasing-power sensibility. Their report to the president portrayed a "dark picture" of the industry. Espionage, terror, discrimination, speedups, subsistence annual wages, and the fear of being laid off made for terrible conditions. "Look out the window," the foreman told workers, "and see the men waiting in line for your job." After reading the Henderson-Lubin report, the *Nation* editors declared: "The automobile wage-earner continues to groan under the heavy burden of tyrannical foremen and straw bosses."[6]

The disclosures of conditions on the shop floor gained wide publicity, but, for Henderson and Lubin, the bigger point was that antiunion industrial labor policies undermined recovery efforts. Henderson won national media attention when he held business accountable for the Depression's longevity. In a controversial study, he claimed that profits had risen substantially more than wages in the 1920s and declined considerably less in the 1930s: "Corporate security holders not only profited most from the boom in the Twenties, but suffered least from the Depression in the Thirties." While production and wages had fallen precipitously during the Depression, dividends had grown. As he explained, "The play of economic forces is not permitted to cut the wages of capital as easily as it cuts the wages of labor."[7] Only through collective bargaining could the country's purchasing power be restored. Labor rights required tougher enforcement measures than Section 7a provided.

The lurch to the left in the 1934 elections facilitated the passage of a labor bill with teeth. Democrats now commanded a 45-seat margin in the Senate and a 219-seat margin in the House. Buoyed by the electoral victories, Wagner assigned Keyserling to draft a new National Labor Relations Bill. Keyserling consulted the NLRB lawyers regarding the practical, jurisdictional, and constitutional problems of protecting collective bargaining. The attorneys advised him not only because they understood the technical, administrative, and legal issues but also because the president and his staff had qualms about Wagner's bill, worried that FDR's backing would only embolden an already militant labor movement. More problematically, Roosevelt doubted its political feasibility and temporized on the question of company unions. The only concession Wagner was able to obtain from the president was a promise not to interfere with the bill's drafting.[8]

The NLRB lawyers pushed for the creation of a stronger permanent board to act as a "Supreme Court of Labor" that would uphold and enforce the right to unionize rather than merely arbitrating labor-management disturbances. As Keyserling put it, the law was granting a "new type of power to labor, not a new kind of mediations service. It legalized a new form of negotiation—collective bargaining by majority rule and strikes, if necessary." For that reason, they insisted on the administrative independence of a new board. If placed under the jurisdiction of the Labor Department, a demand made by Secretary Perkins, Keyserling feared the new board would pressure labor to submit to mediation of its disputes. Instead the sole purpose of the NLRB was to protect the right to organize and engage in collective bargaining. These were new rights, which placed the "emphasis upon the rights of men rather than upon property concepts involved in the flow of interstate commerce." According to Keyserling, "The Wagner bill crystallizes this new approach. It necessarily refers to interstate commerce in order to give the federal board jurisdiction to act, but it states emphatically that the objective of the board is not primarily to protect commerce, but to preserve equality of bargaining power."[9]

How, then, to justify these new rights? Milton Handler, the NLRB's general counsel, helped to formulate the constitutional rationale. Congress had permitted industry to unite through merger and consolidation into powerful corporate units and had encouraged business to form trade associations covering entire industries. To offset that power, Handler argued, new legislation should seek "to effect an economic balance through collective bargaining and the free association of workers in labor organizations." Congress had the right to regulate business practices only when they impinged on interstate commerce. But jurisdiction had to expand beyond labor disputes to cover anything that burdened the free flow of commerce, including workers' lack of purchasing power. Handler explained that "labor organizations are essential . . . in order to keep wages in line with prices and effect a proper distribution of purchasing power." The National Labor Relations Board would draw its authority to act from the underconsumptionist theory that unequal bargaining power led to insufficient purchasing power, which in turn interfered with commerce.[10] The AFL had articulated the importance of unions to national prosperity in the 1920s; now the labor movement and its allies used this argument to sell this historic departure in federal labor policy.

The Wagner coalition that drafted this bill traced its lineage directly to the purchasing-power advocates of the 1920s. One of the act's most ardent supporters was Edward Filene. He spoke as a prominent businessman and also as the president of the Twentieth Century Fund. In 1934 the fund's director, Evans Clark, commissioned a study of the relationship between government and labor unions. Clark had been interested in labor affairs since the time he had helped found the Labor Bureau. At Filene's suggestion, the fund's board established a Labor Committee and appointed Leiserson and William H. Davis, formerly national compliance director of the NRA, to serve on it. Clark himself had been a member of the New York NRA Adjustment Board. He hired Alfred Bernheim and David Saposs, old friends from the Labor Bureau, to become the fund's research staff.[11]

Who were these labor experts? Many were first- or second-generation Jewish immigrants, whose own experience reinforced their belief in the American Dream of social mobility and economic progress. Even labor activists did not expect their children to become factory workers. Their ambitions were largely fulfilled as the number of white-collar workers expanded. Whereas in 1900 60 percent of American Jews held blue-collar jobs, by 1930 only 30 percent did manual work. Leiserson and Saposs, both Jewish immigrants from Russia, had traveled the path up from the shop floor. Leiserson worked in New York's garment industry, Saposs in Milwaukee's breweries. Both attended the University of Wisconsin in their early twenties and worked with the famous labor economist John Commons. Between semesters, Leiserson had combed the streets of Chicago, before landing a job at Sears. Both went to Columbia University for graduate work in economics. They met while working for the U.S. Commission on Industrial Relations in 1914. Leiserson was the assistant director of research and Saposs a field investigator of company towns.[12]

These immigrant intellectuals had one foot in their new white-collar world and one in their ethnic communities, where millions of Jews still

FIGURE 4.1. William Leiserson, second from the left, inspected western labor camps in 1914 as part of a government-commissioned study on U.S. industrial relations. A Jewish immigrant from Russia, Leiserson became a leading arbitrator and key supporter of the National Labor Relations Act of 1935, which protected workers' rights to form unions and to collective bargain, a measure he favored as the way for upward mobility of the immigrant masses.

labored, mostly in the needle trades. While supporting the AFL, they were critical of its member unions' craft orientation and nativist policies, which left out the millions of unskilled immigrant workers in mass-production industries. Saposs and Leiserson believed in mass unionization as a collective path to progress. If nineteenth-century Americans had moved west hopeful of advance through land acquisition, now these experts envisioned unions as the route for upward mobility. As participants in an Americanization study for the Carnegie Corporation, they criticized the restrictive nature of the AFL for driving unskilled immigrants and ethnic minorities into company unions. In the 1920s, Leiserson worked in Rochester, New York, Baltimore, and Chicago, where he became a leading arbitrator in the men's clothing industry. With seven children to support, he decided to look for a job that would pay him a "living wage." Beginning in 1926, he taught economics at Antioch College and served on the board of the Consumers' League of

Ohio. He ran for elective office on a progressive platform, but his future was as a labor expert. During the Depression, he drafted unemployment insurance legislation for the state of Ohio. He was in regular contact with the social-reform community, which included Frances Perkins, Paul Douglas, the staff of the Labor Bureau, and David Saposs.[13]

Saposs, too, had been instrumental in constructing the new unionism of the interwar period. After a brief stint as education director for the Amalgamated Clothing Workers, Saposs joined the Labor Bureau, where he helped to formulate new wage theories. Saposs then taught at Brookwood College, which had been founded to educate and support the progressive elements of the labor movement. Known as "Mr. Labor History," he was particularly knowledgeable about left-wing unionism. When Brookwood's leadership turned too far to the left, the AFL cut back its funding. By 1934, Saposs was heavily in debt and needed another job. He had in mind to undertake a study of industrial unions, prompted by "the urgent need to organize the integrated, mass production industries." This proposal recommended him to Edward Filene, who believed that "craft unions do not fit into modern industrial organizations and are causes of many of the present troubles. The remedy may be found in vertical unions."[14] Though separated by class and age, Filene and Saposs shared a hopeful outlook about improving capitalism through collective action.

The immigrant intellectuals' brand of New Deal liberalism conflated economic advance with a broadened definition of American citizenship. Leiserson explained, "Paying inadequate wages means that employers are restricting the consuming power and the markets of the nation. The liberty to do these things is not guaranteed by the Constitution." Instead, Leiserson argued, "Wage-earners and salaried people ... [have] rights that are inherent in American citizenship." "There is no doubt that the New Deal, by freeing wage-earners to combine for bargaining in large national labor organizations ... is endangering the feudal liberties of combined capital. But by doing so it promotes the liberties of common citizens."[15] The labor community would soon fragment under the weight of conservative attacks and internecine struggles. And even Leiserson would come to defend the right of craft unions to preserve their organizations alongside industrial unions. But, for an important moment, the need for stronger labor legislation unified and embodied the hopes of labor reformers across the spectrum.

These reformers combined their insistence on systematic change with optimism about the potential of American productive power. The life experiences and vision of Senator Wagner's aide, Leon Keyserling, are instructive. Keyserling was raised in the Sea Islands off the coast of South Carolina, where his father, William, a German Jewish immigrant, grew cotton, a crop that had not been planted there since Reconstruction. In the post–World War I recession, when commodity prices dropped precipitously, the young Keyserling saw his father lose everything. But William turned to ice manufacturing and demonstrated to his son that America was indeed a land of "golden opportunities." Because of his background, Leon disapproved of the immigration restrictions of the 1920s. As an idealistic high-school student, he wrote, "After all, is it just that we with acres upon acres of uninhabited land, and millions upon millions of idle dollars, should turn away human beings searching bread, meat, and liberty?" Keyserling, though, was not naive. Growing up in a community of only six white families surrounded by black neighbors and then living in New York City during the Depression, he witnessed harsh social, economic, and political realities. As an undergraduate, Keyserling studied institutional economics with Rexford Tugwell at Columbia University and then attended Harvard Law School, where he studied sociological jurisprudence with Roscoe Pound. He returned to Columbia to continue work with Tugwell. Whereas Tugwell focused on the imbalance between the agricultural and industrial sectors, Keyserling studied the distribution of wages and profits within industry. By the time he came to Washington, he was firmly committed to the spread of unionization as a crucial step in reforming capitalism.[16]

The Wagner Act, as it became known, not only affirmed the right to organize and bargain; it also specified the technical details that would enable a strong mass-union movement. It outlawed the company union, forbade unfair employer practices, such as the intimidation, discrimination, and blacklisting of union workers, and required employers to bargain with worker-elected representatives. It also affirmed the principle of majority representation, which stipulated that the union supported by a majority of workers in a place of employment would represent all workers. The NLRB would have final authority in certifying a single union as an appropriate bargaining unit and granting it exclusive jurisdiction. Keyserling expressed concern that, given American unionism's relative weakness in mass-production industries, a majority rule might place an insuperable burden on new unions that had not yet recruited large numbers. The policy also worked against the existing AFL arrangement, which permitted workers within a given factory to belong to many different unions based on their crafts. But NLRB staff argued that majority rule would prevent management from trying to reach separate deals with minority groups in order to thwart a strong, unified majority. As Paul Douglas explained, anything else would leave open the possibility of company unions, "a sham situation."[17]

The Wagner Act drafters called on the Twentieth Century Fund to provide expert evidence during congressional deliberations in early 1935. The fund released its report to the press when Wagner introduced the bill.

Together, Clark and Wagner also presented the findings to President Roosevelt. Titled *Labor and the Government*, the study endorsed the creation of a strong labor board independent of the Labor Department and with no mediation powers. The board's sole purpose, it said, ought to be the protection of labor's right to organize and bargain, not the inhibition of strikes. The Twentieth Century Fund experts also supported majority rule and compiled enough evidence to substantiate the common assertion that company unions constricted bargaining. They reported that 2.5 million workers belonged to company unions, compared with 4.2 million who were members of trade unions, out of a total of 32 million wage earners. The fund experts argued that only independent trade unions could do the job adequately. In its press release, the fund supported federally regulated unionism "as the most suitable means yet devised of approaching an equality of bargaining power between employers and employees."[18]

The framers of the Wagner Act saw the right to organize as the middle way between an outdated laissez-faire system and an intrusive, even totalitarian, state. With the rise of the Nazis, fascists, and communists in Europe, the specter of totalitarianism was real. As Wagner explained, "The National Labor Relations Bill is the only key to the problem of economic stability if we intend to rely upon democratic self-help by industry and labor instead of courting the pitfalls of an arbitrary or totalitarian state." Congress now faced a choice. With the NRA about to expire, what would replace it? Any kind of direct intervention to set wages seemed unlikely. To redistribute income, the federal government could rely either on powerful unions or on public spending. As much as organized labor posed a daunting specter, antipathy to federal spending was also intense, and Wagner exploited these fears. Business found both repugnant, but Wagner described unions as the only alternative to running permanent government deficits for relief and job programs. The former was preventive and prescriptive, the latter remedial. Wagner warned that if Congress did not institutionalize collective bargaining, then "either we shall have to sustain the market indefinitely by huge and continuous public spending or we shall meet the certainty of another collapse." The way to avoid both eventualities was by not "allowing section 7(a) to languish." He and his allies sought a redistribution of political and economic power, so that well-organized workers could themselves shift the wage structure upward. By checking the power of big business to determine the country's wage scales, collective bargaining would provide the means to revitalize the nation's economy and renew democratic participation. Political empowerment of labor for the sake of economic growth was the essence of Wagner's New Deal liberalism.[19]

Wagner couched the National Labor Relations Bill as part of a program for economic renewal. Strikes and industrial violence proliferated, cutthroat competition plagued many industries, and recovery remained out of sight. All those problems made some type of labor legislation likely. But it was the reliance on purchasing-power logic that made the Wagner Act politically palatable to a diverse set of interests. In a draft of the bill's preamble, Keyserling linked underconsumption to workers' inability to organize. "The tendency of modern industry toward integration and centralized control has long since overturned the balance of bargaining power between the individual employer and the individual employee, and generally has rendered the individual, unorganized worker helpless to exercise actual liberty of contract, to secure a just reward for his services, and to preserve his standards of living." The Wagner Bill rested on the same rationale as the 1925 AFL Frey Resolution and reflected the culmination of at least a decade of thinking about underconsumption. As Keyserling put it to Leiserson, "The failure of the total volume of wage payments to advance as fast as production and corporate surpluses has resulted in inadequate purchasing power, which has accentuated periodic depressions and disrupted the flow of interstate commerce."[20] The solution, then, was passage of the Wagner Act, which linked workers' rights in the factories to their roles as consumers in the marketplace. "Purchasing power" was no longer a static category defined simply by the amount of money in one's pocket; rather, the term now denoted a dynamic, politicized relation between wages, prices, and profits that was subject to collective bargaining.

When Senator Wagner introduced his bill to Congress in February 1935, he described it, in part, as a measure for economic recovery and reiterated that collective bargaining would be part of a permanent solution for achieving national prosperity. "When employees are denied the freedom to act in concert, . . . they can not participate in our national endeavor to coordinate production and purchasing power. The consequences are already visible in the widening gap between wages and profits." Without a more rigorous Section 7a and a permanent labor board, Wagner warned, "the whole country will suffer from a new economic decline." Despite improvements in productive capacity, "the wage earners' share in the product created by manufacturing has declined steadily for nearly a century, . . . [a trend that was] becoming most pronounced in that glittering era [between 1922 and 1929] which we regarded as the zenith of American prosperity."[21]

This purchasing-power logic received legitimacy from various quarters. While united in their opposition to new labor legislation, beginning in the 1920s many prominent businessmen had advocated higher wages for workers, following Henry Ford's lead. Though he could find few business voices to endorse his bill, Wagner hardly had to invent his arguments out of whole cloth. He pointed to two Brookings Institution studies, *America's*

Capacity to Produce and *America's Capacity to Consume,* to lend academic credibility to his argument. Written under Edwin Nourse and Maurice Leven, respectively, who both viewed labor's new power cautiously, these reports largely affirmed Wagner's analysis. "There has been a tendency, at least during the last decade or so, for the inequality in the distribution of income to be accentuated." As a result, the authors concluded, "Even in lines of basic necessities great wants among masses of the people go unsatisfied. The trouble is clearly not lack of desire but lack of purchasing power." As one reviewer of *America's Capacity to Consume* wrote, "It treats in [a] cold and detached manner the powder that now blazes in the New Deal conflagration." "The evidence of maldistribution revealed in this study will prove shocking to every honest conservative."[22]

NLRB members shared a purchasing-power vision. In his congressional testimony, the NLRB's Francis Biddle decried the failure of wage gains to keep pace with productivity increases. "Our domestic consumers' market has been gradually drying up. . . . The problem, therefore, is to increase consumption and broaden buying power." Edwin Smith, another NLRB member and former personnel director of Filene's, echoed those claims. "This concentration of income in the hands of the investing class, not compensated by equivalent gains to industrial wage earners and farmers, helped to bring about a condition where the products of industry could no longer be successfully marketed at current prices, and thus accelerated the general collapse." Lloyd K. Garrison, also of the NLRB, articulated a defense of the Wagner Act that would drive labor liberalism for the next decade. "As costs decrease and profits increase it is absolutely essential that the level of wages should be increased. The mass of the consumers are to have the necessary purchasing power to keep industry going." To achieve this goal required unionization. "It is essential to have collective bargaining, preferably through industry-wide agreement between organized labor and organized management. In no other way will the wage structure of the country be maintained at a proper level."[23]

From middle-class reformers to labor leaders to workers themselves, supporters adopted the language of purchasing power to defend labor's rights. On behalf of the nation's leading clergy, Rabbi Sidney Goldstein asserted, "There can be no recovery from the economic collapse until the working classes recover their purchasing power. The chief hope lies not in the employers' groups and their codes, but in the National Labor Board that this Bill is designed to establish that in turn will protect the workers and promote their welfare." In addressing the League of Women Voters, Secretary Perkins explained, "If $50 or $100 a year could be added to the buying power of each cotton textile worker in the country, the mills would not be able to turn out enough cotton materials to meet the increased consumption of the workers." Expressing his support for the proposed Wagner Act, a Kroger grocery chain-store worker in Cleveland, Ohio, declared, "We of the laboring class want this bill passed. The right of collective bargaining belongs to us, but under present set ups it is impossible for us to do without fear of losing our position." Conflating his roles as worker and consumer, he demanded, "Give the 2/3 buyers of all national production a break by [passing] the Wagner Bill."[24]

Opponents responded to the government's transfer of power to workers with great alarm. The *Schechter* case then before the Supreme Court, which would ultimately declare the NRA unconstitutional, revealed the depth of business opposition to this new exercise of governmental authority. New York poultry dealers like the Schechter brothers found it difficult to comply with NRA wage-and-hour restrictions. They also were squeezed by competitive pressure from the chain stores. One Bronx resident recalled reading the papers for the special sales at the local A & P. "It meant a lot when you could buy three pieces of soap for what you used to pay for two pieces. And the chicken was so much cheaper at A & P than it was at the kosher butcher." The Schechters were supported in the fight against the NRA by the anti–New Deal American Liberty League and the Steel and Iron Institute, two powerful allies that funded the case.[25]

The *Schechter* decision in May 1935 encouraged opponents, but it also left the president without a recovery program. Sensing the pro-labor shift in Congress and seeking to reap political gains, FDR finally endorsed the Wagner Act, which had just managed to pass in the Senate days before. The president's support for the measure increased the likelihood of its passage in the House, where it was expected to encounter tougher resistance. Some senators may have voted yes assuming that the House would defeat it. Wagner urged approval in the House, for only then, he said, will "economic as well as political freedom . . . be protected in this country." After the Supreme Court struck down the NRA, Wagner's staff modified the language of the bill's preamble to emphasize the burden of strikes rather than the impact of inadequate wages on commerce.[26]

The final act still pointed to the centrality of bargaining rights for mass-purchasing power. "The inequality of bargaining power between employees who do not possess full freedom of association . . . and employers who are organized in the corporate or other forms . . . tends to aggravate recurrent business depressions, by depressing wage rates and the purchasing power of wage earners in industry." The House voted in favor of the bill a month later, with many members still expecting the Supreme Court to render it unconstitutional. When he signed it on July 5, 1935, Roosevelt underscored the historic shift in policy. This was not a mediation bill but rather its sole purpose was to facilitate and support the creation of a new collective-bargaining regime. He named Francis Biddle as chairman of the NLRB and appointed Edwin Smith to serve as a member, in order to assure a sympathetic interpretation of new labor law. David Saposs became the NLRB's chief economist. From this post, he provided the same kind of assistance for unions that he had supplied at the Labor Bureau a decade earlier, but he had the added clout of the federal government behind him.[27]

Near-unanimous business opposition attests to the Wagner Act's radicalism. The business community rejected the idea that an inescapable conflict of interest between employers and employees required federal oversight of labor relations. Even Newton Baker, Filene's longtime personal friend and a supporter of organized labor, could not approve. At Filene's invitation, Baker, a prominent liberal businessman, had served on the Twentieth Century Fund Board since its inception. But the fund's labor study gave him pause. He rejected the report because, he claimed, it rested "on the assumption that all employers are frauds and that the relations between employers and employees both are and ought to be relations of armed hostility. With this view I have no intellectual sympathy." He characterized the study as a "report upon the alliance of government and labor against the employer." Signaling the limits of business liberalism, Owen Young and Henry Bruere had already resigned from the fund. In what was a painful blow to Filene, Baker too resigned.[28]

Wagner Act opponents charged that it would undermine recovery by creating a labor monopoly that would hold private industry hostage to union interests. The U.S. Chamber of Commerce announced its "unalterable opposition" to the Wagner Act. The Supreme Court's invalidation of the NRA suggested that the Wagner Act might meet the same fate, a possibility that inspired noncompliance. *Business Week* egged on its readers under the banner "No Obedience!" "Business will not obey this edict. . . . It is injustice aggravated by usurpation. It is tyranny. It is a piece of despotism which business will unitedly resist. It will be fought to the finish." Though the business journal was sympathetic to a purchasing-power argument, this shift in federal labor law went too far. Arthur Young, vice president of U.S. Steel, defiantly proclaimed, "I would rather go to jail or be convicted as a felon" than comply with the Wagner Act.[29]

For the moment, the New Deal was triumphant. The purchasing-power argument had helped to legitimize the growth of the New Deal state, winning support from both the working and middle classes and linking their interests to form a new Democratic majority. After years of severe depression, wage increases and collective bargaining became synonymous with money in consumers' pockets. By appropriating the language of consumers, President Roosevelt solicited middle-class support to make the New Deal more than just a vehicle for labor and farm reform and to assure its survival beyond the crisis of the Depression. No measure better guaranteed the New Deal's continuing support among the middle classes than the passage, in August 1935, of the Social Security Act, which established a nationwide system to give unemployed and retired workers a steady income. According to Senator Wagner, who served as one of the act's chief architects, the intention was to distribute purchasing power widely.[30] From the Wagner Act to the Social Security Act to programs like rural electrification and home mortgage insurance that gave tangible benefits, policymakers now relied on the language of consumption to institute new government policies and bind Americans to the New Deal state.

Labor and Consumer Strikes, 1936–1937

How, though, to translate the legislative victories of 1935 into real gains and still retain political support for such a radical reorienting of the American political economy? That remained a tricky question. Neither the Wagner Act nor the Social Security Act immediately boosted income. Summer food protests over the price of meat coincided with the passage of these acts, as Americans continued to scramble to meet basic needs. Within six months, labor staged a series of dramatic sit-down strikes that finally forced unions on many of the nation's mass producers. New Deal purchasing-power rhetoric lent legitimacy to these popular demonstrations at the market and on the shop floor. But explosive forces built into the New Deal coalition threatened to break it apart. It was one thing to support the idea of mass purchasing power but quite another to endorse the sit-down strikes, industrial capitulation, and inflationary prices that resulted from higher wages and the administration's farm policy. The tensions inherent in the New Deal coalition— between farmers and consumers, between labor and the middle class, and even within labor itself—would become increasingly manifest.

With an election year approaching and the Agricultural Adjustment Act under attack from the Supreme Court, Roosevelt tried to build bridges among members of his constituency. In defending higher prices for farmers, Roosevelt invoked a purchasing-power explanation. "Farm prosperity cannot exist without city prosperity, and city prosperity cannot exist without farm prosperity." It was up to the New Deal to save an economy that was "dying for lack of the blood of purchasing power." Having increased farm income by half, he assured the rest of the nation, "This buying power has been felt in many lines of business." Secretary Wallace claimed that industrial workers could afford slightly higher food prices if business increased production, paid better wages, and created more

FIGURE 4.2. On the Saturday before the 1936 election, President Franklin
D. Roosevelt (*left*), appearing with Governor Herbert Lehman (*center*) and
Senator Robert Wagner (*right*), denounced "economic royalists" before a mass
rally at New York's Madison Square Garden. With this radical rhetoric, FDR
signaled his commitment to the working classes, which in turn gave the
president labor's near-unanimous support.

jobs. Given Leon Henderson's prominence as a spokesman for those
issues, his stature rose higher, and the White House recruited him as
an economic adviser for the 1936 campaign.[31]

To solidify its electoral coalition at this crucial political moment, the
administration condemned business for monopolistic prices and subsistence wages. While promising to protect farmers, the 1936 Democratic
platform also promised lower prices to the middle-class consumer and
the wage earner. "We will . . . insure fair prices to consumers," it proclaimed. "We will continue to protect the worker and we will guard his
rights, both as wage-earner and consumer, in the production and consumption of all commodities." For the moment, the Democratic Party
successfully assembled the various groups behind a program of farmer
parity, high wages, and low industrial prices by attacking monopolies.
The platform proclaimed, "Monopolies and the concentration of

economic power, the creation of Republican rule and privilege, continue to be the master of the producer, the exploiter of the consumer, and the enemy of the independent operator." To a packed Madison Square Garden, Roosevelt delivered the most radical speech of his campaign. He attacked the "forces of selfishness." He promised improved working conditions, aid to the farmer and the needy, and protection of the consumer against unfair prices. In another radical step signaling a shift to the left, Roosevelt announced a "soak-the-rich" tax that had been crafted by Rexford Tugwell to compel industry to invest undistributed profits.[32]

Republicans exploited the inflationary aspects of New Deal policies, blaming them for the high cost of living and condemning government intervention in the market. Rejecting the Democrats' charge against monopolistic pricing, the Republican platform denounced "New Deal policies that raise production costs, increase the cost of living, and thereby restrict buying." In their view, security would come not from government efforts to stimulate consumption or to provide for unemployment and pensions. Instead, "real security will be possible only when our productive capacity is sufficient to furnish a decent standard of living for all American families and to provide a surplus for future needs and contingencies. For the attainment of that ultimate objective, we look to the energy, self-reliance and character of our people, and to our system of free enterprise." Gilbert Montague, a former lawyer for businesses promoting resale price maintenance and a spokesman for the New York State Bar Association and the Merchants Association, explained that the New Deal had driven up the cost of living by billions of dollars and predicted that it would soon double. "What to some of us may seem a holocaust of all that is best and dearest in American life may be welcomed by others as the blazing sunrise of the newest New Deal, in a nationally planned and magnificently regimented and gloriously sovietized America." In Westchester, New York, the Republican County Committee announced, "The women of New York are in 'rebellion' against New Deal high food prices." The committee distributed buttons and bumper stickers displaying potatoes as symbols of the revolt against high grocery bills.[33]

The New Deal programs vowed to save capitalism by reforming private enterprise. But critics considered that promise as precisely the problem. As early as 1934, Herbert Hoover spoke out against New Deal "regimentation." Hoover, of course, understood that there were flaws in the modern economy. But the New Deal "propose[d] to solve the remaining problem of distribution of a hard-won plenty by restrictions which will abolish the plenty." He saw the New Deal measures as posing a fundamental "challenge to liberty." "We cannot extend the mastery of government over the daily life of a people without somewhere making it master of people's souls and thoughts." The American Liberty League, made up of wealthy former Democratic supporters, spent one million dollars to oppose FDR and what they believed to be the New Deal attack on private property. They combined a denunciation of the "higher prices, subsidies, and regimentation" of the AAA with an appeal to the "consumer" as "the forgotten man of this administration." Consumers, they warned, "are paying the costs of misguided experimentation."[34] With business on the defensive after more than half a decade of depression, these arguments had no traction.

Roosevelt scored a sweeping victory in 1936, winning all but two states. Republican strategies played on tensions within the New Deal, but Roosevelt retained his widespread popularity. Congressional Democrats strengthened their grip on power. In the House, Democrats controlled three-quarters of the seats, and in the Senate they held an impressive 80 percent. Voters responded to the relief and jobs the New Deal had provided. Rural voters in the South, faithful Democratic supporters, registered their appreciation of programs like the Rural Electrification Act and the Electrical Home and Farm Authority, which offered installment financing and easy credit for electric appliances, such as refrigerators, ranges, and hot-water heaters. Labor, too, rewarded the Democrats with its overwhelming support, as did African Americans and urban ethnic voters. These New Deal converts would remain loyal Democrat voters for the next three decades.[35]

Nothing better illustrated and cemented the transformation in American power structures than the six-week strike at General Motors (GM) in the winter of 1936–1937. Reacting against GM's arbitrary power and their insecure work status, autoworkers staged a sit-down strike at GM's Fisher Body plants in Flint, Michigan. Strike leaders understood that they could make the Wagner Act a shop-floor reality and build a mass union only through decisive action. By sitting inside the plant for six weeks, the workers stopped production and defused company efforts to use force and strikebreakers. The strike came at a moment when General Motors was eager to capitalize on an upswing in the market. The fledgling United Automobile Workers (UAW) also took advantage of the Democrats' electoral landslide. When FDR campaigned in Michigan, thousands of workers laid down their equipment to cheer on the presidential motorcade. The strike leaders now counted on the neutrality of New Deal governor Frank Murphy, who, in an unprecedented move and with support from President Roosevelt, refused to send in troops to break the strike. After forty-four days, the UAW announced a victory, and its numbers instantly swelled. By the end of the summer, UAW membership had mushroomed from a few hundred to four hundred thousand.[36]

The victory set labor on a new course. In 1937, five million workers participated in industrial actions, thousands staged sit-downs, and nearly three million joined unions. Officially separated from the AFL, the Congress of Industrial Organizations (CIO) took the lead in organizing semiskilled laborers in mass-production industries where millions of immigrants and African Americans worked. Myron Taylor of the U.S. Steel Corporation recognized the CIO's Steelworkers Organizing Committee in March. Reacting to the shifting power on the nation's shop floors, Taylor made his decision one month before the Supreme Court heard *Jones v. Laughlin,* a steel-industry case that ruled on the Wagner Act. In partial response to the Democratic landslide in 1936, the sit-down strikes of 1937, Roosevelt's threats to pack the Court, as well as to the NLRB's successful legal strategy, the Supreme Court declared the National Labor Relations Act constitutional in April.[37]

The year 1937 was a triumphant moment for labor. The CIO formed trade unions in all the great mass-production industries of the early twentieth century. Unions in steel, meatpacking, auto, and electronics not only pushed for higher wages but also secured signed contracts, elaborate grievance procedures, and elected shop stewards. Encouraged by those victories, they sought to create a new kind of democracy on the shop floor, curbing the arbitrary authority of the foremen and forcing managers to recognize the self-worth of a new generation of workers. Just as significantly, the CIO sponsored and was part of a broader political and cultural reorientation. For Italians from Naples to Slovakians from central Europe to African Americans from Greene County, Alabama, the CIO meant a new kind of citizenship. The rise in union membership was the engine that propelled FDR to victory after victory and escalated standards of living. Union power was not uncontested, and business would soon mount a ferocious counterattack, confining labor to a limited arc that stretched from the Pacific Northwest to the industrial Midwest and Northeast. But at its moment of greatest triumph, this new union movement drew support from the lower middle class. White-collar workers at Ford, five-and-dime salesgirls at Woolworth's, back-office workers at the New York Stock Exchange, and waitresses in restaurants across the country clamored to join the CIO. The CIO leadership understood that to be successful it had to be inclusive, and thus it brought in a whole generation of workers ignored by the AFL. To be sure, the CIO had many flaws in its ideology and racial practices, but it pushed the citizenship rights of African Americans and Mexican Americans toward the forefront of American politics. Under the leadership of A. Philip Randolph, the Brotherhood of Sleeping Car Porters signed its members into the union while promoting their rights as minorities. In the 1930s, one million women joined CIO unions, and female workers led sit-down strikes in hotels, drugstores, offices, and auto-parts plants. For more than two generations after 1938, the institutional power of the union movement gave a social democratic voice to the nation's majority party.

Labor liberalism was a defining idea of the New Deal, and its porous quality allowed it to grow in power. The CIO recruited communists and socialists to gain the benefit of their organizing skills. The so-called Popular Front mentality united labor and liberals with radicals in the fight against business and their Republican allies at home and fascism abroad. Ultimately its fluidity opened the Left to attack, but in the crucial early stages this expansiveness enhanced unions' strength. In addition to drawing needed support from political activists on the Left, the union movement also was made more radical by its symbiosis with the consumer movement. Often the union movement was the consumer movement. The CIO was not feminist, but it was organically linked to a consumer, feminist mentality as it was drawn into support for rent strikes, milk boycotts, food cooperatives, and women's trade union auxiliaries, which in turn lent crucial support to striking workers and built community solidarity. The CIO shared many of the rhetorical and organizational strategies of middle-class consumer groups in their joint pursuit of more purchasing power, better quality standards, and fair prices. Though they had varying degrees of political commitment, labor and middle-class organizations subscribed to a consumerist agenda that had deep roots and now reached culmination in powerful political and institutional reform.

As an essential complement to labor's new power, left-wing New Dealers renewed their attack against monopoly prices. In the early spring of 1937, Mordecai Ezekiel at the Department of Agriculture and Leon Henderson, now an economist at the Works Progress Administration (WPA), predicted that the economy would worsen unless prices declined as wages increased. On national radio, Henderson forecast higher prices and explained that the "deficit in purchasing power" was "already evident" in slumping sales and rising installment purchases. "The threat of price rises" meant "that the painfully won gain of collective bargaining will be cruelly destroyed by increased prices." "At long last a sympathetic administration and strong labor leadership are fortifying the equality of bargaining power, but wage gains are being nullified by the rising cost of living." Lest his audience think that inflation resulted from unbalanced budgets, he argued, "They are just plain monopolistic price rises." He circulated his views within the administration in an influential memo titled "Boom and Bust."[38]

Labor, too, castigated rising prices, in part to evade attacks on itself. In May 1937, the AFL announced its "vital concern" with "the rapid rise of prices." "All our efforts to raise wages and living standards, and to provide industry's life blood of buying power will avail nothing whatever if the rise of living costs cancels every wage increase." Labor followed the New Dealers' lead in fixing blame for rising prices on "price profiteering." As the economy began to pick up, industries raised prices higher than necessary to reap immediate profits. The AFL denounced this behavior as morally reprehensible: "To profiteer by raising prices when more than 9,000,000 are still without work in private industry is an act of treason against the welfare of the nation. For every unnecessary price increase cuts production and eliminates possible jobs."[39] By demanding that business hold prices steady as wages increased, these reformers were insisting on a radical redistribution of America's income.

In January 1937, leading civic organizations formed the Consumers National Federation to "put the High Cost of Living on trial." Robert Lynd and Paul Douglas served as officers, as did Helen Hall of the Henry Street Settlement House. Uniting a wide range of labor-liberal reformers under the consumer umbrella, the federation brought together unionists, consumer advocates, settlement house workers, home economists, housewives, and labor activists. The group called for better consumer organization, rent control, federal housing programs, and investigation into the monopolistic practices of the food industries. Whereas many other aspects of New Deal reform were divisive, challenging corporate pricing practices won broad backing. Assistant Attorney General Robert Jackson, an ardent antitrust prosecutor, insisted that "business must boldly reduce prices to the point necessary to cause a normal flow of goods to the consumer."[40]

By now, the search for cheaper prices was receiving organized support from many quarters. In Cincinnati, housewives established an effective Consumers Conference. In Chicago, the United Conference against the High Cost of Living campaigned against hikes in gas prices. In New York, Mayor LaGuardia endorsed labor and consumer groups' united fight for cheaper milk. The Consumers Institute of Massachusetts hosted daily radio programs featuring grocery-market tips. Farm women participated in the consumer movement through the Department of Agriculture's Extension Service, cooperatives, and the Associated Women of the American Farm Bureau Federation. National church groups, too, set up consumer divisions, including the Federal Council of Churches of Christ in America, whose twenty-four national denominations represented twenty million members. Working-class housewives also organized against higher living costs through women's trade union auxiliaries. In December 1937, the National Federation of Settlements sponsored a conference called "People vs. the High Cost of Living," which convened local activists from across the country.[41]

Consumer activism drew strength from across the political spectrum as Popular Front groups worked closely with more moderate social organizations. In the world of consumer politics, there was often no clear boundary between Communist Party activists and other left-wing New Dealers. The League of Women Shoppers (LWS) helped to sustain the High Cost of Living Conferences in New York, Washington, Chicago, and Baltimore. Formed in 1935 in response to a strike at Ohrbach's department store in New York, the league quickly grew to twenty-five thousand members, with branches in fourteen cities from New York to Colorado to California. These women operated as a "flying squadron," generating community support for striking workers. They capitalized on their social prominence by staging successful publicity stunts, including picketing a nightclub in evening gowns while carrying placards that read "We Won't be Wined and Dined Until a Union Contract is Signed."[42] The league also promoted collective consumer action in its regular newsletter, *The Woman Shopper*. "An individual shopper's action as a consumer passes unnoticed," a pamphlet instructed. "But many shoppers organized bring results." New York member Mary Dublin, who would become the National Consumers' League president in 1938, explained, "We the consumers can have a functioning democracy only as we consciously organize to break the bonds of a monopolistic dictatorship which now can control prices, wages, and production." League members staffed local New Deal organizations, such as the Saint Louis County Consumer Council, and worked closely with other organizations of housewives. Along with Communists and fellow travelers, their membership included wives of liberal New Dealers Leon Henderson, Mordecai Ezekiel, William Douglas, James Landis, and Henry Wallace.[43]

The Chicago branch illustrates how the Left embraced the consumer mantle and endowed it with radicalism. Jessie Lloyd O'Connor, a longtime activist who was the granddaughter of the famous reformer Henry Demarest Lloyd, headed the local branch. O'Connor was born in Winnetka, Illinois, in 1904 to socialist William Bross Lloyd and pacifist Lola Maverick, the sister of Texas New Deal congressman Maury Maverick. After earning a B.A. in economics from Smith College in 1925, she traveled to London and Moscow, where she worked as a foreign correspondent for the Federated Labor Press. Returning to America in 1929, she covered everything from the textile strikes at Gastonia to the coal miners' bloody strike in Harlan County, Kentucky, to the organizing drives of steelworkers. In 1930, Jessie married Harvey O'Connor, an editor for the Federated Press and a former member of the International Workers of the World. Her family's radical background and her own experiences in the labor movement attracted her to the Communist Party. The O'Connors went to Moscow in 1932 to work for the English-language *Moscow Daily News*. In the mid-1930s, Jessie became a full-time community organizer in Chicago, where she lived at Hull House and was general secretary of the LWS. League members left calling cards in nonunion stores

FIGURE 4.3. The League of Women Shoppers distributed calling cards to its middle-class members and urged them to patronize only those stores that sold union-made goods. At the time, the league was one of many national women's organizations that used their consuming power to call for fair labor standards and better-quality consumer goods.

throughout the city and joined labor picket lines. Its invited speakers included CIO leaders and local academics close to the labor movement, like Paul Douglas. The league also joined forces with other local consumer groups "to bring down the high cost of living." Among its leaders were the wives of New Dealer Harold Ickes and writer Carl Sandburg.[44] In America, left-wing politics had become indelibly stained with consumerism.

Purchasing-power New Dealers encouraged consumer resistance to high prices. Donald Montgomery cheered on housewives' strikes against high rents in Akron, Chicago, and Detroit and against high milk prices in New York. "While it is not up to the Consumers' Counsel or any other Government official to advise consumers whether or not they should resort to strikes, if you're asking me whether consumers could do any good for themselves by striking, I think they not only could help themselves immediately as consumers, but if they succeed in putting an end to this alarming steady increase in prices, they would probably be performing a very real public service." When bread prices again made front-page news in 1937, Montgomery used his AAA podium to declare them too high. He insisted that at no time since World War I had the spread between costs and retail prices been larger. He urged consumers to organize against increases.[45]

Indeed the 1930s saw the rise of experimentation by consumers in response to a new awareness of their collective power. NRA codes had exempted cooperatives from price-fixing agreements, thus inadvertently encouraging their growth. Over 1,000 cooperatives sprang up to supply cheaper gasoline on the West Coast, in midwestern farm communities, and in Massachusetts, Illinois, and Ohio. From 1935 to 1940, the New Deal's Rural Electrification Agency established 670 rural cooperative associations. Credit unions, too, fared well during the Depression, accruing assets of forty-five million dollars and nearly half a million members. None of the 1,800 branches established by Filene's Credit Union National Extension Bureau failed. The rise of cooperatives, according to Cooperative League president James Warbasse, revealed "a more rebellious attitude on the part of the consumers to higher prices." Retail expert Paul Nystrom told an audience of advertising executives, "High prices, dictatorial methods and attempts to drive or force the consumer are just the conditions to start a rapid development of consumers' cooperatives." Horace Kallen, a leading political theorist, believed that higher prices made a consumer movement inevitable. "The consumer must either acquiesce in the degradation of his standard of living by the organized producers to the level of subsistence or a little lower, or he must organize."[46]

Edward Filene should have felt triumphant. No other businessman had lent more political support to the high-wage, low-price agenda. He had thrown his name and research money behind the Wagner Act and had even endorsed sit-down strikes. He also continued to promote lowering living costs through more efficient distribution, and he gave one million dollars for the establishment of the Consumer Distribution Corporation as an advisory body for cooperative retailing. Yet, despite a life that had taken him from his shop in Lynn to the inner corridors of power, Filene remained pessimistic. Departing for his annual summer trip to Europe in July 1937, he reflected on the economy's continuing problems. Delivering what would be his last public address, he explained that there was an "enormous latent demand in the United States" that only businessmen could release by "increas[ing] buying power." Even after several years of bitter strikes and industrial violence, Filene continued to endorse labor's demands for union recognition and higher wages, explaining that "[they] are necessary to enable higher profits." He urged management to heed labor's requests "for the mutual benefit of both—for the creating of a market." Feeling that he had failed to convince his fellow businessmen of the importance of low prices and high wages and aware of continuing opposition to redistributive policies, he came up with what he considered an appropriate title for his biography, "The Story of an Unsuccessful Millionaire." Filene died of pneumonia in Paris later that summer at the age of seventy-two.[47]

Part of Filene's pessimism stemmed from the fierce resistance to a highly mobilized labor movement. Labor's seizure of private property in sit-down strikes alienated the business community and many potential union supporters. The reality of millions of unskilled immigrant workers insisting on their right to higher wages was frightening to many. So frightening, in fact, that the AFL backed away from lending support to what its leaders correctly identified as a major social revolution. The AFL, whose base was among skilled workers, understood that there was a limited amount of work to be shared or captured by its members. They valued their skilled jobs and the preservation of craft jurisdiction more than a high-wage political economy of mass consumption. The AFL perceived that the gains of unskilled industrial workers came at the price of lower wages for skilled employees. John Frey, the original champion of the idea of workers' purchasing power, insisted that vertical unions organized along industrial lines, "if successful, would tend to level wages downward instead of upward."[48] He had made that statement just months before the UAW struck in Flint, Michigan. The rise of a New Deal state sympathetic to mass industrial unionism made the AFL all the more fearful of such an outcome.

John Lewis of the United Mine Workers and Sidney Hillman of the Amalgamated Clothing Workers became national leaders for mass industrial unionism. They argued that without union gains in mass-production industries like auto, steel, rubber, glass, and oil there could be no labor justice or economic recovery. At the 1935 AFL convention, a heated argument between John Lewis and the president of the United Brotherhood of Carpenters and Joiners led to blows. One month later, Lewis resigned as vice president of the AFL and established the Committee of Industrial Organizations (CIO) with the support of Sidney Hillman and David Dubinsky of the International Ladies' Garment Workers Union (ILGWU). At the 1936 convention, the AFL suspended the CIO unions and then subsequently watched in horror as the newly organized workers engaged in sit-down strikes. Frey emerged as the leading red-baiter within labor ranks, charging the CIO with Communist influence. By the fall of 1937, the AFL was openly hostile to the CIO. FDR, too, backed away from his support of industrial unionism, as he recognized the political liability of massive unrest. When steelworker strikes in the "Little Steel" companies (little only in comparison to U.S. Steel) turned violent, FDR's response to management and the union was "a plague on both your houses."[49]

Filene did not live long enough to hear FDR's declaration. But this inveterate retail reformer did witness the political victory of some of his most hated business opponents. After seven years of depression, cutthroat competition remained a serious problem, especially for those businesses least able to fix their prices. And now the pleas of small merchants, wholesalers, and manufacturers for protection against large chains and cut prices won political attention. The antichain movement got much of its support from rural areas in the South and the West, where politicians drew on populist fears of outside corporations decimating the local economy. Wright Patman, a Democratic New Dealer best known for his support of the Bonus Army, promoted the attack on chains. Influenced by the writings of Louis Brandeis, Patman believed that chains took money out of local communities and destroyed small merchants. He had grown up in and was then representing Northeast Texas in Congress, a poor rural area where condemnation of chain stores as foreign pariahs resonated with local residents.[50]

As the Depression made consumers more cost conscious, the appeal of chain stores grew. Between 1919 and 1935, the percentage of goods sold by chains had gone from 4 percent to 23 percent. The A & P alone had 15,000 stores that sold over one billion dollars of goods. They manufactured twenty million cans annually and baked three million loaves of bread weekly. Altogether chain stores retailed 45 percent of the nation's groceries. The five-and-ten-cent chains also had grown rapidly, resulting in nearly 1,600 Woolworth's stores in forty-eight states. By 1940, J. C. Penney had opened on average a new store every ten days of its forty-year existence. Montgomery Ward counted over six million customers, and Sears Roebuck did twice as much business. Mom-and-pop stores still claimed the majority of retail business, but urban residents increasingly patronized chain stores and mass retailers. During the 1930s, Filene's Bargain Basement sales grew so rapidly that they kept the rest of the store operating at a profit. From food to drugs to dry goods, chain stores offered better deals, convenient locations, more products, and less customer scrutiny than smaller competitors. In the winter of 1938, as economic conditions grew worse, Gimbels ran bold ads featuring low prices and declaring, "It's human to want bargains. Everyone wants the most for his money."[51]

Chain-store expansion aroused the ire of smaller economic competitors. Many rural residents made them a convenient scapegoat for the Depression. FDR could not have endeared himself to other merchants when he tapped S. W. Brister, the local J. C. Penney store manager, as the only person to ride in his 1937 motorcade through Biloxi, Mississippi. A report of the NRA Wayne County Consumer Council publicized lower prices at Detroit chain grocery stores, another example of government favoritism that must have seemed similarly offensive. Chain stores and their growing appeal not only threatened local proprietors but also aroused opposition to the outside cultural influences that they brought with them. A Louisville department-store manager captured the moralism that suffused the chain-store debate: "A new battle of evolution is raging in the South between the smaller retailer, taking the fundamentalist position, against the chain store, the exponent of modernism in distribution."[52]

Opponents of mass retailers won two legislative victories. In 1936, Congress passed the Robinson-Patman Act. This bill, drafted by the U.S. Wholesale Grocer Association, outlawed the practice of quantity discounts for large retailers. In truth, however, much of the chains' price advantage came from lower operating costs. Legislators could not make smaller merchants more efficient, so they eliminated the discounts. The bill gained momentum when Joseph Robinson, the Senate majority leader from Arkansas, cosponsored the measure. Robinson had fought to suppress the Southern Farmer Tenant Union of black and white poor sharecroppers that had formed to protest evictions by large landowners complying with AAA crop restrictions. Now he attacked chain stores as another disruptive intrusion in local economic relations. Chain-store representatives and consumer groups opposed this measure. Filene told Roosevelt that the act "is directly against what you are working for—a better distribution of wealth for the masses—and would tend to decrease the buying power of the people instead of increasing it." Yet protection of the small proprietor had much political appeal, and the bill became law. A year later, Congress passed the Miller-Tydings Act to allow manufacturers to fix minimum prices for their branded goods. One of the bill's sponsors, Representative John Miller from Arkansas, explained in chauvinistic language, "New forces, strange forces, forces alien to the true American way of doing things have long been at work chiseling away the foundation upon which the country rests." Macy's economist, Q. Forrest Walker, warned that politicians had to "protect the great American pocketbook" by rejecting such measures. Roosevelt opposed the bill, but congressional supporters attached it as a rider to a District of Columbia revenue bill to assure the president's signature.[53]

Congress passed these measures, but their impact was more symbolic than real. The Robinson-Patman Act allowed ample room for retailers to justify their discounts and gave ultimate authority to the Federal Trade Commission. Opposition from consumer advocates and most of the nation's economists had succeeded in watering down the bill. The Miller-Tydings Act also had limited application, as it covered less than 15 percent of all goods, specifically drugs, liquor, books, and cosmetics, industries that had long been fair-trade advocates and were the bill's most vociferous proponents. By now, lower prices had proved successful and were beginning to make sharp inroads into corporate America. During the Depression, General Electric introduced a new line of low-priced refrigerators. Fair-trade advocates had pushed for price-fixing measures since the Progressive Era. But, even in their success, it was clear that legislative remedies could not forestall destabilizing economic change.[54]

Chain stores' cheaper prices carried the day, but not without a final challenge. More worrisome than the new fair-trade laws was the growing support for a national tax on chain stores. By 1937, twenty-six states, desperate for revenue, had enacted chain taxes. That same impulse led to demands for regressive sales taxes. In February 1938, Wright Patman introduced a severe national chain-store tax whose proceeds would have exceeded the annual profits of chains like A & P and Woolworth's. The Federal Trade Commission insisted that such a tax would unfairly penalize consumers who shopped at chains because of their price advantage. *Labor World* seconded that opinion: "Throughout the depression the chain store has been a friend of the poor man because the cost of living has been kept within reason." After the A & P agreed to unionize its stores, the AFL opposed the Patman Bill. So too did the American Farm Bureau, the National Council of Farmer Cooperatives, the National Grange, and the National Association of Manufacturers.[55]

Opposition to the Patman Bill mobilized consumer groups. Mrs. Ernest Howard of the District of Columbia Federation of Women's Clubs feared that the tax "would put an end to a system or method of distribution which justifies its survival by economies of operation and low prices to consumers." Harriet Howe of the American Home Economics Association (AHEA) and Caroline Ware of the American Association of University Women (AAUW) also testified in opposition. Ware had just coauthored a book with her husband, Gardiner Means, *The Modern Economy in Action*, which began by acknowledging that "almost every recent effort to fathom the causes of our present ills sooner or later raises the purchasing-power issue." The antichain measure would restrict a mass market and cut into already limited purchasing power. Raymond Moley, a former Brain Truster and now a columnist for *Newsweek*, gave credit to consumers who were now organized "to defend the chain stores and themselves against measures that threatened to increase retail prices." Patman lobbied for this bill for three years, but in the face of this unified opposition it died.[56]

The Consumers National Federation lent coherence to the burgeoning consumer movement. In February 1938, its leaders met with Roosevelt. Their delegation included representatives from the League of Women Shoppers, housewives' leagues, consumer leagues, milk cooperatives, tenant leagues, African American organizations, and union leaders. Collectively, as they explained to FDR, they represented the "pocketbook problems of low income groups." Out of necessity Americans of all classes now paid attention to costs. But enhanced purchasing power required more than good deals or even consumer consciousness. As Robert Lynd, a delegate, wrote, "In a democratic culture in which the consumer occupies a position of such relative disadvantage in relation to business, one turns finally to the role of the government as a surrogate." If the consumer was to exert his necessary influence, it would come "through the action of the agencies of public administration in

Washington." "The primary concern," as Lynd saw it, "is whether the government is prepared to give to the spending of the national income the same degree of concern that it at present bestows upon the earning of that income."[57]

America's Price Watchdog, 1937–1939

In the fall of 1937, a new economic decline added more stress on already stretched budgets. Once again production and income fell faster than the price index. Conservative critics quickly dubbed this downturn the "Roosevelt Recession." The recent Republican vice presidential candidate Frank Knox declared, "Political action destroyed confidence and dammed up the flow of capital." To which Roosevelt responded, "One of the things . . . that brought on the . . . recession was the fact that [the price of] some things . . . went clear through the roof and people quit buying." Democratic congressman Robert Allen insisted that business had raised "prices to such an extent . . . that people could not buy back the very goods which they made." Progressive William Borah repeated a now-familiar charge: "I can see no recovery . . . so long as private interests fix prices and thereby continue to deplete purchasing power."[58]

The growing consumer and labor movements united in blaming industry for paying inadequate wages, charging inflated prices, and engaging in a "capital strike." Their logic appealed to the administration as a way to deflect attacks on the New Deal and hold together a coalition of middle-class consumers, organized labor, and farmers. In well-publicized political speeches, Secretary of the Interior Harold Ickes and Assistant Attorney General Robert Jackson held monopolies and the concentration of wealth accountable for the current recession. Beginning in the summer of 1936, they claimed, monopolists had engaged in a "sit-down strike" of capital to undo New Deal reforms and had raised prices. Leon Henderson echoed their charges. In a nationwide radio address, he asked, "What has happened to recovery?" "Were monopolies responsible for this rise, which crippled workable relationships in the American economy by reducing the general public's capacity to consume? My answer is emphatically yes. I believe the unbalance was touched off by the monopolistic prices."[59]

Purchasing-power progressives devised the administration's response to the recession. Henderson, who had gained credibility by predicting the 1937 downturn, favored "full use of government powers to prevent excessive price increases in the monopolistic industries" and legislation to lift the wages of low-income groups. He agreed with an emerging group of public-spending advocates that ending the recession required "some new vigorous burst of purchasing power." But, he cautioned, recovery would falter once again without an end to administered prices. Known publicly as the "Believers," Henderson and his allies constituted the left wing of the New Deal. Its key players included Tommy Corcoran, Benjamin Cohen, Jerome Frank, Robert Jackson, Mordecai Ezekiel, Isador Lubin, and Thurman Arnold, many of whom lived together in what was known as the "Little Red House" in Georgetown.[60] They disagreed with the "Unbelievers," the fiscal conservatives who maintained that the real problem was a lack of confidence stemming from government debt. The Unbelievers argued that the nature of particular industries and organized labor's wage gains made high prices inflexible. Flexible prices, they claimed, would bring only greater instability.[61]

Yet the Believers were not a monolithic body of economists. One group connected with the Federal Reserve, including New Dealers Marriner Eccles and Beardsley Ruml, was strongly influenced by Keynesian economics, which considered government spending the primary means of modern statecraft. In 1936, John Maynard Keynes had published his *General Theory* in Britain at a time when Britain's economy suffered from declining population growth, stalled technological innovation, and shrinking markets. In a theory that would transform modern economics, Keynes argued that parliamentary government should use its fiscal powers to compensate for economic inactivity in the private marketplace. Harvard economist Alvin Hansen, who would emerge as a leading advocate of spending, embraced Keynesian ideas of economic maturity. Hansen developed a theory of secular stagnation, pointing out that no new industry had emerged to play a role in spurring economic growth comparable to that performed by the auto industry in the 1920s. Now it was up to the government to stimulate the economy by acting as a consumer through public spending.[62]

In general, purchasing-power progressives rejected a Keynesian theory of economic maturity and secular stagnation, or at least an apolitical version of it. For them theories of stagnation were based on a critique of capital, its unwillingness to invest, and subsistence wages. As Gardiner Means would express it, "American consumers, if they had sufficient money income, would constitute a market sufficient to absorb all the production which American industry has the resources to turn out. It is not for lack of wants to be filled that economic activity is carried on at the low level of recent years." The recession of 1937 generated a political crisis for the New Deal, threatening to erase political support. In that context, Roosevelt's advisers embraced a Keynesian spending remedy to save New Deal. They retained their long-standing commitment to higher wages and lower prices to redistribute income, boost purchasing power, and spur demand. Yet they recognized that a compensatory program of government spending could provide momentary relief, stimulate heavy industry, and win votes, and it would avoid the disruptive social tumult of union and consumer mobilization.[63]

A firm believer in balanced budgets, Roosevelt had consistently rejected deficit spending as a remedy to the Depression. One year earlier he had cut WPA spending, eliminating 1.5 million relief jobs in an effort to restore a balanced budget, a move many blamed for causing the current recession. The first collections of Social Security taxes in January 1937 also drained two billion dollars out of the economy. But new spending programs, administration officials hoped, would bring immediate economic and, therefore, political payoff in an election year. Arthur Krock of the *New York Times* cynically captured these political maneuverings: "There can be only one more attempt made by this Administration to increase purchasing power. . . . This time the plan must work—or else." In the days leading up to his announcement of a new policy, the president sought advice from purchasing-power progressives, men like Robert Jackson, Leon Henderson, Harry Hopkins, Aubrey Williams, and Benjamin Cohen, as well as from proponents of spending, like Beardsley Ruml.[64]

When Roosevelt appeared before Congress in April 1938, he put himself firmly in the camp of the Believers. "During the processes of overspeculation and overproduction—in the Twenties—millions of people had been put to work, but the products of their hands had exceeded the purchasing power of their pocketbooks, with the result that huge surpluses, not only of crops but also of buildings and goods of every kind, overhung the market." The New Deal had committed the government "not only to re-establishing reservoirs of credit but to putting purchasing power in the hands of the consuming public and actually securing a more equitable distribution of the national income." But, according to Roosevelt, high prices and inadequate wages meant that "the buying power of the nation lagged behind." To address the resulting "failure of consumer demand," the president asked for a three-billion-dollar Recovery and Relief Bill to increase government spending and ease terms of credit.[65]

Emergency spending would amount to nothing if consumers had to pay high prices, so two weeks later Roosevelt announced the creation of the Temporary National Economic Committee (TNEC) to investigate the concentration of economic control and its impact on the price problem. The president sympathized with the idea that monopolistic pricing had "spoiled" New Deal recovery. In language that could have been written by Berle and Means, he asserted, "The power of a few to manage the economic life of the nation must be diffused among the many or transferred to the public and its democratically responsible government." Known as the Monopoly Committee, the TNEC won support from antimonopolists like Senator Borah and Senator Joseph O'Mahoney of Wyoming. But the

TNEC was not a trust-busting initiative. Its main intention was to focus on prices. Roosevelt declared, "When prices are privately managed at levels above those which would be determined by free competition, everybody pays." Harry Hopkins, head of the WPA, told Congress that, along with a spending stimulus, they had to launch a simultaneous investigation into monopolies. He believed the economy would not recover until the government restored the market to the "voluntary actions of individual consumers," rather than leaving it up to the "judgement or caprice of a few monopolists." Senator Borah, a committed antimonopolist, was even more blunt. He wanted the TNEC to begin by investigating the oil industry: "There's too much sitting down around the table and agreeing on prices." "We ought to stick them in jail." He argued, "We cannot restore purchasing power . . . if there intervenes between [those on relief] and the government a power which fixes prices they must pay."[66]

The TNEC has long since been confined to the dustbins of history, seen as the last hurrah of antimonopolists.[67] But the committee was organically linked to the purchasing-power program of the New Deal, and its staff came from the ranks of the Believers. It was composed of cabinet representatives and members of Congress; they appointed Leon Henderson as executive secretary. The appointments as well of Assistant Attorney General Thurman Arnold of the Antitrust Division, the Securities and Exchange Commission's (SEC) Jerome Frank, and the Department of Labor's Isador Lubin reflected a continued commitment to attacking monopoly prices. Thomas Blaisdell, former Consumer Advisory Board member, now of the SEC, also worked with Henderson. Influenced by Gardiner Means, all shared the perspective that the problem of monopoly was price rigidity rather than corporate size. They rejected a return to a Brandeisian age of small business and instead addressed a central question: "How to make business men behave in the public interest as their training as business men prohibits them from acting?" They dismissed a nineteenth-century-style attack on big business; instead they stressed the consumer over the small businessman. Henderson's motto was "Keep your eye on the consumer." If the consumer was paying too much, that boded ill for the economy.[68]

Arnold led the campaign against administered prices. In an assertion that business would find both shocking and wrong, he stated, "To keep prices up industry is choking off its own avenues of distribution." In March 1938, Roosevelt had appointed this Yale law professor chief of the Antitrust Division at the suggestion of his predecessor, Robert Jackson, as well as Tommy Corcoran and William Douglas. Rather than continue the government practice of going after specific companies, Arnold boldly attacked entire industries, including auto financing, auto tires, the milk industry in Chicago, the American Medical Association, and the building and construction industry. Even the AFL building trades, whose union practices Arnold regarded as obstructionist, were not exempt, and he filed suit against William Hutcheson, president of the AFL carpenters' union and sworn enemy of the CIO. Under Arnold, the administration strengthened the Justice Department's Antitrust Division. While not the most deadly of weapons, well-publicized antitrust suits did institutionalize public pressure to lower prices. Arnold hoped to receive support from middle- and working-class Americans, who he believed would approve of antitrust activities that promised to lower "the price of pork chops, bread, spectacles, drugs, and plumbing."[69]

The purchasing-power program of the late New Deal gained strength even as it aroused opposition. Its community of backers supported the Wage and Hour Bill, drafted to increase the wages of the least powerful and unorganized workers. The National Consumers' League (NCL) had lobbied for decades for federal enforcement of labor standards. Mary Dublin, president of the NCL, now explained that failure to pass federal legislation would lead "us rushing headlong into an even deeper economic abyss. . . . It is not only that these millions of families know the deep meaning of hardship, but their poverty and exploitation is a burden which does and must affect every person in this land." Testifying in Congress, Henderson argued that the bill would "help to prevent a mass reduction in wages and purchasing power." Robert Jackson, Isador Lubin, and John Lewis also supported it. After stalling in Congress for two years, the bill passed as the Fair Labor Standards Act in June 1938. In July, President Roosevelt signed it, thus outlawing child labor and creating a federalized system of minimum wages and maximum hours. Immediately, more than one million workers in low-paying industries, such as textiles, clothing, tobacco, lumber, and pecan shelling, saw gains in their income as a result of overtime pay. Though necessarily an incremental measure, its supporters intended to expand the income of the lowest-level workers, even if only gradually. Within years, southern textile workers, northern shoemakers, and female retail clerks received mandated wage increases. Getting around intransigent southern opposition required excluding agricultural and domestic workers. But New Dealers considered this compromise acceptable, as their support for the measure was directed not only toward improving the lives of the lowest-paid workers but also toward stanching a massive wage cut in the event of another serious depression.[70]

Purchasing-power progressives scored another victory with the passage of the Food, Drug, and Cosmetic Act of 1938. This measure enhanced government regulation of industrial standards for consumer products. Its passage reflected the muscularity of organized consumer groups in the later years of the New Deal as they mobilized behind this bill, which was loathed by industry and advertising. Fourteen national women's organizations pushed for passage of the measure. Lobbying for legislation prompted national women's groups like the General Federation of Women's Clubs (GFWC) and the AAUW to establish permanent consumer boards.[71] Now the administration's purchasing-power progressives could rely on a well-organized and increasingly coherent consumer voice to support their policy initiatives. The three-pronged initiative of the late New Deal—regulation of consumer goods, an attack on monopoly prices, and a minimum-wage policy—marked the fruition of the NRA Consumer Advisory Board's agenda.

However, limitations to these achievements soon became apparent. In the 1938 congressional election, Republicans made significant gains. The purchasing-power program, while popular, unleashed a host of disruptive forces, manifested clearly in the sit-down strikes. Massive organizing drives in steel, auto, and rubber promised to insert powerful new industrial unions into the center of the American economy. Voters supported low prices and even high wages but were becoming increasingly concerned about the chaotic nature of labor strikes. Michigan citizens voted Frank Murphy out of office for his support of the sit-down strikers. Many people felt that Roosevelt's plan to pack the Supreme Court with sympathetic justices also had gone too far. Republican victories suggested a public wary of labor's growing clout. The election results put into question the power of labor-friendly New Dealers like Hopkins, Ickes, Perkins, Corcoran, Henderson, and Lubin and bolstered the influence of more moderate advisers like Postmaster James Farley.[72]

The public may have balked at labor's aggressive tactics, but the crusade against the high cost of living had fewer enemies and had developed a political momentum. Attacking monopoly prices remained popular, and the administration continued to rely on this ploy as a way to stitch together its coalition. The TNEC hearings lasted from December 1938 to March 1941. Over five hundred witnesses testified, and experts produced forty-three volumes of economic studies. As TNEC executive secretary, Leon Henderson argued forcefully that monopolies created price rigidities that made depression a regular feature of the American economy. Henderson's personal authority was enhanced when, in May 1939, Roosevelt appointed him, at the request of Tommy Corcoran and Benjamin Cohen, to serve on the Securities and Exchange Commission.[73]

The TNEC called on consumers directly to testify. Their appearances, arranged by Consumers' Counsel Donald Montgomery, made front-page news. Alice Belester of the United Conference against the High Cost of Living, who spoke for seventy-five thousand Chicago housewives, expressed the group's mission statement: "We, the people who work for a living, are the consumers as well as the producers. . . . But, will high

money wages alone purchase any abundant living if as individual consumers we lose as poor buyers across the counter the gains made by our
collective bargaining with industry?" This was the same question that
Paul Douglas, Edward Filene, and other purchasing-power progressives
had been asking for two decades. Now an increasingly visible consumer
presence asked those questions before Congress.[74]

Consumer organizations had supported the Food, Drug, and Cosmetic
Act, and they now used the TNEC hearings to push for tougher regulations on all consumer products. Belester and a representative of the
GFWC insisted that, without a standard grading system for all branded
goods, the average housewife had an impossible time "getting her
money's worth." Ruth Ayres, formerly of the Consumers Advisory Board
and representative of the League of Women Voters, arrived at the hearings with twenty-one cans of tomato juice to demonstrate the range in
price and size. "Until we have some basis of judgment we'll never be able
to do our jobs as housewives intelligently." "The problems of the consumer" threatened the whole economy, Montgomery proclaimed. "There
can be no free enterprise if the citizen as a consumer . . . must remain in
ignorance." Dexter Masters of the Consumers Union and Robert Lynd
and Persia Campbell of the Consumers National Federation echoed
Montgomery's fears. The GFWC, AAUW, and the AHEA led the campaign for a nationally recognized system of standards and grading for
food, sheets, clothing, shoes, home furnishings, and other essential consumer products. Mass retailers supported these consumers' demands.
Filene's Louis Kirstein explained, "The retail industry should and does
acknowledge the right of consumers to know what they are buying."
Eager to win the favor of their customers, Kirstein declared, "The retail
trade must necessarily turn to producers and hold them responsible."[75]

Business groups feared what they perceived as a blossoming gov-
ernment-backed consumer movement. A 1939 *Business Week* report on
the consumer movement conjured images of fearless women reading
dog-eared copies of Stuart Chase and F. J. Schlink's *Your Money's Worth*
and the sequel, *100,000,000 Guinea Pigs*. The journal warned its readers,
"The consumer movement is spreading like wildfire across the country
in the past decade and it's gaining in force and vigor every day." The report even endorsed the idea of a Department of the Consumer as a way
to contain the "organized discontent" that posed a "real threat to the
producers and distributors of advertised brands." In the late 1930s, the
consumer movement picked up speed as membership in consumer testing groups grew and dozens of so-called guinea-pig books made best-
seller lists. Consumer education courses were taught in high schools
and colleges, and students formed consumer clubs. In 1939, the Institute of Consumer Education brought together four hundred leaders in

this new field. Women's clubs began to train members not only as better homemakers but also as family purchasing-power advocates.[76]

Vociferous political assaults against consumer groups testified to their blossoming strength. In 1939, J. B. Matthews denounced the League of Women Shoppers as a Communist organization. Matthews had been a leader at Consumers' Research (CR) and deeply resented the support that the league had given to CR's striking workers in 1935. The signing of the Nazi-Soviet pact imperiled Popular Front collaboration, and accusations of Communist sympathies became routine as a way to discredit party activists and, with them, their New Deal liberal allies. In December 1939, Representative Martin Dies of Texas, chairman of the newly created House Un-American Activities Committee (HUAC), recruited Matthews to charge the League of Women Shoppers, as well as the Consumers National Federation, Consumers Union, and local housewife and milk committees with Communist influence. Matthews blamed Consumers' Counsel Donald Montgomery for fueling protests and providing governmental assistance to those who staged them. Lynd and Campbell denounced Matthews's charges, as did Representative Jerry Voorhis of California, a cooperative advocate. President Roosevelt also condemned Dies's questionable witch-hunting tactics. The Consumers National Federation, in its defense, stated, "Every housewife wants to buy intelligently in the market and to get good value for her money. It is a strange outcome of our democratic process if, as Chairman Dies implies, it is 'communistic' or 'subversive' to try to get value for your money or to help housewives get value for their money."[77]

The attack on consumer groups was part of a larger onslaught against the New Deal political economy. Matthews also castigated economist David Saposs of the NLRB as an "economic crackpot." Soon after his appointment, Saposs had charged the National Association of Manufacturers and leading industrialists with illegal antiunion practices. What troubled Matthews about Saposs was not his accusation of antiunionism but his favoring of new industrial unions. Saposs and the entire NLRB staff became targets not just of the business community but also of the AFL, which, correctly, believed that the NLRB gave preferential treatment to CIO unions. John Frey appeared before HUAC to accuse top CIO figures, such as John Lewis, Sidney Hillman, Harry Bridges, and Lee Pressman, of being Communist. In Bridges's case the label was true, but the committee was less concerned with Communist Party membership than with the alliance between the new mass organizations and the government. The AFL campaigned to purge the NLRB of its "pro-CIO" bias.[78] As Frey saw it, the CIO mass unions threatened to diminish the power of AFL craft unions to negotiate for their members. Whereas in the 1920s Frey had once championed the economic rights of all workers, the CIO threat to AFL interests now clearly trumped his earlier advocacy of mass purchasing power.

A widely publicized case involving Filene's demonstrated to critics how the NLRB overstepped its authority in promoting industrial unionism. A House investigation accused Edwin Smith of the NLRB of aiding the American Federation of Hosiery Workers, a CIO union, in its strike against Berkshire Mills by asking Louis Kirstein, Filene's manager, to boycott the mill. Smith himself was a former Filene's employee and was in regular contact with Kirstein, who, throughout the early New Deal, had served on various National Labor Boards. Kirstein admitted that indeed he and Smith had discussed the impending strike but denied that Smith had asked him to boycott the mill. To opponents of the CIO and the NLRB, the distinction was immaterial. What concerned them was the number of important government positions that were occupied by people like Smith, who sympathized with an expansive new industrial union movement. By certifying the American Federation of Hosiery as the legitimate union for these workers, the NLRB put the power of the federal government behind mass unionism. FDR, too, who understood the potentially destructive impact of such an alliance, would soon replace Smith with William Leiserson. Though Leiserson had once been a proponent of the CIO unions, he now tried to check their explosive advance in order to support the interests of the AFL.[79]

The New Deal drew its energy from the entry of labor and consumer power into the corridors of corporate America. Previously unorganized workers now had a voice in determining their wages, while organized housewives were demanding better deals at the market. In different political and economic circumstances, their interests would collide, but both groups found friends in the New Deal administration. When conservatives attempted to amend and weaken the Wagner Act in 1939, with help from the AFL, the Twentieth Century Fund intervened and conducted a major study to demonstrate the effectiveness of new industrial unions. By then, Robert Jackson, Robert Lynd, and Adolph Berle were serving as board members. Consumer groups joined the CIO to rebuff any amendments to the act. The union of their efforts was symbolized by the marriage of Mary Dublin, president of the National Consumers' League, and Leon Keyserling, chief drafter of the Wagner Act; they had met when both were defending the legislation. Within a few years, Donald Montgomery's move from the position of AAA's consumers' counsel to aide to United Automobile Workers' president Walter Reuther signaled another sort of marriage—between government and labor.[80]

Demands for price vigilance and product standards grew louder as the government began mobilizing for war. In one sense, the changing political climate after 1939 chastened the consumer-labor movement and made many of their activities suspect. The outbreak of war in Europe in September 1939 also led to the massive investment in armaments that ended the elusive search for recovery. But, at the same time, these grass-roots activists gained momentum as war mobilization threatened to escalate prices. Memories of the destructive experiences of the World War I era and of hyperinflation in the Weimar Republic made combating inflation a national priority. Consumer groups feared the inflationary consequences of mobilization, and they used the national emergency as an opportunity to further their agenda. The Consumers National Federation warned, "General increases should be avoided to prevent pinching the standard of living of the lower-income groups." They insisted, "If individual prices go up, consumers want to know why." They pushed for consumer representation in all mobilization agencies and recommended a new agency to "measure the extent of price increases, the deterioration of products or reductions in the quality sold at a given price." A newly created "federal price unit" must "help consumers to decide how far these increases in price or reduction in quality and quantity are justified." They praised Bureau of Labor Statistics weekly reports on food prices and called for their extension to nonfood items, a demand echoed by the League of Women Voters. Ruth Ayres explained, "Our problem is to urge that sufficient information be given us to judge whether or not we are getting anything like our money's worth."[81]

New Dealers shared these inflationary concerns and turned to the TNEC to block price increases. In September 1939, Roosevelt called on the TNEC to serve as America's "price watchdog." "None of us wants to see the cost of living unjustifiably increased or prices become so unreasonably high." Recalling the experiences of World War I, the president ordered the TNEC to keep a "constant eye on increases in prices . . . to determine whether there is profiteering." The TNEC had necessary authority to "invoke the forceful check of impartial public inquiry on this kind of un-American activity." Already the Department of Justice was receiving hundreds of letters daily complaining of unjustified price increases.[82]

The president hoped to use the power of publicity and the threat of litigation to thwart price hikes. In December 1939, the TNEC held hearings on prices in response to the president's request. The administration particularly feared the effects of a steel price increase in 1940, as the industry was central to the nation's entire price structure. Henderson pressured steel executives to show restraint as orders increased. At the same time, Arnold's Antitrust Division stepped up its litigations between 1939 and 1943. In spite of opposition, appropriations doubled, and the staff increased fivefold. The number of lawsuits Arnold initiated during this four-year period was almost half of all the proceedings that had been held since the Sherman Act had become law in 1890.[83]

Consumer-oriented organizations were alert to rising prices. In February 1940, the AAUW sponsored an exhibit in Washington, D.C., to demand government grades and labeling. Under the banner "Today's Consumers Live in Blunderland," the exhibit drew national attention. Caroline Ware, head of the AAUW's Consumer Division, explained that marketplace and workplace issues were opposite sides of the same consumer coin. According to Ware, workers and consumers shared a reciprocal interest: "The two are coming very close together as the workers are coming to see [that] what goes out of the pay envelope is as important as what comes into it." These Washington-based consumer demonstrations complemented grassroots activity. In New York, the Henry Street Settlement House staged a baby-carriage parade with the Milk Consumers Protective Committee and the Dairy Farmers' Union to demand public milk depots. They milked a cow, which wore a sign that read, "I am a union cow. I give milk for babies, not for the milk trusts." Their demonstration resulted in a license for the Consumer-Farmer Milk Cooperative.[84]

Consumer groups now identified their campaigns as initiatives to preserve American democracy. Fighting high prices was necessary not just for ensuring mass purchasing power but also as part of the battle against fascism both abroad and at home. The power of large corporations would only increase as they secured a disproportionate share of military contracts, enhancing their power to set terms of production. In 1940, at the TNEC hearings, Caroline Ware explained, "The problem of effective economic citizenship is a twofold problem of effective participation, as a producer and as a consumer." Participation required education and organization. "Insofar as our economic system depends upon the bargaining relationship, whether between employer and employee or between producer and consumer, the parties have to be equipped to bargain if the bargaining relationship is to be a real one. . . . They must have the necessary tools with which to participate actively, if the principles of democracy are to obtain." Robert Lynd, who also testified, warned, "There is a 'consumer problem' of national proportions and it is here to stay as a large white elephant on the doorstep of business." He continued, "The only way that democracy can survive, if indeed it is not now too late for it to survive at all, is through the quality of living it can help the rank and file of its citizens to achieve." Only powerful consumers with both economic and political clout could prevent economic ruin and civic decay. Indeed, he saw the consumer as "democracy's third estate."[85]

By 1940, the purchasing-power program of the New Deal had achieved major advances, but it had also experienced setbacks. The highly mobilizing nature of the new industrial labor and consumer movements, combined with efforts to federalize wage and hour policy, ignited the ire of anti–New Deal conservatives, including the AFL. Their electoral victories in 1938 presaged an alliance between southern Democrats and Republicans whose goal was to check the intrusion of a New Deal state, particularly in labor affairs. But before they could push back the major advances of labor liberalism under the New Deal, U.S. participation in World War II provided one last great opportunity to institute a purchasing-power agenda. To be sure, war mobilization forced Thurman Arnold to call off investigations into the steel, shipbuilding, and aircraft industries. But the war intensified government oversight of prices. Under the direction of Leon Henderson, the newly created Office of Price Administration would put the regulation of the wage-price-profit ratio at the heart of America's wartime political economy.

Part III _____

THE EVILS OF INFLATION IN WAR
AND PEACE, 1940–1960

The Consumer Goes to War, 1940–1946

THE INFLATION of World War II threatened to disrupt the New Deal coalition. Wartime food shortages drove up farmers' commodity prices just as a return to full employment gave unions an edge in negotiations for higher wages and more of a voice on the shop floor. Not satisfied with these gains, labor radicals staged a series of wildcat strikes that alienated much of the middle class. But even as wartime conditions exacerbated the tensions within the New Deal, the dramatic expansion of state power facilitated by the war also strengthened the alliance of labor and consumers in pursuit of more money in their pockets. Now the Roosevelt administration was backed by the patriotic imperative of war to mobilize the public against inflated prices. Fair prices became a rallying cry as consumers and workers united behind the Office of Price Administration (OPA) to restrain inflation and preserve mass purchasing power through a system of rationing and price controls. By the end of the war, New Deal opponents had launched a massive assault against OPA, because they recognized it as the most powerful and effective instrument for extending the New Deal into the postwar era.

Indeed, OPA embodied the New Deal regulatory state that at once put redistributive policies in place and mobilized citizens at the grass roots. Its strength was reflected in its budget, which equaled the amount allocated to the Social Security Board and the Department of Labor, and it received more than ten times the money meted out to the Bureau of the Budget and the National Resource Planning Board combined. Its paid and volunteer staff numbered over 250,000, second in size only to the Post Office, and it boasted twice as many economists as the Treasury Department. With its billions of ration stamps and thousands of field officers, OPA became a constant presence in citizens' daily lives, making itself felt at each step in the consumption cycle, from gathering coupons to checking price lists to recycling fat. Moreover, OPA reached into communities and households and enlisted thousands of shoppers as its shock troops.[1]

This wartime fight against inflation resembled the struggle that had occurred in World War I, but with important differences. Once again, the nation's political leaders employed moral exhortation to restrain the functioning of a free market. From Roosevelt on down, Washington

officials championed consumers' interests, denouncing businesses that
charged excessive prices as unpatriotic profiteers. The war gave birth to
OPA, and patriotism was the key to popular support for its policies. But
characterizing OPA as simply a war agency overlooks its New Deal an-
tecedents, which had institutionalized key dynamics of the purchasing-
power program and facilitated a forceful price-control regime. First,
OPA drew on a well-established New Deal redistributive philosophy and
liberal personnel that placed a premium on low prices and high wages.
Second, price controls gained strength from a grassroots consumer
movement, made up primarily of members of national women's clubs,
that had taken hold during the late years of the New Deal. And third,
labor, now better organized and strengthened by New Deal policies,
threw its full weight behind the price-control program, viewing it as a
means of offsetting the wartime wage freeze that made workers especially sensitive to price increases and displaced much conflict from the
shop floor to the market basket.

The Office of Price Administration served as a radical model of state
management: a popular government agency working in alliance with a
coalition of labor, consumers, and social liberals that challenged the
right of private industries to set their own prices and sell their items
freely. Price controls instituted by OPA relied not only on a vast regulatory state administered by technocratic planners but also on a dense
web of citizen participants, which accounts for both consumers' heightened sense of state-conferred legitimacy and the ferocious opposition
that controls engendered. Members of OPA believed in an invasive
form of management, democratized, they hoped, by reliance on residents in local communities to enforce rationing and controls. Their
vision of fair prices and equitable distribution was both technocratic
and participatory. "The fight against inflation is our fight," announced
consumer activist and OPA employee Caroline Ware in her 1942 book,
The Consumer Goes to War.[2] This synergy of state and society resulted in
what supporters hoped, and opponents feared, was a natural evolution
of New Deal statecraft.

Patriotic Prices under General Max, 1940–1942

In 1940, inflation replaced deflation as the nation's number one
economic problem. Defense spending brought an end to a decade of depression. By the time of the Japanese attack on Pearl Harbor, unemployment had declined from ten million to three million and soon would
disappear. Greater opportunities, better jobs, and longer hours led to
substantial pay increases, resulting in a doubling of blue-collar income.

Yet inflation threatened to wipe out income gains. The prices of food, rent, and clothing, the biggest items in working-class budgets, shot up. With half of all production channeled to the military effort, too much money chased too few goods. The specter of spiraling prices eroded morale and promised to arouse labor militancy. Strikes and popular defiance added to the higher costs of military goods and jeopardized the defense effort. Advancing full production while avoiding social chaos would remain a central challenge for the Roosevelt administration.

In the summer of 1940, President Roosevelt declared that America would serve as "the arsenal of democracy." The Nazis had occupied France and unleashed a bombing blitz on London. To marshal the nation's industrial resources, Roosevelt created the National Defense Advisory Commission (NDAC) in May 1940. Many feared that mobilization, which summoned the nation's leading businessmen to powerful roles as the "warlords of Washington," meant the end of New Deal reform, particularly when Roosevelt appointed Edward Stettinius of U.S. Steel and William Knudsen of General Motors to the NDAC. Indeed, big business would prosper handsomely during the war. More than two-thirds of all contracts went to one hundred corporations. Automobile corporations accounted for one-fifth of all military production, and General Motors alone was responsible for 10 percent. On the eve of the 1940 GOP national convention, Roosevelt invited Henry Stimson and Frank Knox, two prominent Republicans, to join his war cabinet as a way to blunt the isolationist partisan threat. Three years later, in a much-repeated pronouncement, Roosevelt explained that "Dr. Win the War" had replaced "Dr. New Deal."[3]

Yet the administration did not, indeed could not, forget its New Deal roots. At the polls Americans returned Roosevelt to office for an unprecedented third term. As his running mate, FDR tapped Secretary of Agriculture Henry Wallace, one of the foremost New Deal liberals. Labor, particularly the Congress of Industrial Organizations (CIO), rallied behind FDR: 79 percent of the CIO members voted for his reelection. Roosevelt could not turn his back on his labor allies. He appointed Sidney Hillman to the NDAC and assigned Isador Lubin, commissioner of the Bureau of Labor Statistics (BLS), as his assistant. George Soule hailed Hillman, the Amalgamated Clothing Workers' (ACW) chieftain, as the premier labor statesman. In contrast to John L. Lewis, who had declared his independence from the New Deal by endorsing Republican candidate Wendell Willkie and resigning from the CIO, Hillman was a loyal supporter who believed that a mass industrial union movement could survive only with government backing. To ensure a seat at the table of power, he would have to quell factional fights and smooth social frictions within the CIO. Hillman considered labor cooperation

and "responsible unionism" reasonable trade-offs for government support of unionization. Was this so-called Faustian bargain worth it? At the
time, New Dealers hoped, and opponents feared, that the administration would use the war to extend New Deal reforms. Indeed, the ranks
of organized labor would grow by 50 percent, from ten million in 1941
to fifteen million in 1947. Lieutenant General Brehon Somervell of the
Armed Service Forces remarked that war mobilization allowed "Henry
Wallace and the leftists to take over the country." A November 1941
Fortune poll revealed that most businessmen shared those suspicions.[4]

Roosevelt also did not forget his middle-class constituencies and their
pocketbook concerns. Early on, the administration committed itself to
price stabilization. In a fireside chat on May 26, 1940, Roosevelt announced, "This emergency demands that the consumers of America be
protected so that our general cost of living can be maintained at a reasonable level. We ought to avoid the spiral processes of the World War."[5]
The administration was forced to pay more attention to the cost of living as inflation became the central problem in the economy. Women's
groups rallied to protect the working and middle classes, especially people with fixed incomes, such as government employees, teachers, and
members of the military, from being ravaged by inflation.

Perhaps no appointment symbolized New Deal continuity more
than Roosevelt's selection of Leon Henderson as NDAC's price boss.
Henderson brought with him his administrative experience, his
purchasing-power philosophy, and his reputation as a left-wing New
Dealer. His recent posts, especially his years as executive secretary of the
Temporary National Economic Committee (TNEC), had trained him
well for the position. One TNEC committee member commented, "The
million dollars spent on the investigation may justify itself in the education it gave Henderson for his present job."[6] Roosevelt called on Harriet
Elliott, a prominent member of the American Association of University
Women (AAUW), a consumer advocacy group of the late New Deal, to
become head of NDAC's Division of Consumer Protection. Two decades
earlier, she had joined Mary Rumsey in spearheading the World War I–era
fair-price campaign. Henderson's and Elliott's appointments signaled to
Roosevelt's labor and middle-class constituencies that he was taking
price stability seriously.

Rising prices became a real problem as the military appropriated an
increasing share of goods. The army alone placed orders for 250 million pairs of pants, 250 million pairs of underwear, and half a billion
socks. In her magazine column, Eleanor Roosevelt bemoaned the BLS
announcement that the cost of living had gone up by 12 percent in
1941. *Life* editors illustrated what that meant to the average American
family by displaying grocery items with old prices crossed out and

replaced by their new, inflated ones. The caption noted wryly that American housewives did not need BLS statistics to tell them that their marketing bill was going up.[7]

Consumer and labor representatives pushed for a vast expansion of industrial production as the way to protect living standards. In many industries, nearly half of the plants lay idle. "National Defense requires that business profits come through large volume rather than through high prices," said Elliott. United Automobile Workers (UAW) president Walter Reuther boldly called upon Detroit auto manufacturers to plan collectively for the production of five hundred planes a day. Henderson, Jerome Frank, and Harry Hopkins applauded Reuther's imaginative scheme, if for no other reason than to prod industry toward diversifying and expanding into war production. Emerging from years of depression, many firms did not want to cease civilian production in a booming market and feared that wartime expansion would leave them with surplus capacity. After winning reelection, FDR increased the pressure on industry to expand, offering favorable tax advantages and lower interest rates.[8]

In January 1941, Roosevelt coupled the call for mobilization with a declaration of the Four Freedoms. At bottom, these freedoms— freedom from want, freedom from fear, freedom of worship, and freedom of speech—amounted to a New Deal vision of security on a global scale. The occasion for their promulgation was Roosevelt's introduction of the Lend-Lease Bill, which would enable the United States to supply the war-torn and cash-depleted Allies with matériel and munitions. While inching America into a closer alliance with Britain, FDR designed his stirring rhetoric to reassure Americans that the postwar years would not repeat the boom-and-bust cycle that had followed the last war. The private aspirations of the middle class were captured by Norman Rockwell's famous rendering of freedom from want, which showed a table decorated with a sumptuous turkey and all its trimmings, a vision of abundance that some found distasteful amid the ravages of war and starvation abroad.[9] Rockwell's representation would have been more accurate had he added a framed portrait of Roosevelt hanging on the wall, as millions of Americans derived their sense of security and hopes for postwar abundance from their faith in Roosevelt's vision of a protective state.

In April 1941, the president enhanced the government's ability to fight inflation by establishing the Office of Price Administration as its own agency under Leon Henderson's control. That move signaled Roosevelt's recognition of the seriousness of the inflationary threat and freed Henderson from the corporate influences that permeated the NDAC. Henderson made it clear that he would be tough on price increases, rejecting the idea that expanding production required higher prices. In a move praised by the CIO, Henderson ordered a freeze on steel prices in spite of the wage hike achieved by labor. The steel executives would have to absorb wage increases out of profits. Throwing the moral weight of his office behind restraint, the president denounced "profiteering and unwarranted price increases." A public showdown with Chrysler in June gave Henderson another chance to demonstrate his resolve. "It is the policy of this office to ask companies which are enjoying a good volume of business and profit . . . to absorb cost increases." He bluntly stated, "Refusal by the Chrysler Corporation to cooperate is forcing us to take the pricing of automobiles out of the hands of the industry." Throughout the summer and into the fall, Henderson and his staff of economists issued price schedules for industrial goods. By the time of Pearl Harbor, price schedules directly or indirectly covered half the goods in the BLS price index.[10]

OPA had mixed success. Unable to escape public scrutiny, large oligopolistic industries like steel and auto complied, even though OPA had no enforcement powers or legal authority. They were responding not only to the threat of bad publicity and loss of military contracts but also to Henderson's dominating presence. In a profile for *Saturday Evening Post*, journalist Samuel Lubell captured him perfectly. "Most persons who try to describe Henderson arrive at the same appraisal—he looks and acts more like a truck driver than a cap-and-gown economist or a Government dignitary. Forty-six, black-haired, and black-eyed, he is five feet seven, with his best fighting weight around two hundred pounds. He has a barrel-like paunch, which makes his clothes look wrinkled and sloppy the moment he dons them. He chews gum and smokes cigars simultaneously, littering himself with ashes, is profane, and spits out of windows, which has promoted some anti-Hendersons to dub him a 'spittoon economist.'" This was the man who was in charge of setting prices for the nation's businessmen. Lubell reported that, as a young professor at Carnegie Tech, Henderson gave class credit to students for going to hear Eugene Debs talk in Pittsburgh.[11]

Henderson gathered around him a coterie of young, liberal-minded economists. He demanded that his staff match his own clear-cut commitment to price control. He explained, "We believe deeply in what we are doing in OPA. . . . We believe we should not allow a society to commit hara-kiri. We believe in stability and balance." No mere bureaucratic mission, this declared vision operated almost as a political litmus test for the career civil servant. Indeed, OPA was a magnet for mass-consumption activists, many of whom had served with Henderson on the National Recovery Administration (NRA) and the TNEC. Like Henderson, they believed in the possibility of determining a proper balance between prices and profits. Dexter Keezer of the Consumer Advisory Board, for

FIGURE 5.1. The Office of Price Administration put into place a national system of price controls and rationing. Many OPA executives, including the chief, Leon Henderson, had served in the New Deal. Seated here in 1942, left to right, are John Kenneth Galbraith, Leon Henderson, John Hamm, and David Ginsburg. Standing, left to right, are Dexter Keezer, Paul O'Leary, Paul Porter, Edward Hay, and Robert Horton.

example, had left his job as president of Reed College to head NDAC's Research Division. Henderson also worked with New Dealers Louis Bean, Isador Lubin, Gardiner Means, Mordecai Ezekiel, and young new Keynesians Richard Gilbert, John Kenneth Galbraith, Alvin Hansen, Gerhard Colm, and Robert Nathan, who were scattered throughout the war mobilization agencies.[12]

Conviction and moral suasion, however, were not enough to stem the inflationary tide. For one thing, rapid mobilization meant a reduction in consumer goods. Soon, by executive order, industry would stop turning out washing machines, irons, radios, refrigerators, and automobiles at a time when wages were rising in response to a tightening labor market and the flexing of union muscle. In 1941, two million workers participated in more than four thousand strikes, a majority led by CIO unions. The most dramatic victories came with the unionization of Ford and Bethlehem Steel, two of the last holdouts among the leading industrial corporations. As paychecks rose, even industries that had shown restraint would find it difficult to resist price increases. Furthermore, price control by voluntary participation had not been effective in all industries. As Gardiner Means, now in the Bureau of the Budget, explained, the administration could not enforce restraint in competitive fields like textiles. Unable to stop deflation during the Depression, firms in these industries now rushed to recoup losses.[13] And farmers too, a key constituent of the New Deal, saw an opportunity to charge higher prices. They would fiercely resist any effort to curb their gains after two decades of depression. Finally, many local markets, such as those for rental housing and milk, were beyond OPA's influence.

Under Elliott's direction, OPA's Consumer Division concentrated on price restraint at the local level, where community pressure and grassroots groups, if properly mobilized, could work most effectively. In a national broadcast, Elliott assured listeners, "We don't want Mr. and Mrs. John Public to pay unjustified prices for the things they need. And we want them to get just as good meat and shoes and clothes for their money as they ever have." Consumers could "help prevent local speculation or profiteering, by inquiring into any apparently unjustified increase in the cost of living—food, rent, clothing, fuel, furniture, recreation—and by informing proper authorities." Elliott appealed to women as "the purchasing agents of the American family. They can tell whether a merchant is charging too much for his goods by checking the prices." To define what "too much" meant, division members conducted price surveys of meat, woolen blankets, work shoes, and denim overalls. In November 1940, the Consumer Division began releasing *Consumer Prices*, a biweekly price bulletin.[14]

The Consumer Division drew on an established community of activists. Within hours of her appointment, Elliott recruited the help of Caroline Ware, who sent her a who's who list of the consumer movement that included hundreds of names and organizations. The NRA's Consumer Advisory Board, when it was created in 1933, had "virtually no self-conscious consumer movement upon which the Board could rely." By contrast, Ware noted approvingly, "In the past seven years, the consumer movement has gained great momentum." In August 1940, the Consumer Division summoned leaders of nearly one hundred national civic groups to Washington to solicit their support. Many, including the General Federation of Women's Clubs (GFWC), the American Home Economics Association (AHEA), and the AAUW, had fought side by side for the Food, Drug, and Cosmetics Act. Their agenda reflected no "mere preoccupation with problems of buying" but rather a concern with better information, quality standards, government representation, and equitable distribution as matters of national defense. Elliott pushed these women's groups to introduce price-recording projects for house-wives to make sure that merchants did not cheat them. The staff also encouraged communities to air radio shows, using Works Projects Administration (WPA) funds to publicize local prices. Since the late 1930s, many cities had established daily radio broadcasts announcing good deals in municipal markets. New York's program had over one million listeners. The division joined with the League of Women Voters for a national weekly radio show, *The Consumer Wants to Know*, to discuss the best market buys.[15] These groups embraced the fight for fair prices as part of their patriotic civic duty.

Though the consumer movement had been largely middle class, OPA used rising prices as a way to educate lower-income groups and recruit their support in government regulation of consumer goods. Its Consumer Division distributed millions of leaflets with titles like *132 Million Consumers* and *Shock Troops* to arouse the "economic consciousness of the consumer." Caroline Ware believed that "the defense program re-quired active, democratic, understanding participation of the public, and that the Division had a responsibility for mobilizing that participa-tion." "It must be, as far as possible, a grass-roots program, rather than one which is superimposed from above." Effectively regulating the mar-ket "implies working through every sort of group, and also finding ways to tap the unorganized." To mobilize a "consumer front," the division quickly recruited the aid not only of middle-class women's groups but also of more radical consumer groups, like the League of Women Shoppers, trade-union groups and their women's auxiliaries, black orga-nizations, and ethnic associations. The division also hired Minnie Fisher Cunningham from the Agricultural Adjustment Administration (AAA), a founder of the League of Women Voters and the Women's Democratic National Club, to organize rural women and working-class wives.[16]

In the fall of 1941, the Consumer Division institutionalized price watching by creating consumer information centers throughout the country, beginning with Detroit. "In each and every community," Elliott explained, "American consumers must be equipped to perform their function as economic citizens." Each center had an official complaint desk for reporting price increases. "In protesting against rising prices," Elliott declared, "not only are citizens democratically right, but they are also economically right." The committees could police prices, but they lacked the legal authority to punish gougers. However, the Consumer Division urged the consuming public "to use the force of publicity to keep prices in line." As Henderson explained, "Our biggest weapon is the moral support of the community." The Consumer Division recommended using WPA staff and funds to locate centers in settlement houses, union halls, churches, and women's clubs, as well as in "neutral" places, such as public libraries, post offices, and schools. In one crucial area, rent, the Consumer Division demonstrated impressive results by helping to set up 210 Fair Rent Committees in thirty-four states, primarily in key production areas where housing shortages were most acute.[17]

Labor and consumer groups rallied to support the Consumer Division. Members of the League of Women Shoppers staffed consumer information centers in Washington, Chicago, and New York and sat on Fair Rent Committees. At its 1941 annual convention, the CIO passed a resolution calling "upon all trade unionists to implement the crusade against profiteering and the high cost of living by cooperating . . . in the organization of local consumer and anti–high cost of living councils." The CIO's Women's Auxiliary distributed form letters to local chapters to send to Leon Henderson, requesting an expanded price-control and rationing program. "As an American housewife," the letter read, "I want to help my country win the war. . . . I cannot do my part to keep up [my family's] health and morale if every day my cost of living rises; if selfish people with money can buy up and hoard, not only their share, but mine, of goods that are short. . . . I therefore urge you, Mr. Henderson, to insure my family its fair share of goods by rationing all scarce goods and by setting prices above which my merchant may not charge me."[18]

The Consumer Division did not stop with organized labor and middle-class consumer groups. Ware and her staff were particularly interested in reaching out to black consumers and other ethnic minorities. As a professor of history at Howard University, Ware had established connections to leading black reformers. The Consumer Division distributed tens of thousands of pamphlets titled *A Negro Community Works in Behalf of Its Families,* explaining how to seek consumer information. Ware also encouraged the formation of "consumer corners," a modified version of formal information centers, in black churches, urban leagues, YWCAs, and rural home-demonstration offices. The division's Frances Williams from the Negro branch of the YWCA met with thousands of black Americans everywhere, from a Harlem Housewives League to branches of the Southern Tenant Farmers Union to rural isolated pockets of Arkansas and Oklahoma.[19]

The campaign against inflation and the presence of the Consumer Division energized demands for fair prices. For consumers, particularly those who faced routine discrimination in the marketplace, the "promotion of economic citizenship" complemented the federal government's aggressive wartime support of employment and civil rights. The

FIGURE 5.2. OPA's Consumer Division solicited mass support at the grass roots, including among African American groups. Here in 1943 Ethel Stephens, organizer of the Consumer Interest Council, a group of African American housewives from Newport News, Virginia, meets with OPA members to discuss point rationing. Left to right are Mrs. M. Barr, Miss A. Wilson, Miss Freedman, Ethel Stephens, Miss Warwick, and Frances Williams.

insertion of public authority into the most basic market transactions transformed this elemental relationship. Such enlarged state ambitions could be carried out and legitimized only by cultivating public activism. The vision sustained by purchasing-power planners—of governmental authority joined with a mobilized citizenry in pursuit of economic fairness, or what Caroline Ware called "the democratic control of our economy"—was a central legacy of the New Deal.[20]

Price restraint would succeed only with retailers' cooperation, but merchants were running "scare advertising," urging consumers to "buy now" before prices went up later. To thwart these tactics, the Consumer Division hosted a conference of 125 leading retailers in September 1940, obtaining their pledges of support for voluntary price restraint, offered largely to forestall the imposition of government-instituted controls.

Some prominent liberals, like Filene's Louis Kirstein, endorsed the administration's program, while Macy's, Filene's, Abraham & Straus, and other big department stores cooperated to prevent hoarding of items like silk stockings. But the majority of retailers regarded the Consumer Division as a threat. After all, the division's staff featured the same cast of characters that had sought greater state regulation over the retail trade in the Progressive Era and more recently during the New Deal. Now they were reappearing, ominously, in the guise of government officials. Retailers rightly feared getting caught in a "squeeze," as Kirstein explained to FDR, between frozen prices and rising costs. Kirstein reported that many of his peers went to the Washington conference "in a very skeptical frame of mind and figuratively speaking, carried tomahawks, axes, etc." In the keynote address, Fred Lazarus of Federated Department Stores warned his fellow merchants, "Unless by our own action we can prevent price increases and shortages at the pre-retail levels we shall be drawn into a situation in which government regulation becomes inevitable."[21]

That moment was drawing closer as successive months of inflation threatened the New Deal's commitment to economic citizenship and security. Between December 1940 and December 1941, the wholesale price index increased by an average of 1.3 percent per month, while the retail food price index in the same period went up by an average of 1.24 percent per month. OPA staff argued that inflation would undermine social stability and lower the living standards of the masses, especially those on fixed incomes. The solution, then, was tougher, more extensive controls. At Henderson's urging, the president asked for price legislation in July 1941, asserting to Congress: "We are determined that the sacrifice of one shall not be the profit of another. Nothing will sap the morale of this Nation more quickly or ruinously than penalizing its sweat and skill and thrift by the individually undeserved and uncontrollable poverty of inflation." With the disastrous reminders of Weimar Germany and prefascist Italy fresh in their minds, Washington officials feared the inflationary threat of a full-employment, war production economy. Because the Roosevelt administration chose a loose monetary policy to finance wartime borrowing and Congress could not yet impose a tax for a war that many were hoping to avoid, direct price controls would be essential to keep the economy on an even keel. The lesson the OPA staff drew from World War I was the importance of getting statutory authority for price controls early on, rather than relying on what they derisively called "price regulation through negotiation."[22]

Price controls faced enormous opposition in Congress. The battle lines were similar to the divisions over the Lever Food Control Act in World War I. Farmers were reluctant to have the government impose controls when wartime conditions provided them with booming markets. To the extent that they relented, they insisted on prices being set 10 percent higher than the parity rate established under the AAA. Since parity fluctuated with the cost of living, the provision made controls meaningless. The American Farm Bureau Federation, then at the peak of its influence, succeeded in defending the interests of the farm bloc. It received support from nearly all Republicans, who resisted controls on behalf of industrialists, especially the canners, millers, meat packers, and small businessmen. The latter were die-hard opponents of price ceilings, which could impose real hardships, especially as labor costs increased. Opposition to OPA solidified the anti–New Deal coalition that had been gaining steam since the election of 1938 and would make the mobilization effort that much more difficult. Unlike the situation that Wilson had faced in World War I, however, labor, a key, powerfully organized constituent, was squarely in the Democratic camp. And thus, the tension between food prices and urban costs of living was the greatest challenge, further straining the divisions within the New Deal's coalition. Proponents pushed for OPA as an emergency measure. But the fact that these policymakers had crafted much of the New Deal and continued to use the same rationale—of protecting consumers' purchasing power—gave OPA's opponents reason to fear.[23]

Pearl Harbor provided the final impetus for passage of the Emergency Price Control Act of 1942. Continued opposition could not undo the institutional structure and the ideological framework that had already been established and had received a final boost from the attack. Senator Robert Wagner, chair of the Senate Banking and Currency Committee, played a key role in passage of the bill. His committee explained, "Rising prices and increases in the cost of living bring misery to our people, cause industrial unrest, and undermine our unity. . . . The need for price stability is urgent. The cost of living must be stabilized." Thus, in January 1942 Congress delegated to OPA the authority to enforce rationing, rent control, and price controls, though its powers would terminate on June 30, 1943, and would have to be reviewed each year thereafter. The final act empowered OPA "to prevent speculative, unwarranted, and abnormal increases in prices and rents" and "to protect persons with relatively fixed and limited incomes . . . from the undue impairment of their standards of living." FDR explained, "The fight against inflation is not fought with bullets or with bombs, but it is equally vital. It calls for unflagging vigilance and effective action . . . to prevent profiteering and unfair returns." Despite OPA's increased authority and the moral imperative invoked by a wartime president, the act's exclusion of agricultural prices seriously hampered OPA's effectiveness. Appearing before the National Defense Forum of the General Federation of Women's Clubs, Henderson predicted that this measure "would not keep your prices in line."[24]

Henderson and his administrators immediately got to work to devise a practicable price schedule. The main task fell to John Kenneth Galbraith. Born in Canada, Galbraith received his Ph.D. in agricultural economics from the University of California, Berkeley, in 1934. For a short time, he worked at the AAA and then at the National Resources Planning Board. Galbraith then joined the faculty at Harvard, where he was part of an emerging group of young Keynesian economists who saw a bold and essential role for the government in stabilizing modern capitalism. Though Galbraith had hoped to use selective controls, administrative and economic necessities soon dictated a general freeze on all retail prices. In April 1942, President Roosevelt announced the General Maximum Price Regulation, better known as "General Max." In accordance with the provisions of that order, OPA instructed each seller to take as his ceiling the highest price he had charged in March for the same or a "similar" item with "fairly equivalent serviceability." All prices were to be "generally fair and equitable."[25] Obviously those terms left a good deal to the discretion of individual merchants and manufacturers.

On the eve of General Max's implementation, Roosevelt delivered his third fireside chat since the United States had entered World War II, in which he warned of the dangers of inflation. The president explained to his radio audience that winning the war abroad required sacrifice at home, what FDR called "equality of sacrifice." In addition to price controls, he also recommended increased taxes, urged people to buy war bonds, and asked for an end to installment purchases to siphon off consumer spending. It was becoming increasingly clear that the administration would have to take tougher measures, particularly against farm prices and rising wages, but the president's hands were tied as each group proved unwilling to make sacrifices without assurances that the other would also have to do so. His speech was intended to arouse public support for stricter price controls and put pressure on Congress, especially the farm bloc.[26]

General Max was highly elastic, and yet its scope was unprecedented. It was the first time the U.S. government had attempted to regulate and codify consumption by dictating retail prices throughout the economy. Unlike the code authorities of the NRA, OPA deputies were the sole arbiters of price levels. Moreover, in cases where OPA issued or adjudicated a specific ceiling, Henderson and his staff based their pricing decisions on the "overall company earning standard." Under that formula, OPA deemed irrelevant the cost of any one product in determining profits. If a company was not showing a loss, the price of any one item would not be adjusted. The leading alternative, articulated forcefully by Bernard Baruch, the former director of the World War I War Industries Board, was for profits under price control to be calculated on a "cost-plus" basis that accounted for cost increases and fixed a minimum profit level. The idea was that each product should "pay its own way."[27]

Although Baruch's approach had the support of all business groups, Henderson succeeded in structuring a far more radical pricing policy. In fact, OPA soon expanded this overall earnings standard to cover a whole industry, thereby ignoring the profit-and-loss sheet of any given company. The agency rejected bulk-line pricing, whereby the high-cost marginal producer set the maximum price. As Henderson explained, "Consideration of profits makes it clear that industries can well afford to absorb even substantial cost increases and by doing so make a contribution to the stabilization of the price level." Henderson minced no words in broadcasting this policy. If companies tried to lead OPA through "mazes" of complicated cost justifications, Henderson announced bluntly, "We refuse to follow." Of course, this strategy could easily bankrupt a high-cost producer or retailer. If a company was unable to lower its costs and streamline its operations, it could justifiably blame OPA for forcing it out of business. The leading trade associations denounced this radical transformation of the pricing mechanism. One year before opponents chased him from office, Henderson accurately prophesied, "It's only a matter of time till I shall be the most damned man in the country."[28]

OPA failed to prevent inflation. Here the farm bloc was the main culprit. General Max proved ineffective largely because farm lobbyists continued to ensure that many agricultural commodities fell outside OPA's regulatory sphere. In the first six months under General Max, lamb prices increased 12 percent, eggs went up 43 percent, and butter rose 18 percent. By contrast, sugar and coffee prices, both under controls, decreased. FDR soon acknowledged that agricultural interests would undermine the entire stabilization program, and he recognized he could no longer coddle farmers, even at the risk of jeopardizing Democratic votes in the South and Midwest in the upcoming election. In a tremendous show of bravado, he took them on directly in the fall of 1942. If Congress did not pass legislation in less than one month to bring down the cost of food, "I will act," Roosevelt threatened. "You cannot expect the laborer to maintain a fixed wage level if everything he wears and eats begins to go up drastically in price. . . . War calls for sacrifice."[29]

FDR's gambit succeeded. The Economic Stabilization Act, passed in October 1942, brought an end to agricultural privilege by extending OPA's coverage to 90 percent of food products. OPA also set specific dollar-and-cents ceiling prices for pork, an item that accounted for 10 percent of the average housewife's food budget. In addition, OPA required packers to grade all beef products according to government standards to prevent the sale of cheaper cuts of meat at high-grade prices. OPA justified those actions on the grounds that "maintenance of existing prices on meat [was] absolutely basic to [the] success of [the] cost of living control program." Galbraith denied that "peace time reform . . . is being put through in time of war." Instead, he claimed, "It is the old idea that you can't price unless you know what it is you are pricing." The women's clubs could not have agreed with him more.[30]

But inflation continued. The lack of sophisticated means to chart and control the economy hindered OPA's success. In addition, the contradictory and fragmented nature of the government's economic policymaking exacerbated its efforts to fight inflation. Congress passed the Revenue Act of 1942, which taxed millions of Americans for the first time, but the measure still left too much money in consumers' hands. The Treasury Department beseeched Americans to save and buy war bonds, but it insisted on low interest rates to finance public debt, adding inflationary pressure on the economy. Those fiscal and monetary policies necessitated harsher tactics to hold prices steady, such as going after the black markets, preventing quality deterioration, and uncovering willful evasion. Local stores commonly charged exorbitant under-the-counter prices, sold shoddy merchandise at regular prices, or simply closed down and reopened as a ploy to set new, higher prices. Hardware stores, for instance, began to branch out into selling toys, while candy makers reduced the weight of each candy bar. One inventive tactic to get around price ceilings was the "tie-in": a merchant would sell a regulated item to a customer only if she purchased another product whose quality and price was determined by the merchant himself. Even neglecting to trim fat from a cut of meat before weighing it constituted a breach of the law. Retailers, acknowledged OPA's Richard Gilbert, were in "open rebellion."[31]

For some merchants, the war offered irresistible opportunities to make money. But, for many others, price controls presented a real hardship. Fred Lazarus explained, "The squeeze on retailing is most acute. Tremendous protest has already come from the food people." Even assuming that most wanted to comply, they were faced with tight deadlines for complicated and cumbersome regulations. Filene's Toiletries Department, for example, had to print up ceiling price lists for 172 brands of soap, 52 toothpastes, and 31 shaving creams. Management ran full-page ads announcing the store's compliance in order to justify cutting back services like free delivery and gift wrapping and to explain why the store no longer installed fancy show windows. The Boston OPA office, administered by a particularly enthusiastic leadership, recruited "an army of shoppers" to visit Filene's and other department stores on the first day General Max went into effect.[32]

OPA had allies in labor and the organized consumer groups. After Pearl Harbor, the unions signed comprehensive no-strike pledges. Without that essential weapon, unions became dependent on the newly created National War Labor Board (NWLB) to compel wage increases and adjudicate contract disputes. In July 1942, the NWLB announced a "Little Steel formula," whereby the government sanctioned a one-time wage boost of 15 percent to allow workers to keep up with the hikes in the cost of living since January 1941. Thereafter, by presidential mandate, wages would be stabilized. Leon Henderson, a strong supporter of organized labor, pushed for this wage freeze, because he feared that "popular resentment would follow" from wage increases that threatened price controls. "On the basis of this resentment," he warned the president, "Congress would sooner or later . . . strike at the very heart of collective bargaining." Thus he pushed for the wage freeze "in return for a guarantee of stable living costs."[33]

Militancy on the inflation front was essential to America's trade-union leadership, because the wage freeze and the no-strike pledge made their jobs exceedingly difficult. Although job upgrades and huge amounts of overtime pay increased real weekly wages for most industrial workers, shop-floor discontent was rife by early 1943. The NWLB did begin to equalize the wages of textile, retail-trade, and food-processing workers, whose pay increased by almost 50 percent during the war, but anger arising from hundreds of thousands of examples of wage inequities festered throughout industrial America. From the West Coast, labor journalist Mary Heaton Vorse reported, "The chaotic state of the [aircraft] industry finds two people working with identical tools on the same job, one paid twenty cents an hour more than the other. Parts made at the Ford plant in San Diego at $1.00 an hour minimum are shipped to Douglas in Los Angeles and paid 65 cents an hour in assembly." And from Pittsburgh in 1942 came the complaint, "A man at the blast furnace does the same work another fellow does at the open hearth, but gets a few cents an hour less. Now frankly it's not a question of starving, much as he could use the money. It's just not right. A man does not see any sense in it and gets pretty mad. Who wouldn't?"[34]

Tying the hands of organized labor, the wage freeze converted labor leaders into militant supporters of price control. As labor historians have shown, labor and liberals were being pushed back in certain realms, from shop-floor issues to wages to decision making in war production agencies. But those defeats added urgency to consumption issues and moved price questions to the center of political debates about economic security and the fate of labor liberalism. Long hours, combined with workplace speedups, continued to generate shop-floor unrest and wildcat strikes. Yet labor leaders and their allies, fearful of generating public hostility, encouraged workers to shift their attention from the shop floor and the pay packet to the market basket. American Federation of Labor (AFL) president William Green informed President

Roosevelt that he planned to persuade all his union members to join in making controls work, and he distributed twenty-four million consumer pledges. The CIO unions became OPA's biggest boosters. The League of Women Shoppers, too, urged members to police prices collectively instead of marching on picket lines. "Buying power in wartime is a grave responsibility. Alone the consumer may be duped and confused but together consumers can be wise and strong and can Shop for Victory of the Democratic Principle." The league's Minneapolis secretary, Norma Olson, explained, "President Roosevelt's price freezing order . . . gives us, as consumers, a united program, behind which we must work together to endorse these price ceilings." In March 1942, the League of Women Shoppers met with OPA's Richard Gilbert to advocate distribution of price lists to enable shoppers to record purchases, and soon after the league began to mass-produce its own wartime price-checking booklets. Feeling rank-and-file pressure, labor and consumer groups began to demand a more aggressive price-control program.[35]

Mobilizing citizens to make price controls work was a democratic alternative to totalitarian enforcement. But to New Deal opponents, this strategy, combined with the cultivation of economic citizenship, was a terrifyingly muscular extension of the state. When OPA's political enemies derided the bureaucratic nature of wartime regulations, they did not have in mind just Washington red tape. Instead, they were responding to the filtering and penetration of government authority deep into society. They regarded as alarming the congressional delegation of power to OPA, and thus its congressional opponents continued to attack OPA and harass it with threats, investigations, and appropriations cuts. Ironically, lack of funds required OPA to look to ordinary citizen volunteers for enforcement of its policies. Representative Jed Johnson, a Republican from Oklahoma, declared that the encouragement of price watching was "inexcusable, un-American, and absolutely unconscionable." "The American people," he said, "do not need watching." Price controls could work "without a Gestapo and without paid snoopers."[36]

A young Richard Nixon found the extension of government power frightening. An unenthusiastic OPA employee, he regarded his fellow employees as "slide-rule boys" and "snoopsters." The son of a grocer, Nixon shared the mentality of small merchants everywhere who regarded OPA as an unwarranted intrusion. After only seven months as a lawyer in the tire-rationing department, Nixon had grown thoroughly disillusioned. He left in August 1942 to join the navy. Years later, Nixon was to claim that it was this brief wartime Washington experience that shaped his hostility to big government and overzealous bureaucrats. Nixon's friend and the only other Republican on the staff, J. Paul Marshall, explained, "We both believed in the capitalist system, but the other lawyers were using rationing and price control as a means of controlling profits." Both of their observations were correct.[37]

By the end of 1942, OPA had no choice but to inaugurate a stronger program. The lesson of the first year of war was that temporizing did not work. Half measures failed to restrain inflation and generated resentment among those who felt unfairly singled out to make sacrifices. That became clear with gasoline rationing. Consumers had registered few complaints in response to the rationing of tires, typewriters, sugar, bicycles, work shoes, fuel oil, and coffee. But when Henderson implemented a policy of gasoline rationing only in certain areas during the summer of 1942, he precipitated an avalanche of criticism because it was perceived as inequitable. In addition, the farm bloc made political hay over the initially small rations issued to farmers, a group already feeling victimized by price controls. In the fall election campaign, politicians capitalized on anger over OPA programs, resulting in more defections from New Deal ranks, especially because GIs and relocated war workers, many of whom were Democrats, did not vote. The Democrats held on to their majority by only the slimmest margin, losing forty-four representatives and seven senators, many from the Midwest. Michigan senator Prentiss Brown, who had pushed the farm bill in defiance of the agricultural interests of many of his constituents, was among those who lost their seats. Henderson became the scapegoat for this political debacle, and he resigned.[38] But because the administration was committed to fighting inflation, the political and social conflict generated by controls was just beginning.

Holding the Line, 1943–1944

FDR scored a victory for OPA when he issued his "Hold the Line" order on April 8, 1943. As OPA's official history asserts, this executive command was the turning point "legally, psychologically, and administratively." The order bolstered OPA's stand against higher prices by eliminating the agency's authority to sanction any increases and by instituting price rollbacks. It also created a subsidy for agricultural producers, whereby the government purchased commodities and resold them below market price. The added decision to introduce standardized dollar-and-cents community ceiling prices for food signaled OPA's new commitment. Such a tactic made it easier for the individual shopper to check prices, and it was enhanced by a coordinated effort to enforce compliance rigorously in the field.[39]

This executive order was a political calculation as much as an economic one. Ineffective price controls would alienate Americans living on fixed incomes, including the families of those in military service.

With half of all Americans purchasing war bonds and even more putting away savings, the government had to guarantee that inflation would not erode the value of their nest eggs. A more pressing problem was that spiraling prices would cause labor to chafe against the Little Steel formula. In the winter of 1943, meat prices took center stage when, in the absence of rationing, packers and butchers sold meat to the highest bidders and low-priced cuts disappeared. "High-priced restaurants and swanky hotels are still selling juicy steaks and fancy meat cuts to a select few," Harry Bridges, the West Coast director of the CIO, wrote to Roosevelt. "Baloney from government officials is no substitute for good red meat." Bridges charged that the meat shortage generated absenteeism on the docks, as workers took time off to scour local markets. Bridges had close ties to the Communist Party and was a firm supporter of the no-strike pledge and wage freeze to ensure essential production for the war effort. Thus, he considered it crucial for OPA to resolve the meat crisis, as shortages of meat on the West Coast were causing resentment among thousands of shipyard, airplane, dock, and other war workers.[40]

John L. Lewis tapped into this growing dissatisfaction when he led six hundred thousand coal miners on strike in four separate industry shutdowns during 1943. Lewis excoriated the Little Steel formula and the NWLB, and he bristled at labor's declining influence in Washington. With strong support throughout the key Midwest industrial cities, especially Detroit, Akron, and Pittsburgh, Lewis threatened to upset the industrial-relations bargain that union leaders had forged with industry and government in the weeks just after Pearl Harbor. Responding to Lewis's moves, Congress passed the Smith-Connelly War Labor Disputes Act, which enabled the government to seize struck plants, enforce a thirty-day cooling-off period, insist on majority approval before a strike, and prevent unions from contributing to political campaigns. Philip Murray, president of the CIO, and other American trade-union leaders feared additional antiunion retribution from Congress, the military, and the public. Yet they recognized the need to ameliorate the growing sense of rank-and-file wage grievances and to counter the political challenge from mavericks like Lewis. Thus, they began to insist militantly on a more effective price-control apparatus. The CIO *Labor Herald* announced, "It's time we make it clear to all officials and agencies of the government that we want real price control and rationing. We want food and clothes at a price we can afford to pay."[41]

The possible defection of labor groups posed a serious challenge for OPA. One of the most outspoken pro-labor critics of lax price controls was Donald Montgomery, who had resigned from his post as the AAA consumers' counsel in December 1942 in protest over rising food prices. Victor Reuther, Walter's brother, recruited Montgomery to the UAW as the chairman of its consumer committee, reflecting labor's growing institutional commitment to consumer issues. For the next decade and a half, Montgomery would be one of Walter Reuther's confidants. By 1943, the UAW had come to regard OPA as a "complete phoney." Even after the announcement of the Hold the Line policy, together Montgomery and Reuther devised a national anti-OPA campaign and ran full-page national newspaper advertisements condemning the agency's "do-nothing policies" and the resulting "sky-high prices." "Yes, We Have No Potatoes," the headline read. The AFL, too, denounced the "feeble, fumbling half-hearted efforts of the OPA."[42]

In that context, Prentiss Brown, ex–Michigan senator and now OPA's new administrator, announced a crackdown on prices. "We are retaking the price ground we have lost," announced Brown. A dramatic demonstration of the administration's commitment to the working classes came with meat rationing as a complement to subsidy payments to farmers for select commodities to keep their prices down and specific dollar-and-cents ceiling prices for foods. OPA pushed for these programs, even at the risk of further angering the farm bloc, which despised the use of subsidies to curb market prices because they created public expectations for artificially low prices. Their use turned farmers and their allies into sworn enemies of price control. At the same time, Roosevelt sought to preserve labor support by vetoing the Smith-Connelly Act. With few good choices and fearing further congressional attacks, the AFL and CIO fell in line behind OPA. "OPA should be strengthened, not destroyed," declared a new UAW advertisement. The UAW now blamed the farm bloc for high prices, claiming that farmers hated Roosevelt more than Hitler.[43] When OPA created the Labor Advisory Committee, Montgomery accepted appointment as its chair.

OPA's aggressive new policy entailed an expansion of its authority at the local level. OPA staff, which had gone from three thousand to thirty thousand, grew to sixty thousand by the end of 1943. More than 90 percent of the staff worked in regional, district, and local War Rationing and Price Control Boards. "Hold the Line" served as a powerful rallying slogan that boosted the morale of both OPA staff and consumers. Reflecting OPA's new toughness, the agency announced plans to distribute individual price lists, "which the housewife can put in her handbag when she goes to market." These policy declarations added muscle to OPA and gave consumers weapons to fight inflation. Throughout the remainder of the war, the consumer price index rose by only 2 percent. Total food costs, constituting one-third of the average family budget, actually decreased by 4 percent. Price controls succeeded in putting the inflationary genie back in its bottle because they worked in conjunction with the sale of war bonds and the introduction of payroll withholding taxes in 1943. But the public credited OPA with blocking inflation. Through its active campaign to expand its operations at the local level—to build the state from the bottom up—OPA became a highly effective agency.[44]

Under the Hold the Line policies, the entire population had immediate, intimate contact with price control and rationing. By 1944, OPA was affecting more than three million business establishments and issuing regulations controlling eight million prices, stabilizing rents in fourteen million dwellings occupied by forty-five million tenants, and rationing food to thirty million shoppers. The state was now reaching into the kitchen and closets of every home, influencing daily economic decisions like fashion choice and menu planning. Ads boasted of "footwear that requires no ration coupons," while Filene's and other department-store windows featured hair-removal products and leg paint as "substitutes for silk." Ladies' magazines and newspapers ran special ration-free recipes. New cookbooks with titles like *How to Cook a Wolf* offered novel suggestions about "making do." To be sure, OPA asked Americans to restrict their consumption, particularly of scarce goods. But, as John Kenneth Galbraith remarked years later, never before had there been so much talk of sacrifice amid so little actual want. Indeed, the goods and services available in 1944 exceeded those of 1940. The average department-store purchase rose from two dollars in 1940 to ten dollars in 1944.[45]

To the extent that OPA asked for sacrifice, it justified the request by linking it to patriotism. To help win the war, Chester Bowles, who succeeded Brown as head of OPA in November 1943, called on American families to plant two million more "victory gardens." OPA appealed to housewives to do their "patriotic duty" by turning in their waste kitchen fat for salvage to be used in the production of munitions, medicine, and manufacturing. Procter & Gamble sponsored an advertisement that read, "Our fighters are lean and lanky—but they can't fight without FAT!" The Campaign for Waste Paper also encouraged large-scale recycling efforts. Public announcements called on "Boy Scouts, school children, [and] housewives" to "Save Waste Paper for War!" The explanation for this appeal was that "one hundred pounds of newspapers will make 200 containers for blood plasma."[46]

OPA also sold wartime sacrifice by encouraging high expectations about better living in the future. Americans' anticipation of a prosperous postwar economy was based on a vision constructed by OPA and other government agencies, which reinforced a growing consumer mentality. In its massive bond campaign, the Treasury Department stressed that patriotic sacrifice for the war effort would result in personal gains at its end. As Secretary of the Treasury Henry Morgenthau Jr. explained, the bond campaign used promises of postwar plenty to sell the war, rather than using the war to sell bonds. Reliance on private firms to develop and pay for bond ads underscored the link between public aims and private interests. One ad sponsored by an appliance company proclaimed, "You, personally, have an important job in winning the war—buying War Bonds. It's not glamorous—no, not even a sacrifice, really, because you are only *lending* your money, to be returned with interest," interest, coincidentally, that could be put toward a new radio or refrigerator. A Treasury Department survey confirmed that Americans bought bonds to preserve the "American way of life" and to save for postwar purchases.[47]

As much as it appealed to visions of postwar plenty or patriotism, the OPA grounded its program in a New Deal sense of equity and fairness. A nationwide system of rationing bolstered this claim of equal sacrifice. The *Woman's Home Companion* readers' poll found near-unanimous support for rationing as the best way to make distribution equitable. Along with meat, coffee, and sugar, OPA introduced shoe rationing, claiming that without this essential program, "war workers, farmers and busy housewives might be unable to find shoes that fitted them. Millions of pairs of shoes would disappear uselessly into the closets of hoarders." In addition to rationing, the government required manufacturers to shorten heel heights, eliminate two-tone shoes and extra trimmings, and discontinue formal evening footwear. The hope was to enable the production of fifteen million pairs of work shoes. James Byrnes, who had stepped down from the U.S. Supreme Court to become director of the Office of Economic Stabilization, which oversaw all mobilization agencies, promised, "The shoes will be there."[48] Rationing and price control were not simply measures made necessary by war. They reflected the administration's best effort to preserve labor and consumer support at a time when war had temporarily displaced much conflict from the shop floor to the marketplace.

The Roosevelt administration understood the relation between consumption, patriotism, and citizenship, and the president readily transposed his intangible, elusive Four Freedoms into specific benefits. Roosevelt accomplished this most clearly in his 1944 State of the Union address. Written with the help of OPA's Chester Bowles, the speech called for an economic bill of rights. FDR defined America's war aims in terms of the economic expectations of its people: "The one supreme objective for the future . . . can be summed up in one word: Security. And that means not only physical security which provides safety from attacks by aggressors. It means also economic security, social security, moral security." He insisted that a "second Bill of Rights" would provide citizens with the right to a job, medical care, good education, housing, and enough income to secure food, clothing, and recreation. Encouraging Americans' sense of entitlement, FDR insisted that "our fighting men abroad and their families at home expect such a program and have the right to insist upon it."[49]

Who, though, would enforce these so-called rights? Congressional conservatives had already begun to eliminate New Deal agencies like the WPA, the Civilian Conservation Corps, and the National Resources Planning Board as part of a broad dismantling effort. Like the farm bloc, they viewed OPA as another New Deal body, one that was more meddlesome than most. To its opponents' dismay, OPA succeeded in winning popular support and selling itself as the government agency that would protect American standards of living. Its Information Department issued scores of consumer manifestos with titles like "What You Can Do To Make Price Control Work," "Of the People, By the People, For the People, Price Control," and "How You Can Tell Top Legal Prices—The Wartime Consumer's Bill of Rights." This propaganda emboldened consumers to speak up in their corner grocery store. When they spotted price violations, consumers had the right to sue for three times any overcharge or fifty dollars, whichever was greater. Such policies led consumers to believe that the government would serve as their arbiter in disputes over prices or quality of goods. Bowles claimed that, in any given week, OPA received 4.5 million phone calls and 2.5 million letters.[50] As the end of the war approached, Americans would worry about keeping their jobs and preserving their wages, but they had come to believe that fair prices were also essential to their postwar economic security.

The success of rationing and price control rested largely on the support of women as the principal "purchasing agents." In the fall of 1943, OPA launched a massive Home Front Pledge campaign, starting with Eleanor Roosevelt at the White House. In New Orleans, 250,000 citizens signed the pledge within forty-eight hours, and food prices declined by 5 percent. Nationwide, twenty million shoppers signed on, and the cost-of-living index dropped for the first time in nearly three years. Pledge takers posted placards in their parlor windows showing a housewife in an apron and affirming, with her right hand raised, "I pay no more than top legal prices. I accept no rationed goods without giving up ration stamps." It was their duty "to stamp out the activities of all chiselers, profiteers and black market operators"—or, in other words, free-market entrepreneurs. For rationed goods like meat, housewives had to surrender coupons to the grocer, who in turn had to hand them in to replenish his supply. In addition to these elaborate controls, OPA lobbied for government-grade labeling, a system whereby government-sanctioned standards and specifications would inform the consuming public what typical marketing terms like "fancy" and "choice" actually meant. That policy, bitterly resisted by farm and business groups, appeared at the top of consumers' and labor's lists of necessary steps for making price controls more effective.[51]

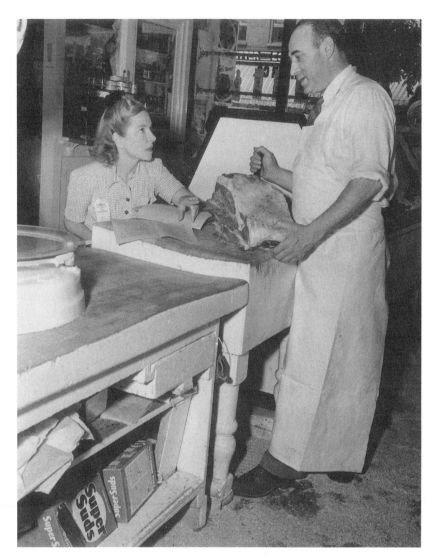

FIGURE 5.3. OPA relied on thousands of volunteers to inspect local merchants to make sure they complied with and posted price controls. Here, in 1944, an OPA volunteer, wearing her OPA official badge, scrutinizes the quality and cost of this butcher's meat selection.

The main institutional mechanism for mobilizing the community in the fight against inflation came with the implementation of "little OPAs," the 5,525 local War Price and Rationing Boards. Located strategically between the policymaking elite at the top and a diffuse consumer constituency at the bottom, these local volunteer boards played an essential role in stabilizing prices. In one month, July 1945, 127,075 volunteer price- and rationing-board members served 1.5 million hours. In addition to the "regular" volunteers, more than 300,000 "peak-load" volunteers were recruited for special tasks, such as distributing ration books. Each local board had between ten and twelve "price panel assistants," who acted as OPA's advance army. Drawn from their local communities, they were, according to OPA, the "'front-line forces' in the fight against inflation." It was their job to conduct regular price checks in their neighborhoods, in some cases assisting ignorant merchants, and in others reporting willful, repeated violators. They also investigated consumer complaints of overcharging and convened public hearings to bring offenders into compliance.[52]

These volunteers were mostly women. The customary ritual of buying and comparing prices had become thoroughly politicized. Not only were women familiar with all the intricacies of shopping, but they also typically had participated earlier in established volunteer networks. California's program, for example, demonstrated the effectiveness of relying on housewives. The Office of Civilian Defense solicited the help of Geraldine Dodge, identified as a housewife, mother of grown children, and experienced volunteer. For twenty years, she had been affiliated with the League of Women Voters, the Junior League, and the Community Chest. When asked to head up the San Francisco region's recruiting drive, she turned to the Red Cross and the American Women's Voluntary Services. Within a few months, Dodge matched eighty-eight volunteer supervisors with each Price and Rationing Board, and they in turn brought in twenty-four thousand regional volunteers.[53]

One of the more celebrated OPA staff members was the writer Jessica Mitford, who was a prominent American Communist Party activist. The daughter of British aristocrats, Mitford took a job in the federal OPA office after her wartime emigration to the United States. She viewed her experience "as close to the front line of the war against Fascism as anything in Washington." Not only did she help supervise the restriction of pleasure driving in an effort to conserve American resources for the "anti-Fascist struggle," but as a field investigator she regularly entered local stores to "hold the line against war profiteers, price gougers, greedy landlords, [and] violators of rationing regulations." After cutting her teeth in Washington, Mitford relocated to the San Francisco regional office, where she was placed in charge of inspecting secondhand machine-tool dealers. To educate herself about the details of lathes, dies, molds, and punch presses, on her first day Mitford went undercover into a local shop and asked seemingly innocuous questions about the style and make of various tools. Though having no cause for suspicion, she had a strong feeling that this unsuspecting retailer might be a "front for a vast second-hand machine tool black market ring." She returned later in the day when the owner was out, this time "armed with [her] OPA identification card," and demanded that the secretary hand over the store's books. When the proprietor came storming into the OPA office brandishing a gun and demanding his confiscated records, Mitford's boss asked her if she had ever read the U.S. Constitution.[54]

The advocates of consumer participation found a friend in Chester Bowles. In reaction against Henderson and his henchmen, OPA opponents had amended the price-control act to limit employment in the agency to those with practical business experience. Their intention was to prevent "long-haired professors," a derisive term for New Deal liberal economists, from serving in executive positions. The CIO initially opposed Bowles's appointment in November 1943, on the grounds that he was an advertising executive with ties to big corporations. But Bowles was a dyed-in-the-wool New Dealer whose passion for price controls ran as deep as Henderson's had. Bowles announced that OPA would not be a "walking doormat." A vision of low prices and high volume informed his ideological convictions and business strategy. He had built his advertising firm into one of the nation's ten largest by convincing clients like Maxwell House, General Foods, Palmolive, and Columbia Records to make their products affordable for the lowest third of the population. He claimed as his influences Donald Montgomery and Stuart Chase, both anathema to the advertising community for their charges of inefficient, costly distribution and gross deception. In his politics, too, Bowles was also liberal leaning. Like Roosevelt, Bowles came from a political family, went to elite schools, and married a prominent, college-educated woman, Dorothy Stebbins, who was active in social work. Bowles, too, had a charm that would make him a celebrated public servant in an inherently difficult job. As FDR had done in his fireside chats, Bowles cultivated a close relationship with the public through his weekly national radio broadcasts.[55]

Building on his success as OPA state director in Connecticut, Bowles understood the need for community outreach and consumer participation. He called on OPA field representatives to visit national women's organizations to recruit "as many price panel volunteers as possible." He told associates, "The metropolitan retail price problem could be licked by using price panels recruited from and supported by labor unions and consumers' groups." Bowles also set up a consumer advisory committee under the direction of Caroline Ware. Ware assembled a formidable cast of consumer, labor, and women's representatives.[56] These groups helped to recruit thousands of price-panel assistants. In March 1944 alone, forty-one thousand volunteers marched into 430,000 food stores around the country to monitor what merchants were charging and how they were transacting their sales. Ware also appealed to minority leaders, distributing pamphlets with titles like "Negroes, too, are Consumers." In Washington, D.C., blacks served on six of the fifteen price panels.[57]

These volunteer women could be divided into two broad categories. First, as Bowles suggested, previously organized groups, such as labor unions, working-class women's groups, and consumer groups made up a reliable core. Many of those organizations had consumer agendas that meshed with OPA's goal of stabilization and equalization. Union groups continued to support price controls as an essential complement to the Little Steel wage-freeze formula, while rent-control advocates saw OPA as an ally in their fight against slumlords. The second pool of volunteers consisted of previously unorganized shoppers from all communities and income groups. Teachers, feeling the pinch on their fixed salaries, were particularly active. By calling on citizens to volunteer and providing them with a legally established institutional framework, OPA fostered and legitimized the organization of consumers. Under OPA, the labor-liberal vision of an organized, broad-based, cross-class popular movement reached its apogee.[58]

Throughout the country, women's organizations rallied to enforce price control. The General Federation of Women's Clubs, the American Home Economics Association, the League of Women Voters, and the AAUW threw the weight of their millions of members behind OPA. Spanning the social spectrum from left to right, dozens of other national groups joined them, including the Parent-Teachers Association, the Red Cross, the Daughters of the American Revolution, the United Daughters of the Confederacy, the American Legion Auxiliary, the Farm Bureau, and Home Demonstration Clubs. These groups urged members to serve on price boards as OPA volunteers, to be "the eyes and ears of OPA," as the League of Women Shoppers put it. New York City's OPA launched an aggressive campaign to recruit one "price warden" for every ten stores. After signing up, the women were trained through "practice checking." Under the caption "Volunteer Price Wardens Get First-Hand Information," a *New York Times* photograph captured a group of disgruntled-looking women "inspecting food that is not price controlled."[59]

To opponents, the only thing that was more repugnant than these snoopers was OPA's distribution of ten million price-ceiling lists directly to housewives. OPA recruited women's clubs to get these lists to consumers and instruct them how to check merchant compliance on each shopping trip. The Parent-Teachers Association (PTA) of the South, for example, sent a quarter of a million price lists to its members in seven southern states. Mrs. R. A. Long, president of the Georgia PTA Congress, told her 685 local presidents, "Our own personal security, the security of our country, and the length of the war depend upon prices being held down. I am depending upon you to see that your members not only receive a copy of the Wartime Shopping List but use it." Mrs. W. H. Beckham, president of the Florida PTA, urged her 600 local leaders, "Our government has given us a job to do and has given us the tools with which to do it. The Community Price List is the weapon with which we can control rising prices." In even more strident language, Mrs. Berry D. Willis of the Virginia PTA called women to battle. "The opportunity and responsibility to fight are ours. The Community Price Lists . . . I am sending you are the weapons."[60]

This reliance on consumers amounted to a policy revolution. Bowles proclaimed the efforts of the price-panel assistants a great accomplishment in the history of local self-government; OPA was "democracy in action." FDR asserted, "We are the only Nation in the world where volunteers are doing this job. In the way it has been done, it's as American as baseball." For many people, Caroline Ware observed, volunteering was "a first experience in civic responsibility." Such appeals to traditional American symbols and rhetoric belied or, more accurately, signaled an effort to domesticate the new programs by deflecting their radical edge. OPA drew upon a long American history of popular civic engagement, but its dependence on citizens for regulatory enforcement extended the government's reach to an unprecedented degree. OPA turned to consumers for enforcement in part because of restrictions on federal power and in part because relying on heavy-handed statist solutions while fighting totalitarian enemies would have appeared contradictory. In the end, though, its adopted strategy made OPA's presence all the more pervasive because it mobilized the public behind the campaign for fair prices. Ware and other OPA policymakers viewed the volunteers' activities as the necessary "duties of economic citizenship in a modern state and in a war economy." She explained, "As the Government plays a larger and larger part in controlling the economy . . . our duties as economic citizens are more and more centered around governmental economic policies and their administration."[61]

By mobilizing thousands of volunteer price checkers, OPA reinforced the wartime confluence of public and private spheres. The enlistment of the household into the political arena and the resultant organized, state-backed consumer army was a highly potent combination. As one editorial writer commented, "OPA's plan to mobilize groups of housewives throughout the country—euphemistically designated as 'price panel assistants'—to inform against their neighborhood shopkeepers concerning deviations in ceiling prices becomes a haunting specter." Congressional Republicans and members of the business press saw a "kitchen gestapo," reminiscent of the block wardens deployed in Nazi Germany and the Soviet Union. OPA

FIGURE 5.4. Unlike an earlier government poster featuring a docile housewife raising her hand, solemnly swearing to pay legal prices and surrender coupons, the aggressive woman in this 1944 poster actively fights the black market. Such images aroused strong opposition from OPA opponents.

opponents were alarmed by posters featuring a snarling housewife, with fist clenched, growling, "I'm out to lick runaway prices." Indeed, in localities where volunteers conducted regular weekly checks on prices, compliance reached almost 100 percent. In a survey conducted by the Office of War Information in February 1945, 7 percent of the women interviewed claimed to have reported a price violation. Given that housewives depended upon these local merchants for scarce goods, that number was in fact high. When such displeased consumers were added to the hundreds of thousands of volunteers and millions of members of women's groups who lent support to OPA, it appeared that housewives had become organized and militant.[62]

Price Control or Profit Control, 1944–1946

The fate of OPA played itself out in the annual congressional battle over renewing price controls in 1944. OPA bolstered its strength by mobilizing the public, but its congressional foes retained the power to rein in this price agency. Because OPA had broad-based, popular support, opponents could not attack it directly. Instead, they tried to limit OPA's authority. As Saul Cohn of the National Retail Dry Goods Association explained, businessmen favored a "price control, not profit control mechanism." Thus, while claiming to endorse OPA, they attached various "hardship amendments" that essentially would have reversed Leon Henderson's "overall industry earning standard," instead guaranteeing every company a minimum level of profits—the policy, in other words, of "cost plus" that Bernard Baruch had proposed. The most widely debated amendment called merely for the elimination of the word "generally" before "fair and equitable" in the description of ceiling prices. In practice, this slight semantic difference meant that prices would be pegged to the highest-cost producers and merchants. Appearing before the House Committee on Banking and Currency, Chester Bowles denounced these machinations as an effort to institute the "greatest orgy of wartime profiteering this nation has ever seen," and he called on all consumer groups to stand strong against such "crippling amendments." Shortages and black markets may have made their shopping more complicated, but all the consumer representatives vigorously supported extension of a strong OPA. "We will back you and the Congress in resisting emasculating amendments," announced eleven national labor, consumer, and veterans' groups with a total membership exceeding ten million members.[63]

Trade unions forcefully defended OPA and sought a radical expansion of its authority. Donald Montgomery crafted the UAW-CIO's defense of OPA, while Philip Murray appealed to all CIO unionists to petition their congressmen. Under Montgomery's guidance, OPA's Labor Advisory Committee pushed to have OPA extended for two years after the end of the war. The committee also lobbied to require companies to reveal their profits under wartime controls. In her testimony, Annie Stein of the Women's Auxiliary of the CIO and a Washington price-panel assistant pushed for government funding of inspections as a way of strengthening price investigations. Rather than just relying on housewives to report overcharges and file a complaint, Stein wanted the government to issue OPA volunteers the money and authority to make "test purchases" as evidence, a measure supported by OPA itself. This was a bold suggestion, considering that price-panel assistants were trying to shed their ignominious reputation as "snoopers." To justify this request, Stein did not identify herself as a unionist (or a member of the Communist Party, which she probably was) but instead as a housewife. "I don't set myself up as an expert. I explained to you I am just a housewife and I am a member of a woman's auxiliary, and I have studied the regulations as much as I can without a technical training."[64]

A new authority was now conferred on housewives. Indeed, OPA encouraged housewives to see themselves as uniquely qualified advocates. As the nation's chief purchasing agents, they had intimate, street-level contact with the problems of price control. One of their main complaints was that price control lowered quality, as merchants and manufacturers tried to pass off shoddier goods as first-rate merchandise. An AHEA survey reported that 55 percent of all women found that the quality of clothes and shoes for sale was deteriorating. In addition, many low-end clothing items simply disappeared from the stores. At the hearings, Gladys Wycoff, AHEA field secretary, brought in as evidence baby "pajamas that didn't last the night out." When the War Production Board removed decorative trim from the essential items list, members of the New York Women's Trade Union League protested, insisting that such "luxuries" were useful accessories that helped working-class women to extend the life of their limited wardrobes.[65]

OPA's Consumer Advisory Committee constantly emphasized this low-end "merchandise problem." This predominantly female committee appreciated the problems of insufficient children's clothes and the general deterioration of all civilian apparel. During the 1944 hearings, it made a formal recommendation to Bowles that dollar-and-cents ceilings, already applied to many foods, be expanded to cover work clothes, underwear, hardware, sheets, and other dry goods. Laura Somers of the League of Women Shoppers also demanded a reinstitution of government-grade labeling, which had been eliminated the previous year. As she told the oversight House committee, "It is fully consistent with the American way of life for the American consumer to know what he is buying with his

American dollar." Whereas the Communist-aligned League of Women Shoppers had once occupied a position on the margins of political discourse, now its members successfully advanced their claims in the language of wartime patriotism, speaking not just on behalf of the working class but also in the name of all consumers. Indeed Katharine Armatage, the national chairman of the league, was in charge of consumer mobilization policy for the OPA Consumer Advisory Committee.[66]

If the consumer movement had begun as a middle-class movement for better labels and truth in advertising, now its leaders linked quality issues directly to the preservation of mass purchasing power. Labor, too, made this connection most forcefully when the AFL and CIO publicly repudiated the official BLS statistic that reported a 23 percent increase in the wartime cost of living, claiming that this number understated the increase by half. The acrimonious fight between labor and the BLS raged for months and ultimately forced FDR to appoint a special committee to resolve the question. This huge battle over a seemingly technical issue reflected the wartime transfer of the labor-capital conflict from the factory to the marketplace. Although no doubt a ploy to win an upward revision of the Little Steel formula, labor's claim that the actual number was double captured some truth. The BLS measured changes in prices only; thus its statistics did not reveal hidden cost-of-living hikes resulting from quality downgrading and the dislocations of war that required eating out, shopping at more convenient if not cheaper stores, and child care. "If I am compelled to take my choice between [the BLS] and some steel worker's wife," Philip Murray announced to the CIO executive board, "my inclinations will naturally run to the facts presented to me by the housewife."[67] Murray's ability to keep his rank and file in check depended on effective price curbs. Defending the housewife also made political sense when millions of Americans, not just wage earners, felt the pinch of inflation.

OPA's Ware and the UAW's Montgomery organized middle- and working-class consumers in the congressional fight for OPA renewal. They formed the Consumer Clearing House to bring together organized consumer groups and helped the Congressional Committee for the Protection of the Consumer to plan a price-control week. They launched a major media blitz and galvanized local communities to mobilize mass support. New York's Brownsville Consumer Council, a hotbed of radical consumer activity since the famous World War I–era rent strikes and food boycotts, rallied to the cause. Now these Communist activists were joined throughout the city by settlement house workers, unions, and middle-class consumer groups, who handed out tens of thousands of pamphlets printed with the slogan "Price Control or Panic" and shouted, "OPA must be defended."[68]

Both opponents and supporters understood that OPA had become thoroughly politicized. OPA relied on consumer, labor, and left-wing groups to implement its policies successfully, and in turn these groups invoked OPA's authority to advance their own agendas. Many middle-class groups viewed OPA as an extension of their efforts to regulate the consumer marketplace. Some thought OPA was tinged with a protofeminist culture that was socially progressive and even liberal on racial matters. The New York League of Women Shoppers, a staunch supporter of OPA, exemplified this culture. Many of its members were the spouses of New Deal progressives and active themselves as academics, intellectuals, and artists. The league counted Margaret Bourke-White, Lillian Hellman, Dorothy Parker, Mary Beard, Helen Lynd, and Freda Kirchwey among its ranks. Appreciating the way in which OPA injected a protective governmental presence into every market transaction, women's groups, including African American organizations, pushed for OPA reenactment without amendments. Thomasina Walker Johnson, legislative representative of the black Alpha Kappa Alpha Sorority, explained, "As Negro women we have had a particular interest in rent control."[69]

The 1944 renewal of OPA represented the agency's apogee as a strong interventionist agency. Though its supporters failed to enhance OPA's arsenal of regulatory weapons, they staved off crippling amendments, and OPA remained a powerful institution that could thwart market forces. Bowles beseeched women, consumers, and labor organizations to continue their active support of OPA. He wrote directly to Jessie Lloyd O'Connor of the Chicago League of Women Shoppers, for example, to solicit "the continued help of you and your membership." He named Esther Cole Franklin, director of the AAUW national consumer education program, as his consumer relations adviser. He also instructed regional administrators to set up district committees to recruit more community organizations into OPA enforcement. Price controls—by enlisting consumers at the grass roots to extend state supervision of private marketplace transactions—represented an attractive, vigorous model of New Deal economic management. From the time of their initiation through the spring of 1946—almost one year after the end of the war—roughly 75 percent of Americans approved of price controls. The widespread support revealed by polls and by participation in price panels signaled more than just wartime patriotism. Indeed, many believed that OPA would help deliver the postwar world of affordable abundance for which they longed. In recognition of its broad-based popularity, Republicans would not campaign against OPA in the 1944 elections.[70]

But OPA's very strength led to a forceful countermobilization. In mid-1944, Representative Howard Smith, a southern Democrat from Virginia, appealed to Republicans to "live up to your campaign promises that you were going to save the country from bureaucracy." As a landlord in Alexandria, Virginia, Smith felt persecuted by OPA rent controls, but his opposition to OPA was as much ideological as personal. For years, he had led the attack on New Deal agencies, especially the National Labor Relations Board. After the 1942 elections, he had pushed through the creation of the Special Committee to Investigate Acts of Executive Agencies beyond the Scope of Their Authority. What its name lacked in felicity, Smith made up for in zeal. In his opinion, OPA was perhaps the worst embodiment of New Deal efforts to regulate the market by issuing endless orders and mobilizing plebian groups. Congressional Republicans shared that perception. Senator John Bricker of Ohio regarded the seemingly innocuous consumer pledge program as a threat to local business. When the local League of Women Shoppers spearheaded the Columbus, Ohio, campaign, Bricker blocked it. Senator Robert Taft, also from Ohio, declared that OPA was doing too good a job. OPA is "holding the line so tight that everybody is making stuff for the Government practically at cost." "Price control," he declared, "has been overdone."[71]

OPA's consumer campaigns—for grade labeling, low-end production, and quality standards as well as for price control—faced stiff opposition from trade associations, merchants, and the farm bloc. Business representatives, from the local grocer to the leader of the National Association of Manufacturers, hated OPA because it insisted on making their private pricing decisions a matter of public debate. Industries with narrow profit margins, such as grocery, dry goods, textile, and meat, felt particularly aggrieved, for they could no longer take advantage of the wartime sellers' market. Grocery stores, for example, routinely resisted OPA's order to hang official price lists in easy-to-see locations. Smaller retailers found objectionable OPA's "free advertising" of cheaper prices at chain stores. Grocers eventually agreed to display price posters in exchange for OPA's ending the distribution of pocketbook-size lists directly to individual consumers.[72]

The fight over price lists typifies the compromises that OPA was forced to make. When the Consumer Advisory Committee heard of this deal with the grocers, its members became enraged, finding it morally repugnant and politically disastrous, on par only with sabotage. As the committee put it, "The objective of OPA is to keep prices in line rather than to decorate store interiors with posters of various kinds." They angrily told Chester Bowles, "To drop a plan for putting these ceiling prices into the hands of consumers would be tantamount to denying the principle of public participation in the enforcement of price control." For months they pushed for a reversal of this decision, claiming "that the only practical way, under wartime conditions of time problems, scarcities, and discrimination on the part of sellers, to arm the consumer with her weapon against inflation, is to give her a price ceiling list of her own." In some areas where OPA had already distributed the lists, consumer complaints had increased by 50 percent. But the generation of that kind of conflict was precisely the problem. Grocers could not abide the direct distribution to consumers of material that they saw as OPA price propaganda, and they fought to end the practice.[73]

OPA also lost the battle over low-end clothing. In the year and a half following the Hold the Line order, clothing costs went up by more than 10 percent, and the $1.98 dress that had been a staple of working-class budgets disappeared. The textile and garment industries proved extremely difficult to regulate. There were 3,500 mills, 18,000 apparel manufacturers, 3,400 wholesalers, and 900,000 retailers. New firms were constantly replacing old ones, and the fluidity of styles made many price rules irrelevant. As Bowles explained, no sooner did OPA set a price for the "dress with the rose on the left shoulder" than the manufacturer simply switched the rose to the right shoulder. In a sellers' market without competitive restraints or self-regulation, producers readily shifted to high-end, often poor-quality, merchandise. Many of those businesses had suffered during the Depression, but now the combination of wartime prosperity and scarcity brought the prospect of enormous short-term gains. During the 1944 extension hearings, Dr. Claudius Murchison, president of the Cotton Textile Institute, made it clear that OPA could expect an all-out revolt from the congressional cotton bloc.[74]

In their efforts to resist OPA regulation of their production and pricing decisions, businessmen received help from other government agencies, especially the War Production Board (WPB), whose control over materials could influence the supply of various commodities. Production of low-end commodities became the main source of controversy between OPA and WPB. According to OPA executives, mass consumption required not only universal purchasing power but also cheaply priced merchandise in large quantities. Yet manufacturers switched to higher-end goods to reap bigger profits. Only WPB had the authority to issue allocation orders, and it rarely heeded OPA's requests.

The conflict between OPA and WPB came to a head over the issue of work clothes. At the 1944 congressional hearings, Donald Montgomery, representing the UAW, complained of a dearth of low-end work clothes, children's clothes, sheetings, heavy-knit underwear, and other low-cost, low-profit items. He told the House committee, "Mr. Bowles is quoted as having said that the manufacturers engaged in a sit-down strike. Whether or not he said it, we believe it." I. J. Walz, president of the Big Jack Overall Company, insisted that producers would continue to turn away from low-end lines unless OPA granted them price relief. But OPA refused to comply. WPB issued a host of fashion directives, banning double-breasted jackets, wide skirt sweeps, and pant cuffs, but those orders then became an excuse for WPB not to take further action. OPA thus found itself unable to deliver the goods to its labor allies. Senator John Bankhead from Alabama proposed an amendment to raise the price of cotton goods that almost passed and surely would have exacerbated the clothing crisis that seemed imminent.[75]

OPA therefore faced a catch-22 dilemma. Only an effective, strong government agency could hold together an organized, cohesive consumer interest. But the very strength of this general consumer interest engendered fierce opposition and would soon be challenged by well-organized interests with more discrete agendas and strong congressional backers. With much success, OPA had united and relied upon a cross-class coalition of consumers who defended price stability in the public's interest. In the summer of 1944, the New York City Consumer Council sent fifteen thousand postcards to President Roosevelt, thanking him for his "inspiring leadership in the struggle to protect consumers' interests" and his "help fighting for renewal of price control and more funds for OPA." Thousands hailed Bowles as the "housewives' hero," a label that fueled an attack on him by Senator Robert Taft. "What you are doing is organizing consumers against business. . . . It is absolutely un-American and contrary to law and contrary to the Constitution. . . . OPA goes out and organizes one class of the community, say consumers, and says to them: 'Get together and help us enforce the law.'" As the end of the war approached, textile, dry goods, and other trade associations honed their arguments against OPA's "profit-squeezing intentions." Farm representatives fought an all-out battle against controls. And even most labor groups, who strongly identified with consumer interests, would abandon OPA as a sinking ship and worry first about securing a wage increase.[76]

OPA's weakness became apparent in the battle over meat. During the war, Americans had actually enlarged their annual consumption of meat from 127 to 150 pounds per capita. Thanks to larger incomes and the equity of rationing, the poorest third of the population increased their protein consumption by nearly 17 percent, compared with a roughly 4 percent decline among the wealthier two-thirds. OPA's emblem of a scale connoted a balance both among income groups and within diets as people adopted more nutritious eating habits.[77] But these wartime gains, combined with increased purchasing power, only fueled Americans' desire for more meat.

Though meat-company profits soared during the war, packers vociferously condemned price controls. Their complaints could be attributed in part to a structural transformation of the meat industry. Throughout the first half of the twentieth century, meat slaughtering had been dominated by five, and then four, large packers—Armour, Swift, Wilson, and

Cudahy. Together they accounted for more than half of the packing industry's output. Their production increased from nineteen billion to
twenty-five billion pounds in five wartime years. But the big packers experienced much frustration and anger. First, meat was not as profitable
overall as other food industries; and second, independent slaughterers
had eroded the packers' market share. The imposition of compulsory
federal grading during the war, which standardized meat cuts, making
brand names and private grading systems less important, allowed the independents to compete directly with the Big Four. And the big packers
found themselves subject to stricter enforcement than the independents, for the simple reason that these large firms were easier to regulate
than the thousands of new, fly-by-night slaughterhouses. As one black-
market butcher said, "All you need is a club or knife, a rope, a truck, and
a tree to hang the carcass while it drains, and you're in business."[78]

The American Meat Institute, which was the packers' trade association, therefore routinely blamed OPA policies for the disruption and
contamination of the country's meat supply. In ads and press releases, it
regularly invoked the specter of the black market and forecast "ex-
tremely serious" shortages. While retaining price controls, government
officials had derationed pork, veal, lamb, and mutton in 1944, partly in
response to the packers' lobbying pressure and partly because the regu-
lators had miscalculated the timing of the war's end. The Consumer
Advisory Committee protested vehemently, warning that this would result in shortages, particularly for working women, who would find empty
shelves by the time they got to the market. In December, OPA reversed
itself and announced the return of rationing. Real shortages did appear
in 1945, lending fuel to the packer-inspired predictions of scarcity,
famine, and black markets. According to trade representatives, price
controls that did not allow for "adequate profit margins" pushed producers out of the legitimate market and into the black market. One packer
summed up the industry's views by charging that OPA forced the industry to choose between "going broke or going black." Farm-bloc politicians sympathized with the packers' sense of frustration and condoned
their lawlessness. Republican senator Harlan Bushfield of South Dakota
declared, "If my family needs meat I am going to get it wherever I can."[79]

OPA was the lightning rod for a major showdown over the future of
the New Deal state. Roosevelt handily won reelection in 1944, and the
Democrats regained some lost ground. Labor, especially the newly organized CIO Political Action Committee, made a well-financed, sustained
push to get out the vote, and Democrats did well in urban areas. But the
election confirmed the trend that had begun in 1942, with Republicans
scoring their greatest victories among some of OPA's fiercest opponents
in the Midwest. OPA was so alarming because its power manifested itself

daily in all aspects of American business and because it was, rightfully, considered only the boldest part of a broader New Deal project to institutionalize regulatory authority and mass economic citizenship. In early 1945, food wholesalers issued a denunciation of the agency: "The overseers are the real saboteurs of this country and Chester Bowles is a traitor." Furious at OPA's unwillingness to raise clothing prices, Representative Fred Hartley, a New Jersey Republican, excoriated OPA executives as "blundering bureaucrats" and insisted that "OPA has no business in using its powers to control a man's profits."[80]

Bowles viewed the preservation of price controls as part of an implied social contract. "The American people will insist that the fight against runaway prices be continued until the danger is over," he wrote to Roosevelt on April 7, 1945, just before the president's death. Strong presidential leadership to maintain controls during reconversion to a peacetime economy would be essential in the face of mounting congressional opposition. Bowles explained that many workers had benefited substantially from higher wages, new jobs, overtime pay, and longer hours. But, at the urging of government voluntary savings campaigns, Americans had stored away one-quarter of their disposable income. Controls, Bowles believed, would still be essential to preserve the value of those savings. In addition, Bowles's vision of postwar prosperity rested on the New Deal purchasing-power agenda of low prices and high wages. Pent-up demand would provide an enormous peacetime market, but only if the government guaranteed that runaway prices did not wipe out savings. Bowles turned on his former advertising colleagues by explaining that products would basically sell themselves, thus enabling manufacturers to cover the costs of reconversion to civilian products without higher prices. In early 1945, he made a major enemy of mass-market retailers by insisting that distributors also would have to absorb increased costs of reconversion. Not only would businesses have to keep their prices in check; they would also have to pay high wages to maintain mass markets, especially when labor would face job and hour cutbacks after V-E day. Bowles concluded, "Mass purchasing power is the indispensable basis of the prosperity we seek."[81]

Labor threw its energy into preserving OPA and forcefully advanced a purchasing-power argument. Donald Montgomery, now chairman of the CIO Cost of Living Committee, argued that weakened stabilization policies would not "assure adequate real purchasing power in the hands of workers necessary to support full employment." The cost-plus pricing that OPA opponents were seeking "curtails purchasing power of workers' incomes and inevitably spells disaster." The end of overtime and the downgrading of jobs would mean a decline in the annual payroll. Basic wage rates would thus have to be increased to offset cutbacks, layoffs, and loss of overtime. It was essential to "assure equity to workers now and to maintain the purchasing power of wages when V-E day arrives." At the 1945 OPA renewal hearings, Philip Murray insisted, "Wages must be substantially increased now to prevent a disastrous fall in workers' purchasing power after V-E day." A "deflationary gap" would have consequences for all Americans. "If labor loses purchasing power, it will lose jobs. If labor loses jobs, all other workers—farmers, white collar, professional and middle class—will suffer." An aide to Montgomery put it succinctly: "The C.I.O. is showing that the only investment opportunity now existing is in so increasing wages and purchasing power that the goods now possible of manufacture can be sold to increase the profit opportunity of business."[82] Rising prices would only widen the deflationary gap between workers' declining income and national production.

Popular support for OPA remained high. In May 1945, women's and labor groups united to call for a postwar extension of OPA and insisted that they would not settle for a "negotiated peace." They joined together to launch a Fight Inflation Week campaign. Through boycotts and buyers' strikes, they planned to oppose any efforts to weaken OPA and raise prices. Ruth Lamb Atkinson appeared at the 1945 hearings on behalf of twelve middle-class national women's organizations that collectively had millions of members. The League of Women Shoppers denounced the packers' argument that higher prices would lead to more meat as based on a "false economic theory." Ten other national consumer groups also endorsed OPA. At the same time, New York City women marched with baby carriages through the local shopping district and chanted, "Keep prices down, pay no more than ceiling."[83]

OPA defenders saw price controls as more than just a wartime measure. To them, OPA represented the culmination of the drive for the government's guarantee of economic citizenship. They defended their position as consumers who had to make the most of their family income. "We are an organization of housewives and we are the women who actually go out to the stores and spend the pay checks," asserted Eleanor Fowler of the CIO Women's Auxiliary. Catherine Gelles of the UAW-CIO Women's Auxiliary explained, "Housewives don't know statistics, but they do know what it costs them to get essential food and clothing for the family." They insisted that OPA was the key to protecting their family income from erosion, especially as the end of the war would bring a reduction in paychecks. While controls would clearly not last forever, they viewed OPA's temporary extension as a down payment on future governmental protection. Helen Hall of the National Federation of Settlements explained, "Long since, [housewives] had to transmute much of the pioneering woman's household enterprise into ability to bargain well in the modern marketplace. But they have only gradually become aware of how helpless they are there as individuals, and what kinds of protection they should have at their elbows. That is what they are asking you to supply them."[84]

The Price Control Act passed largely intact and extended OPA's life for another year. A Roper poll in June 1945 reported that 80 percent of the public favored a continuation of controls. Polls conducted by the American Institute of Public Opinion, the National Opinion Research Center, and the Office of War Information discovered similar widespread support. A Bureau of the Budget survey of public opinion found that "the fear of removing controls too soon submerges fear of keeping them too long."[85] As all middle-aged Americans remembered, prices had shot up in the months after the last war.

Widespread popular support for OPA lasted beyond V-J day. The more OPA seemed to be effective, the more support it garnered. Indeed, by 1945, OPA had enhanced its enforcement division, adding to its strength. OPA enforcement staff investigated over 1 million cases and initiated serious actions in over 250,000 of them. By 1945, these cases accounted for 10 percent of all federal court cases, including war offenses; 4,000 were being filed a month. The ending of the war did not slow operations at the local level. The total number of violations reported by volunteer price panels between January 1945 and June 1946 was 1,375,380.[86]

The tougher OPA stood against price agitation by trade associations, the more consumers supported it. The public understood that OPA's enemies were certain producer groups, not generalized inflation or labor in particular. Addressing himself to Chester Bowles after OPA's refusal to increase auto prices, one pleased constituent wrote, "We who have to buy cars are for you and are deeply appreciative of the guts you have displayed in standing up [for] the consumer. Come to Texas and we'll elect you Governor." Housewives looked up to OPA as their personal champion. "I speak for thousands of housewives who want prices kept under control. . . . [L]et the National Association of Manufacturers sweat." Another claimed that her "knowledge of economics is equal to that of a new-born babe. But . . . if the moral support of a mere housewife is of any use to you, it is yours." Regardless of income or occupation, OPA supporters identified themselves as consumers who belonged to one big group of underrepresented citizens. "From one of the 125 million without a pressure group to lobby for us. Wish to commend your stand on the Auto prices as a means of combating inflation." Another wrote on behalf of the "twenty-five girls who work in the same office as I [and] are one-hundred percent for the O.P.A." She lamented that "individuals are not organized as thoroughly as big business so that they could really get behind the O.P.A." Several months after the return to peace, three-quarters of the public continued to pin their hopes for affordable abundance on the extension of OPA price controls. A spring 1946 *Fortune* survey showed 67.2 percent of the public favoring price controls for another year with 70.7 percent of all women, 75.9 percent of all Democrats, and even 60 percent of the "well-to-do" also voting in favor of extension.[87]

OPA did not only serve immediate consumer interests. More broadly it represented a political culture based on popular participation and economic rights. OPA mobilized citizens to enforce cheap prices and the equitable distribution of goods. And, indeed, consumption increased during the war, gains that OPA convinced consumers were something they deserved. Their sense of entitlement and expectation had deep roots in the promise of the mass market itself. What had begun in the marketplace gained political confirmation during World War I, the New Deal, and, most dramatically, World War II, when government officials legitimized the notion of a fair price and turned to consumers to institute market policies that exceeded the authority of a democratic regime. But that popular mobilization made an expanded regulatory government all the more threatening, especially when organized labor also lined up behind this consumer agenda. With broad popular support, OPA easily survived into peacetime and found itself at the center of a highly charged debate over America's postwar political economy.

Pocketbook Politics in an Age of Inflation, 1946–1960

WITH the end of the war, all the earlier conflicts over the nation's economy and social structure resurfaced and quickly assumed top place on the political agenda. The Office of Price Administration (OPA) had succeeded too well in conveying the image that inflation was an evil that could be controlled. Consumer groups were mobilized to defend their interests. They were joined by a trade-union movement that in five wartime years had grown from ten million to fifteen million people, representing 30 percent of the nonagricultural workforce. Like labor, organized consumers were now equipped and ready to protect their wartime gains. Supporters and opponents alike viewed OPA as the culmination of twelve years of politicized bargaining over prices and wages, resulting in powerful unions, mobilized consumers, and a strong state that institutionalized and legitimized an expansive notion of economic citizenship.

The National Association of Manufacturers (NAM) labeled this system "regimented chaos," a phrase that suggested a large bureaucratic state with the ability to rally disruptive grassroots forces. At the end of the war, Alfred Sloan of General Motors captured the business community's resolve to do away with this government-sponsored anarchy: "It took fourteen years to rid this country of prohibition. It is going to take a good while to rid the country of the New Deal, but sooner or later the ax falls and we get a change."[1] In 1946, NAM launched an enormous public-relations campaign, claiming that prosperity and abundance would be possible only with the demise of OPA. This marked the beginning of an all-out assault on the New Deal and its allies.

Eliminating price controls in the fall of 1946, opponents then sought to dismantle organized labor's capacity to politicize wages and prices through strikes, political mobilization, and interunion solidarity. A perennial, potentially fatal, fault line in the purchasing-power program was labor's ability to push up prices. Inflation, or rather the lack of control over rising prices, emerged as the Achilles' heel of postwar labor liberalism. Middle-class consumers supported labor's right to higher wages and to organize, but not when those rights resulted in higher prices, disruptive strikes, and general social chaos. As labor became more powerful and as its leadership gained a reputation for being corrupt and self-serving, its interests increasingly seemed at odds with those of the general public. New Deal opponents moved to exploit this tension as a way of unhinging the coalition of consumers and labor that had been forged during the Depression and World War II.

Had Enough? 1946

The renewed debate over price controls after the war precipitated another full-scale battle for consumers' hearts, minds, and stomachs. Business wanted to abolish controls and let the market take over. But in pleading for OPA's renewal in 1946, price executives insisted that only its continuation could assure postwar plenty at affordable prices. The greatest inflationary threat, they warned, would come after the war, and thus they asked for an extension of controls until the summer of 1947. In December 1945, OPA's Chester Bowles condemned NAM's call for the elimination of price controls by February 15, 1946, as "reckless in the extreme." Days before, Bowles had told his congressional enemies, "Among the most punishing blows of war—next to the loss of life—is the devastating effect of inflation. While prices are soaring it destroys the value of savings deposits, bonds and insurance policies, and puts pensioners, disabled veterans, people living on annuities and white-collar workers in a tragic squeeze." "At all costs the nation must be protected from postwar inflation."[2]

Business representatives, of course, were quick to reject OPA's vision of prosperity under controls. No longer constrained by wartime patriotism, NAM spent three million dollars in a major media blitz against OPA. The National Retail Dry Goods Association hosted a "chambers of horrors" exhibit in the Senate and House office buildings that featured shoddy goods tagged with high prices. Describing these items, Senator Kenneth Wherry, a Republican from Nebraska and leading opponent of OPA, fumed, "That's the kind of sacks Chester Bowles is hanging on the women of America."[3] OPA's enemies promised that a return to free enterprise would bring high levels of production at stable prices.

This postwar conflict over OPA was fought on two fronts. The first battle for popular support was waged in butcher shops and kitchens. The second took place among the policymaking elite in the executive offices of Detroit, Pittsburgh, and Washington. On Capitol Hill, OPA's congressional critics became more vocal and aggressive, while the Truman administration inadvertently undermined OPA's position by bungling postwar reconversion. Top economic policymakers had no coherent strategy to deal with the upward pressure on prices that resulted from burgeoning postwar demand, wartime savings, and the huge increase in the money supply and short-term government bonds. Secretary of Agriculture Clinton Anderson's suggestion that there would be a quick end to controls caused the meat packers to hold their products back. In addition, a serious international food crisis forced the diversion of wheat from feed for cattle to exports. The administration was internally divided on both agricultural policy and labor relations, while conflicting economic forecasts complicated planning. Proposals ranged from Bernard Baruch's call for rapid removal of all controls to Secretary of Commerce Henry Wallace's vision of a nationally planned economy, which he laid out in his book *Sixty Million Jobs.*[4]

The wage-price policy dominated the reconversion debate. Within the administration, Bowles argued forcefully that the end of the excess-profit tax, combined with increases in productivity and profits, would enable companies to absorb higher wages without initiating price increases. Inflationary pressures would be temporary during reconversion. In Bowles's view, insufficient purchasing power brought on by a reduction in overtime pay, job reclassification, and surplus labor posed larger threats. *New Republic* editor George Soule asserted, "Both social and economic policy demand that a general increase of purchasing power and real income should be directed as far as possible toward the lower-paid strata of the population." "In the end," he concluded, "a gain in currently earned purchasing power will be necessary for full employment." Soule and his Labor Bureau allies had made this argument at the end of World War I, but now their logic held sway at the highest levels of government. After V-J day, President Truman endorsed lifting the lid on wage controls, without ending OPA.[5]

Labor began to craft its own postwar strategy. Union leaders continued to support price controls while insisting on higher wages. In August 1945, Walter Reuther of the United Automobile Workers (UAW) demanded a 30 percent wage hike from General Motors (GM) with no corresponding price increase. Reuther understood that labor demands could alienate public support if business passed on higher wages to consumers. If GM refused to honor either its wage or its price demand, the UAW would strike. Reuther's announcement was a gambit to force concessions from industry while putting pressure on the administration to maintain price controls. Higher prices would not only anger consumers but would also put Reuther and other labor leaders in the unenviable position of having to insist on continuous wage hikes as inflation eroded income gains.

Union leaders had been under enormous rank-and-file pressure for years. Workers in higher-paid industries had routinely contested the Little Steel formula, not least because the weekly earnings of textile and retail workers, for example, rose 50 percent faster than the pay of steel and auto workers, while the overall wages of black workers expanded twice as quickly as the wages of white workers. Unions wanted higher wages, and they were also determined to preserve wartime improvements in vacation pay, sick leave, paid mealtimes, seniority, and grievance handling. Yet industry stood poised to refuse all wage demands, thus guaranteeing a massive strike wave.

The slogan "Purchasing Power for Prosperity" that the UAW used for its strike against GM was a deliberate ploy to couch its wage demands in the public interest. Taking their cue from OPA economists, unionists argued that only their formula of high wages and low prices would prevent depression and sustain postwar prosperity. National production had nearly doubled in just five wartime years. Without adequate consumer purchasing power, Reuther maintained, the marketplace would choke on its own products. With the advice of longtime consumer advocate and trusted counselor Donald Montgomery, Reuther argued for an increase in real wages accompanied by price stability. Thus the UAW leader rejected GM's offer of a thirteen-and-a-half-cent wage increase without a guarantee of price restraint, and in November 1945, he led the autoworkers on a strike that lasted 113 days. Reuther explained, "We will not be a party to sand-bagging the American customer." Instead, he said, "We fight to make progress with the community and not at the expense of the community."[6]

The key issue for both the UAW and GM was price control. Public support for OPA ran as high as 70 percent; support for union wage demands was only slightly lower. Reuther prodded GM executives to "open their books" in order to demonstrate their "ability to pay" wage increases without imposing higher prices. As consumers' counsel, Montgomery had fought for open-book clauses in the Agricultural Adjustment Administration's (AAA) marketing agreements. Now the UAW highlighted that demand in its public-relations campaign. The UAW leader insisted, "The American people are entitled to know all the facts with respect to industries' current pressure campaign to smash price control." This battle with GM represented the culmination of consumer demands for reasonable prices that Walter Lippmann had observed on the Lower East Side three decades earlier. GM refused and aptly summarized what was at stake. "The UAW-CIO is reaching for power. . . . It leads surely to the day when union bosses . . . will seek to tell us what we can make, when we can make it, where we can make it, and how much we can charge." George Romney of the Automobile Manufacturers' Association demonized Reuther as "the most dangerous man in Detroit." "No one is more skillful in bringing about the revolution without seeming to disturb the existing forms of society."[7]

In the winter of 1945–1946, conditions did seem revolutionary as millions of workers across the country struck for higher wages. Labor walked out in the oil, electrical goods, coal, railroad, glass, steel, rubber, and meat industries, causing the loss of more workdays in January and February alone than during the entire war. Thus 1946 became the record year for man-days lost and workers on the picket lines. Even amid this turmoil, or perhaps because of it, consumer groups continued to support OPA. Leading liberals, including Eleanor Roosevelt and Leon Henderson, formed the Citizens Committee to Save OPA. These New Deal voices joined labor's in a strong defense of OPA. The allied groups recognized that, without OPA, it would be hard to maintain a united front and sustain the New Deal's momentum.[8]

The great steel strike of early 1946 ended in a critical defeat for the purchasing-power program. When the United Steelworkers walked off the job to gain a thirty-cent wage hike, steel executives insisted to the administration that they could not afford to accede to the union's demands without a five-dollar-per-ton price increase. Bowles recognized the necessity of moderate relief, but other policymakers who were hostile to OPA and the social unrest it generated ignored his economic data and instead argued for granting industry's demands. John Snyder, director of the Office of War Mobilization and Reconversion, encouraged steel-industry intransigence by promising favorable price concessions behind closed doors. Truman, who had been in office for less than a year, thought labor's program was nothing more than a grab for power. Following Snyder's lead, in January 1946 the administration promised steel a price increase of twice the amount OPA had calculated as necessary. In turn, steel put on the table an eighteen-and-a-half-cent wage increase, which Philip Murray, president of the United Steelworkers, readily accepted. Murray was unwilling to prolong the steel strike to defend OPA. Reuther kept his workers out, even when GM offered the same deal, but his stance was undermined by the administration's capitulation. Although Truman claimed that this price concession did not represent "a new line . . . [but] a bulge in the old line," his decision to compromise on steel gave business the opening it was seeking.[9]

Legislative opposition to price control, especially by congressmen representing ranchers, textile makers, and wheat growers, gathered strength and dimmed any chances of extending OPA into the postwar years in its existing form. On June 28, 1946, two days before its authorization was set to expire, Congress presented the president with a severely weakened price-control bill that made OPA a paper tiger. Senator Robert Taft of Ohio and Senator Kenneth Wherry of Nebraska inserted amendments that effectively required a cost-plus pricing scheme. In announcing his veto on June 29, Truman claimed that Congress had given

'Grass Roots' Lobbyists March for OPA Extension

FIGURE 6.1. Women from across the nation gathered in the nation's capital to demand OPA renewal in the spring of 1946. Teachers, veterans' wives, and other middle-class activists joined organized labor in defending this agency against its legislative enemies.

him "a choice of inflation with a statute or inflation without one." Organized consumer groups rallied behind OPA throughout the spring, leaders of women's groups from all parts of the country journeyed to Washington, D.C., to demonstrate their support for the agency, and opinion polls reflected its continuing popularity. Emboldened by public sentiment, Truman's advisers hoped the veto might scare Congress into scaling back the attempt to gut price controls, but that plan soon backfired. On July 1, OPA became defunct. In three days, wholesale prices went to their highest level since 1920. Within two weeks, retail meat prices rose 30 percent. From June 15 to July 15, the cost of living went up 5.5 percent, the single highest one-month jump ever recorded by the Bureau of Labor Statistics (BLS). Confirming the politicized nature of meat supply and prices, packers instantly rushed undernourished cattle to market at exorbitant prices. By September, the cost of meat had doubled, from thirty-five cents to seventy cents per pound.[10]

Despite the administrative retreat and the apparent victory of organized business and farm interests, OPA remained amazingly popular. Within days of Truman's veto, thousands of letters streamed in to the Senate Banking and Currency Committee, with supporters for OPA's renewal outnumbering opponents by twenty to one. Not since President Roosevelt's court-packing plan had citizens sent as many letters and telegrams on any single issue, though in this case they were backing strong governmental action. In the nation's capital, Annie Stein of the CIO's Women's Auxiliary led a successful consumers' boycott of meat to protest prices. Within two weeks, the Washington Committee for Consumer Protection collected forty thousand signatures and spread "Don't Buy High" buttons throughout the city. They distributed cards listing old and new prices that read "Compare your prices" and urged consumers not to pay more than 60 cents per pound of meat. Many stores soon announced "sale on steak for 59 cents a pound." Meanwhile, in Cadillac Square, labor's new rallying ground, Reuther urged forty thousand Detroit citizens to inaugurate a meat buyers' strike to "terrorize profiteers" and gain lower prices. Labor came out in numbers, proclaiming "CIO Fights for OPA Extension." Workers did not stand alone. As *Business Week* reported, "What really bothers the businessman is not the parades and the speeches—though their nuisance value is unquestioned—but the attitude that the great, inarticulate mass of consumers will adopt." In response to this popular outpouring, Congress quickly reinstituted controls at the end of July, though they were no stronger than the ones Truman had vetoed. One provision exempted meat and several other agricultural products until a special board could review the situation. Only on September 1 did meat return to price controls. And even then the secretary of agriculture had the right to raise prices, which he subsequently did.[11]

Now meat producers moved in for the kill. They sought to bring an end to OPA once and for all. Advancing the battle lines from the halls of Congress to the local butcher shops and into household kitchens, the packers withheld their meat from the market in an attempt to create panic and force the public into submission. After a week of the renewed controls, they decreased the rate of slaughter by 25 percent. Secretary Anderson urged the packers to send meat to market and insisted that "price adjustments are now behind us," but his rhetoric came too little and too late. By the middle of September, slaughtering had dropped 80 percent from the level recorded for the same period in 1945. The BLS soon ceased making comparisons because there was not enough beef, pork, and veal in the stores to measure. Ninety percent of the butcher shops in Chicago were closed. While their cattle grew fatter, the packers could afford to wait out the situation. All they had to do was win the public to their side.[12]

The missing meat became the top news event, exaggerated in the press as a "famine." In story after story, journalists relayed tales of housewives mobbing local stores, hospitals serving horse meat, and "steakleggers" making meat runs across the Canadian border. Fanning the hysteria, a typical *Times* headline announced, "Queens Restaurateur, Worried over Meat, Dives off Brooklyn Bridge," while another proclaimed, "Horse Meat Consumption by New Yorkers Is Rising." Journalist A. J. Liebling described Americans as suffering from "the great Gouamba," an African expression with no English equivalent that meant "inordinate longing and craving of exhausted nature for meat." Though indeed sensational, especially in the context of the real food shortages spreading across Europe, this coverage accurately reflected the pandemonium generated by the meat crisis.[13]

The methods OPA had chosen to legitimize and constitute its authority contributed to its defeat. By uniting consumers, labor, and the state in pursuit of "fair prices," OPA drew its strength from a sea of forces that was at once too wide and too shallow. Precisely because OPA mobilized consumers and gave them a sense of entitlement, it came under severe attack from producers and, as it turned out, from the same people who composed its support. Meat producers' decision in 1946 to withhold their product from market in a "packers' strike," rather than sell under controlled conditions, precipitated the final showdown. After weeks of bare butcher shops and a rampant black market, the public lost confidence in OPA. NAM took out full-page ads against controls, asking, "Would you like some butter or a roast of beef?" Echoing the question, one disgruntled consumer wrote a curt letter to President Truman that demanded, "How About Some Meat?"[14]

Consumers now regarded OPA as ineffectual, no longer able to control inflation and distribute goods equitably. With plenty of meat apparently in reserve, waiting to come to market, the public lost its faith in OPA's ability to act as its defender. A New York housewife summarized the situation: "We, the consumer have three alternatives. No meat, Horse Meat, or exorbitant under-counter dealings." Fed up with OPA's inability to face down its enemies and force meat from the hoof to the table, the public mood turned to anger and apathy. From May to October of 1946, approval of price controls fell from roughly 80 percent to just over 40 percent. As another disheartened consumer explained, "There is no more hope of enforcing O.P.A. than of Prohibition. . . . Why not call it a day and quit?"[15]

Unable to deliver the goods, the agency alienated and disappointed the very consumers who had been its backers, while its labor allies scrambled to shore up their positions at the bargaining table. Indeed, consumers who had relied on OPA to represent them against better-organized interests became resentful when OPA seemed to be capitulating to powerful lobbies. As a Hartford housewife complained, "the OPA might just as well be passed with all its emasculating amendments if you are going to grant increases to individual industries. . . . [I]f increases are going to be granted to certain favored industries such as steel, the farmers, and various others, then I'm obliged to assume you're not doing your job as the people hope and expect you to." A Brooklyn resident claimed that rising gasoline and car prices "indicate a decided tendency on your part to cater to the whims of the high pressure lobby boys who seemingly occupy offices adjacent to your own."[16]

When confronted with the choice of no meat or high-priced, free-market meat, Americans chose the latter. A transformation of political consciousness was at work. Up to that time, more than three-quarters of the public had implicitly favored the highly intrusive government agency because they viewed OPA and the restrictions it imposed as a necessary component of wartime sacrifice and patriotism. But they had also supported OPA because it worked. Prices had remained relatively steady, and rationing ensured an equitable distribution. Now the packers' strike undermined the legitimacy of controls, making OPA powerless to remedy this situation. Though seemingly simple, the question, "How About Some Meat?" reflected a deeper debate about the efficacy and authority of the New Deal regulatory state. Opposition to OPA that had once been concentrated among particular producer interests spread among urban and middle-class consumers who had been OPA's strongest supporters and put mounting electoral pressure on politicians to address the situation.[17]

Women, in particular, felt betrayed. They wanted meat back in their diet and now looked on price control as the culprit. "How long are the American housewives going to stand this O.P.A.," wrote one New York housewife. "We are sick and tired of it." Another asked, "Just what kind of nerves does your administration believe a housewife has? . . . [signed] Another meatless weekend." Many women perceived themselves as unfairly victimized. "I am just one of the many thousands of harassed housewives trying to feed a family and keep them healthy during these days of 'no Meat.'" If the OPA presence had once emboldened them on their daily marketing trips, these housewives now felt abandoned. Another letter to Paul Porter, OPA's new administrator, began, "You, obviously, are not a housewife or the family cook. Were I addressing Mrs. Paul Porter, she would probably know a little about my problem. It, therefore, would be my suggestion that you take over the shopping chores for the household for just one week. And I would like to be there at the end of the week to hear you yell 'uncle.'" These women made it clear that they planned to avenge their sense of powerlessness in the voting booths. As one woman put it, "The angry voice of the un-organized housewife, who is helpless at the moment, will have her day of being heard at the FORTHCOMING ELECTIONS." Many insisted, "We are going to have some new faces in Washington."[18]

Fearing voter retribution and feeling pressure from Democratic politicians across the country, Truman finally capitulated and lifted controls on October 15, two weeks before the election. But this last-minute tactic further angered voters, especially those who continued to hold out hope for OPA, and fueled a sense of "administrative bungling" and "mismanagement." The charges its opponents had always leveled took on added resonance as OPA indeed appeared as an inefficient and ineffective Washington bureaucracy that interfered with the successful functioning of a free market. Moreover, the administration's about-face did not bring meat to market. The year 1946 marked the beginning of the Cold War era, in which foreign policy and fears of communism shaped political discourse. But domestic issues, particularly the labor strikes and the debate over OPA, dominated the so-called beefsteak elections of 1946, in which voters blamed ineffectual government price controls for their meatless dinner plates. While unions flexed their muscles in defense of their members, the OPA stood by powerless, unable to offer the public any price protection. With OPA in shambles, the Republicans' promise of a control-free prosperity gained appeal. The subsequent Republican victory prompted President Truman—in an undelivered speech—to criticize American voters for "desert[ing] your president for a mess of pottage, a piece of beef—a side of bacon."[19]

For the first time since 1930, the electorate returned control of Congress to the Republicans. In 1946, voters responded in the affirmative to the Republicans' simple slogan, "Had Enough?" That question referred to the panoply of New Deal and wartime controls and regulations. Republican strategy played on anticommunist fears, targeting price controls as the centerpiece of a debate that played up the specter of Soviet-style "bureaucratic regimentation" and "totalitarian shackles." In southern California's Twelfth Congressional District, Richard Nixon won his first election by beating five-time Democratic incumbent and OPA supporter Jerry Voorhis. Nixon defeated Voorhis by associating him with ineffective price controls and the Congress of Industrial Organizations' Political Action Committee. As one Nixon voter put it, "If you are for the continuation of the New Deal and its bureaucratic control and regimentation of the American people, then you would naturally vote for Jerry." Soon after the elections, the administration dissolved OPA. Within the year, livestock prices went up 47 percent, wholesale meat prices soared 89 percent, and retail meat prices rose 61 percent. Overall, consumer prices shot up 16 percent. Those dizzying jumps would lead Americans to demand the renewal of controls, but once Republicans were securely in place, it was too late to bring OPA back to life.[20]

The damage to the Democrats went beyond even their original fears. The party lost eleven seats in the Senate and fifty-three in the House. The election solidified the voting patterns that had begun to take shape in the 1942 and 1944 elections, when Republicans scored victories in rural and small-town America. Democrats experienced devastating defeats in all rural districts in the Midwest. Conservative Democrats retained the South, and these representatives would join the Republicans in thwarting labor's power and blocking further New Deal ambitions. The decisive votes occurred in the border states and suburban areas between the Democratic urban strongholds and the Republican-dominated rural areas. That was largely because ten million disenchanted Democrats, many from working-class, urban communities, who had voted in 1944 now simply stayed home. In suburban Westchester County, New York, no Democrat received more than a third of the vote, while in New York City, working-class people did not go to the polls, giving the Republicans a victory. Democrats lost Philadelphia, Boston, Saint Louis, Pittsburgh, Detroit, Cleveland, and Los Angeles as a result of low voter turnout. Whereas OPA's success had earlier galvanized the public, its failure now demobilized millions and diminished public support for an activist state.[21]

Industrywide Bargaining Is No Bargain for You, 1947–1952

Just as problematic an enemy to conservatives was the power of organized labor. OPA was dead, but the labor movement most definitely was not. From wages to prices to politics, unions yielded considerable influence. As the strikes of the postwar years showed, strong unions could challenge employers' right to manage the shop floor. Even more threatening, especially to competitive industries in low-wage areas, large unions could make bargains for wages and benefits that affected the cost structure of an entire industry. Industrywide bargaining was a thorn in the side of small producers everywhere, for those who struggled to rebuff unionization efforts, and especially for those who failed and thus paid higher costs than their nonunionized competitors. Many small producers felt particularly besieged given the competition that resulted from labor's uneven success at unionizing outside the Northeast and Midwest. Moreover, labor's demand for union security in mass-production industries meant that, as a condition of employment, employees had to join the trade union that represented the workforce in their factory or office. During the war, the National War Labor Board institutionalized a system that made employers responsible for automatically collecting union dues from workers' paychecks. Those dues funded huge union war chests for political campaigns and popular appeals. Containing union power was thus the number one goal of the Republican-controlled Eightieth Congress.

In their effort to restrict the power of collective bargaining, congressional conservatives and industry leaders sought to hold labor accountable for soaring living costs. Into the 1950s, labor opponents gained a growing audience for their warnings about the evils of inflation that resulted from "monopoly unionism." This catchphrase was a linguistic inversion of an earlier left-wing attack on monopoly capitalism. It spoke to both the real and the ideological concerns of small producers, who, unlike General Motors and General Electric, could not afford to pay high wages or to protect themselves from the costs of inflation by administering high prices in oligopolistic markets. The message of monopoly unionism, even if not an apt description of labor's power, appealed to unorganized, middle-class salaried workers and even to skilled blue-collar workers, who complained that their incomes grew more slowly than the pay of their less skilled counterparts. NAM now redirected its attack from OPA to the Congress of Industrial Organizations (CIO) and ran ads that declared, "Industry-wide bargaining is no bargain for you." In another, NAM blamed "labor monopoly" and industry-wide bargaining for "rais[ing] the prices of the things you need." A full-page ad read, "The price of MONOPOLY comes out of your pocket." "How about some Pro-Public legislation?" another NAM ad asked.[22] If successful, that campaign would not only undermine labor's power but also would weaken the New Deal consumer-worker coalition.

The acceleration of postwar inflation made the push for wage advances increasingly unpopular. Middle-class sympathy for labor's demands ran only so deep, especially as strikes continued. As inflation eroded income gains, union leaders came under constant pressure from their members to press for higher wages. Each round of annual contract negotiations produced what the business press labeled the "wage-price spiral." To prevail in their negotiations, unions engaged in mass picketing in front of factories, in downtown squares, and outside the homes of hostile businessmen and politicians. Moreover, sympathy strikes and secondary boycotts suggested the expansive, unpredictable quality of labor's actions. Truckers interrupted delivery of basic commodities like milk and newspapers, while transportation and coal strikes interfered with daily routines. General Electric president Charles Wilson, in a national ad paid for by the Bank of New York, declared, "The time has come when we must, not as business men but as citizens, examine and define that word 'strike.' It has been said for a long time that nothing must deprive labor of the right to strike." But, Wilson argued, "If today we mean by 'strike' such a situation as the Pittsburgh power strike, the maritime strikes, the New York tugboat and truckmen's strikes, and the threatened strikes of transportation workers, then labor has no such right, any more than any group has a right to starve, endanger, or destroy the society of which it is a part." As House Republican Francis Case of South Dakota put it, "There is no natural right to conspire against the public welfare."[23]

The absence of a strong government agency to restrain prices put labor on the defensive, especially when manufacturers used wage increases to justify raising their prices. Walter Reuther ruefully lamented, "Labor has no way to bargain collectively for price reductions." Workers grew disheartened while they watched price increases outpacing their wage gains. As higher prices ate into their savings and industry remained intransigent, workers became reluctant to strike. Autoworker Edward Pachowicz explained, "I don't like to strike. If I had a fortune in my pocket, I wouldn't care." Years of experience as a wartime presidential adviser led Bernard Baruch to sum up the situation with these dramatic words: "Inflation . . . next to human slaughter, maiming, and destruction, is the worst consequence of war. It creates lack of confidence of men in themselves and in their Government."[24]

The Truman administration, especially the newly created Council of Economic Advisers (CEA), endorsed labor's repeated demands for higher wages. Congress had created the CEA when it passed the Employment Act of 1946, which committed the government to maintaining "maximum production, maximum employment, and maximum purchasing power." The act reflected an ideological commitment to keep the wage-price question on the political agenda. Truman appointed Edwin Nourse, a well-respected conservative economist, as the CEA chairman in order to blunt the council's threat. But the president also appointed Leon Keyserling to the council in recognition of labor's continuing political influence. Keyserling had the support of Senator Robert Wagner and other congressional sponsors of the bill. Keyserling was also CIO president Philip Murray's top choice. Truman announced Keyserling's appointment when he signed a weakened version of the price-control bill in July 1946. With little authority or policymaking capacity, the CEA was hardly a substitute for OPA. But Keyserling's presence on the council did reflect labor's standing as a key constituent of the Democratic Party. Another Truman appointee, John D. Clark, was a New Deal supporter whose views coincided with Keyserling's.[25]

From the beginning, Keyserling and Nourse crossed swords. Nourse had been recommended for the post by NAM. As a former president of the American Farm Economics Association and the American Economic

Association, Nourse commanded considerable respect within the academic economic community. He had found a home in the Brookings Institution as vice president and, since 1942, had also been chairman of the Social Science Research Council. Nourse accepted the chairmanship begrudgingly. He wrote to Truman, "To accept this appointment would completely disrupt the program of professional work which I had laid out for myself for the coming years." However, in the name of "rendering public service," he continued, "I feel I cannot do other than accept." Throughout his tenure on the council, he maintained that the nature of his involvement was "science" and therefore above politics. He insisted to other CEA members, "There is no occasion for the Council to become involved in any way in the advocacy of particular measures or in the rival beliefs and struggles of the different economic and political interest groups." Keyserling responded, "While we economists have long talked in the refined atmosphere of theoretical underpinnings, we live in a world where prices and wages and profits are being made." In spite of Nourse's position as chairman, Keyserling's influence on the council and within the Truman administration would grow steadily.[26]

The rest of the staff shared Keyserling's laborite vision of political economy. Most of the economists had served in New Deal and wartime agencies. Walter Salant, Benjamin Caplan, and Susannah Calkins came from OPA. Edgar Hoover and Joseph Fisher had worked at the National Resources Planning Board. Many had also been at the Bureau of the Budget and the War Production Board and retained their liberal sympathies. Most regarded the Council of Economic Advisers as an extension of the New Deal state. And they accepted Keyserling's emphasis on mass purchasing power as the key to economic prosperity. In addition, they forged close contacts with White House staff members Clark Clifford, David Bell, Robert Turner, and Richard Neudstadt.[27]

The CIO saw Keyserling as a natural ally. In late 1946, it released the Nathan Report to popularize its purchasing-power platform. Robert Nathan, a former liberal planner with the War Production Board, left the government when John Snyder took over reconversion policy. Commissioning his services to the CIO, Nathan argued that corporations, flush with wartime profits, could afford to increase pay by 38 percent while keeping prices stable. Keyserling set out to prove the Nathan Report correct. Arguing that the council's responsibilities extended beyond "mere forecasting," he announced that it was up to the CEA, not the free market, to determine what the "components and composition of the g.n.p. *ought to be*." Keyserling worked closely with Gerhard Colm to formulate wage and price guidelines. Colm had been raised in Germany, where he served as an economist in the Weimar Republic, an experience that shaped his social democratic, statist orientation. As head of the CEA's Stabilization Devices Committee, he collaborated with Keyserling on formulating a reliable national income and pricing scheme to guide labor-management negotiations. The committee called for a $300 billion economy with a universal annual salary of $4,000 in the next decade. That was more than double the average income at the time.[28]

Their formulations struck fear into the hearts of the nation's businessmen, who repudiated this "purchasing power fallacy." As NAM explained, "The Nathan report is an attempt to fool the public into choosing higher wages which means higher prices. That obviously cannot be in the public interest." Emboldened by their victories in the 1946 elections, conservatives escalated their attack on the New Deal and its support of collective bargaining. General Electric president Charles Wilson criticized both labor and the administration. "Higher Prices are the legitimate result of the national wage-increase pattern which the present Administration has tolerated, if not actively abetted." Large producers in capital-intensive industries could afford to pay higher wages as the price of industrial stability. But those payments conflicted with funds needed to modernize production and develop new products. Moreover, small producers, whose labor costs were high, found the projected numbers alarming.[29] Without major gains in productivity, they could not pay these higher wages unless they also substantially raised prices. And the public was still deeply sensitive to spiraling prices.

OPA's defeat and the impressive Republican victory did not signal the end of pocketbook politics. Within months of the agency's demise, former OPA supporters from labor and the consumer movement pushed for the reintroduction of price controls on meat. In early 1947, Caroline Ware helped to form the National Association of Consumers, a body claiming to speak for ten million Americans. Their ranks came from the organized consumer movement, both left-wing and moderate. And their leadership included Stuart Chase, Robert Lynd, Evans Clark, Leon Henderson, Isador Lubin, and Eleanor Roosevelt. As inflation continued and business failed to deliver on its promise of abundance and stable prices, these consumer advocates had a ready audience. To conservatives' horror, the public began to clamor for controls as a remedy for inflationary prices.[30]

Alive to this issue, the White House appealed for voluntary price restraint. The small town of Newburyport, Massachusetts, gained national attention when, responding to Truman, 171 local merchants cut over-the-counter retail prices by 10 percent. Banners lined the streets, proclaiming, "Newburyport—Leading the Nation, Lowering Prices, Fighting Inflation." Within a week, the Newburyport Plan spread to Flushing, New York, Columbus, Ohio, Sherman Oaks, California, and 413 other communities across the country. Macy's and other mass retailers who feared consumer resistance demonstrated price restraint. But most businessmen, including the merchants of the president's hometown, Independence, Missouri, refused to participate. Truman's old haberdashery partner, Eddie Jacobson, declared the Newburyport Plan "ridiculous." The president's "price control by harangue" was undermined when major industries announced another round of price increases in the spring of 1947.[31]

The business community seized on this inflationary specter to hold labor accountable for disruptions to postwar prosperity. Their efforts crystallized in the Taft-Hartley Act of 1947. Under the leadership of Senator Robert Taft of Ohio, its conservative advocates argued that the public suffered from an excess of labor power. The goal of the act was to take back control of the shop floor. A key provision banned foremen from joining unions, to assure that they would be management's representatives in the factories. But the act's advocates fought just as hard to end unions' ability to politicize wages, profits, and prices by subjecting them to public debate. To that end, the law outlawed secondary boycotts and forbid the direct expenditure of union dues in political campaigns. The act also allowed states to pass "right-to-work" laws that would prohibit unions from requiring all workers in a factory to join the union as a condition of employment. That provision was intended to break the power of unions within individual factories as well as across industries nationwide.[32]

Defenders of the act demonized union leaders as labor bosses who subverted an individual's liberty of contract and the public welfare. Even Averell Harriman, FDR's secretary of commerce, a liberal businessman, and Mary Rumsey's brother, told a sympathetic NAM convention, "Labor power has grown to the point where we find one man defying the government and recklessly tearing down the life of the nation." Harriman had in mind United Mine Workers chief John Lewis, whom liberals ostracized as a "labor dictator," if only to differentiate him from more responsible union leaders. But Harriman's audience did not make such distinctions. At the Taft-Hartley hearings, George Kennedy, president of Kelsey-Hayes Wheel Corporation, raged, "Today Mr. Lewis has more control over the coal-mining business than the owners of the business. He can turn them on and off at his will. Mr. Murray can do the same thing in the steel business, and Mr. Reuther can do the same thing in the UAW-CIO." A House committee report explained, "The American working man has been deprived of his dignity as an individual. He has been cajoled, coerced, intimidated and on many occasions beaten up. . . . His whole economic life has been subject to the complete domination and control of unregulated monopolists."[33] Whereas fifty years ago, and even only a decade earlier, the term monopolist referred to Standard Oil or the meat packers' trust, these politicians now used it as a derisive label for union bosses.

Industrywide bargaining was not only un-American—it caused higher prices. That was the charge made by Taft, who laid blame on the Truman administration and its pro-labor policies. This condemnation reflected efforts to win middle-class support and also real fears that higher prices would revive calls for controls. In spite of its postwar floundering, OPA's wartime effectiveness remained a vivid popular memory. Thus, NAM president Ira Mosher warned, "Government intervention can become a habit leading to regulation of wages, hours, and other conditions of employment, and also of prices." Addressing the Republican National Committee, Alf Landon declared high prices as "more dangerous to free enterprise than the Communist Party." Smaller competitive industries also worried that they could not easily pass on higher labor costs to consumers.[34]

Organized labor devoted all its resources to defeating Taft-Hartley. The AFL and CIO unions had fought an internecine war in the late 1930s, but they stood united against this bill. To a packed protest rally at Madison Square Garden, CIO president Murray warned, "This bill turns the clock back. . . . It announces . . . that the forces of reaction want a show down with free American labor—and they want it now." He voiced his belief that it might bring about "years of depression and economic chaos." In Detroit, five hundred thousand autoworkers walked off the job for five hours. The AFL also condemned the "Slave-Labor Act." George Meany, secretary-treasurer of the AFL, saw it as enforcing "involuntary servitude." It "completely demolishes the natural, organic development which is collective bargaining, and substitutes, instead, what at best is paternalistic statism, and at worst, out and out dictatorship."[35]

The debate over Taft-Hartley accompanied a general rightward shift in American politics that was precipitated by the Cold War and fears of communism. In this environment, organized labor, especially the CIO, was particularly suspect because of its reliance on Communist leaders in key unions. Indeed, the Taft-Hartley Act required all union officials to pledge that they were non-Communist before their unions could stand in National Labor Relations Board–sanctioned elections. Truman was a fierce Cold Warrior, and the left-leaning tendencies of some CIO unions increased his innate suspicion of organized labor. But the political logic of the situation required Truman to support labor and its purchasing-power agenda, putting him in league with the New Deal elements he most disliked. While pursuing the Cold War, Truman pushed hard for an extension of the New Deal. His embrace of labor began with his opposition to Taft-Hartley.

Given his desire to be reelected, Truman had no choice but to defend labor against this legislative onslaught. The White House recruited Keyserling to draft Truman's veto. The Wagner Act had justified the right to organize and strike for the sake of "further[ing] a sounder distribution . . . of the proceeds of industry between management and labor." "By this test," Keyserling argued, "labor has not yet become 'too strong' compared with management," because "the distribution of purchasing power through the price-wage-profit relationship is still unbalanced." The president had to challenge "the fallacious idea" that "high wages and other privileges accorded labor are substantially responsible for the high cost of living." This idea "needs to be hit on the head—not once, but repeatedly." He wanted Truman to "torpedo the fallacy that high wages necessitate and justify high prices, and that only through lower wages can we have lower prices. Point out that this is contrary to the whole history of America's economic progress."[36] In the end, the results of the 1946 election deprived Truman of the congressional votes, and Taft-Hartley became law over his veto.

Truman's defense of labor became central to his 1948 presidential campaign. Since 1946, a group of liberal Democrats had met every Monday to plan Truman's electoral strategy. Called the Wardman Group after the Washington apartment house where they gathered, it consisted of Oscar Ewing of the Federal Security Administration, Assistant Secretary of Labor David Morse, Assistant Secretary of Agriculture Charles Brannan, White House adviser Clark Clifford, and Keyserling. All ardent New Dealers, this group plotted Truman's shift to the left, leading with his crucial veto of Taft-Hartley. This shift, they hoped, would reverse the disastrous electoral results of 1946 and return voters from the Democrats' base in northern cities to the pulls, particularly the urban working classes and ethnic minorities.[37]

The need to shore up a labor-liberal coalition became imperative when Truman faced challenges on his right and left. After having been fired as secretary of commerce for denouncing the administration's hard-line stance against the Soviets, Henry Wallace announced his candidacy on the Progressive Party ticket. Wallace's backing by Communists substantially diminished his potential support, but Truman had to be sure to hold on to his labor and urban constituencies. That need motivated the Democrats to support a civil rights platform, a move that prompted Strom Thurmond to lead the southern Dixiecrats out of the Democratic Party. To check the power of conservative planter oligarchs in the South and win support among small farmers, particularly in the Midwest, the Wardman Group persuaded Truman to sponsor the Brannan farm plan. That proposal called for paying cash subsidies to small farmers to produce meat and milk instead of surplus crops like grain and cotton. The hope was that these payments would yield a high volume of food at low costs. They crafted this proposal to reconcile the interests of farmers with those of middle-class consumers.

To appeal to the latter group, they also called for standby price controls.[38]

OPA opponents had promised too much, and New Dealers seized the moment. As prices continued upward in May 1947, former OPA administrators Chester Bowles, Leon Henderson, and Paul Porter pushed for a Price Adjustment Board. In his "Blueprint for a Second New Deal," Bowles recommended the reintroduction of grain controls, meat rationing, price ceilings for steel and other essential commodities in short supply, and government construction of steel mills if necessary. Bowles was a member of the Americans for Democratic Action (ADA), a leading liberal organization that counted all the OPA heads and other purchasing-power New Dealers among its ranks. Together, the ADA, the National Association of Consumers (NAC), the CIO Women's Auxiliary, and the League of Women Shoppers initiated a "Buy No Meat Week" in the summer of 1947. While Keyserling formulated Truman's economic platform, his wife, Mary Dublin Keyserling, a leader of NAC, mobilized consumers behind a bill for meat rationing and standby controls. As John Kenneth Galbraith explained before Congress, "To keep the society free from controls, one must use controls."[39]

Truman took up the anti-inflation battle as the theme of the 1948 election. He kicked off his campaign by convening a special congressional session in November 1947 to combat high prices. His program featured selective price controls and rationing measures. Immediately, Senator Taft, a likely contender for the upcoming presidential race, denounced Truman's agenda as "a step toward a completely totalitarian nation." But the platform appealed to Truman, who was more comfortable attacking big business and monopoly prices than supporting union rights. He also recognized that he had to shift blame away from organized labor if he was to hold together FDR's carefully constructed alliance of consumers and workers. In addition, Truman had to challenge the charge that his spending on European recovery, especially food aid, was the true source of inflation. Thus, he placed all the blame for inflation on his opponents, and, just as FDR had done in 1936, he came out swinging against big business as a way to keep his electoral coalition intact.[40]

Truman's shift to the left coincided with the crafting of a Cold War agenda. In March 1947, he announced the Truman Doctrine, committing the United States to a policy of communist containment worldwide. At home he initiated loyalty oaths for federal employees. According to journalist Samuel Lubell, for every one progressive step forward this Missouri populist took, he took two backward. But the 1948 campaign was a tribute to the politics of purchasing power. Although strongly influenced by the advice of many of his conservative cronies, in this election Truman presented himself as more radical than Roosevelt. Winning the

1948 election required him to be. This meant that while he was calling for anticommunist loyalty oaths he was also exchanging friendly letters with the president of the League of Women Shoppers, whose support he was happy to have.[41]

Truman turned the election into a referendum on OPA. In June of 1948, during the campaign, Truman insisted, "We should have a stand-by price control law to be put into effect when necessary—and it is necessary right now." Truman's call for controls played well. Consumer groups had renewed their protests against packers' high prices and called for reinstating rationing and price controls for meat. The nation's magazines printed pictures of boycotters picketing in the streets with placards that read "Bring Prices Down—Buy No Meat" and "Don't Bring Home the Bacon; Bring Down Prices." Helen Gahagan Douglas, glamorous Hollywood star turned California congresswoman, made national headlines when she shopped with her old OPA price list and expressed outrage at meat prices. Even retailers joined in the campaign. "We endorse consumer resistance," proclaimed the executive secretary of the Associated Food Dealers. Anthony D'Amelio, a New York meat dealer, declared "Down with These Drastic Meat Prices" and closed his doors to business. He hung a poster explaining, "The management of this store will not continue to sell meat. Prices are entirely too high!"[42]

The Democratic Party's Women's Division mobilized voters around this issue. Under India Edwards, former *Chicago Tribune* journalist, the division campaigned to get out the vote of young new housewives, a cohort that leaned to the Democrats but did not necessarily go to the polls. Accompanying Truman on his famous whistle-stop campaign, Edwards organized the "Housewives for Truman," a series of trailers in which household items were on display along with their high price tags that were blamed on the Eightieth Congress. At the Democratic convention, the first to be televised, Edwards addressed the delegates in a prime-time speech, dramatizing her fiery rhetoric by shoving a raw piece of high-priced meat at the camera with its blood dripping down her arm. The Women's Division followed up on this rousing performance with a series of "Headaches for Housewives" radio commercials.[43]

On the campaign trail, Truman seized any opportunity to blame inflation on the "Do-Nothing" Eightieth Congress. In Reading, Pennsylvania, he declared, "The Republicans don't want any price control for one simple reason: the higher the prices go up, the bigger the profits for the corporations." Truman called a second special congressional session in July 1948 to push again for controls. In October, at a mass rally in Kentucky that was broadcast nationwide, Truman accused NAM and big business of conducting an "organized conspiracy against the American consumer." After OPA, "prices adjusted themselves all right. They adjusted themselves

FIGURE 6.2. Organized labor saw a Democratic victory in the 1948 campaign as being essential for reversing the Taft-Hartley Act, which restricted their power and blamed them for postwar inflation. Like President Truman and his Council of Economic Advisers, the CIO argued in this 1948 cartoon that business was driving up the cost of living while the Republican-dominated Eightieth Congress refused to reinstate OPA-style price controls.

the NAM way, the big business way, the Republican way, up and up and up." He warned that a Republican victory would lead to even higher prices. Thomas Dewey, the moderate New York governor, was the Republican candidate for president, but Truman ran against Senator Taft and the Republican Congress that had refused to reinstate controls. The Republican National Committee predicted that Truman's anti-inflation plan would result in the "same old 50-cent price tag in the empty steak counter that we had under OPA." But its warnings fell on deaf ears.[44]

Truman's tactics worked, and, in spite of third-party challenges, he squeaked out a surprise victory against Dewey. Labor turned out in large numbers, with 89 percent of autoworkers supporting the president. A *Fortune* cover story dubbed Truman "Our Laboristic President." Not only had Truman won reelection; he did so without the help of either the Deep South or the leftists in Henry Wallace's Progressive Party campaign. Democrats reclaimed Congress and sent Paul Douglas of Illinois and Hubert Humphrey of Minnesota to the Senate. Both would become leading liberals during the next decades. Chester Bowles was elected governor in Connecticut, and Adlai Stevenson became governor of Illinois. Truman and his laborite allies convinced the public that they, and not their Republican adversaries, held the key to mass prosperity.[45]

Truman used his 1949 State of the Union address to press for a radical program. Its centerpieces were a four-billion-dollar corporate and estate tax and the issuance of a warning to the steel industry that, unless it expanded production, the government would build its own plants. In essence, this proposal would do for steel what the Tennessee Valley Authority had done for electricity. Greater steel production was essential for cars, homes, appliances, and other major consumer goods, especially as increased defense spending was siphoning off part of the supply. In addition, Truman called for building more public housing, expanding Social Security, raising the minimum wage, extending rural electrification, and implementing the Brannan farm program to lower food costs. And he continually reiterated the importance of repealing Taft-Hartley. Dubbed the "Fair Deal" by its supporters, Truman's proposals were a legacy of the New Deal purchasing-power agenda that held to the view that expanded production along with high wages and low prices were essential to prosperity.[46]

To give the president the authority to build steel mills, Representative Brent Spence, a Democrat from Kentucky and chairman of the House Banking and Currency Committee, introduced the Economic Stabilization Bill in early 1949 as an amendment to the Employment Act. Senator O'Mahoney, chairman of the Joint Economic Committee and former Temporary National Economic Committee (TNEC) chairman, cosponsored the bill. Keyserling and the newly appointed secretary of agriculture, Charles Brannan, had drafted the legislation, which called for standby price controls, allocation powers for scarce resources, and government loans to expand steel. After Truman's victory, the industry journal *Iron Age* had ominously predicted to steel executives, "You can bet your bottom dollar that President Truman and the new Congress are getting ready to roll up their sleeves, spit on their hands and go to work. Their working-over may be done with (a) an axe, (b) a broom, (c) both." Testifying on the bill's behalf, John Clark of the CEA argued that it might be necessary for "the Government itself to become a producer" and warned that the president "is not afraid to take that final step." The CIO endorsed the attack on the steel industry, and Walter Reuther, echoing his 1941 proposal, called for a major industrial expansion.[47]

The Spence Bill generated fierce opposition from all business factions, ranging from the moderate Committee for Economic Development to the conservative NAM. Although the call for state-run steel mills was little more than political bluster, its place on the agenda indicated the

New Deal was ongoing. Senator Taft warned that the Spence Bill proposed "a completely planned and controlled economy." The bill "makes all previous illustrations [of government authority] look like practice performances," wrote the *New York Times* editorial board. "If the Administration is extraordinarily coy and diffident when it comes to asking for authority to deal with labor crises, its inhibitions disappear as if by magic when the question is one that concerns industrial prices, profits, and production." To Keyserling's great irritation, Edwin Nourse joined the chorus of dissenters.[48]

Calls for steel expansion grew louder when the president announced that the economy was in a recession in the spring of 1949. In May, the congressmen who had supported the Economic Stabilization Bill renamed it the Economic Expansion Bill. Whereas in the winter the legislation was sold as an anti-inflation measure, now it became part of an antirecession strategy. Reporter Edward Collins called the two measures for "all intents and purposes identical twins." While the downturn undercut the push for price controls, steel expansion became necessary to stimulate the economy. If industry did not accept government loans, then the government would open its own mills. The Economic Expansion Bill's main sponsors included Senators James Murray, Hubert Humphrey, and Elbert Thomas, and Representatives Helen Gahagan Douglas, Wright Patman, and Andrew Biemiller. It received instant praise from the liberal community and a ringing endorsement from the Americans for Democratic Action, whose members included Leon Henderson and Chester Bowles.[49]

Conservatives opposed the bill with equal vehemence. Senator Harry Byrd denounced the bill as "the certain road to ruin." The American Bar Association warned that it "would make the President of the United States an economic dictator." Harold Moulton of the Brookings Institution condemned it as "essentially totalitarian, since it embodies a master plan in which the state determines the allocation of productive resources, in line with what the Government conceives to be required." Such measures, he claimed, went far beyond the New Deal and were the legacy of "the vast control mechanism" that had prevailed during World War II. Indeed, the Joint Economic Committee, again under Democratic control, recommended making steel a public utility. In April, the Antitrust Congressional Committee, led by New York Democrat Emanuel Celler, conducted an investigation of the steel industry that was even more rigorous than the one completed earlier by TNEC. Its goal was to expose the companies' restrictive practices.[50]

In the fall of 1949, Keyserling became the head of CEA when Nourse finally quit. Keyserling had the support of the CIO and the UAW, which considered him a key ally. A CEA report, written by Keyserling, insisted,

"The 'enlarging production' of an industrially efficient nation must go increasingly to filling in the consumption deficiencies of the erstwhile poor," by which he meant that an increased proportion of the productivity dividend had to go to wages rather than to profits. The National Industrial Conference Board derided the report as "embod[ying] the very essence of Marxism," while labor embraced it as a justification of wage demands.[51] Truman now firmly adopted Keyserling's rhetoric and declared, "We can achieve within a few years a national output well above 300 billion dollars," but only "if the real needs and aspirations of our people are translated into effective demand through constantly growing employment and purchasing power." Truman adopted the CEA national economic budget numbers, calling for a $4,000 annual salary by 1958.[52]

American Cold War commitments, however, began to dominate government economic policy and impede its leftward movement. Truman appointed Keyserling to sit on the National Security Council (NSC), a new body charged with constructing America's foreign policy. Its leadership was dominated by Cold Warriors who believed that the Soviet government was bent on the worldwide spread of communism. Only a policy of containment whereby the United States checked the spread of communism wherever it emerged could prevent its growth. This required an enormous increase in military spending as well as spending for European recovery. After the end of World War II, the percentage of gross national product devoted to the military had declined to less than roughly 5 percent. In response to the fall of China and the Soviets' explosion of an atomic bomb in 1949, the NSC advocated doubling that number.

A committed Cold War anticommunist, Keyserling supported increased military spending. Fearing that such spending could interfere with a liberal domestic agenda, he argued that America could have both guns and butter provided that the economy expanded. Such expansion, Keyserling argued, was possible only by implementing his radical proposals for higher wages and government-run steel mills. But military spending, it turned out, undercut the need for redistributive programs, especially when it boosted the economy. Government expenditure on the Marshall Plan, roughly sixteen billion dollars, had already helped to mitigate the 1949 downturn.[53]

A bigger obstacle to the purchasing-power agenda was the fate of organized labor, which was experiencing two major difficulties. First, organized labor had not expanded significantly beyond its base in the industrial core of the Northeast and Midwest. A CIO effort to unionize the South had failed. The consequences became clear when firms began to shift production to the nonunionized, low-wage, low-tax areas in the South and the West. The recession of 1949 sped the decline of New England mill towns, bringing local levels of unemployment equal to those of the Great Depression. In Connecticut, when the Chance Vought aircraft plant moved production of its planes from Bridgeport to Texas, the city's unemployment rate soared to 28 percent. As part of Truman's antirecession program, the CEA devised the Aid to Depressed Areas program, which offered federal contracts and loans as a way to address regional decline. Under the direction of Special Assistant to the President John Steelman and Secretary of Commerce Sawyer, two of Truman's conservative advisers, the program did not get off the ground. Senator Paul Douglas would revive this structural approach to the problems of poverty in the late 1950s, but the aid was not enough to stanch capital flight and resuscitate dying industries, like textiles and coal, that had been mainstays of organized labor.[54]

The second problem grew out of organized labor's acceptance of a private solution to labor's price squeeze. In its 1948 contract, GM offered the UAW "cost-of-living adjustments" (COLAs) that, in effect, institutionalized the notion of the "wage-price" spiral. When prices went up, hourly wages would follow, giving workers protection on a per hour basis, but at the expense of consumers and salaried workers. In 1950, autoworkers signed a new five-year contract that linked wage increases to the consumer price index (CPI) and allowed an annual improvement factor of 2 percent, a figure smaller than the amount of GM's productivity gains. The contract also included pay deferments, pensions, and other benefits that reduced labor's support for Fair Deal programs. *Fortune* writer Daniel Bell, who, like Walter Reuther, had been a former Socialist Party member, captured the historic nature of this "Treaty of Detroit." This contract "unmistakably accepts the existing distribution of income between wages and profits as 'normal' if not as 'fair.' . . . It is the first major union contract that explicitly accepts objective economic facts—cost of living and productivity—as determining wages, thus throwing overboard all theories of wages as determined by political power, and of profits as 'surplus value.'" Bell concluded, "GM may have paid a billion for peace but it got a bargain."[55]

Organized labor was at the peak of its membership, capturing over one-third of the nonagricultural workforce. Yet it no longer spoke for the larger community. That was especially the case as it became clear that, in the absence of world war, Truman could not translate his campaign rhetoric into the basis of any kind of national income policy that would unite consumers and labor. Labor leaders continued to utilize the language of mass purchasing power, but given the structure of collective bargaining and labor's political weakness, their actions belied their ideological rhetoric.

High Prices Are Just Driving Me Crazy, 1950–1960

In his 1951 classic work, *The Future of American Politics,* journalist Samuel Lubell predicted that inflation would remain an insurmountable problem for the labor left. Lubell correctly pointed to the New Deal Democratic coalition as the formative bloc in American politics. And yet he also underscored tensions within this alliance. Inflation was one of the divisive issues. Above all, the new Democratic coalition was made up of the demographic groups that were fighting to get into the middle classes. And the rise of these new middle classes—the product of "the march of the masses"—paralleled the growth of the government. The New Deal state, with its political rhetoric of mass abundance and promises of more, then generated heightened expectations among its favored sectors. "Our class struggle, if it can be called that, arises not from the impoverishment of the masses but from their progress. It is evidence not of the failure of the American dream but of its successes." And yet inflation threatened to undo this progress and tear apart the Democratic alliance because, as Lubell explained, inflation made it harder to give to one group without taking away from another. "No new economic gains can be promised any group of Democrats today without threatening the gains of other Democrats." Thus, Lubell concluded, "Inflation has clearly become the breaking point of the Roosevelt coalition."[56]

The outbreak of the Korean War in May 1950 escalated the concern over inflation. Very quickly it became clear that Americans would have to devote 20 percent of their national production to the defense effort. In this circumstance, inflation posed a larger threat than it had at the beginning of World War II, because the economy now had less slack to absorb the increased defense production. And the Korean War was not World War II. Unlike World War II, when OPA was so central, the government approached the problem of mobilizing for the Korean War in a different fashion, relying on credit controls and a gradual increase in military production. With Keyserling's help, the Economic Expansion Act now became the Defense Production Act, once again calling for an expansion of steel. But industry intransigence and the foreign-policy decision to "stretch out" production in order to avoid alarming China and the Soviet Union eliminated the chances of a rapid increase in industrial capacity. Only at government expense did the steel industry finally expand.[57]

Throughout the war, the public advocated the use of wage and price controls, testifying to the popular memory of their effectiveness in World War II. But Congress and the president took no immediate action. The stretch-out mentality differed markedly from the sense of urgency that had prevailed in the early days of World War II. Wage and price controls were imposed only in January 1951, after the Chinese entered the war. Labor and liberals argued loudly that these measures were insufficient. In May 1951, the Americans for Democratic Action sponsored an anti-inflation conference that was attended by many former OPA employees and supporters, including CIO leaders, who called for stronger controls.[58]

From 1950 through 1953, the high cost of living rivaled the public concern with ongoing war. Between June 1950 and January 1951, when controls began, the consumer price index went up 6.6 percent; retail prices for food rose 9.9 percent. In 1951 and 1952, the rates of increase slowed considerably, but the public still feared rising prices. As one North Carolina housewife stated in June 1951, after the Depression and World War II came "a catastrophe as great as those two—the great inflation; which I choose as the most horrible, for it is a cancerous growth, without reason or order, incomprehensible, parasitic, living on the good life of this nation until that life must become drab and invalid or dead. Is there no doctor in the house?" These sentiments translated into demands for tougher controls. Mrs. David Green of Brooklyn, New York, wrote to the president, "I know that I am expressing the sentiments of millions of homemakers when I write to you to continue the struggle against inflation. . . . Please continue this struggle for a high American standard of living."[59]

Korean War controls were pale imitations of their World War II predecessors. From the beginning, the government set price ceilings on a cost-plus basis, which enabled sellers to pass on higher costs of production. In addition, soon after the establishment of controls, Congress granted weakening amendments to favored industries and producers. Meat packers once again challenged controls and undermined popular confidence in them. Economist Gardner Ackley understood public frustration with beef prices: "The cost of living is high when hamburgers, or T-bone steak, is expensive. Price control works well if beef is available, of good quality, and low in price." Thus the administration insisted on a rollback in beef prices in April 1951. But cattle producers lobbied for and won an antirollback amendment. When Congress allowed the Defense Production Act to expire at the end of June 1951, meat prices climbed to new highs. Militant housewives resumed their regular protest tactics in Washington, releasing balloons into the capital's sky to symbolize that the "cost of living [is] flying higher."[60]

The Korean War marked an important shift in the government's management of the economy. To the extent that controls were effective, it was because they worked in tandem with monetary restraint to keep inflation at 2.6 percent a year. The government had accrued a substantial debt during the Depression and World War II, leading the Treasury to favor low interest rates. Until 1951, the Federal Reserve went along with that policy, contributing to the inflation of the immediate postwar years. The Federal Reserve–Treasury Accord of March 3, 1951, finally loosened interest rates from the decade-long control of the Treasury Department. Thereafter, monetary policy played a decisive role in achieving economic stability. Policymakers could also count on increased military spending to stimulate demand. The Korean War assured the high levels of military spending that Cold Warriors sought. These fiscal and monetary policies would obviate the need for much of the purchasing-power agenda as they helped to stabilize demand and prices. And because these strategies were far less invasive than wage and price controls, they won moderate business support.[61]

Indeed, the leading Keynesian economists now believed they had the technocratic tools necessary to achieve economic prosperity. To be sure, there would be a trade-off between growth and slight upward price instability. Liberal economists, including the prominent business economist Sumner Slichter, began to support modest inflation because it facilitated both full employment and increased government spending. *Business Week* told its readers that inflation would not disappear anytime soon. "If you want full employment you have to have a continuously rising price level." As Harvard professor Slichter argued in a widely discussed article, "How Bad is Inflation?" "A slowly rising price level is actually preferable to a stable price level. . . . [T]he maintenance of a stable price level would conflict with other important interests of the country." Increasingly, Fair Deal economists accepted the concept of a "slow inflation" of 1 to 2 percent annually as healthy because it allowed expansion that in turn generated higher living standards.[62]

But the public did not abide even this low level of price creep. According to yearly public opinion polls of the 1950s, when annual inflation averaged less than 3 percent, Americans cited inflation as the most important domestic problem in eight years out of ten. World War II propaganda had demonized inflation, and this evil force loomed over postwar life, threatening to undermine the security and abundance Americans had achieved. With large wage settlements, a commitment to Cold War spending, and a full-employment policy, the postwar economy came under continuous inflationary pressures. And though many firms and industries increased their productivity, the gains were not evenly distributed, leaving behind the service and construction industries. Faced with heavy demand and higher labor costs, those growing sectors continued to raise their prices. In addition, the steel industry sought larger profits to support necessary modernization. Those forces combined to put stresses on any labor-management peace while passing on higher costs to the public.[63]

Part of the problem stemmed from changing consumer expectations. Americans lived in an affluent society where many goods once considered luxuries became necessities. Between 1941 and 1960, family income doubled. By 1956, more Americans worked in white-collar jobs than in manual labor. The GI Veterans Bill guaranteed education and home loans, and millions of Americans moved to the suburbs, purchased a home, and obtained a college degree. By 1960, 80 percent of American families owned at least one car, and 90 percent owned a television set. "If few can cite the figures," historian David Potter wrote in his 1954 classic work, *People of Plenty*, "Everyone knows that we have, per capita, more automobiles, more telephones, more radios, more vacuum cleaners, more electric lights, more bathtubs, more supermarkets and movie palaces and hospitals, than any other nation." Americans felt entitled to material goods and demanded more. Although the cost of basic goods did not increase substantially, Americans desired more expensive items. These hankerings fostered a constant sense that the cost of living was going up as shoppers spent more of their income on high-end consumer durables. Public opinion polls consistently revealed a new car or a new house at the top of Christmas gift lists. In May 1952, *Business Week* dubbed inflation "the permanent dilemma." Four years later, its reporters explained, "A prosperous country can have its own brand of discontentment. . . . The complaint isn't that things are bad, but the price of keeping them good is so high."[64]

Indeed, during the 1950s individuals felt under growing pressure to demonstrate their social standing through material possessions, particularly as large sectors of the new middle classes struggled to assert their place in the fluid social structures of the postwar suburbs. Popular social critic Vance Packard captured that sense of striving in his 1959 bestselling book, *The Status Seekers*. Packard argued that although class lines had softened because of considerable economic gains, social stresses had in fact become exaggerated. "Many people are badly distressed, and scared, by the anxieties, inferiority feelings, and straining generated by this unending process of rating and status striving. The status seekers, as I use the term, are people who are continually straining to surround themselves with visible evidence of the superior rank they are claiming." The concept of status anxiety, first delineated by Richard Hofstadter and Seymour Martin Lipset, while much debated, contained a kernel of truth for the new middle classes. In this context, small increases in the price of new items could generate stress disproportionate to their significance in a person's or family's overall budget or lifestyle.[65]

Blue-collar workers shared the general sense of striving and entitlement and now found themselves with the union strength to assert their demands. The National Labor Relations Act was created to institutionalize

higher wages through collective bargaining. The postwar gains by organized labor demonstrated the success of that policy. Before the war, nearly
80 percent of a steelworker's income went toward a very basic standard of
living. He could afford a new pair of shoes only every two years and a new
coat every six. In 1942, 30 percent of steelworkers lived in homes without
indoor bathrooms. But, in the fifteen years after the war, the same steelworkers came to expect paid vacations, holidays, pensions, and health insurance as part of their earned benefits. And not just skilled workers but
also semiskilled assembly-line workers in unionized industries took home
much larger paychecks. *Fortune* editors understood that the American
union was the worker's "tool for gaining and keeping as an individual the
status and security of a full citizen in capitalist society. That the union
has made the worker to an amazing degree a middle-class member of a
middle-class society—in the plant, in the local community, in the
economy—is the real measure of its success." Three-fifths of all families
now had some discretionary income.[66]

   But workers' gains did not occur automatically. They came about because of productivity gains, because other industrial economies had
been bombed during the war and could not compete, and because
workers continuously went on strike. In the postwar years, annual work
stoppages reached all-time highs. In 1955, nearly four hundred strikes
involved one thousand workers or more. *Fortune* editors correctly claimed
that "the American union is a militant union—more militant, perhaps,
than its European counterparts." In contrast to other industrialized
Western countries where the labor movement was stronger, American
unions had to fight regularly because of their comparative weakness.
Bell's description of a "treaty" reflected an ideal more than a reality.
Strikes continued throughout the decade. The idea of a labor-management accord, much in evidence in historical and labor-relations literature, represented but a wishful fable at best.[67]

   By all accounts, the group that fared worst from the wage-price spiral
comprised those on fixed incomes: teachers, public servants, white-
collar workers, pensioners. Creeping inflation typically reflects a successful alliance of corporations and unions against middle-class proprietors,
pensioners, and savers. The demographic fact that more workers were
obtaining employment in professional and service-sector jobs during
this period created a real split between blue-collar workers and their
white-collar, middle-class counterparts. These Americans constituted
roughly one-third of the workforce, with 6.3 million government employees, 4 million Social Security pensioners, and another 4 million
retired Americans. Salaried workers also feared losing their savings to
inflation. Price increases became problematic as a larger share of families' savings was being invested in insurance policies, whose fixed nature

meant an erosion of their value and hence less security, not more. Inflation also raised interest rates and discouraged entrepreneurship. Even the well-off began to complain about the "Great Squeeze." *Nation's Business* reported the hardships of John Statistic, a fictionalized composite of a businessman, and his family, who had to make do on twelve thousand dollars (about eighty thousand dollars today): "[he] has understandable regrets over . . . the dreams of affluence which have failed to materialize." Although the emerging Keynesian consensus on the left maintained that mild inflation would alleviate distributional conflict, the "creeping inflation" of the 1950s fueled tensions between social groups and encouraged the very conflict this technocratic elite sought to avoid.[68]

In this inflationary environment, both unions and large corporations were criticized as "vested interests" that had the power to generate the wage-price spiral, thereby undermining the general welfare. Economist Walter Morton explained, "Laying the blame for economic evils on trade-unions and monopolies has a wide appeal. It is easy to succumb to this temptation because it is not likely to receive severe scrutiny. On the contrary, an attack upon such unpopular groups as unions and monopolists is quite welcome and therefore likely to meet with uncritical acceptance." Detractors of the new Keynesian economics pointed out that compensatory thinking simply fueled these groups' demands because of their confidence that the government would support them. As conservative ideologue Henry Hazlitt argued, "The pressure on the politicians to continue a policy of inflation is enormous. For the fetish of today is 'full employment.'" Keynesians themselves also attacked "special interests" and, indeed, the leading Keynesian, Alvin Hansen, had already begun to decry the lack of "restraint" exhibited by labor unions, calling on them to demonstrate "social responsibility."[69]

Labor stood defenseless before these charges, having lost a key ally as the consumer movement of the New Deal–World War II era waned. Since the 1930s, middle-class women's groups had supported labor's demands for higher wages, government monitoring of monopolistic prices, and better regulations for consumer products. Amid the anticommunism of the 1950s, their programs came under attack as too left leaning. Mary Keyserling, for example, found herself subject to the red-baiting tactics of Joe McCarthy and the House Committee on Un-American Activities. The porous quality that had characterized consumer politics since the 1930s now resulted in a cloud of suspicion settling on noncommunist leaders, undercutting their strength. In addition, women's groups like the General Federation of Women's Clubs shifted their attention to Cold War issues such as civil defense against nuclear attack and world hunger. While fears of inflation were pervasive, administered prices and income distribution were no longer on the agenda of any middle-class social movement.[70]

The decline of a consumer movement sympathetic to labor reform, income redistribution, and mass purchasing power reflected broader transformations of American society. The general prosperity, growth in real income, and movement to suburbia all contributed to relegating the consumer movement to the margins. If consumers found themselves short of cash, they could make up the difference with their newly issued credit cards, a practice that began when Diners' Club introduced the first all-purpose charge card in 1950. To the extent that the public was concerned about inflation, they tended to blame trade unions, whose leaders negotiated deals that substantially boosted the pay of their members. In the popular mind, labor was becoming associated with communism, corruption, and disruptive strikes. Just as important, union gains in securing wage increases made labor susceptible to charges of acting as a "special interest" and causing what many perceived as "ruinous inflation." Indeed, organized labor's wage gains in key industries seized income not from big business, which simply passed on higher costs, but rather from the salaried middle class, retired people, savers, and government employees, who had to pay the higher prices. The middle classes, including many highly skilled blue-collar workers who suffered from wage compression, began to consider union power as illegitimate.

Republicans embraced the fight against inflation as a key electoral issue in 1952. The Democratic Party could not safely disavow its labor allies or repudiate their gains. That political reality left Democrats vulnerable to Republicans' attack on this cost-of-living issue. On June 15, the Bureau of Labor Statistics released a report that placed the cost of living at an all-time high. According to the CPI, the American dollar now bought less than half the goods and services than it had in 1939. Even though Americans had largely come to expect a higher standard of living that included a car, a radio, a paid vacation, and a five-day workweek, most people were not only able to save less; they also found themselves in debt. *U.S. News and World Report* summed it up: "Most people are on a treadmill, or losing ground."[71]

Republicans portrayed inflation as symptomatic of New Deal–Fair Deal irresponsibility. "The wanton extravagance and inflationary policies of the Administration in power have cut the value of the dollar in half," read the Republican platform. "If this Administration is left in power, it will further cheapen the dollar, rob the wage earner, impoverish the farmer and reduce the true value of the savings, pensions, insurance and investments of millions of our people." Of the forty-two freshmen Republican candidates running for Congress, almost all discussed inflation in their campaigns as much as, if not more than, any other issue, including taxes, "creeping socialism," and the Korean War.[72] High prices brought support for government controls that business viewed as anathema. Thus the attack on inflation and the anticommunist crusade reinforced each other.

Republican candidate Dwight Eisenhower took advantage of this electoral topic, using television to dramatize the issue. Political spots were first used in 1952, when approximately 40 percent of American households owned sets. These commercials did not determine the election, but they revealed the salient concerns of the day. In one ad, a middle-aged woman holding her groceries declared, "I paid twenty-four dollars for these groceries—look, for this little." Eisenhower responded, "A few years ago, those same groceries cost you ten dollars, now twenty-four, next year thirty—that's what will happen unless we have a change." Another elderly woman lamented, "You know what things cost today. High prices are just driving me crazy." Eisenhower soothed, "Yes, my Mamie gets after me about the high cost of living. It's another reason why I say, it's time for a change. Time to get back to an honest dollar and an honest dollar's work." In another ad, when a man asked which party would lick inflation, Eisenhower replied, "Well, instead of asking which party will bring prices down, why not ask which party has put prices up?" In many spots, the general broke a piece of wood in half to demonstrate the decrease in the nation's purchasing power since the end of World War II.[73]

After winning the election, Eisenhower took on the evil of inflation as his main domestic priority. As a fiscal conservative, the new president was staunchly committed to balanced budgets, a sound dollar, and minimal inflation. When Democrats regained control of Congress in 1954, their unwillingness to cut expenditures led the administration to adopt a more restrictive monetary policy. Federal Reserve chairman William Martin shared Eisenhower's disdain for inflation and soon moved to restrict the money supply. Even when this policy resulted in more price stability, inflationary fears were never far from people's minds. Martin's tighter credit coincided with the end of the Korean War and cuts in the federal budget. There ensued a thirteen-month recession in 1953–1954, during which unemployment reached a peak of 5.8 percent. After the recession, prices held steady throughout 1955 but then began to creep up, accompanied by constant press reports that the CPI was at an "all-time high." According to reports, by 1956, the dollar's value had declined to fifty-two cents since 1939.[74]

By that year, the CPI was growing at a rate of 3.5 percent annually, seemingly confirming administration warnings about the overwhelming threat that inflation posed to the economy. At a time when most people held bonds, not equity, in pension accounts, Secretary of the Treasury George Humphrey warned, "Inflation is the great thief. The young, the old, the sick, the small saver, all those least able to protect themselves are the helpless prey of wicked inflation. It must be held in check." White

House aide Gabriel Hauge warned about the "Problems of Prosperity" and challenged the "depression-born thinking, that the difficulty with our economy is oversaving and underconsumption." He rejected the idea that "creeping inflation is a tolerable price to pay for avoiding unemployment. . . . If we retain our depression psychosis about the tendency of the economy to run down, we become resigned to a more or less perpetual pumping up of our prosperity—hardly the way to keep it healthy."[75] To these officials, the cure came through balanced budgets, restrictive monetary policy, and government pressure to restrain wage increases.

By now, the idea of "wage-price inflation" was cemented in the public imagination. Both the public and the popular press translated abstract economic phenomena into concrete numbers. Business reports in the summer of 1956 explained that if United Steelworkers' president David McDonald succeeded in winning his demands of a sixty-cent hourly increase, then the cost of a refrigerator would increase by fifteen dollars. Labor's case was weakened politically by the inclusion of COLAs in over half of all union contracts, protecting labor from price increases while loading the burden on nonunionized sectors. In 1955, the UAW won a guaranteed annual wage for its workers. The 1955 merger of the American Federation of Labor and the Congress of Industrial Organizations amplified the idea of big labor as a monolithic force that was capable of subverting the nation's economic well-being. Although unions had only limited reach in certain industries and firms, the wages they won for their members exerted upward wage pressure even on nonunionized sectors.[76]

Amid continued popular concern over escalating prices, prostability forces stepped up their assault on organized labor. U.S. Steel lambasted labor's established practice of industrywide bargaining. "The abuse of labor monopoly privilege and the monetary policy that transfers to the public in higher prices the penalty of that abuse appear to be the main elements of institutionalized inflation." Steel directors warned that this amounted to a "permanent and alarming peacetime trend." U.S. Steel president Roger Blough had his own solution to beating "Old Man Inflation": tax cuts, wage cuts, and higher prices. From his point of view, higher wage demands led to "phantom profits," by which he meant profits not large enough to modernize and expand steel's capacity. "As a result of postwar inflation, it is possible for a company to earn what appears to be a most substantial profit, and still wither away." In the end, he appealed to the public to support higher steel prices as a necessary investment in the nation's economic growth and national defense.[77]

This campaign against wage-hike inflation reinforced a renewed legislative attack on organized labor. In the spring of 1956, NAM released another public-relations barrage, denouncing the "purchasing-power fallacy." "The wage-price spiral gets no one anywhere." The association

FIGURE 6.3. Business representatives repeatedly blamed organized labor for raising the cost of living, insisting that labor's wage demands automatically raised production costs and forced higher prices on the consumer. The National Association of Manufacturers promoted this idea of a futile wage-price spiral in national media campaigns with illustrations such as this one from a 1955 pamphlet.

painted a picture of an endless cycle: Labor demanded higher wages, which raised production costs, which in turn led to higher prices. "The obvious remedy in this situation is to curtail the power of industrywide unions to engage in monopolistic practices and restore bargaining to the local level." Business leaders and a reinvigorated conservative movement launched a major effort to nationalize "right-to-work" restrictions against union organizing that heretofore had been confined to the South and the Mountain West.[78]

Although labor flexed its political muscles in the 1958 and 1960 elections, which helped Democrats make substantial gains at the polls, the victories did not give labor any political dividends. It did not help organized labor that two-thirds of union workers were concentrated in ten states. Under the direction of Senator John McClellan of Arkansas, the Senate held well-publicized hearings on corruption in 1958 that further discredited labor, reinforcing charges that unions constituted nothing more than a corrupt and self-serving interest group. Though these hearings focused on the corruption in the Teamsters under Jimmy Hoffa, the public did not make such distinctions. Republican senator Barry Goldwater said, "I would rather have Hoffa stealing my money than Reuther stealing my freedom." The passage of the Landrum-Griffin Act in 1959 allowed for more government regulation of union affairs and clamped down on union secondary boycotts and picketing. These challenges to labor's power led to a downward cycle. Even as labor waxed in numerical strength, representing nearly one in every three nonagricultural workers, political defeats constricted its vision and helped transform it into a special interest. In popular imagination, and to a certain degree in reality, the wage-price spiral was the real culprit in the inflationary patterns, and it symbolized labor's crooked dealings. John Kenneth Galbraith, the former deputy administrator of OPA in 1942 and architect of the price freeze, explained that, in the competition to assign blame, "The public will always attribute the whole of the price increases at such a time to the presumed rapacity of the unions."[79]

Purchasing-power progressives were now a minority voice, but they were still present. Gardiner Means's writings in the 1950s, which pointed out that two hundred corporations controlled over half of all corporate assets, renewed interest in his theory of administered prices. Beginning in 1957, Senator Estes Kefauver, a Tennessee Democrat and chair of the Antitrust and Monopoly Subcommittee of the Senate Judiciary Committee, pushed for an investigation into steel and auto prices. Kefauver explained, "Every day in our lives monopoly takes its toll. Stealthily it reaches down into our pockets and takes a part of our earnings. . . . [T]he deed is done so smoothly, so deftly, that we are not even conscious of it." A graduate of Yale Law School, Kefauver was first elected to Congress in 1939 as a New Deal Democrat. After gaining national attention by leading an investigation into organized crime, he ran for president in 1956. Between 1957 and 1963, Kefauver interrogated the steel, auto, bread, and drug industries, among others. Kefauver called before him U.S. Steel president Roger Blough, who, as a young attorney, had first made his mark defending U.S. Steel before TNEC. Senator Paul Douglas joined Kefauver in reading from the same scripts they had helped to write in the 1930s. Donald Montgomery served as Douglas's assistant before retiring from his lifelong career as a consumer advocate.[80]

The administered price hearings served as the backdrop for one of labor's last midcentury gambits to win public opinion to their side in the battle against their corporate adversaries. In June 1957, when steel announced plans to increase prices, Kefauver invited Walter Reuther to testify before Congress. The UAW president characterized the proposed increases as "unjustifiable, socially irresponsible, and dangerously inflationary." In August, as the United States plunged into the worst recession since 1938, Reuther called on auto leaders to cut car prices for 1958 by one hundred dollars. All Big Three automakers rejected this as a stunt. Reuther captured the spotlight months later by proposing customer rebates, which he called a profit-sharing plan for consumers. Reuther defended these proposals as "motivated primarily for a deep concern for all American consumers." He insisted that a federal review board should be appointed to "protect the American consumer from the high prices rigged by the giant corporations exercising monopoly control in the vital sectors of our economy." This bold rhetoric was vintage Reuther, and he articulated the same ideology that had shaped the fight against General Motors in 1945–1946. His proposals earned him the number one place as the most hated labor leader in the country. Senator Goldwater denounced him as "a more dangerous menace than Sputnik or anything Soviet Russia might do to America."[81]

In truth, Reuther's enemies had little to fear. For all its radicalism, Reuther's rhetoric revealed labor's defensive posture. The recessions of the late 1950s and the rapid introduction of automation resulted in unemployment levels not seen since 1940. Between 1948 and 1967, Detroit lost almost 130,000 manufacturing jobs as industries fled to low-wage, nonunionized areas in the South and abroad. The precipitous decline generated tensions within the working class, particularly between black and white workers. African Americans had migrated in large numbers to Detroit to take advantage of the opportunities presented by the wartime labor shortage and the CIO's commitment to interracial solidarity. But a philosophy of racial progress soon triggered resentments and racial strife as workers competed for increasingly scarce homes and jobs. At a national level the CIO firmly supported civil rights, but locally many of its unions enforced discrimination. These hostilities, which at times turned violent, put more pressure on Reuther to make real gains for his workers.

As economic conditions gutted Detroit industry, Reuther's consumer rebate plan represented a desperate attempt to bolster labor's position by winning public support. In 1946, his demand that General Motors hold prices steady had showed an awareness that labor's strength could alienate the public. A decade later, this similar appeal signified labor's weakness. Reuther coupled this call for price restraint with promises that the UAW would not push for higher wages. His conciliatory offer reflected labor's waning power more than any concern for the general welfare. With slack demand and a backlog of production, the auto companies felt no need to make further concessions to the union. Why not, then, offer to forgo wage demands in exchange for price restraint, as he might thereby succeed in turning the union's stalemate into a victory for the consumer?[82]

The public did not buy this kind of warmed-over New Deal bargain, especially when David McDonald called the steelworkers out for a massive strike in 1959. Lasting 116 days, this was the largest strike in American history in terms of man-hours idled. The steelworkers themselves had not been anxious to strike and claimed that they too would forgo wage increases. But steel executives, sensing that the union was weakening, precipitated a strike by threatening to eliminate work rules that the steelworkers felt they needed for protection against speedups and job reclassifications. The executives overplayed their hand. While workers were willing to moderate their wage demands, they could not accept such a direct challenge to their authority on the shop floor, and they stood united against management. In an impressive show of labor's enduring organizational strength, steelworkers rebuffed the challenge. But their success won them little public sympathy.[83]

Kefauver's hearings lasted until 1962, but they were no substitute for OPA. In opinion polls, the public continued to rank inflation as an important problem, but such sentiments no longer shaped liberal politics.[84] No organized social movement or political strategy existed to translate the attack on monopoly prices into a political force capable of reform. Without a governmental commitment to restraining prices, a commitment of the sort that had proved possible only in a time of war, labor leaders knew that Kefauver's attack on industry was a dead end. Indeed, by 1960, their main concern was preserving jobs for their union members in the face of a slowing economy, automation, and foreign competition. And the consumer movement that had once supported antimonopoly campaigns no longer existed. In fact, the direct result of the Kefauver hearings was the spawning of a new consumer movement that was substantially different from its New Deal–World War II predecessor.

While Kefauver was attacking the drug industry for its monopolistic prices, a scandal broke involving the drug thalidomide. A tranquilizer given to pregnant mothers, the drug caused birth defects, and the press ran pictures of deformed children. This event aroused public anger at the apparent hubris of large corporations unrestrained by competition or government regulation. In 1957, Vance Packard had published a best-selling book, *The Hidden Persuaders*, which argued that corporate America exerted undue influence over consumers through suggestive advertising that could "channel our unthinking habits, our purchasing decisions, and our thought processes." After the thalidomide scandal, Congress introduced a series of consumer protection measures. In 1962, President John F. Kennedy proclaimed his commitment to a "consumer's bill of rights" and appointed a Consumer Advisory Council to the Council of Economic Advisers. Although Caroline Ware sat on this body, the meaning of a consumers' interest had radically shifted since she had emerged as a leading advocate in the 1930s.[85]

Consumer issues now had little to do with prices or income distribution. Instead, the consumer movement of the 1960s and 1970s, personified by activist Ralph Nader, stressed safety and health issues. When Stuart Chase and F. J. Schlink first published exposés in the 1920s, their attention to fraud and consumer safety was just one aspect of what would become the New Deal–era consumer movement. Now concerns over dangerous products and dishonest advertisements predominated. In 1962, Congress passed the Truth in Lending Act to protect credit borrowers. Four years later, Congress enacted the Truth in Packaging Act to require better labeling and created the Consumer Protection Safety Commission. At the state level, consumer offices for fraud proliferated. Ralph Nader's *Unsafe at Any Speed* (1965) prompted the passage of the National Traffic and Vehicle Safety Act. Nader and his team of lawyers spearheaded the public-interest movement that extended government regulation of safety and health issues to the environment and workplaces. Their success did not depend on broad grassroots support but, rather, resulted from a combination of skilled lobbying and corporate willingness to reform in a period of relative affluence. As American corporations faced growing foreign competition, the labor movement, which had long sought to link itself with middle-class concerns, now allied itself with its corporate adversaries. Although labor leaders paid lip service to the public-interest movement, they actually gave it little support, as they feared that additional regulations would threaten American jobs. The consumer movement of the 1960s and 1970s, with its narrow focus on the prevention of fraud and accidents, had little to say about the broader pocketbook issues that had once made it a unifying, multifaceted social force.[86]

This shift away from pocketbook politics mirrored a transformation in American liberalism in the last third of the twentieth century. In contrast to earlier generations, whose critique of materialism constituted just one strand among many concerns, liberal intellectuals of the 1950s and 1960s, like Dwight MacDonald, David Riesman, and Daniel Bell, had grown increasingly disenchanted with the idea of consumption as the embodiment of American progress. These writers did not view affluence as an unmitigated blessing, citing the decline of personal autonomy and the rise of conformity that accompanied the mass market's pervasiveness. The result, they feared, was the deadening of progressive politics as Americans retreated into a private world of abundance and mind-numbing acquisitiveness—what Daniel Boorstin piercingly called "national self-hypnosis." In *The Affluent Society* (1958), John Kenneth Galbraith argued that private affluence resulted in the abandonment of public spending. "The family which takes its mauve and cerise, air-conditioned, power-steered and power-braked automobile out for a tour passes through cities that are badly paved, made hideous by litter blighted buildings." Mass consumption now seemed the problem rather than the solution to society's ills.[87]

The reasons for this shift in liberalism were many: a revulsion against mass consumption, a decline in support of class-based issues, the rise of the civil rights movement, the sprouting of the New Left and student protest, and an increasingly critical stance toward American Cold War policy. The decline of a vision of economic citizenship that had animated liberal reform also resulted from the New Deal's success as well as the inherent tensions in its political agenda. From the 1920s through the Great Depression and World War II, organized labor had argued that society could prosper only if the country met its demands for mass purchasing power and redistribution. In a single generation, the ranks of organized labor more than doubled, as did blue-collar income. Labor had been key to building a New Deal coalition, and it was able to do so with middle-class support.

The consumer was a pliable and therefore politically useful label, but the politics of purchasing power were too difficult to manage when the constituent groups had different, and at times conflicting, agendas. The inflationary economic culture of the postwar years presented liberal policymakers with an insoluble dilemma. Unable to escape blame for the wage-price spiral, labor alienated other members of the community who felt that even a mild inflation threatened their standard of living. Throughout the 1950s, conservative, and even moderate, politicians and businessmen correctly perceived that substantial wage gains signified union power, and they succeeded in using these gains to delegitimize organized workers and the New Deal state that had empowered them. No longer a victim, labor had become one of the most powerful forces in the economy. With a single command, union leaders could call hundreds of thousands of workers off the job and shut down entire industries. Such power belied the efforts of labor to speak on behalf of a general consuming public.

In retrospect, it became clear that the late 1950s signaled the height of labor's institutional power. Soon after Kennedy's success in the 1960 election, liberal policymakers embraced Keynesian tax cuts as a way to stimulate economic growth. That policy paid little attention to the relationship between wages, prices, and profits. Keynesian economics rendered the decisions of each buyer and the buyer's capacity to consume less important than aggregate spending. For a while, these fiscal policies seemed to work, and organized labor continued to do well throughout the 1960s. But the affluence of this decade, like labor's power, would not last. The year 1959 turned out to be the last time the steelworkers engaged in a nationwide strike. As the number of unionized jobs, especially in the manufacturing core, fell and the nonunionized sectors of the economy picked up speed, the percentage of jobs controlled by organized labor began a precipitous decline. At the end of the twentieth century, organized labor accounted for less than 16 percent of the nonagricultural workforce. By the time that the labor movement's fate became clear, the rhetoric of mass purchasing power that had first helped labor win popular support had disappeared as well.

Epilogue

Back to Bargain Hunting

TODAY'S mainstream American politics holds no place for a purchasing-power agenda. But for nearly sixty years, from World War I through the Nixon administration, the question of how much things cost fueled American liberalism. The driving desire to secure mass purchasing power put in place a set of institutions and public policies to promote high wages and low prices. Two iconic incidents in the postwar history of the waning New Deal reflected both the continuing influence of this economic policy and its obvious constraints. The first, in the spring of 1962, was the face-off between President Kennedy and U.S. Steel president Roger Blough, called by some the "Battle of Blough Run." By the early 1960s, concern over international competitiveness, a balance-of-payments deficit, a potential gold crisis, and increased military expenditure coincided, making the Kennedy administration determined to keep a tight lid on inflationary pressures. Secretary of Labor Arthur Goldberg worked behind the scenes to construct a rock-bottom wage-price steel agreement in this pattern-setting industry during the 1961–1962 collective-bargaining round. Goldberg, who had served as an influential legal counsel to the United Steelworkers for many years, thought he had succeeded when his old union friends agreed to an exceedingly modest settlement.

Within days, Blough shocked Goldberg, Kennedy, and much of the nation by announcing substantial price increases throughout U.S. Steel's entire product line. Blough claimed that the industry needed more income to finance modernization and forestall an import invasion. But President Kennedy felt betrayed. In a famous fit of rage, Kennedy is said to have declared, "My father always told me that steelmen were sons of bitches, but I never realized till now how right he was." He mobilized the entire apparatus of the U.S. government to force the steel industry to rescind the increases. When Inland Steel, a smaller producer heavily dependent upon defense contracts, broke ranks with U.S. Steel and other big firms, Big Steel was forced to back down, at least temporarily.

This dramatic confrontation, less than two decades after the great postwar wage-price battles, unsettled many businessmen. In May 1962, the stock market dropped some thirty-five points, at that time the largest single one-day decline since 1929. Shaken by the business reaction to his uncharacteristic militancy, Kennedy responded with a program of appeasement. That June, in a signal speech at Yale University, the president declared that ideology had no place in the formulation of economic policy. "What is at stake in our economic decisions today is not some grand warfare of rival ideologies which will sweep the country with passion but the practical management of a modern economy." Soon thereafter he supported a large, probusiness investment tax-credit designed to lower corporate taxes and restore relations with industry executives. When the steel corporations raised their prices in 1963, Kennedy made no objection. Thereafter both Kennedy and his successor, Lyndon Johnson, retreated from heavy-handed wage and price policies as a remedy for economic woes, relying instead on "jawboning." At the same time, Kennedy and his Council of Economic Advisers pushed for across-the-board permanent tax cuts to stimulate consumption. That kind of tax policy, which emphasized tax cuts rather than increased government spending, had always been denounced by New Deal liberals. John Kenneth Galbraith agreed with Socialist Michael Harringtons's label of "reactionary Keynesianism" while Leon Keyserling, true to his purchasing-power ideology, denounced its lack of attention to income distribution. Now a voice in the wilderness, he urged bigger breaks for tax payers in the lower income brackets.[1]

The second episode in the long New Deal twilight came in August 1971, when none other than the Republican president Richard Nixon imposed a ninety-day wage and price freeze. Vietnam spending and a huge increase in the money supply had set off an accelerating spiral that would become the Great Inflation of the 1970s. As in 1946, more than half the American public favored wage and price controls. Indeed, as Vietnam-era inflation accelerated, the Democratic Congress had already offered the president standby authority to impose World War II–style economic controls. Facing reelection in 1972 and fearing an inflation backlash, Nixon cast aside his ideological aversions and, on August 15, 1971, put in place the most dramatic set of economic controls since the end of World War II. Despite his disdain for the Office of Price Administration (OPA), where he had worked briefly before resigning in disgust, the president instituted a program that OPA liberals might well have designed. But, in sharp contrast to the situation during World War II, the Nixon controls came without local price-checkers, labor support, or any redistributive ideology. Instead, the freeze was offered as a remedy to what policymakers and the public saw as the problem of excessive wage settlements. Indeed, Nixon policymakers let their conservative constituents know that the program was designed to "zap labor."[2]

In contemporary America, the relation between wages, prices, and profits is not subject to national political debate. There is no longer a language of purchasing power that links individual bargain hunters to collective bargaining and a larger economic citizenship. Bargains abound in the malls across America, from Best Buy and Wal-Mart to the cyberspace market occupied by eBay and Amazon.com. But, whereas mass consumption was once part of a political outlook that called for a fundamental redistribution of wealth and power, today there is no such agenda.

In part, the purchasing power of the American masses has become a less prominent political issue as a result of the globalization of the economy since the 1970s. During that decade, the value of imported manufacturing goods trebled from 14 percent of domestic product in 1970 to almost 40 percent in 1979, while many manufacturers shifted their production to low-wage areas abroad. Facing foreign competition, General Motors slashed its payroll in half and moved a portion of its production to Mexico. Whereas General Motors, once the largest American employer, had driven up wages across the economy, today Wal-Mart heads the list of big employers that have adopted the opposite strategy, paying its workers subsistence wages and importing its shoes, clothing, and household products from over fifty countries. In this global market, a purchasing-power program for American workers is no longer sufficient.

Sam Walton, founder of Wal-Mart Discount Stores, became the late-twentieth-century successor to Edward Filene. Walton was everything that Filene was not: a family man, an athlete, an outdoorsman, Protestant, and popular. Walton got his start in Bentonville, Arkansas, not Boston, and he made his billions by opening up 3,500 discount stores in small-town America. The only dream these two retail pioneers shared was the over-riding desire to sell underwear, soap, toothpaste, and tens of thousands of other goods as cheaply as possible. There the similarities end. Filene's vision of mass consumption included a commitment to high wages, a powerful union movement, and a world of interclass harmony and coop-eration. In contrast, Walton was renowned as a union fighter, and he built his success by employing low-wage, part-time, nonunionized workers in his Wal-Mart stores. As Walton explained, "When it comes to Wal-Mart, there's no two ways about it: I'm cheap."[3]

Today's consumer politics is a mixture of many strands, but they look very different from the story told in this book. First, there was the "Buy American" campaign in the 1980s, spearheaded by Sam Walton. Osten-sibly designed to save American jobs, this campaign put pressure on domestic manufacturers to cut costs and then drove down wages in third-world sweatshops as well. Another theme represents a revival of the kind of conscientious consumption promoted by Florence Kelley and the National Consumers' League a century ago. In 1995, Kathie Lee Gifford, ABC's morning television show host, became the subject of a scandal when a labor activist revealed that Honduran children, working under terrible conditions and earning twenty-two dollars a week, were making the clothes for her label sold by Wal-Mart. Though Wal-Mart denied the charges, Gifford pleaded mea culpa and joined other celebrity designers and Clinton administration officials in promoting independent inspections in overseas factories. Another thread of today's consumer politics is the attempt by local communities to block megastores and national chains from locating in their areas. In contrast to the antisweatshop crusade, this "Stop Wal-Mart" campaign has aroused grassroots support among residents in small towns from Iowa to Ithaca, New York. As in the anti-chain-store movement a century ago, small merchants have tried to keep discount giants from moving in, fearing that they will destroy local business. Out of an aesthetic disdain, many middle-class residents have joined them, claiming that the presence of large impersonal corporate retailers ruins a sense of community.[4]

Such Wal-Mart politics draw few connections between what people earn, the prices they pay for retail products, and the state of the larger economy. But, for more than half a century, the issue of what people could afford to buy animated liberal politics. Twentieth-century consumerism was not merely a distraction for the working class nor simply a by-product of national prosperity. It was the linchpin in an ongoing political debate about how to organize, reform, and regulate American capitalism. The rise of an interventionist state drew its legitimacy and strength from a broad coalition, one that united Americans behind the idea that a high living standard was their right as citizens. In the twentieth century, the fulfillment of an expansive economic citizenship relied on a mutually reinforcing dynamic between a strong state and an active public. Although now in eclipse, this vision and its turbulent history makes clear the democratic potential of an engaged citizenry pursuing the promise of a better, richer life.

Notes

Abbreviations Used in Notes

Archives and Libraries

BPL	Boston Public Library, Special Collections, Boston, Massachusetts
CUA	Catholic University of America, History Research Center and University Archives, Washington, D.C.
CUNA	Credit Union National Association, Madison, Wisconsin
FDRL	Franklin D. Roosevelt Presidential Library, Hyde Park, New York
GTL	Georgetown University, Lauinger Library, Special Collections Division, Washington, D.C.
HBS	Harvard Business School, Baker Library, Historical Collections, Boston, Massachusetts
HML	Hagley Museum and Library, Wilmington, Delaware
HSTL	Harry S. Truman Library, Independence, Missouri
LOC	Library of Congress, Manuscripts Collection, Washington, D.C.
NARA	National Archives and Record Administration, Washington, D.C.
NARA-II	National Archives and Record Administration II, College Park, Maryland
NMAH	National Museum of American History, Smithsonian Institution, Washington, D.C.
NYSA	New York State Archives, Cultural Education Center, Albany, New York
SC	Smith College, William Allan Neilson Library, Northampton, Massachusetts
TCF	Twentieth Century Fund, New York, New York
UVA	University of Virginia, Alderman Library, Charlottesville, Virginia
WHS	Wisconsin Historical Society, Manuscript Collections, Madison, Wisconsin
WSU	Wayne State University, Archives of Labor History and Urban Affairs, Detroit, Michigan

Manuscript Collections

AAA Papers	Agricultural Adjustment Administration Records, RG 145, NARA-II
ADA Papers	Americans for Democratic Action Papers, WHS
Clinard Papers	Marshall B. Clinard Papers, WHS
Colm Papers	Gerhard Colm Papers, HSTL
Davis Papers	William H. Davis Papers, WHS
Deverall Papers	Richard L. G. Deverall Papers, CUA
Edwards Papers	India Edwards Papers, HSTL

FDR Papers-OF	Franklin D. Roosevelt Papers, Official File, FDRL
FDR Papers-PP	Franklin D. Roosevelt Presidential Papers, FDRL
Filene Papers	Edward A. Filene Papers, CUNA
Filene's Store Papers	Filene's Marketing Archives, BPL
Gilbert Papers	Richard V. Gilbert Papers, FDRL
Henderson Papers	Leon Henderson Papers, FDRL
Keyserling Papers-GTL	Leon H. Keyserling Papers, GTL
Keyserling Papers-HSTL	Leon H. Keyserling Papers, HSTL
Kirstein Papers	Louis E. Kirstein Papers, HBS
Lauck Papers	W. Jett Lauck Papers, UVA
Leiserson Papers	William M. Leiserson Papers, WHS
Lincoln Filene Papers	Lincoln Filene Papers, HBS
Lusk Papers	Lusk Committee Records, NYSA
LWS Papers	League of Women Shoppers Papers, SC
Lynd Papers	Robert S. Lynd Papers, LOC
NAM Pamphlets	National Association of Manufacturers Pamphlets Collection, HML
NRA Papers	National Recovery Administration Records, RG 9, NARA
O'Connor Papers	Jessie Lloyd O'Connor Papers, SC
OPA Papers	Office of Price Administration Records, RG 188, NARA-II
RNC Pamphlets	Republican National Committee Pamphlet Collection, NMAH
Sachs Papers	Alexander Sachs Papers, FDRL
Salant Papers	Walter S. Salant Papers, HSTL
Saposs Papers	David J. Saposs Papers, WHS
Steelman Papers	John R. Steelman Papers, HSTL
TCF Papers	Twentieth Century Fund Records, TCF
Truman Papers-OF	Harry S. Truman Papers, Official File, HSTL
Truman Papers-PP	Harry S. Truman Presidential Papers, HSTL
UAW-Montgomery Papers	United Auto Workers—Donald Montgomery Papers, WSU
VACU Papers	Virginia Credit Union Records, UVA
Ware Papers	Caroline F. Ware Papers, FDRL

Periodical Literature

AAAPSS	*Annals of the American Academy of Political and Social Sciences*
AER	*American Economic Review*
AHR	*American Historical Review*
BG	*Boston Globe*
BHR	*Business History Review*
BW	*Business Week*
DGE	*Dry Goods Economist*

JAH	*Journal of American History*
LD	*Literary Digest*
LHJ	*Ladies' Home Journal*
NB	*Nation's Business*
NR	*New Republic*
NYT	*New York Times*
NYTM	*New York Times Magazine*
SEP	*Saturday Evening Post*
USNWR	*U.S. News, U.S. News & World Report*

Introduction
Economic Citizenship in the Twentieth Century

1. Steve Lohr, "Is Wal-Mart Good for America?" *NYT*, December 7, 2003, 1, 4; Leon Harris, *Merchant Princes: An Intimate History of Jewish Families Who Built Great Department Stores* (New York: Harper and Row, 1979), 3–35.

2. David A. Hounshell, *From the American System to Mass Production, 1800–1932: The Development of Manufacturing Technology in the United States* (Baltimore: Johns Hopkins University Press, 1984).

3. Werner Sombart, "American Capitalism's Economic Rewards," in *Failure of a Dream? Essays in the History of American Socialism,* ed. John Laslett and Seymour Martin Lipset (Garden City, NY: Doubleday Anchor, 1974), 599; William Leach, *Land of Desire: Merchants, Power, and the Rise of a New American Culture* (New York: Pantheon Books, 1993), 7. For recent studies that emphasize the political nature of consumption, see Lizabeth Cohen, *Making a New Deal: Industrial Workers in Chicago, 1919–1939* (New York: Cambridge University Press, 1990), and Dana Frank, *Purchasing Power: Consumer Organizing, Gender, and the Seattle Labor Movement, 1919–1929* (New York: Cambridge University Press, 1994).

4. Simon Kuznets and Dorothy Swaine Thomas, *Population Redistribution and Economic Growth: United States, 1870–1950* (Philadelphia: American Philosophical Society, 1957–64), vol. 1, pp. 353, 357, 684; Bureau of the Census, *Historical Statistics of the United States: Colonial Times to 1970* (Washington, DC: GPO, 1976), series D 167–77, p. 139; Stanley Lebergott, *Manpower in Economic Growth: The American Record since 1800* (New York: McGraw-Hill, 1964), table A-4, p. 513; David Hackett Fischer, *The Great Wave: Price Revolutions and the Rhythm of History* (Oxford: Oxford University Press, 1996), 181–90.

5. Walter Lippmann, *Drift and Mastery* (Madison: University of Wisconsin Press, 1985 [1914]), 54, 56.

6. In her recent book, Lizabeth Cohen examines grassroots social movements among women and blacks and the importance of consumer issues to them. *Pocketbook Politics* also sees grassroots movements as important but puts particular emphasis on the crucial and relatively unexamined role of the national state and liberal policymakers in encouraging and channeling grassroots consumer activism. In contrast to Cohen's focus on the racial and gendered differentiation of consumption, this book stresses the importance of fundamen-

tal economic questions concerning wages and prices to a pre-1970s consumer agenda. In addition, by examining the purchasing-power program and its radical redistributive claims, I see the postwar period not as one of consensus among labor, consumers, and management, as does Cohen, but rather as continuing the contentious political battles around the cost of living that spanned much of the twentieth century. Lizabeth Cohen, *A Consumers' Republic: The Politics of Mass Consumption in Postwar America* (New York: Knopf, 2003).

7. For the development of Keynesianism, see Robert M. Collins, *The Business Response to Keynes, 1929–1964* (New York: Columbia University Press, 1981), and Alan Brinkley, *The End of Reform: New Deal Liberalism in Recession and War* (New York: Knopf, 1995). The most important books on the rise of the American welfare state include Theda Skocpol, *Protecting Soldiers and Mothers: The Political Origins of Social Policy in the United States* (Cambridge, MA: Belknap Press, 1992), and Linda Gordon, *Pitied but Not Entitled: Single Mothers and the History of Welfare, 1890–1935* (New York: Free Press, 1994).

8. Caroline Ware testimony, Temporary National Economic Committee, *Investigation of Concentration of Economic Power, Part 30: Technology and Concentration of Economic Power,* Hearings, 76th Cong., 3d sess., April 8–26, 1940, 17214.

9. Lippmann, *Drift and Mastery,* 55. See also Frederic C. Howe, *The High Cost of Living* (New York: Scribner's, 1917); David P. Thelen, *The New Citizenship: Origins of Progressivism in Wisconsin, 1885–1900* (Columbia: University of Missouri Press, 1972); and Daniel Horowitz, *The Morality of Spending: Attitudes toward the Consumer Society in America, 1875–1940* (Baltimore: Johns Hopkins University Press, 1985).

Chapter One
From the Bargain Basement to the Bargaining Table, 1900–1917

1. *A Brief History of the Filene Automatic Bargain Basement* (Boston: William Filene's Sons and Company, 1914), Filene Papers, Box 55, Folder 7; Edward Filene, "17 Stockturns a Year through the Bargain Appeal," *System,* April 1924, 469–73, 569–71; Edward Filene testimony, House Committee on Interstate and Foreign Commerce, *Regulation of Prices: Hearings on H.R. 13568,* 64th Cong., 2d sess., January 5–11, 1917, 212–13.

2. Filene's advertisements, *BG,* September 5, 1909, 31; January 2, 1910, 37.

3. Milton Friedman and Anna J. Schwartz, *A Monetary History of the United States, 1867–1960* (Princeton, NJ: Princeton University Press, 1963), 41, 89–134. See also Eric Rauchway, "The High Cost of Living in the Progressives' Economy," *JAH* 88 (December 2001): 898–924.

4. Simon Kuznets and Dorothy Swaine Thomas, *Population Redistribution and Economic Growth: United States, 1870–1950* (Philadelphia: American Philosophical Society, 1957–64), vol. 1, pp. 353, 357, 684; Bureau of the Census, *Historical Statistics of the United States: Colonial Times to 1970* (Washington, DC: GPO, 1976), series D 167–77, p. 139; Stanley Lebergott, *Manpower in Economic Growth: The American Record since 1800* (New York: McGraw-Hill, 1964), table A-4, p. 513.

5. Walter Lippmann, *Drift and Mastery* (Madison: University of Wisconsin Press, 1985 [1914]), 54, 52–56.

6. Leon Harris, *Merchant Princes: An Intimate History of Jewish Families Who Built Great Department Stores* (New York: Harper and Row, 1979), 3–35; George E. Berkley, *The Filenes* (Boston: International Pocket Library, 1998), 120–21.

7. Susan Strasser, *Satisfaction Guaranteed: The Making of the American Mass Market* (New York: Basic Books, 1989), 210–11; Tom Mahoney, *The Great Merchants: The Stories of Twenty Famous Retail Operations and the People Who Made Them Great* (New York: Harper and Row, 1955), 6, 7, 14; Daniel J. Boorstin, *The Americans: The Democratic Experience* (New York: Vintage Books, 1973), 101; Paul H. Nystrom, "An Estimate of the Volume of Retail Business in the United States," *Harvard Business Review* 3 (January 1925): 150–59; Thomas K. McCraw, "Rethinking the Trust Question," in *Regulation in Perspective: Historical Essays,* ed. Thomas K. McCraw (Cambridge, MA: Harvard University Press, 1981), 1–55; William Leach, *Land of Desire: Merchants, Power, and the Rise of a New American Culture* (New York: Pantheon Books, 1993), 15–38.

8. Susan Porter Benson, *Counter Cultures: Saleswomen, Managers, and Customers in American Department Stores, 1890–1940* (Urbana: University of Illinois Press, 1986), 32, 34.

9. "Made a Holiday," *BG*, September 4, 1912, 13; Berkley, *Filenes*, 120–21, 126–27.

10. Elaine S. Abelson, *When Ladies Go A-thieving: Middle-Class Shoplifters in the Victorian Department Store* (New York: Oxford University Press, 1989), 52; "Made a Holiday," *BG*; Leach, *Land of Desire*, 39–111.

11. Theodore Dreiser, *Sister Carrie* (New York: New American Library, 1980 [1900]), 26; Leach, *Land of Desire*, 61, 77; William Leach, "Transformations in a Culture of Consumption: Women and Department Stores, 1890–1925," *JAH* 71 (September 1984): 319–42; Abelson, *Ladies*, 63–90.

12. Edgar J. Goodspeed, "Buying Happiness," *Atlantic*, September 1925, 343–47; Benson, *Counter Cultures*, 12–30.

13. Mary Antin, *The Promised Land* (Princeton, NJ: Princeton University Press, 1985 [1904]), 187. Andrew R. Heinze, *Adapting to Abundance: Jewish Immigrants, Mass Consumption, and the Search for American Identity* (New York: Columbia University Press, 1990), 89–115, 133–44; Sarah Deutsch, *Women and the City: Gender, Space, and Power in Boston, 1870–1940* (New York: Oxford University Press, 2000), 21; Mamie Garvin Fields with Karen Fields, *Lemon Swamp and Other Places: A Carolina Memoir* (New York: Free Press, 1983), 153. Lizabeth Cohen, *Making a New Deal: Industrial Workers in Chicago, 1919–1939* (New York: Cambridge University Press, 1990), 147–56.

14. Benson, *Counter Cultures*, 98; Leach, *Land of Desire*, 116–18.

15. Nystrom quoted in Strasser, *Satisfaction Guaranteed*, 210; Leach, "Transformations," 329–42; Deutsch, *Women and the City*, 15; Benson, *Counter Cultures*, 82–91, 76.

16. This of course is not meant to suggest that women did not previously play economic roles, but the notion of women as female purchasing agents rapidly took hold around the turn of the century. Abelson, *Ladies*, 13–32; Leach, "Transformations," 333. Canned foods statistics: Bureau of the Census, *13th*

Census 1910 (Washington, DC: GPO, 1911), vol. 8, p. 382; Bureau of the Census, *Historical Statistics,* Series G 881–915, pp. 330–31.

17. Josephine Preston Peabody, *Diary and Letters of Josephine Preston Peabody,* ed. Christina Hopkinson Baker (Boston: Houghton Mifflin, 1925), 280; Elizabeth Ewen, *Immigrant Women in the Land of Dollars: Life and Culture on the Lower East Side, 1890–1925* (New York: Monthly Review Press, 1985); Heinze, *Adapting,* 200.

18. Boorstin, *Americans,* 91–100; Wendy Gamber, *The Female Economy: The Millinery and Dressmaking Trades, 1860–1930* (Urbana: University of Illinois Press, 1997), 137; Berkley, *Filenes,* 50; Susan Strasser, *Never Done: A History of American Housework* (New York: Henry Holt and Company, 2000), 125–44.

19. Filene's advertisements, *BG,* December 20, 1908, 31, and December 6, 1908, 33; Boorstin, *Americans,* 108; Alfred D. Chandler, Jr., *The Visible Hand: The Managerial Revolution in American Business* (Cambridge, MA: Harvard University Press, 1977), 224–39; Susan Porter Benson, "The Cinderella of Occupations: Managing the Work of Department Store Saleswomen, 1900–1940," *BHR* 55 (spring 1981): 1–25.

20. Along the East Coast and in major cities, cash registers became common just after the turn of the century and achieved saturation in the next few decades. See Walter A. Friedman, "John H. Patterson and the Sales Strategy of the National Cash Register Company, 1884 to 1922," *BHR* 72 (winter 1998): 552–84.

21. Dreiser, *Sister Carrie,* 345, 64; William Leiserson, Diary, June 23, 1906, Leiserson Papers, Box 48, Diaries—1906, vol. 1.

22. Sears catalogue quoted in Boris Emmet and John E. Jeuck, *Catalogues and Counters: A History of Sears, Roebuck and Company* (Chicago: University of Chicago Press, 1950), 150–89; Tom Schlereth, "Country Stores, County Fairs, and Mail-Order Catalogues: Consumption in Rural America," in *Consuming Visions: Accumulation and Display of Goods in America, 1880–1920,* ed. Simon J. Bronner (New York: W. W. Norton, 1989), 339–375; Hal S. Barron, *Mixed Harvest: The Second Great Transformation in the Rural North, 1870–1930* (Chapel Hill: University of North Carolina Press, 1997), 155–91.

23. Zelie Leigh, "Shopping Round," *Atlantic,* September 1925, 198–201; Robert Hendrickson, *The Grand Emporiums: The Illustrated History of the Great Department Stores* (New York: Stein and Day, 1978), 122; Benson, *Counter Cultures,* 51.

24. "From Tunnel to Filene's a Step," *BG,* December 1, 1908, 5; Hendrickson, *Grand Emporiums,* 130–31.

25. *Brief History of the Filene Automatic Bargain Basement;* Filene's advertisement, *BG,* February 11, 1912, 41.

26. Filene testimony, *Regulation of Prices,* 1917, 212–13; Filene, "17 Stockturns a Year," 469–73, 569–71.

27. Harris, *Merchant Princes,* 14; Berkley, *Filenes,* 166–67; "Basement Business: Use It to Interest Masses and Advertise the Entire Store," *DGE,* April 22, 1916, 43.

28. Mahoney, *Great Merchants,* 257–60; Hendrickson, *Grand Emporiums,* 143–44.

29. Heinze, *Adapting,* 111–12, 187, 192–202; Ewen, *Immigrant Women,* 168–70.

30. Clara Belle Thompson, "Bargains and Basements," *SEP,* June 6, 1925, 19, 174, 177–78; Ad Man, "Do You Believe in Ads?" *Outlook,* August 4,

1926, 475–77; Heinze, *Adapting*, 111; Louis Rothschild, "Shopping Around: A Feminine Habit That Blocks Profiteering," *Independent*, August 15, 1925, 187–88.

31. Edward L. Ayers, *The Promise of the New South: Life after Reconstruction* (New York: Oxford University Press, 1992); Grace Hale, *Making Whiteness: The Culture of Segregation in the South, 1890–1940* (New York: Pantheon Books, 1998).

32. Mary Wood testimony, *Regulation of Prices*, 1917, 286; Ewen, *Immigrant Women*, 67–71; Richter quoted in Steve Fraser, *Labor Will Rule: Sidney Hillman and the Rise of American Labor* (New York: Free Press, 1991), 227; Goodspeed, "Buying Happiness," 343–47.

33. Leach, *Land of Desire*, 232–33, 192; T. J. Jackson Lears, *Fables of Abundance: A Cultural History of Advertising in America* (New York: Basic Books, 1994), 52–53, and *No Place of Grace: Antimodernism and the Transformation of American Culture, 1880–1920* (New York: Pantheon Books, 1981), 54, 96; John F. Kasson, *Amusing the Million: Coney Island at the Turn of the Century* (New York: Hill and Wang, 1978), 96, 98–100, 232–33; *Dry Goods Reporter* quoted in Abelson, *Ladies*, 73; Abelson, *Ladies*, 173–74; Vice Commission of Chicago quoted in Benson, *Counter Cultures*, 135; Willard Thorp, afterword to Dreiser, *Sister Carrie* (1961), 470. For treating, see Kathy Lee Peiss, *Cheap Amusements: Working Women and Leisure in Turn-of-the-Century New York* (Philadelphia: Temple University Press, 1986).

34. Chandler, *Visible Hand*, 209–39; Leach, *Land of Desire*, 27; Emmet and Jeuck, *Catalogues and Counters*, 150–68; Strasser, *Satisfaction Guaranteed*, 215–21; Schlereth, "Country Stores," 371–72; Emmet and Jeuck, *Catalogues and Counters*, 152; David A. Horowitz, *Beyond Left and Right: Insurgency and the Establishment* (Urbana: University of Illinois Press, 1997), 115–37.

35. Leach, *Land of Desire*, 182–85.

36. Charles Miller, "The Maintenance of Uniform Resale Prices," *University of Pennsylvania Law Review* 63 (November 1914): 33.

37. Strasser, *Satisfaction Guaranteed*, 3–57; Richard S. Tedlow, *New and Improved: The Story of Mass Marketing in America* (New York: Basic Books, 1990), 3–111.

38. William Hard, "Better Business," *Overland Monthly* 64 (July–December 1914): 203.

39. Thomas K. McCraw, "Competition and 'Fair Trade': History and Theory," *Research in Economic History* 16 (1996): 188.

40. H. R. Tosdal, "Price Maintenance in the Book Trade," *Quarterly Journal of Economics* 30 (November 1915): 86–109; "The War against Cut-Throat Prices," *Current Opinion*, January 1914, 61–64.

41. *Bobbs-Merrill Company v. Straus et al. Doing Business as R. H. Macy & Company*, 210 U.S. 339 (1908); 231 U.S. 222 (1913); *Great Atlantic & Pacific Tea Co. v. Cream of Wheat Co.*, 224 Fed. 566 (1915); Sumner H. Slichter, "The Cream of Wheat Case," *Political Science Quarterly* 31 (September 1916): 392–412; McCraw, "Competition and 'Fair Trade,' " 189–91.

42. R. D. Eastman (Kellogg Toasted Corn Flake Co.) to the Editor, "The Right of the Manufacturer to Maintain Prices," *Outlook*, September 20, 1913, 124–27; Philip Scranton, *Endless Novelty: Specialty Production and American Industrialization, 1865–1925* (Princeton, NJ: Princeton University Press, 1997).

43. Pabst Extract advertisement, *Life*, October 5, 1911, 593; Cascarets Cathartic Candy advertisement, *Los Angeles Times*, June 3, 1900, 8; Welch's Grape Juice advertisement, *SEP*, April 5, 1913.

44. McCraw, "Competition and 'Fair Trade,' " 189; Scranton, *Endless Novelty*, 247–59; McCraw, "Rethinking the Trust Question," 6, 32; Chandler, *Visible Hand*, 207–344.

45. Joseph Palamountain, *The Politics of Distribution* (Cambridge, MA: Harvard University Press, 1955), 38–48; McCraw, "Competition and 'Fair Trade,' " 198–99; Jonathan J. Bean, *Beyond the Broker State: Federal Policies toward Small Business, 1936–1961* (Chapel Hill: University of North Carolina Press, 1996), 17–36; Paul T. Cherington, "Price Maintenance—Discussion," *AER* 6 (March 1918): 206; E. M. Patterson, "Co-operation among Retail Grocers in Philadelphia," *AER* 5 (June 1915): 279–91.

46. *Congressional Record*, 63d Cong., 2d sess., September 29, 1914, 51, 15857; "The Supreme Court of the United States on Price Maintenance," *Scientific American*, June 14, 1913, 545; William H. Spencer, "Recent Cases on Price Maintenance," *Journal of Political Economy* 30 (April 1922): 189–200; H. R. Tosdal, "Price Maintenance," *AER* 8 (March 1918): 34; McCraw, "Competition and 'Fair Trade,' " 197–209.

47. "Dealers Champion Price-Fixing Bill," *NYT*, May 31, 1916, 20; Miller, "Maintenance of Uniform Resale Prices," 34; "Opposition to the 'Stevens Bill,' " *Current Opinion* 59 (August 1915): 135–36; U.S. Chamber of Commerce quoted in "Referendum for Resale Price Plan," *NYT*, May 19, 1916, 15; Kelly quoted in " 'The Stevens Bill,' for the Maintenance of Resale Prices," *Current Opinion* 58 (May 1915): 370; Norman Hapgood, "Why Price Maintenance Is Right," *Harper's*, December 11, 1915, 567–68; Palamountain, *Politics of Distribution*, 90–106.

48. McCraw, "Competition and 'Fair Trade,' " 195; Louis Brandeis, "On Maintaining Makers' Prices," *Harper's*, June 14, 1913, 6; "War Against Cut-Throat Prices," 64; Gilbert Montague, "The Proposed Patent Law Revision," *Harvard Law Review* 26 (December 1912): 136; Tosdal, "Price Maintenance," *AER*.

49. James H. Collins, "She Spends $20,000 Every Minute," *Mother's Magazine*, January 1917, as reprinted in *Regulation of Prices*, 1917, 620–24.

50. C. E. LaVigne testimony, *Regulation of Prices*, 1917, 375.

51. Christine Frederick, "The Woman Who Buys Wisely," *LHJ*, November 1913, 95. See also Christine Frederick, "What You Should Know about the Can You Buy," October 1916, 54, and "How I Learned Food Values," November 1917, 56, both in *LHJ*. "Ad Clubs Debate Anti–Price Cutting," *NYT*, June 29, 1916, 11; H. C. Brown testimony, *Regulation of Prices*, 1917, 557–62.

52. J. Newcomb Blackman testimony, *Regulation of Prices*, 1916, 75; Edward Rogers, "Predatory Price Cutting as Unfair Trade," *Harvard Law Review* 27 (December 1913): 151.

53. Louis Brandeis, "Cut-Throat Prices: The Competition That Kills," *Harper's*, November 15, 1913, 12; House Committee on Interstate and Foreign Commerce, *To Prevent Discrimination in Prices and to Provide for Publicity of Prices to Dealers and the Public: Hearings*, 63d Cong., 2d sess., February 6, 1914–January 9, 1915, 39–40; Brandeis, "Co-operation vs. Cut-Throat Competition," *Harper's*, June 12, 1915, 573–74.

54. Edmond Wise testimony, *Regulation of Prices*, 1917, 10–11; F. Colburn Pinkham, "Fixed Prices and the Public Pocketbook," *Harper's*, December 4, 1915, 532; J. M. Barnes testimony, *Regulation of Prices*, 1917, 80–82; "Problems of the Bargain Basement," *NYT*, February 22, 1925, E13.

55. Cherington, "Price Maintenance—Discussion," 207, 201; F. W. Taussig, "Price Maintenance," *AER* 6 (March 1916): 170–84; Tosdal, "Price Maintenance," *AER*.

56. Mary Wood testimony, *Regulation of Prices*, 1917, 285–87; Edward Filene testimony, ibid., 214. For AFL testimony, see Samuel Gompers to Lew Hahn, reprinted in ibid., 94.

57. Daniel Horowitz, *The Morality of Spending: Attitudes toward the Consumer Society in America, 1875–1940* (Baltimore: Johns Hopkins University Press, 1985), 67–68.

58. Rebecca Edwards, *Angels in the Machinery: Gender in American Party Politics from the Civil War to the Progressive Era* (New York: Oxford University Press, 1997), 59–61, 68–74, 87, 147; Joanne R. Reitano, *The Tariff Question in the Gilded Age: The Great Debate of 1888* (University Park: Pennsylvania State University Press, 1994), 89–95; Lodge quoted in David P. Thelen, "Patterns of Consumer Consciousness in the Progressive Movement: Robert M. LaFollette, the Antitrust Persuasion, and Labor Legislation," in *The Quest for Social Justice: The Morris Fromkin Memorial Lectures, 1970–1980*, ed. Ralph M. Aderman (Madison: University of Wisconsin Press, 1983), 32.

59. "Beef Trust Is Beaten," *BG*, May 21, 1902, 1, 2; Steven L. Piott, *The Anti-monopoly Persuasion: Popular Resistance to the Rise of Big Business in the Midwest* (Westport, CT: Greenwood Press, 1985), 21–22, 32, 82–88; Jimmy M. Skaggs, *Prime Cut: Livestock Raising and Meatpacking in the United States, 1607–1983* (College Station: Texas A & M University Press, 1986), 88–106.

60. Russell quoted in Skaggs, *Prime Cut*, 101, 100–105; Gwendolyn Mink, *Old Labor and New Immigrants in American Political Development: Union, Party, and State, 1875–1920* (Ithaca, NY: Cornell University Press, 1986), 102; Piott, *Anti-monopoly Persuasion*, 85.

61. Seymour Martin Lipset and Reinhard Bendix, *Social Mobility in Industrial Society* (Berkeley: University of California Press, 1959), 48–56; Olivier Zunz, *Making America Corporate, 1870–1920* (Chicago: University of Chicago Press, 1990); Horowitz, *Morality of Spending*, 67–84; Richard Hofstadter, *The Age of Reform: From Bryan to F.D.R.* (New York: Alfred A. Knopf, 1955), 170.

62. For quotes see Hofstadter, *Age of Reform*, 170, 216.

63. Quoted in Piott, *Anti-monopoly Persuasion*, 64, 99.

64. Henry Leffmann, "Who Is to Blame for the High Prices? Why the Trusts Are to Blame," *LHJ*, November 1, 1910, 21; Horowitz, *Morality of Spending*, 52–53; U.S. Bureau of the Census, *Historical Statistics of the United States: Colonial Times to 1970* (Washington, DC: GPO, 1976), Series G 470–79, p. 320.

65. Paula E. Hyman, "Immigrant Women and Consumer Protest: The New York City Kosher Meat Boycott of 1902," *American Jewish History* 70 (September 1980): 94; Herbert G. Gutman, *Work, Culture, and Society in Industrializing America: Essays in American Working-Class and Social History* (New York: Vintage Books, 1977), 61–63.

66. Hyman, "Immigrant Women," 95.

67. "Big Crowds Out," *BG*, May 22, 1902, 8; "Check Meat Riots," *BG*, May 22, 1902, evening edition, 1, 9; Deutsch, *Women and the City*, 198, 200.

68. Jenna Weissman Joselit, "The Landlord as Czar: Pre–World War I Tenant Activity," in *The Tenant Movement in New York City, 1904–1984*, ed. Ronald Lawson (New Brunswick, NJ: Rutgers University Press, 1986), 39–50; Ronald Lawson, "The Rent Strike in New York City, 1904–1980: The Evolution of a Social Movement Strategy," *Journal of Urban History* 10 (May 1984): 235–38; Annelise Orleck, *Common Sense and a Little Fire: Women and Working-Class Politics in the United States, 1900–1965* (Chapel Hill: University of North Carolina Press, 1995), 29–30; Ewen, *Immigrant Women*, 126–27.

69. Orleck, *Common Sense*, 23–30; Hyman, "Immigrant Women," 99.

70. Hyman, "Immigrant Women," 103; Werner Sombart, "American Capitalism's Economic Rewards," in *Failure of a Dream? Essays in the History of American Socialism*, ed. John Laslett and Seymour Martin Lipset (Garden City, NY: Doubleday Anchor, 1974), 599; Walter Lippmann, *Drift and Mastery* (Madison: University of Wisconsin Press, 1985 [1914]), 56.

71. Lippmann, *Drift and Mastery*, 54.

72. Lemlich quoted in Nan Enstad, *Ladies of Labor, Girls of Adventure: Working Women, Popular Culture, and Labor Politics at the Turn of the Twentieth Century* (New York: Columbia University Press, 1999), 146–47.

73. Quotes in Orleck, *Common Sense*, 6, 133.

74. Ibid., 64–65.

75. Quote in Allis Rosenberg Wolfe, "Women, Consumerism, and the National Consumers' League," *Labor History* 16 (summer 1975): 380; Kathryn Kish Sklar, *Florence Kelley and the Nation's Work: The Rise of Women's Political Culture, 1830–1900* (New Haven, CT: Yale University Press, 1995); Landon R. Y. Storrs, *Civilizing Capitalism: The National Consumers' League, Women's Activism, and Labor Standards in the New Deal Era* (Chapel Hill: University of North Carolina Press, 2000), 20.

76. Theda Skocpol, *Protecting Soldiers and Mothers: The Political Origins of Social Policy in the United States* (Cambridge, MA: Belknap Press, 1992), 328–33; Kathryn Kish Sklar, "The Consumer's White Label Campaign of the National Consumers' League, 1898–1918," in *Getting and Spending: European and American Consumer Societies in the Twentieth Century*, ed. Susan Strasser, Charles McGovern, and Matthias Judt (New York: Cambridge University Press, 1998), 17–35. On women's clubs, see Elizabeth S. Clemens, *The People's Lobby: Organizational Innovation and the Rise of Interest Group Politics in the United States, 1890–1925* (Chicago: University of Chicago Press, 1997); Michael Kazin, *The Populist Persuasion: An American History* (New York: Basic Books, 1995), 79–106; Paula Baker, "The Domestication of Politics: Women and American Political Society, 1780–1920," in *AHR* 89 (June 1984): 620–47; and Robyn Muncy, *Creating a Female Dominion in American Reform, 1890–1935* (New York: Oxford University Press, 1991).

77. Orleck, *Common Sense*, 63–80, 123; J. Joseph Huthmacher, *Senator Robert F. Wagner and the Rise of Urban Liberalism* (New York: Atheneum, 1968).

78. Fraser, *Labor Will Rule*, 28; Eileen Boris, *Home to Work: Motherhood and the Politics of Industrial Homework in the United States* (New York: Cambridge University Press, 1994), 49–122.

79. Filene's advertisements, *BG*, December 6, 1908, 33; December 20, 1908, 31.

80. Edward Filene, "Why the Employees Run Our Business," *System*, December 1918, 805–10; Edward Filene, "Basic Regulations under Which We Are Working," Address before the Council Meeting, January 31, 1919, Filene Papers, Box 32, Folder 40.

81. Herbert Croly, *The Promise of American Life* (New York: MacMillan, 1909), 205–6.

82. Horowitz, *Morality of Spending*, xxvi; Gompers quoted in Lawrence Glickman, *A Living Wage: American Workers and the Making of Consumer Society* (Ithaca, NY: Cornell University Press, 1997), 64–65, 82–83.

83. Glickman, *Living Wage*, 31, 60, 63, 69, 70, 76–77.

84. Fraser, *Labor Will Rule*, 77–113.

Chapter Two
Business without a Buyer, 1917–1930

1. "President Determined upon Food Inquiry," February 21, 1917, 7; "Women in Uproar at a Food Meeting" and "Women in Bread Riot at Doors of City Hall," February 21, 1917, 1, 7, all in *NYT*.

2. Robert Cuff, *The War Industries Board: Business-Government Relations during World War I* (Baltimore: Johns Hopkins University Press, 1973), 93–98; "High Prices Tottering," *LD*, January 25, 1919, 14.

3. "Plan to End War Profits," *NYT*, November 2, 1917, 11; Paul A. C. Koistinen, *Mobilizing for Modern War: The Political Economy of American Warfare, 1865–1919* (Lawrence: University Press of Kansas, 1997), 262–67; Dana Frank, "Housewives, Socialists, and the Politics of Food: The 1917 New York Cost-of-Living Protests," *Feminist Studies* 11 (summer 1985), 257.

4. "Women in Uproar at a Food Meeting"; "Women in Bread Riot at Doors of City Hall."

5. See, for example, "Food Riots in the United States," *LD*, March 3, 1917, 533–34; Bruno Lasker, "The Food Riots," *Survey*, March 3, 1917, 638–41; "Potato Boycott Move Spreads; Price Drop Due," February 26, 1917, 3; "Women Start 'Food Strike,' " February 21, 1917, 1, both in *Chicago Tribune*; and "Boycotting Housewives Shout Their Defiance," February 23, 1917, 1; "Food Takes Drop, Due to Boycott," February 28, 1917, 3, both in *Philadelphia Evening Bulletin*. See also Tom G. Hall, "Wilson and the Food Crisis: Agricultural Price Control during World War I," *Agricultural History* 47:1 (1973): 25–46.

6. "President Determined upon Food Inquiry," February 21, 1917, 7; "Women Denounce Brown's Food Bill," August 7, 1917, 4; "May Delay Food Bill Vote," August 19, 1917, 4, all in *NYT*.

7. Cuff, *War Industries Board*, 95–98, 128–31; Koistinen, *Mobilizing for Modern War*, 194.

8. Ray Lyman Wilbur, foreword to *We Pledged Allegiance: A Librarian's Intimate Story of the United States Food Administration*, by Edith Guerrier (Stanford, CA: Stanford University Press, 1941), v–vii; George H. Nash, *The Life of Herbert Hoover, Vol. 3: Master of Emergencies, 1917–1918* (New York: W. W. Norton, 1996), 3–44.

9. "Organize Food-Saving Teams," June 19, 1917, 2; Roosevelt quoted in "How to Save in Big Homes," July 17, 1917, 3; "President Appeals for Food Canning," July 30, 1917, 10; "Women Help Hoover," August 19, 1917, E7, all in *NYT*. See also Stephen Ponder, "Popular Propaganda: The Food Administration in World War I," *Journalism & Mass Communication Quarterly* 72 (autumn 1995): 539–50; and Nash, *Herbert Hoover*, 41–44. Mary Jean Houde, *Reaching Out: A Story of the General Federation of Women's Clubs* (Chicago: Mobium Press, 1989), 153–54; Clara S. Lingle, "Social Conditions and War," *GFWC Magazine*, July 1917, 14–15.

10. David Burner, *The Politics of Provincialism: The Democratic Party in Transition, 1918–1932* (New York: Knopf, 1968), 28–32.

11. "New York Will Aid in Saving of Food," June 19, 1917, 2; "Retailers of Sugar Agree to Cut Price," October 27, 1917, 12; "Food Canvass This Week," October 28, 1917, 18; "Plan for Women's Aid," June 22, 1917, 3; "Food Pledge for Women," August 4, 1917, 3, all in *NYT*. Christopher Capozzola, "Uncle Sam Wants You: Political Obligations in World War I America" (Ph.D. diss., Columbia University, 2002), 137, 143–46, Chapter 3. See also Marsha Gordon, "Onward Kitchen Soldiers: Mobilizing the Domestic during World War I," *Canadian Review of American Studies* 29:2 (1999): 61–87.

12. "Control of Food by Government to Begin on Nov. 1," *NYT*, October 10, 1917, 1, 22.

13. "Must Save to Win War, Hoover Warns Public," July 4, 1917, 4; "Hoover Is Elated over Food Outlook," July 29, 1917, 2, both in *NYT*. Alice Ames Winter, "What War Is Doing to Club Life," *GFWC Magazine*, November 1917, 5. For a good overview of volunteer efforts, see Maxcy Robson Dickson, *The Food Front in World War I* (Washington, DC: American Council on Public Affairs, 1944); and David M. Kennedy, *Over Here: The First World War and American Society* (New York: Oxford University Press, 1980), 117–23.

14. On the WIB, see Cuff, *War Industries Board*; Ellis W. Hawley, *The Great War and the Search for a Modern Order: A History of the American People and Their Institutions* (New York: St. Martin's Press, 1979), 20–27; and Kennedy, *Over Here*, 126–37.

15. "Wilson Warns Foes," June 19, 1917, 2; "House Rejects Food Bill Changes," June 22, 1917, 3, both in *NYT*; Nash, *Herbert Hoover*, 45–74; Burner, *Politics of Provincialism*, 35–36; I. A. Newby, "States' Rights and Southern Congressmen during World War I," *Phylon* 24:1 (1963): 34–50.

16. Sherman quoted in "House Rejects Food Bill Changes," June 22, 1917, 3; "Pushing the Food Bill," June 23, 1917, 8; "Food Bill Passed, with Prohibition Clause, 365 to 5," June 24, 1917, 1, 2; "The Food Bill Delay," June 28, 1917, 10; "Senate Speeds Up Food Bill Debate," July 4, 1917, 4; "The Food Bill Muddle," July 10, 1917, 12; "Senate to Vote on Food Bill July 21," July 11, 1917, 1, 18; "Blocking the Food Bill," July 11, 1917, 8; "Keep to the One Purpose," July 15, 1917, 18; "Farmers Ask Food Control," July 16, 1917, 7; "Curb Hoover's Power in Revised Food Bill," July 18, 1917, 3; "Progress of the Food Bill," July 23, 1917, 8; "May Veto Food Bill Because of War Board Rider," July 24, 1917, 1, 3; "Give Us the Food Bill," July 24, 1917, 9; "Fight over War Board On Today," July 25, 1917, 1, 2; "New Deadlock over Food Bill," July 30, 1917, 1, 10; "President

Wins; Hoover to Be Sole Food Controller," July 31, 1917, 1; "Food Bill Victory Expected This Week," August 6, 1917, 3, all in *NYT*.

17. "Food Bill Passed by Senate, 81 to 6," July 22, 1917, 1, 4; *NYT* quoted in "Food Bill Signed: Hoover in Office; Warns Profiteers," August 11, 1917, 1; "16,000 Women to Aid City Food Campaign," October 1, 1917, 22; "Start City Food Drive," October 7, 1917, 14; U.S. Food Administration quoted in "Will Reduce War Profits on Food," October 28, 1917, 1, 18; "7,406,544 Food Pledges," November 7, 1917, 20, all in *NYT*. "The Problem of Food Conservation," *GFWC Magazine*, November 1917, 12–13; Mrs. Joseph C. Gawler, "Emergency Work," ibid., November 1917, 28–33; William Clinton Mullendore, *History of the United States Food Administration, 1917–1919* (Stanford, CA: Stanford University Press, 1941), 18–20; Ivan L. Pollock, *The Food Administration in Iowa* (Iowa City: State Historical Society in Iowa, 1923), 126–57; Joseph Carruth, "World War I Propaganda and Its Effects in Arkansas," *Arkansas Historical Quarterly* 56 (winter 1997): 385–98; Koistinen, *Mobilizing for Modern War*, 255–56; Cynthia Brandimarte, "Using Government Documents: The Food Administration Papers for Texas," *Southwestern Historical Quarterly* 104 (October 2000): 262–81.

18. "Plan for Women's Aid," June 22, 1917, 3; "Hints to Housewives on Food," July 11, 1917, 12; "Food Pledge for Women," August 4, 1917, 3; "Food Canvass This Week," October 28, 1917, 18; Hoover quoted in "Food Pledge Week," October 28, 1917, E2; Van Norden quoted in "Public-Spirited Men Help in Saving Food," November 12, 1917, 20; " 'Hoover' Prices on Menu," November 19, 1917, 18, all in *NYT*. Joan Sullivan, "In Pursuit of Legitimacy: Home Economists and the Hoover Apron in World War I," *Dress* 26 (1999): 31–46.

19. "Churches in Food Saving," July 11, 1917, 12; "Churchmen Indorse Hoover," July 18, 1917, 3; "Churches Back Hoover," July 21, 1917, 3; "Rabbis Urge Food Saving," July 24, 1917, 3; "Chain Stores Aid Food Saving," July 21, 1917, 3; "Ousts Servants Who Spurn Food Cards," October 30, 1917, 14; "500,000 Food Pledges In," November 4, 1917, 17, all in *NYT*. See also, Nash, *Herbert Hoover*, 152–62.

20. Quotes from "Control of Food by Government to Begin On Nov. 1," October 10, 1917, 1, 22, and "Hoover Assumes Control of Prices," November 4, 1917, 17, both in *NYT*. See also "Proclaims Food License System," October 11, 1917, 1; "To Control Retail Prices Now," October 12, 1917, 10; "Cuts Food Profits to Pre-war Figures," December 1, 1917, 9; "Jail for Profiteers," December 12, 1917, 4, all in *NYT*; and George Soule, *Prosperity Decade: From War to Depression, 1917–1929* (New York: Rinehart, 1947), 23–26.

21. "State Merchants Join in Food Saving," October 2, 1917, 13; "Food-Saving Campaign On," October 7, 1917, 14; "Hoover Predicts Drop in Prices," October 19, 1917, 1; "Some Prices Are Far Too High," October 20, 1917, 12; "Administration Gives Chicago Food Prices," October 24, 1917, 15; "To List Food Prices for the Housewives Here," October 26, 1917, 5; "Women's War Work Chief Forum Topic," November 17, 1917, 13; "Ousts Servants Who Spurn Food Cards," October 30, 1917, 14; "500,000 Food Pledges In," November 4, 1917, 17; "Jail for Profiteers," December 12, 1917, 4, all in *NYT*. Kent Lutey, "Lutey Brothers Marketeria: America's First Self-Service Grocers," *Montana* 28 (spring 1978): 50–57.

22. "Meat Investigation to Be Country-wide," July 26, 1917, 9; "To List Food Prices for Housewives Here," October 26, 1917, 5; "Packing Industry under Restriction," November 25, 1917, 19; "Food Saved in Massachusetts," December 3, 1917, 20; "Packers' Profits Increased by War," January 18, 1919, 4, all in *NYT*. Soule quoted in Robert Cuff, "Herbert Hoover, the Ideology of Voluntarism, and War Organization during the Great War," *JAH* 64 (September 1977): 369; Jimmy M. Skaggs, *Prime Cut: Livestock Raising and Meatpacking in the United States, 1607–1983* (College Station: Texas A&M University Press, 1986), 86–88, 105, 117; Robert Cuff, "The Dilemmas of Voluntarism: Hoover and the Pork-Packing Agreement of 1917–1919," *Agricultural History* 53:4 (1979): 727–47; Nash, *Herbert Hoover*, 163–96, 314–46.

23. "State Plans to Act on Advance in Milk," October 1, 1917, 22; "Milk Going Higher, Dairyman Predicts," October 7, 1917, 14; "Says Farmers Make Good Profit on Milk," October 13, 1917, 14; "Federal Officials After Milk Dealers," October 14, 1917, 16; "To Adjust Milk Prices," November 21, 1917, 10; "Federal Milk Body Named for City," November 22, 1917, 13, all in *NYT*. James Guth, "Herbert Hoover, the United States Food Administration, and Dairy," *BHR* 55 (summer 1981): 171, 174, 180.

24. Frederic C. Howe, *The High Cost of Living* (New York: Scribner's, 1917). "Has a Food Plan to Best Middlemen," July 29, 1917, 2; "Club Plan Proposed to Cut Living Costs," October 24, 1917, 15; "City Gets Privilege of Dealing in Food," November 2, 1917, 11, all in *NYT*.

25. David Montgomery, *The Fall of the House of Labor: The Workplace, the State, and American Labor Activism, 1865–1925* (New York: Cambridge University Press, 1987), 330–85; Melvyn Dubofsky, *The State and Labor in Modern America* (Chapel Hill: University of North Carolina Press, 1994), 61–81; Steve Fraser, "Dress Rehearsal for the New Deal: Shop-Floor Insurgents, Political Elites, and Industrial Democracy in the Amalgamated Clothing Workers Union," in *Working-Class America*, ed. Michael Frisch and Daniel Walkowitz (Urbana: University of Illinois Press, 1983), 218–19; Gary Gerstle, *Working-Class Americanism: The Politics of Labor in a Textile City, 1914–1960* (New York: Cambridge University Press, 1989), 42–45; Michael Kazin, *The Populist Persuasion: An American History* (New York: Basic Books, 1995), 69–72; Joseph McCartin, *Labor's Great War: The Struggle for Industrial Democracy and the Origins of Modern American Labor Relations, 1912–1921* (Chapel Hill: University of North Carolina Press, 1997).

26. Florence Kelley to Edward Filene, October 25, 1918, December 5, 1918, Filene Papers, Box 11, Folder 2; House Committee on District of Columbia, *Minimum Wage for Women and Children: Hearings*, 65th Cong., 2d sess., April 16, 1918, 27; Landon Storrs, *Civilizing Capitalism: The National Consumers' League, Women's Activism, and Labor Standards in the New Deal Era* (Chapel Hill: University of North Carolina Press, 2000), 41–59; Theda Skocpol, *Protecting Soldiers and Mothers: The Political Origins of Social Policy in the United States* (Cambridge, MA: Belknap Press, 1992), 306–9, 419–21. Steve Fraser, *Labor Will Rule: Sidney Hillman and the Rise of American Labor* (New York: Free Press, 1991), 118–19.

27. "All Labor Disputes Go to New War Board," *NYT*, August 11, 1917, 1. Daniel Horowitz, *The Morality of Spending: Attitudes toward the Consumer Society in America, 1875–1940* (Baltimore: Johns Hopkins University Press, 1985),

120–27; Leon Fink, *Progressive Intellectuals and the Dilemmas of Democratic Commitment* (Cambridge, MA: Harvard University Press, 1997), 214–41.

28. F. W. Taussig, "Price-Fixing as Seen by a Price-Fixer," *Quarterly Journal of Economics* 33 (February 1919): 213; Brookings, Peek, and Baruch quoted in Cuff, *War Industries Board*, 233–34, 237.

29. "Pursuing the Profiteers," *NR*, September 3, 1919, 140. Irving Fisher, "Will Prices Drop to Pre-war Levels?" July 1921, 68; "High Prices; and a Remedy," September 1919, 272, both in *American Review of Reviews*; O. M. Kile, "Other People's Prices," *Outlook*, July 25, 1923, 471–73. Robert Himmelberg, "Business, Antitrust Policy, and the Industrial Board of the Department of Commerce, 1919," *BHR* 42 (spring 1968): 14, 12–22; Koistinen, *Mobilizing for Modern War*, 262–88.

30. "Text of President's Message," *New York Sun*, August 8, 1919; "Wilson Urges U.S. Control of Clothing, Fuel and Feed and Time Limit on Cold Storage," *New York Herald*, August 9, 1919; "Palmer Plan to Cut High Cost Futile," *New York Globe*, August 19, 1919; "Sure Public Will Compel a Conviction," *New York Tribune*, September 18, 1919, all in Lusk Papers, Newspaper Clippings, Reel 7. "Department of Justice May Appoint Women to Detect Profiteers," *New York Tribune*, August 21, 1919; "Appeal to Earners of High Wages," *New York Journal*, August 27, 1919, both in Lusk Papers, Newspaper Clippings, Reel 6; Palmer quoted in "Retail Profiteers," *NYT*, August 22, 1919; "The Housewives' Brigade," *NYT*, September 13, 1919.

31. "Women to Discuss Foods," *NYT*, March 9, 1919, 13; "Housewives Join to Quiz Middlemen and Retailers on High Cost of Living," *New York Telegram*, August 21, 1919, in Lusk Papers, Newspaper Clippings, Reel 7. See also "Housewives of Denver Demand Prosecution of Food Profiteers," August 5, 1919, 1, 2; "State 'Fair Price Board' Meets to Quell Gougers," August 12, 1919, 1, both in *Denver Post*; "Fair Profits Committees Are Formed," *San Francisco Examiner*, August 21, 1919, 2; and "Committee to Consider Fair Prices Named," *San Francisco Examiner*, August 26, 1919, 4.

32. "Woman's Service League," April 29, 1919, 11; "Battle Names Committee," September 15, 1919, 24; "Mrs. Rumsey Wants Bargaining for All," September 19, 1919, 23; "Mrs. Rumsey to Aid Barnard Drive," February 2, 1920, 26, all in *NYT*. Persia Campbell, "Mary Harriman Rumsey," *Notable American Women, 1607–1950, Vol. III* (Cambridge, MA: Harvard University Press, 1971), 208–9.

33. "Shoe and Clothing Men Now Helping to Set Fair Prices" and "Food Hoarders Indicted," *NYT*, August 26, 1919, 13.

34. "War on Prices Won, Food Chief Says," September 3, 1919, 4; "Women Plan Drive on High Food Prices," September 11, 1919, 10; Rumsey quoted in "Women to Inspect Markets by Night," September 22, 1919, 19; "Clearing House for Clubs," October 5, 1919, 104, all in *NYT*; "Women Start New Fight on Profiteering," *New York Tribune*, September 11, 1919; "Women Meet To-Day to Try to Force Food Prices Down," *New York Post*, September 11, 1919, both in Lusk Papers, Newspaper Clippings, Reel 7.

35. Williams and Brooklyn woman quoted in "Shoe and Clothing Men"; "War on Prices Won, Food Chief Says"; "Fair Price Committee's List of What Groceries Should Cost New York Consumers," August 26, 1919, 13, all in *NYT*; "Packers

Deny Straus' Plea to Check Prices," *New York Tribune*, September 20, 1919, in Lusk Papers, Newspaper Clippings, Reel 7. Mullendore, *United States Food Administration*, 224.

36. Friedsam quoted in "Shoe and Clothing Men"; "Heney Assails Packers," January 18, 1919, 4; "Decrease Revealed in Clothing Prices," December 31, 1919, 18, all in *NYT*. Soule, *Prosperity Decade*, 93; Cuff, *War Industries Board*, 227–33.

37. "U.S. May Sell Army Food at Cheyenne," *Denver Post*, August 12, 1919, 1. "25,000 Sales of Army Supplies," *New York Globe*, September 21, 1919; "Women Faint at Army Sale," *New York Sun*, September 25, 1919; "698,000 Here Buy Army Foodstuffs," *NYT*, September 28, 1919, all in Lusk Papers, Newspaper Clippings, Reel 7. Edward Filene, "The High Cost of Living, Its Causes and Possible Remedies," address before City Federation of Women's Clubs, Boston, MA, March 19, 1920, Filene Papers, Box 42, Folder 66, p. 6; Louis Rothschild, "Shopping Around: A Feminine Habit that Blocks Profiteering," *Independent*, August 15, 1925, 187–88.

38. "Pursuing the Profiteers"; Meeker quoted in "Higher Prices Predicted," *LD*, January 17, 1920, 16; Fisher, "High Prices," 268–75; L. K. Frank, "To Bring Down Prices," *NR*, 175–76; Byron W. Holt, "Rising Prices and Security Values," *Review of Reviews*, September 1919; Koistinen, *Mobilizing for Modern War*, 262–67.

39. "Pursuing the Profiteers," 139.

40. "Says Daugherty Aids Mail Order Houses," *NYT*, February 17, 1922, 8.

41. "Thousands Join Bread Boycott on East Side," *New York Tribune*, May 15, 1919; "Women Threaten Strike to Cut Meat Prices Ten Cents," *New York Tribune*, May 27, 1919; "Bronx Winning in Meat Strike," *New York American*, June 5, 1919; "Boycotts and Cheaper Breakfasts," *NYT*, October 28, 1919, all in Lusk Papers, Newspaper Clippings, Reel 7; Annelise Orleck, *Common Sense and a Little Fire: Women and Working-Class Politics in the United States, 1900–1965* (Chapel Hill: University of North Carolina Press, 1995), 220–22.

42. "Tenants Threaten A General Strike," *NYT*, May 15, 1919; "Big Tenement Strike Looms on East Side," *New York American*, August 31, 1919; "Women Fight in Rent Strike," *New York Post*, October 13, 1919; "Tenants' League Is Socialists' Tool, Say Witnesses," *New York Herald*, October 18, 1919; "No Americans Admitted by Rent Strikers," *New York American*, October 22, 1919; "Leaders Tell How Tenants' Leagues Control Landlord," *New York Tribune*, November 1, 1919; "2,000 Men, Women and Children Go on Rent Strike in Brooklyn," *New York Herald*, November 2, 1919; "3 Sub Committees Named to Take Up Complaints against Rent Profiteering," *New York Telegram*, September 22, 1919; "Irate Tenants Break Up Rent Hearing," *New York Journal*, September 24, 1919; "Tenants' Meeting with Landlords Ends in Riot," *New York American*, September 24, 1919; "Tenant Riot at Rent Hearing," *New York Globe*, September 24, 1919, all in Lusk Papers, Newspaper Clippings, Reel 6. Joseph Spencer, "New York City Tenant Organizations and the Post–World War I Housing Crisis," in *The Tenant Movement in New York City, 1904–1984*, ed. Ronald Lawson (New Brunswick, NJ: Rutgers University Press, 1986), 51–93.

43. "Women for Peace Meeting," March 5, 1919, 10; "Speak for Women Workers," March 30, 1919, 2; "Woman for Senator Is Named by Labor," May 31,

1920, 2; "Replies to Amos Pinchot," July 19, 1920, 3; "Clubwomen Drop War on Gauzy Gown," November 1, 1919, 14; "Cut Out the Teas for Women Voters," June 19, 1920, 23; "Asked to Indorse Dry Law," June 22, 1920, 10, all in *NYT*. John Spargo, "Make Way for the Consumer!" *Independent*, June 18, 1921, 640–41. Orleck, *Common Sense*, 111–12, 117–20, 184, 191.

44. "House Denies Fund for Food Inquiry," *NYT*, September 12, 1919, 24; Burner, *Politics of Provincialism*, 36–39.

45. "Sex Told to Stick to 2 and Smite High Costs," *New York Journal*, October 18, 1919; "Palmer Seeks Aid of Women to Cut Prices," *New York Tribune*, October 18, 1919, both in Lusk Papers, Newspaper Clippings, Reel 6.

46. "Profiteers' Accomplices," *NYT*, August 17, 1919, 33; "Refusal to Buy as a Remedy for High Prices," *LD*, January 24, 1920, 81; Christine Frederick, "The Economic Strike of the American Housewife," *Current Outlook*, June 1921, 751.

47. "Links Socialists with Beef Inquiry," *NYT*, October 21, 1919, 19.

48. Hillman quoted in Fraser, *Labor Will Rule*, frontispiece; Dana Frank, *Purchasing Power: Consumer Organizing, Gender, and the Seattle Labor Movement, 1919–1929* (New York: Cambridge University Press, 1994), 15–39; Montgomery, *Fall of the House of Labor*, 387–89; John Morton Blum, *Joe Tumulty and the Wilson Era* (Boston: Houghton Mifflin, 1951), 204–7.

49. "391 Alien Reds Now under Arrest," November 11, 1919, 1; "Refuse Hearing to Howe," November 29, 1919, 3; "Hustling Reds Back to Europe Well Under Way," December 1, 1919, 1, 7; "Arrest Speakers at Street Rally," October 13, 1920, 17, all in *NYT*. Montgomery, *Fall of the House of Labor*, 463–64; Leon Harris, *Merchant Princes: An Intimate History of Jewish Families Who Built Great Department Stores* (New York: Harper and Row, 1979), 33.

50. Palmer quoted in Dubofsky, *State and Labor*, 78. See also A. Mitchell Palmer, "How to Bring Prices Down," *Independent*, December 13, 1919, 167, 203–4. McCartin, *Labor's Great War*, 173–98; Montgomery, *Fall of the House of Labor*, 300–302, 438–39, 454–57; Gerstle, *Working-Class Americanism*, 76.

51. Lauck quoted in "Says Huge Profits Raise Living Costs," May 8, 1920, 17, and "Profit on $66 Suit is $27.64, He Says," May 17, 1920, 3, both in *NYT*. See also "Says Retail Sugar Could Be 11.5 Cents," May 14, 1920, 17; "Asserts Shoes Sell at Double the Cost," May 15, 1920, 4; "Cost of Steel Trebled," May 21, 1920, 22; "Offers Labor Plan to Curb Profiteers," May 22, 1920, 2; "Says Profits Took Third of Flour Bill," May 24, 1920, 10; "Dress Goods Profits Called Enormous," May 27, 1920, 3; "Says Packers Lay Burden on Public," May 31, 1920, 18; "Charges Gouging by Coal Monopoly," June 29, 1920, 17, all in *NYT*.

52. "Shoe Workers Deny Blame," *NYT*, August 26, 1919, 13; Edward Filene, "Obstacles in the Way of Maximum Production," speech before the American Academy of Political and Social Science, May 8, 1920, Filene Papers, Box 32, Folder 75, p. 10; Edward Filene, "Counterfeit Wages," typescript, 1920, in Filene Papers, Box 32, Folder 71, p. 2.

53. Evans Clark, "Union Labor Takes New View of Wages," *NYT*, October 18, 1925, XX24; Dubofsky, *State and Labor*, 87; Montgomery, *Fall of the House of Labor*, 406.

54. "Wage Cutting: A Vicious Circle," *NR*, January 5, 1921, 158; Lauck quoted in Fink, *Progressive Intellectuals*, 219.

55. National Association of Manufacturers quoted in "Fight 'Buyer Strike' by National Drive," *NYT*, January 8, 1921, 21; "Is Distributing 'Buy Now' Cards," *NYT*, January 9, 1921, 41; "How to Break the Buyers' Strike," *LD*, March 26, 1921, 7–9; Christine Frederick," The Economic Strike of the American House-wife," *Current Outlook*, June 1921, 750–52; "High Retail Prices Holding Back Prosperity," *LD*, April 30, 1921, 7–9.

56. "9 Women Leaders Discuss Ideal Minimum Wage Law," *NYT*, June 3, 1923, sec. 8, p. 13.

57. "287 Wage Advances in May Reported," *NYT*, June 11, 1923, 14.

58. *Annual Report, 1921*, Labor Bureau, Inc., Saposs Papers, Box 24; "144 Unions Aided by Labor Bureau," *NYT*, June 24, 1923, sec. 2, p. 7; "Labor Bureau Aids Unions," *NYT*, July 22, 1927, 19.

59. "Evans Clark," *Current Biography*, 1947, 115–17; "Evans Clark, Writer, Is Dead," August 29, 1970, 21; "Lists Americans as Pacifists," January 25, 1919, 1, 4; "War Department Sells to the Soviet," February 28, 1920, 1; "Soule Makes Statement," October 7, 1921, 6; "Attacks 'Radicals' in Church's School," October 18, 1921, 11; "Puts Blame on Employers," December 9, 1921, 10, all in *NYT*; Evans Clark, "What the Shop Strike Cost the Railroads," *Nation*, December 27, 1922, 715–16.

60. Ellis Hawley, "Herbert Hoover, the Commerce Secretariat, and the Vision of an 'Associative State,' " *JAH* 61 (June 1974): 116–40; Guy Alchon, *The Invisible Hand of Planning: Capitalism, Social Science, and the State in the 1920s* (Princeton, NJ: Princeton University Press, 1985), 64–111; Robert Zieger, "Herbert Hoover, the Wage-Earner, and the 'New Economic System,' 1919–1929," *BHR* 51 (summer 1977): 161–89.

61. Stuart Chase, *The Tragedy of Waste* (New York: Macmillan, 1925), 9–10, 13–14, 135, 154, 126–74; Evans Clark, "This Wasteful, Wabbling, Ill-Conducted World," November 15, 1925, sec. 3, p. 5; "Waste," September 21, 1925, 18; "Labor Bureau Warns against Inflation," December 7, 1924, X7, all in *NYT*.

62. George Soule, "The Productivity Factor in Wage Determinations," *AER* 13 (March 1923): 129–40.

63. Lynn Dumenil, *The Modern Temper: American Culture and Society in the 1920s* (New York: Hill and Wang, 1995); David J. Goldberg, *Discontented America: The United States in the 1920s* (Baltimore: Johns Hopkins University Press, 1999).

64. Burner, *Politics of Provincialism*; Douglas B. Craig, *After Wilson: The Struggle for the Democratic Party, 1920–1934* (Chapel Hill: University of North Carolina Press, 1992).

65. Hillman quoted in Fraser, *Labor Will Rule*, 195; Evans Clark, "Clothing Trade Signs New Treaty of Peace," August 10, 1924, VIII, 8; Clark, "Size and Strength of Trade Unions," April 19, 1925, sec. 3, p. 14; Clark, "Labor's Concerted Move to Do Its Own Banking," January 28, 1923, sec. 8, p. 1, all in *NYT*.

66. Orleck, *Common Sense*, 111–12, 117–20, 184–93; Edward Filene to William Neisel, November 23, 1926, Filene Papers; Richard Altenbaugh, *Education for Struggle: The American Labor Colleges of the 1920s and 1930s* (Philadelphia: Temple University Press, 1990), 249–68.

67. Owen Young to Edward Filene, April 24, 1923, Filene Papers. See also Josephine Young Case and Everett Needham Case, *Owen D. Young and American Enterprise: A Biography* (Boston: D. R. Godine, 1982), 247, 252–53, 267, 270–71.

68. Annual Reports for the Twentieth Century Fund, TCF Papers.

69. Edward Filene, "Distribution of the Future," Address to the Taylor Society, October 29, 1925, Filene Papers, Box 37, Folder 29, p. 15.

70. "American Business Backs Dawes Plan," *NYT*, May 7, 1924, 32.

71. Edward Filene, memo, April 14, 1926, Filene Papers.

72. Edward Filene, "Ford: Pioneer, not Superman," *Nation*, January 3, 1923, 17–18.

73. John Commons, "Why Mary Smith Wants to Work at Filene's," *Independent*, August 7, 1920, 137–38, 163; *Handbook of the Filene Co-operative Association* (Boston: F.C.A. Publicity Committee, 1924), Filene Papers, Box 56, Folder 1.

74. "Filene Attacks Coolidge's Record," *NYT*, October 26, 1924, 8. On welfare capitalism, David Brody, "The Rise and Decline of Welfare Capitalism," in *Workers in Industrial America* (New York: Oxford University Press, 1980), 48–81; Sanford Jacoby, *Employing Bureaucracy: Managers, Unions, and the Transformation of Work in American Industry, 1900–1945* (New York: Columbia University Press, 1985); Lizabeth Cohen, *Making a New Deal: Industrial Workers in Chicago, 1919–1939* (New York: Cambridge University Press, 1990), 159–211.

75. Edward Filene, *The Way Out: A Forecast of Coming Changes in American Business and Industry* (Garden City, NY: Page & Company, 1924), 42.

76. Orleck, *Common Sense*, 223–25; "Rents Go Up with Wages," October 25, 1923, 28; "Begin Fight on High Rents," December 24, 1923, 2; "Wages and Living Costs," December 15, 1924, 24; "Sees Wages in a Race Upward with Prices," February 12, 1925, 21; "Cost of Living Continues to Increase," August 24, 1925, 15; "Wages Have Risen, but So Have Costs," February 8, 1926, 12, all in *NYT*.

77. Evans Clark, "Milk Monopoly Plan Designed to Cut Waste," *NYT*, March 29, 1925, IX, 8.

78. "Women to Oppose Tariff Increases," October 31, 1921, 8; "League and Grange Fight Tariff Plan," November 11, 1921, 14; "Tariff Valuation Fought by Women," November 20, 1921, sec. 2, p. 9; "Women Hit Fordney Plan," April 13, 1922, 23; "Women Join in Move to Sift Living Costs," September 30, 1929; "Women Here Urged to Fight Tariff Bill," October 29, 1929, 18, all in *NYT*. Fraser, *Labor Will Rule*, 194–96; Frank Costigliola, *Awkward Dominion: American Political, Economic, and Cultural Relations with Europe, 1919–1933* (Ithaca, NY: Cornell University Press, 1984), 103, 142–43.

79. Hazel Kyrk, *A Theory of Consumption* (Boston: Houghton Mifflin, 1923), 94.

80. William Ogburn, "The Standard-of-Living Factor in Wages," *AER* 13 (March 1923): 127. For a discussion of AFL policy in this era, see Benjamin Kline Hunnicutt, *Work without End: Abandoning Shorter Hours for the Right to Work* (Philadelphia: Temple University Press, 1988), 76–84; and Gary S. Cross, *Time and Money: The Making of Consumer Culture* (London: Routledge, 1993), 28–33.

81. Frey quoted in "Labor on the Brink of New Wage Policy," *NYT*, October 13, 1925, 6; Evans Clark, "Union Labor Takes New View of Wages," *NYTM*, October 18, 1925, 1, 24. Irving Bernstein, *The Lean Years: A History of the American Worker, 1920–1933* (Boston: Houghton Mifflin, 1960).

82. Clark, "Union Labor Takes New View"; "Labor Demands Gradual Time Cut," *NYT*, October 10, 1926, 1, 22.

83. Herbert Feis, John Frey, Waddill Catchings, and W. A. Berridge, "Roundtable: The Consuming Power of Labor and Business Fluctuations," *AER* 16 (March 1926): 83, 85, 86.

84. William Trufant Foster and Waddill Catchings, "The Automobile—Key to Our Prosperity," *World's Work*, December 1926, 165–74; William Trufant Foster and Waddill Catchings, "The Dilemma of Thrift," *Atlantic*, April 1926, 533–43. In his review of *Profits*, Evans Clark pointed out that the title was "really a misnomer." "Its authors contend that the great masses of people should have more money to spend if the present economic order is to give ultimate satisfaction." Evans Clark, "Solving Industry's Paradox," *NYT*, January 17, 1926, sec. 3, p. 1.

85. William Trufant Foster and Waddill Catchings, *Business without a Buyer* (Newton, MA: Pollak Foundation for Economic Research, 1927).

86. William Leach, *Land of Desire: Merchants, Power, and the Rise of a New American Culture* (New York: Pantheon Books, 1993), 276–78; Thomas Ferguson, "Industrial Conflict and the Coming of the New Deal: The Triumph of Multinational Liberalism in America," in *The Rise and Fall of the New Deal Order*, ed. Steve Fraser and Gary Gerstle (Princeton, NJ: Princeton University Press, 1989), 3–31; Fraser, *Labor Will Rule*, 262, 267–8.

87. Foster sent Filene a copy of his and Catchings's article "Progress and Plenty: A Way Out of the Dilemma of Thrift," *Century*, July 1928, 257–58 and that was the inscription he wrote. Filene Papers. On Foster and Catchings, see William J. Barber, *From New Era to New Deal: Herbert Hoover, the Economists, and American Economic Policy, 1921–1933* (New York: Cambridge University Press, 1985), 208; Joseph Dorfman, *The Economic Mind in American Civilization, 1918–1933*, vol. 5 (New York: Viking Press, 1959), 339–51; Alan Brinkley, *The End of Reform: New Deal Liberalism in Recession and War* (New York: Vintage Books, 1995), 75–77.

88. Paul Douglas, "The Movement of Real Wages and Its Economic Significance," *AER* 16 (March 1926): 49, 17–53; "Finds Wages up 27% over 35 Years Ago," December 29, 1925, 15; "Soviets Maligned," October 24, 1927, 9; "Injustice to Russia Laid to Americans," November 20, 1927, II, 5, all in *NYT*. Dorfman, *Economic Mind in American Civilization*, 526–34.

89. David Hounshell, *From the American System to Mass Production, 1800–1932: The Development of Manufacturing Technology in the United States* (Baltimore: Johns Hopkins University Press, 1984), 217–61.

90. Samuel Strauss, "Things Are in the Saddle," *Atlantic*, November 1924, 579.

91. Murray French, "Why People Buy Things," *Magazine of Business*, August 1929, 163. Roland Marchand, *Advertising the American Dream: Making Way for Modernity, 1920–1940* (Berkeley: University of California Press, 1985), 18–20.

92. Leach, *Land of Desire*, 341; Lendol Calder, *Financing the American Dream: A Cultural History of Consumer Credit* (Princeton, NJ: Princeton University Press, 1999), 18–19, 195, 201; Shelley Nickles, "Object Lessons: Industrial Design, Household Appliances, and the American Middle Class in a Mass Consumer Society, 1920–1960," (Ph.D. diss., University of Virginia, 1998); Olivier Zunz, *Why the American Century?* (Chicago: University of Chicago Press, 1998), 94–97.

93. "E. A. Filene Defends Coolidge on Economy," April 27, 1925, 18; "Install-
ment Buying Condemned," April 28, 1925, 20; Evans Clark, "Installment Buying
Now Involves Billions," August 2, 1925, VIII, 4; "Sees Economic Crisis in Installment Buying," April 8, 1926, 34, all in *NYT*. Labor Bureau quoted in "Find
Wages Rising, Employment Gaining," May 8, 1926, 30; Stuart Chase, "New
Competition Vexes Business," October 31, 1926, IX, 6, both in *NYT*. Edward
Filene, "The Credit Union—a Crusader against Usury," *American Bankers Association Journal*, January 1925, 363, 439, 461. Calder, *Financing the American Dream*,
211–35, 272.

94. Berridge quoted in Feis et al., "Roundtable: The Consuming Power," 87;
William Berridge, Emma Winslow, and Richard Flinn, *Purchasing Power of the
Consumer: A Statistical Index* (Chicago: Shaw, 1925); Colin Gordon, *New Deals:
Business, Labor, and Politics in America, 1920–1935* (New York: Cambridge Univer-
sity Press, 1994), 43; Marchand, *Advertising the American Dream*, 7, 56, 64, 95.

95. Eugene Grace, "Distributed Prosperity," *SEP*, September 4, 1926,
57–58; Charles Abbott, "Creative Spending," *Magazine of Business*, August 1929,
166, 164.

96. "Money for the Masses," *NYT*, January 18, 1926, 20; Evans Clark, "Where
Capital and Labor Meet," *NYT Book Review*, August 1, 1926, 1; Evans Clark,
"America's Prosperity Reaches New Heights," *NYTM*, November 27, 1927, 4.

97. Evans Clark, "The Farm Issue Moves toward a Climax," January 2, 1927,
VII, 1; Frey quoted in "Labor Leader 'Hits' Prosperity Talk," October 7, 1927, 29;
Clark, "America's Prosperity"; "Consumers' Body Thirty Years Old," November
10, 1929, X, 18, all in *NYT*; Storrs, *Civilizing Capitalism*, 64–67; Barber, *From New
Era to New Deal*, 48–53.

98. "Find Wages Rising, Employment Gaining," *NYT*, May 8, 1926, 30. "Score
Treatment of Labor in South," *NYT*, August 7, 1929, 15; "Unemployment—a
Symposium," *Forbes*, April 1, 1928, 38.

99. Filene quoted in "Filene Pleads for Scientific Retail Training," *Retail Ledger*,
April 5, 1924; Edward Filene, "Mass Buying and Mass Selling, Too," *Nation's
Business*, September 1924, 24–26; Edward Filene, "Finding the Right Price Levels,"
Garment Weekly, October 16, 1923, 3–17; Edward Filene, "What Is Back of a Fast
Rate of Turnover?" *System*, November 1923, 583–86, 658–62; "Warns on Chain
Stores," February 2, 1927, 9; "Cut in Living Cost Aim of New Census," June 27,
1929, 1, 6, both in *NYT*; Edward Filene, "Instructions to My Executors and
Trustees," January 18, 1929, Filene Papers, Box 55, Folder 7; Leach, *Land of Desire*,
283–85, 364–65.

100. Wesley Mitchell, "The Backward Art of Spending Money," *AER* 2 (June
1912): 271; Faith Williams, "Stretching the Household Dollar," *Survey*, November,
1928, 152, 203.

101. Stuart Chase and F. J. Schlink, "Consumers in Wonderland," February 2,
1927, 293; Stuart Chase and F. J. Schlink, "Consumers in Wonderland II—the
Twin Gods of Bad Business: Adulteration and Misrepresentation," February 9,
1927, 320–23; Stuart Chase and F. J. Schlink, "Consumers in Wonderland III—
What We Get for Our Money When We Buy from Quacks and Venders of Cure-
Alls," February 16, 1927, 348–51; Stuart Chase and F. J. Schlink, "Consumers in
Wonderland IV—How Standardization Helps and Hinders the Buyer," February

23, 1927, 12–15; Stuart Chase, "The Tragedy of Waste," August 12, 1925, 312–16, all in *NR*.

102. Day Monroe, "A Conference on the Problems of the Household Buyer," *Journal of Home Economics*, February 1928, 95–97; Caroline Sherman, "The Consumer and Standardization in Food Products," *Journal of Home Economics*, November 1928, 801–3; F. J. Schlink and Robert Brady, "Standards and Specifications from the Standpoint of the Ultimate Consumer," *AAAPSS*, May 1928, 231–39; Robert Brady, "How the Government Standards Affect the Ultimate Consumer," ibid., 247–52. See also Paul Betters, *The Bureau of Home Economics: Its History, Activities, and Organization* (Washington, DC: Brookings Institution, 1930).

103. Susan Strasser, *Never Done: A History of American Housework* (New York: Henry Holt and Company, 2000); Ruth Schwartz Cowan, *More Work for Mother: The Ironies of Household Technology from the Open Hearth to the Microwave* (New York: Basic Books, 1983); Kathy Lee Peiss, *Hope in a Jar: The Making of America's Beauty Culture* (New York: Metropolitan Books, 1998).

104. Helen Sorenson, *The Consumer Movement: What It Is and What It Means* (New York: Harper and Row, 1941), 9; "Consumers' Group Grows," *NYT*, December 8, 1929, sec. 2, p. 10. "Organize New Body to Aid Consumer," *Consumers Research, Inc.*, January 27, 1930; F. J. Schlink to William Leiserson, January 28, 1930, Leiserson Papers, Box 4; Chase and Schlink, "Consumers in Wonderland IV"; Chase and Schlink quoted in Stuart Chase and F. J. Schlink, "Consumers in Wonderland V—in Which the Authors Give Some Suggestions as to the Way Out of Wonderland," *NR*, March 2, 1927, 38–41; Robert S. Lynd, "Democracy's Third Estate: The Consumer," *Political Science Quarterly* 51 (December 1936), 497.

105. "Full Text of Hoover's Speech Accepting Party's Nomination for the Presidency," *NYT*, August 12, 1928, 2; Brian Balogh, "Mirrors of Desire: Interest Groups, Elections, and the Targeted Style in Twentieth-Century America," in *The Democratic Experiment: New Directions in American Political History*, ed. Meg Jacobs, William J. Novak, and Julian E. Zelizer (Princeton, NJ: Princeton University Press, 2003); Anna Harvey, *Votes without Leverage: Women in American Electoral Politics* (New York: Cambridge University Press, 1998), 104–54.

106. "Mrs. M. H. Rumsey Supports Smith," August 6, 1928, 2; "Filene Favors Smith," July 12, 1928, 2; "Filene Says Smith Means Prosperity," October 4, 1928, 8; "Roosevelt Takes Up Fair Wage Question," November 21, 1928, 10; "Roosevelt Opens Labor Bill Fight," March 2, 1929, 9; "Mrs. Rumsey Dies after Hunt Injury," December 19, 1934, 20, all in *NYT*; Orleck, *Common Sense*, 139–68. Kristi Andersen, *The Creation of a Democratic Majority, 1928–1936* (Chicago: University of Chicago Press, 1979).

107. Foster and Catchings, "Progress and Plenty"; "Authors of the Plan," *NYT*, November 22, 1928, 4; "Warn of Dangers in Merger Trend," *NYT*, August 10, 1929, 5; "Organize for Curb on Unemployment," *NYT*, August 24, 1929, 16; William Trufant Foster and Waddill Catchings, *The Road to Plenty* (Boston: Houghton Mifflin, 1928); Alchon, *Invisible Hand of Planning*, 129–51.

108. Chase quoted in "Sees Prosperity Unhurt," *NYT*, November 1, 1929, 3; John Kenneth Galbraith, *The Great Crash: 1929* (Boston: Houghton Mifflin, 1954).

109. "Urges Us to Share Monroe Doctrine," *NYT*, August 30, 1929, 9; "Pay Rise, Time Cut Asked for Workers," *NYT*, November 10, 1929, 17; Michael A. Bernstein, *The Great Depression: Delayed Recovery and Economic Change in America, 1929–1939* (New York: Cambridge University Press, 1987). See also Amy Sue Bix, *Inventing Ourselves Out of Jobs?: America's Debate over Technological Unemployment* (Baltimore: Johns Hopkins University Press, 2000), 9–42.

110. Unemployment Speech of Hon. Robert F. Wagner of New York in the U. S. Senate, March 5, 1928, Keyserling Papers-GTL, Box 2; William Leiserson, "Unemployment in 1929: A Problem of Prosperity," n.d., Leiserson Papers, Box 49; Leiserson, "Overproduction and Soldiering on the Job," n.d., Leiserson Papers, Box 51.

111. Edward Filene, "Mass Production Must Have Mass Consumption," *Magazine of Wall Street*, January 5, 1930; Labor Bureau, Inc., *Facts for Workers*, December 1929, 2, Leiserson Papers, Box 21; "Wage Cuts in June Show Big Increase," July 10, 1930, 44; "Says Jobless Data Give a False View," June 28, 1930, 9; "Labor Bureau Sees Lower Wage Trend," February 9, 1930, 16, all in *NYT*.

112. Labor Bureau, Inc., *Facts for Workers*, 2.

Chapter Three
The New Deal and the Problem of Prices, 1930–1935

1. Edward Filene, "The New Relations Between Business and Government," *AAAPSS* 172 (March 1934): 38; Robert S. Lynd, "The Consumer Becomes a 'Problem,' " *AAAPSS* 173 (May 1934): 1–6. Since the 1930s, scholars have debated the economic causes of the Great Depression. See, for example, Peter Temin, *Did Monetary Forces Cause the Great Depression?* (New York: W. W. Norton, 1976); Milton Friedman and Anna J. Schwartz, *A Monetary History of the United States, 1867–1960* (Princeton, NJ: Princeton University Press, 1963); Charles P. Kindleberger, *The World in Depression, 1929–1939* (Berkeley: University of California Press, 1973); and John Kenneth Galbraith, *The Great Crash: 1929* (Boston: Houghton Mifflin, 1954). For a recent assessment, see Michael A. Bernstein, *The Great Depression: Delayed Recovery and Economic Change in America, 1929–1939* (New York: Cambridge University Press, 1987).

2. For an overview of the New Deal, see Ellis W. Hawley, *The New Deal and the Problem of Monopoly: A Study in Economic Ambivalence* (Princeton, NJ: Princeton University Press, 1966); William E. Leuchtenburg, *Franklin D. Roosevelt and the New Deal, 1932–1940* (New York: Harper and Row, 1963); Anthony J. Badger, *The New Deal: The Depression Years, 1933–1940* (New York: Hill and Wang, 1989); Arthur M. Schlesinger Jr., *The Age of Roosevelt: The Coming of the New Deal* (Boston: Houghton Mifflin, 1958); Jordan Schwarz, *The New Dealers: Power Politics in the Age of Roosevelt* (New York: Knopf, 1993); and David M. Kennedy, *Freedom from Fear: The American People in Depression and War, 1929–1945* (New York: Oxford University Press, 1999). For studies that emphasize the significance of underconsumption thought, see Theodore Rosenof, *Dogma, Depression, and the New Deal: The Debate of Political Leaders over Economic Recovery* (Port Washington, NY: Kennikat Press, 1975); Stanley Vittoz, *New Deal Labor Policy and the American*

Industrial Economy (Chapel Hill: University of North Carolina Press, 1987); Christopher L. Tomlins, *The State and the Unions: Labor Relations, Law, and the Organized Labor Movement in America, 1880–1960* (New York: Cambridge University Press, 1985); Colin Gordon, *New Deals: Business, Labor, and Politics in America, 1920–1935* (New York: Cambridge University Press, 1994); Steve Fraser, *Labor Will Rule: Sidney Hillman and the Rise of American Labor* (New York: Free Press, 1991); Alan Brinkley, *The End of Reform: New Deal Liberalism in Recession and War* (New York: Vintage Books, 1995); and Meg Jacobs, " 'Democracy's Third Estate': New Deal Politics and the Construction of a 'Consuming Public,' " *International Labor and Working-Class History* 55 (spring 1999): 27–51.

3. Curley and *Raleigh News* quoted in "Shall We Spend or Save?" *LD*, October 25, 1930, 46–48; "Each Edison Aide Gets $5 to Start 'Buy-Now' Drive," *NYT*, October 18, 1933, 10. For a discussion of underconsumptionist explanations, see Rosenof, *Dogma, Depression*, 40–45, 67–72.

4. *Journal of Commerce* quoted in "Shall We Spend or Save?" 47; "Buy Now—If You Can!" *NR*, November 12, 1930, 336; "340 Wage Scales Reduced in March," *NYT*, April 8, 1931, 6; Labor Bureau quoted in "10% Wage Decrease Noted in 175 Plants," *NYT*, June 7, 1931, IV, 1. "Business Leaders Look for Leadership at Atlantic City," *BW*, May 2, 1931, 5.

5. John Frey et al., "Shorter Working Time and Unemployment," *AER* 22 (March 1932): 11; "Long Deferred, Wage Cuts Begin to Assume Ugly Proportions," April 11, 1931, 5; "A Platform for American Business," March 4, 1931, 6; "Speaking of Operations," May 6, 1931, 52, all in *BW*.

6. "They Meant Well," August 5, 1931, 40; "Long Deferred, Wage Cuts Begin to Assume Ugly Proportions," 5; "U.S. Steel Cut in Salaries Forecasts General Wage Drop," August 5, 1931, 5; "Rush of Wage Cutting Follows Big Steel's Lead," October 3, 1931, 5–6, all in *BW*; "Wage Cuts Wrong, E. A. Filene Insists," *Women's Wear Daily*, February 17, 1933; Badger, *New Deal*, 23, 30, 47.

7. "Trade Association Is Keystone of Swope Stabilization Plan," September 23, 1931, 12; "Plans to Put End to Depression Offered by Organized Business," October 14, 1931, 7–8; "Demand for Trust Law Changes Increases Steadily on All Sides," November 4, 1931, 8, all in *BW*.

8. "New Party Needed, Economist Writes," August 1, 1932, 13; "Third Party Urged by 500 Economists," August 8, 1932, 4; "Liberals Are Urged to Vote for Thomas," September 24, 1932, 8, all in *NYT*; Robert Wagner to William Leiserson, April 20, 1932, Leiserson Papers, Box 43; William Leiserson, "Dole or Insurance?" *Nation*, February 17, 1932, 193–94; "Urges Labor to Build a Party of Reform," *NYT*, February 2, 1930, 17. For the development of social-welfare programs, see Linda Gordon, *Pitied but Not Entitled: Single Mothers and the History of Welfare, 1890–1935* (New York: Free Press, 1994); Robyn Muncy, *Creating a Female Dominion in American Reform, 1890–1935* (New York: Oxford University Press, 1991); Edwin Amenta, *Bold Relief: Institutional Politics and the Origins of Modern American Social Policy* (Princeton, NJ: Princeton University Press, 1998).

9. Kazin quoted in Beth Wenger, *New York Jews and the Great Depression: Uncertain Promise* (New Haven, CT: Yale University Press, 1996), 108; Paul Nystrom, "A Restatement of the Principles of Consumption to Meet Present Conditions," *Journal of Home Economics* 24 (October 1932): 871; "Buying Power Cut in Half

Since 1929," March 27, 1933, 31; "Cost of Living," July 15, 1933, 10, both in *NYT*; "$22 Wage Makes Manufacturing Worker a Poor Customer," *BW*, October 14, 1931, 26.

10. Paul H. Douglas, *The Coming of a New Party* (New York: McGraw-Hill, 1932), 78.

11. Dexter Merriam Keezer and Stacy May, *The Public Control of Business: A Study of Antitrust Law Enforcement, Public Interest Regulation, and Government Participation in Business* (New York: Harper and Brothers, 1930), 254.

12. For information on Gardiner Means and Adolf Berle, see Frederic S. Lee, "A New Dealer in Agriculture: G. C. Means and the Writing of *Industrial Prices*," *Review of Social Economy* 46 (October 1988): 180–202; and Theodore Rosenof, *Economics in the Long Run: New Deal Theorists and Their Legacies, 1933–1993* (Chapel Hill: University of North Carolina Press, 1997), 28–43. For information about Caroline Ware, see Ellen Fitzpatrick, "Caroline F. Ware and the Cultural Approach to History," *American Quarterly* 43 (June 1991): 173–98. See also Caroline F. Ware, Gardiner C. Means, and Thomas C. Blaisdell Jr., "Consumer Participation at the Federal Level," in *Consumer Activists: They Made a Difference*, ed. Erma Angevine (Mount Vernon, NY: Consumers Union Foundation, 1982), 171–97.

13. William Ripley, "Our 'Corporate Revolution' and Its Perils," *NYT*, July 24, 1932, 21; Tugwell quoted in Allan Gruchy, *Contemporary Economic Thought: The Contribution of Neo-institutional Economics* (Clifton, NJ: A. M. Kelley, 1972), 65.

14. Berle and Means quoted in Joseph Dorfman, *The Economic Mind in American Civilization, 1918–1933*, vol. 5 (New York: Viking Press, 1959), 754. See also Adolf A. Berle and Gardiner C. Means, "Corporations and the Public Investor," *AER* 20 (March 1930): 54–71; Thomas K. McCraw, "Berle and Means," *Reviews in American History* 18 (December 1990): 578–96; and Charles R. Geisst, *Monopolies in America: Empire Builders and Their Enemies from Jay Gould to Bill Gates* (Oxford: Oxford University Press, 2000), 121–25. Stuart Chase, "Eating without Working: A Moral Disquisition," *Nation*, July 26, 1933, 93–94.

15. Gardiner C. Means, "The Consumer and the New Deal," *AAAPSS* 173 (May 1934): 8, 12–13; Gardiner C. Means, "Competition Called Far From Ordinary," *NYT*, November 4, 1934, IV, 5; Frederic S. Lee, "*The Modern Corporation* and Gardiner Means's Critique of Neoclassical Economics," *Journal of Economic Issues* 24 (September 1990): 673–93.

16. Robert S. Lynd, foreword to Persia Campbell, *Consumer Representation in the New Deal* (New York: Columbia University Press, 1940), 9; Robert S. Lynd, "Democracy's Third Estate," *Political Science Quarterly* 51 (December 1936): 496. On Lynd, see Richard Wightman Fox, "Epitaph for Middletown: Robert S. Lynd and the Analysis of Consumer Culture," in *The Culture of Consumption: Critical Essays in American History, 1880–1980*, ed. Richard Wrightman Fox and T. J. Jackson Lears (New York: Pantheon Books, 1983), 101–42; and Mark C. Smith, "Robert Lynd and Consumerism in the 1930s," *Journal of the History of Sociology* 2 (fall–winter 1979–80): 99–120.

17. Rexford Tugwell, Thomas Munro, and Roy Stryker, *American Economic Life and the Means of Its Improvement* (New York: Harcourt, Brace, 1925), 449; "Buying Habits Changing," *NYT*, January 28, 1933, 15; Robert Lynd, "Family Members as

Consumers," *AAAPSS* 161 (March 1932): 86–93; Campbell, *Consumer Representation*, 21, 23.

18. "Keen-Nosed Consumer Is Uncanny at Smelling Bargains These Days," *BW*, July 6, 1932, 9; Lawrence Glickman, "The Strike in the Temple of Consumption: Consumer Activism and Twentieth-Century American Political Culture," *JAH* 88 (June 2001): 99–128.

19. Franklin D. Roosevelt, *The Public Papers and Addresses of Franklin D. Roosevelt*, vol. 1, ed. Samuel I. Rosenman (New York: Random House, 1938), 751–52, 754–56. See also Kennedy, *Freedom from Fear*, 123.

20. "Federal Pay Cut of 15% on April 1 Looms," *NYT*, March 28, 1933, 1.

21. Leuchtenburg, *Franklin D. Roosevelt*, 37–43; Albert Romasco, *The Politics of Recovery: Roosevelt's New Deal* (New York: Oxford University Press, 1983), 64.

22. Roosevelt quoted in Edwin Nourse, Joseph Davis, and John Black, *Three Years of the Agricultural Adjustment Administration* (Washington, DC: Brookings Institution, 1937), 421; Romasco, *Politics of Recovery*, 157–85; Badger, *New Deal*, 147–89; Schlesinger Jr., *Age of Roosevelt*, 27–84.

23. "Agricultural Adjustment Act," in *The Great Depression and the New Deal: Legislative Acts in Their Entirety*, ed. Frederick Hosen (Jefferson, NC: McFarland & Co., 1992), 62; Badger, *New Deal*, 152–56, 163–69, 175–77; Leuchtenburg, *Franklin D. Roosevelt*, 75–76, 86–87; "Roosevelt Signs Cotton Curb Bill," *NYT*, April 22, 1934, 25; "Hog Plan Dooms 5,000,000 Animals," *NYT*, August 19, 1933, 17.

24. "Labor Group Backs Wagner for Senate," *NYT*, October 10, 1926, 22. See also J. Joseph Huthmacher, *Senator Robert F. Wagner and the Rise of Urban Liberalism* (New York: Atheneum, 1968).

25. Badger, *New Deal*, 248; Ira Katznelson, Kim Geiger, and Daniel Kryder, "Limiting Liberalism: The Southern Veto in Congress, 1933–1950," *Political Science Quarterly* 108 (summer 1993): 283–306.

26. On the NRA, see Gordon, *New Deals*, 167, 170–71; Robert F. Himmelberg, *The Origins of the National Recovery Administration: Business, Government, and the Trade Association Issue, 1921–1933* (New York: Fordham University Press, 1976); Hawley, *New Deal and the Problem of Monopoly*, 31–32, 54–62; Vittoz, *New Deal Labor Policy*, 73–134; Irving Bernstein, *The Turbulent Years: A History of the American Worker, 1933–1941* (Boston: Houghton Mifflin, 1969), 26–35; and Badger, *New Deal*, 66–117.

27. "Field Day for Critics," *NYT*, February 28, 1934, 28.

28. Paul Douglas, "The Role of the Consumer in the New Deal," *AAAPSS* 172 (March 1934): 98; A. A. Berle Jr., "The Social Economics of the New Deal," *NYTM*, October 29, 1933, 5; Transcript of Oral History Interview with Leon H. Keyserling, May 3, 1971–May 19, 1971, Oral History Collection, HSTL, p. 8; Robert Wagner, "Planning in Place of Restraint," *Survey Graphic*, August 1933, 395–96.

29. Mark Leff, *The Limits of Symbolic Reform: The New Deal and Taxation, 1933–1939* (New York: Cambridge University Press, 1984).

30. Roosevelt quoted in Dexter Keezer, "The Consumer under the National Recovery Administration," *AAAPSS* 171 (March 1934): 89, 95; "Expect Public to Watch for Undue Price Rises," August 2, 1933, 10; "Consumers' Board Seeks Price Data," September 8, 1933, 13, both in *NYT*.

31. Hugh S. Johnson, *The Blue Eagle: From Egg to Earth* (Garden City, NY: Doubleday, 1935), 255.

32. Johnson quoted in Russell Owen, "Gen. Johnson Wages a Peace-Time War," *NYTM*, July 30, 1933, 3, 18. "Fervor Sweeps Throngs," September 14, 1933, 1; "The Blue Eagle Parade," September 15, 1933, 18; "Text of General Johnson's Address on the NRA in Boston," August 31, 1933, 2; "Purchasing Power of the Nation Rises," April 22, 1934, VIII, 2, all in *NYT*.

33. "Text of Johnson's Speech Opening St. Louis's NRA Drive," August 14, 1933, 2; "Consumers' Blue Eagle on White House Doors," August 14, 1933, 3; "Johnson Opens Consumer Drive," August 28, 1933, 1, all in *NYT*.

34. Mary Hughes to Mrs. Reverdy Miller, Charlotte, NC, September 1, 1933, NRA Papers, Public Relations Division, Women's Section, General Records 1933–35, Box 5, Miscellaneous (North Carolina) Folder. The NRA Women's Division maintained its own files organized by state. The following portrait comes from the records of at least twenty states that include a representative sample of different regions. "Pajaro Valley NRA Executive Committee Maps Program," "Women's Committee Will Meet Tuesday," "Committeemen of Pajaro Valley NRA Survey Work to be Done in Community," "15,000 NRA Signers Goal for Saturday," "Valley-Wide Drive Scheduled Saturday for Consumer Pledges," "City Turns Out in Force for Signup," *Watsonville Register*, August 9–22, 1933; Mrs. M. M. Swisher to Mrs. J. D. Graham, Watsonville, CA, September 16, 1933, NRA Papers, Public Relations Division, Women's Section, General Records 1933–35, Box 1, California Folder. "957,000 Here Sign Consumer Pledge," September 12, 1933, 13; NRA quoted in "Johnson Prepares NRA Drive Wind-Up," August 21, 1933, 3; "Women to Aid NRA by Door-Bell Drive," August 12, 1933, 1, all in *NYT*.

35. "Buy Now to Save, Johnson Appeals," *NYT*, October 9, 1933, 1; Mary Hughes to Esther Taber Fox, August 14, 1933, NRA Papers, Public Relations Division, Women's Section, General Records 1933–35, Box 5, Miscellaneous (New York) Folder; " 'Buy Now' a Duty, Says Mrs. Roosevelt," *NYT*, October 10, 1933, 23; Edward Filene, "September—The 'Buy Now' Month," statement for the *Boston Daily Record*, September 5, 1933, TCF Papers; "Scouts Aid Buying Drive," *NYT*, October 30, 1933, 5.

36. "Living Costs Rise for Wage Earners Keeps Up," August 25, 1933, 18; "Buying Power Declines," October 5, 1933, 40; "Gain in Wages Less Than Living Cost Rise," December 1, 1933, 30; "Retail Food Prices Rose 3.3% in Month to June 15, According to 51 Cities' Reports," July 15, 1933, 15; "Price Survey Brings Opposition to Rises," August 9, 1933, 33; Isador Lubin, "The Cost of Living Starts up Again," July 30, 1933, sec. 8, p. 2, all in *NYT*; "The Crisis in the N.R.A.," *NR*, August 23, 1933, 33–34.

37. "Retailers Divided on Code Price Plan," *NYT*, September 17, 1933, 30; "Price-Fixing Stays in the Retail Code," *NYT*, September 21, 1933, 1; "Price-Fixing and NRA," *BW*, November 25, 1933, 11–12; Hawley, *New Deal and the Problem of Monopoly*, 59–60, 63–64, 85–86, 94, 99, 100, 113, 116; Peek quoted in Schlesinger Jr., *Age of Roosevelt*, 46, 125; Gilbert C. Fite, *George N. Peek and the Fight for Farm Parity* (Norman: University of Oklahoma Press, 1954).

38. "Bread Prices: A Large Economic Issue," July 16, 1933, 1; "39 Cities Complain of Profiteering on Bread," July 19, 1933, 1, both in *NYT*.

39. "Consumer Bureau to Check Prices," June 24, 1933, 22; "Living Costs Rose in May, Food Prices 3.6%," June 26, 1933, 1, both in *NYT*. On Howe, see Maxine Block, ed., *Current Biography* (New York: H. W. Wilson, 1940), 408.

40. "Textile Hearings Will Start Today," June 26, 1933, 1; Mildred Adams, "On the Trail of the Elusive Consumer," October 15, 1933, sec. 7, p. 4, 13; Rumsey quoted in S. J. Woolf, "Champion of the Consumer Speaks Out," August 6, 1933, 5, 14; "Drive Begins Today to 'Stamp out Want' in 6,000 City Blocks," March 28, 1932, 1, all in *NYT*.

41. "Activities of the CAB of the NRA and the Consumers' Counsel of the AAA," Bulletin No. 2, Consumers' Division of the National Emergency Council, NRA Papers, Advisory Bodies, CAB, Office Files of Emily Newell Blair, Entry 363 (PI-44), Box 2, Consumers' Divison, N.E.C. Material Folder; Blaisdell quoted in Memorandum attached to "Suggestions for Code Revision," CAB Report to Hugh Johnson, February 19, 1934, ibid., Box 2, CAB Reports and Speeches (General) Folder, p. 7.

42. Rumsey quoted in "Cotton Code Is Praised," July 15, 1933, 5; "First Label to Go to Mrs. Roosevelt," October 5, 1933, 4; "To Sew NRA Dress Label," January 21, 1934, 20, all in *NYT*; Campbell, *Consumer Representation*, 41; Susan Ware, *Beyond Suffrage: Women in the New Deal* (Cambridge, MA: Harvard University Press, 1981), 87–96.

43. Rumsey quoted in R. L. Duffus, "The NRA Enters upon Its Climactic Stage," August 27, 1933, 21; "Consumers' Board Seeks Price Data," September 8, 1933, 13; "Asks Delay on Oil Price," October 10, 1933, 38; "Warns Consumers on Soft Coal Rise," November 8, 1933, 26; " 'White Collar' Aid Urged," September 19, 1933, 4; "Publicity for Slackers," August 9, 1933, 2; "Warns against Price Rise Fears," August 16, 1933, 7; "Mrs. Roosevelt Urges Consumers to Band and Prevent Gouging in Rise of Prices," August 17, 1933, 1, all in *NYT*.

44. "Price of Bread," July 13, 1933, 18; "Wallace May Label Bread with the Tax," July 3, 1933, 22; "Bread Rises Bring Licensing Threat," July 9, 1933, 15, all in *NYT*.

45. "49 Cities Warned on Bread Prices," July 12, 1933, 8; "Bread Rule Requires Weight on Wrappers," July 27, 1933, 19; "No Bread Profiteers," July 14, 1933, 2; "St. Paul Bread Price Up," July 3, 1933, 22; "The Task of Coordination," July 3, 1933, 10; "Bread Up in Indianapolis," July 6, 1933, 10; "Bread Dearer Up-State," July 9, 1933, 15; "Federal Investigator in Bismark," July 11, 1933, 4, all in *NYT*.

46. Harold Wise to Henry Wallace, July 30, 1933; Celia Mills to Henry Wallace, August 5, 1933, Box 3, Ohio Folder; S.A. Thomas to Henry Wallace, July 2, 1933, Box 3, Pennsylvania Folder; Irene Baker to Hugh Johnson, Box 1, California Folder; Lois Hargett Crane to Hugh Johnson, September 8, 1933, Box 4, Ohio Folder, all in AAA Papers, Records of the Consumers' Counsel, Correspondence Relating to Price Racketeering, Entry 11. This record group contains sample letters from all forty-eight states.

47. Harry Gockel to Henry Wallace, July 5, 1933, Box 2, Missouri Folder; Mayor John Murphy, New Haven, CT, to Henry Wallace, July 13, 1933, Box 1, Connecticut Folder; Charles White to Henry Wallace, July 13, 1933, Box 1, Delaware Folder; Pedro Moya to Henry Wallace, July 22, 1933; Stanley McGilligan to Henry Wallace, July 9, 1933, Box 1, Illinois Folder, all in ibid.

48. Howe quoted in "Publicity Planned to Curb Profiteer," August 4, 1933, 8; "Howe Questions Bread Prices," September 9, 1933, 7; "Howe Questions Some Bread Prices," September 29, 1933, 17; "Reports on Bread Price Rise," October 19, 1933, 10, all in *NYT*.

49. "Radio Food Talks Planned by City," February 3, 1934, 15; Gannon quoted in "Daily Radio Talks on Food Prices Are Started by New City Bureau," February 11, 1934, sec. 2, p. 1; "City Food Survey to Aid Housewives," February 18, 1934, 12, all in *NYT*.

50. "Consumers' Guide," *BW*, September 30, 1933, 10; Howe quoted in "Bread Price Rise Found Moderate," *NYT*, August 15, 1933, 19.

51. " 'Gouging' Charged in Textile Prices," September 12, 1933, 13; "Profiteering Inquiry Ordered by Johnson," October 1, 1933, 30, both in *NYT*; Philadelphia women quoted in Ada Toll to Henry Wallace, August 25, 1933; Frederic Howe to Ada Toll, September 28, 1933; Elton Allison (Chairman, Milk Consumers Protective League of Eastern Pennsylvania) to Mary Rumsey, August 31, 1933; Frederic Howe to Elton Allison, September 28, 1933, all in AAA Papers, Records of the Consumers' Counsel, Correspondence Relating to Price Racketeering, Box 3, Pennsylvania Folder.

52. Darrow quoted in Schlesinger Jr., *Age of Roosevelt*, 133; David Cushman Coyle, "Public Works: A New Industry," *Atlantic*, December 1933, 758.

53. James Martin, " 'Buy Now'—on $30 a week," *Nation*, November 1, 1933, 503.

54. William Ogburn, "The Consumer and the NRA," *Nation*, September 20, 1933, 318; "The Same Old Paymaster," *NYT*, August 15, 1933, 16; "Sniping the Blue Eagle," *BW*, September 9, 1933, 4; "Jobs, Hours, Wages," *BW*, September 23, 1933, 16–17.

55. "Ogburn Quits Post, Warning Johnson," August 15, 1; "Price Statistics Demanded," August 22, 1933, 7; "Jump in Milk Price Fought in Chicago," November 5, 1933, IV, 6; "Means on Consumer Board," September 29, 1933, 3; "10,468 Complaints Sent to NRA Here," October 2, 1933, 6, all in *NYT*; "The Future of the NRA," *Nation*, November 1, 1933, 498; Stuart Chase, "The Consumer's Tomorrow," *Scribner's*, December 1933, 333; "NRA Builds a Machine," September 16, 1933, 5–6; "Balky Consumers," September 23, 1933, 3, both in *BW*.

56. Emergency Conference quoted in "10,468 Complaints Sent to NRA Here"; "Cabinet Department Urged for Consumer," December 12, 1933, 17; "Consumers' Board Is Urged to Resign," December 17, 1933, 24; "Remedies for Too High Prices," December 18, 1933, 3; "Awaits 'with Interest' NRA Consumer Position," December 24, 1933, II, 13; "NRA Is Scored and Defended on Consumers," January 7, 1934, II, 1, 6, all in *NYT*; "New Consumer Champions," *BW*, December 30, 1933, 9; James Rorty, "The Consumer vs. the NRA: What Shall We Do About It?" *Nation*, March 28, 1934, 351.

57. Albert Evans, "Can the NRA Succeed?" *Nation*, September 27, 1933, 347; Rexford Tugwell, *The Battle for Democracy* (New York: Columbia University Press, 1935), 268; Keezer, "The Consumer under the National Recovery Administration," 96–97; NRA field agents quoted in " 'Public Attitude toward the NRA Program,' as Reported by State Directors of the National Emergency Council," May 2, 1934, NRA Papers, Research and Planning Divisions, Subject File of Leon Henderson

1933–35, Box 1, Compliance Folder, 11; Means, "The Consumer and the New Deal," 15.

58. "Councils Planned to Curb Gougers," August 26, 1933, 22; Rumsey quoted in S. J. Woolf, "Champion of the Consumer Speaks Out"; "Text of Roosevelt's Message Read to Congress," January 4, 1934, 2, all in *NYT*. "Activities of the CAB," 11; William T. Foster to Harry Moore, November 22, 1933, NRA Papers, National Emergency Council's Consumer Divison, County Council Files 1933–35, Entry 3(A1), Box 28, New York Administration (Jan 1933–February 1934) Folder; Dexter Keezer to Robert Brady, April 30, 1934, ibid., Box 2, Field Contacts, Brady Folder.

59. "Professor Douglas Gets Post," *NYT*, November 17, 1933, 6; Douglas, "Role of the Consumer in the New Deal," 106; Paul Douglas to Mrs. Raymond Ingersoll, NRA Papers, National Emergency Council's Consumer Divison, County Council Files 1933–35, Entry 3(A1), Box 28, New York Administration (Jan 1933–February 1934) Folder.

60. CAB quoted in "Councils Formed to Protect Buyer," *NYT*, October 26, 1933, 13; "Consumers in County Areas Enter the Recovery Program," *NYT*, January 7, 1934, sec. 9, p. 1; "General Information, Rules, and Regulations," Bulletin No. 1, April 1934, NRA Papers, Consumers' Division of the National Emergency Council, Publications of the Consumers' Division of the National Emergency Council 1934–1935, Box 1.

61. Tillie Kaplan to Sue White, March 12, 1934, NRA Papers, Consumers' Division of the National Emergency Council, County Council Files 1933–35, Box 28, New York Administration (March–May 1934) Folder; "Cent Cut Is Asked by Milk Consumers," November 13, 1934, 19; "Demand Milk Price Cut," November 20, 1934, 24; "Winter Food Costs Listed for Housewives," December 5, 1934, 1; "Study of the Consumer," February 3, 1935, sec. 10, p. 11, all in *NYT*.

62. Robert Lynd, "New Deal Consumer: A Study at Close Range," *Printer's Ink*, March 22, 1934, 44; Helen Christine Bennett, "A Housewife's Everyday Buying," *Scribner's*, July 1934, 43–45; Robert McElvaine, *Down and Out in the Great Depression: Letters from the Forgotten Man* (Chapel Hill: University of North Carolina Press, 1983).

63. "Quality Standards Requested for Codes," October 20, 1933, 2; "Roosevelt Curbs AAA Code Power as Peek Revolts," December 7, 1933, 1, both in *NYT*; Robert Lynd to Meredith Givens, November 1, 1933, Lynd Papers, Container 2, Reel 2; Caroline F. Ware, "Implementing the Consumer," *Survey Graphic*, February 1934, 71; Committee on Consumer Standards of the CAB, "Proposal to Develop Standards for Consumer Goods by Establishing a Consumer Standards Board and Funds for Basic Testing," December 1, 1933, NRA Papers, Consolidated Reference Materials, Misc. Reports and Documents 1933–37, Entry 396 (PI-44), Box 24, Consumer Goods Folder.

64. Philips, Boyle, and Hauck quoted in "Testimony on Standards for Consumer Goods at Canning Industry Hearing," February 8, 9, 1934, NRA Papers, Advisory Bodies, CAB, Office Files of Emily Newell Blair, Box 2 (February–November 1935), CAB Reports and Speeches (General) Folder; "Housewives Give Advice to Canners," *NYT*, February 9, 1934, 21; Lynd committee quoted in "Activities of the CAB," 8.

65. "Consumers Held Chief NRA Victims," June 27, 1934, 21; Macy's quoted in "Warns of Buyers' Revolt," November 9, 1934, 43, both in *NYT*; Business lobbyists quoted in "Tugwell Bill Tension," *BW*, December 16, 1933, 8; Dickinson quoted in James Rorty, "Call for Mr. Throttlebottom!" *Nation,* January 10, 1934, 37.

66. Katharine Dayton, "The Love Letters of a Consumer to Her Congress," *SEP*, April 14, 1934, 87–88.

67. "Holds Consumers Suffer under NRA," *NYT*, February 25, 1934, 15. On Henderson, see Block, *Current Biography* (1940), 377–79; Samuel Lubell, "The Daring Young Man on the Flying Pri-cees," *SEP*, September 13, 1941, 13, 82.

68. "NRA Profiteering to Be Looked Into," November 16, 1933, 1; "Rise on Cloth Laid to Price-Fixing," January 21, 1934, 20; Code Conferences Called For Public," February 14, 1934, 6; "Johnson Invites Criticism of NRA," February 21, 1934, 1; "Follows Montgomery in NRA Division Post," February 27, 1934, 14, all in *NYT*; "Henderson Heads NRA Research Unit," *Baltimore Sun*, February 27, 1934; Henderson quoted in Wayne Parrish, "A Critic of the NRA Gets Important NRA Post," *LD*, April 7, 1934, 38.

69. "Code Showdown," *BW*, February 24, 1934, 20; "Johnson Invites Criticism of NRA," *NYT*, February 20, 1934, 1.

70. "Consumers' Board Urges NRA Changes on Conference Eve," *NYT*, March 5, 1934, 1, 2; CAB quoted in Memorandum attached to "Suggestions for Code Revision"; "Activities of the CAB"; Walton Hamilton, "Consumers' Interest in Price-Fixing," *Survey Graphic*, February 1934, 95; "Asks Grade Rules in All NRA Codes," *NYT*, March 25, 1934, sec. 2, p. 17; Henry Carter, "The Consumer Comes of Age," *New Outlook*, April 1934, 39–41. "Johnson Backs 10% Cut in Hours," *NYT*, March 6, 1934, 3; "NRA Prices Called Unfair to Public," *NYT*, May 19, 1934, 4.

71. "Retailers Ready for Code Meetings," *NYT*, February 25, 1934, sec. 2, p. 15.

72. Nystrom quoted in "Johnson Meets NRA Critics, Proposes 12-Point Revision," February 28, 1934, 11; Filene quoted in "Code Delegates Hesitate to Cut Hours, Raise Pay, without Price Increases," March 7, 1934, 1–2; "23,000 Stores Pledge Aid to Bar Profiteering," August 27, 1934, 1, all in *NYT*. "Sears Slash," *BW*, February 16, 1935, 22; Parodneck quoted in James Rorty, "The Consumer vs. the NRA," *Nation*, March 14, 1934, 295.

73. "Guidance of NRA Put up to Women," *NYT*, December 5, 1933, 2; "NRA Calls Critics to Sessions Today," *NYT*, February 27, 1934, 9. See also Landon Storrs, *Civilizing Capitalism: The National Consumers' League, Women's Activism, and Labor Standards in the New Deal Era* (Chapel Hill: University of North Carolina Press, 2000), 91–123.

74. Peter H. Irons, *The New Deal Lawyers* (Princeton, NJ: Princeton University Press, 1982), 205; Edward Filene, "A Report of a Study Tour of Business Conditions in Fourteen Large Cities in the United States as Affected by the President's Recovery Program," March 1, 1934, Filene Papers, Box 42, Speech 777, p. 3; Letter from employee of Bethlehem Steel Company to Senator Wagner, written on Employee Representation Plan Circular, 1936, Keyserling Papers-GTL, Box 1, Folder 16; Civic League of Westerly and Southern Rhode Island to Senator Wagner, March 10, 1934, ibid., Folder 1.

75. "New Deal Permanent, President Says; Asks Higher Pay, Shorter Hours, Now," *NYT*, March 6, 1934, 1, 2; Gordon, *New Deals*, 211–12.

76. "200 Liberals Ask a Powerful NRA," *NYT*, May 24, 1934, 10; "More and Better Strikes," *NR*, October 11, 1933, 227, 226.

77. "Fall Business Rise Predicted by NRA," July 23, 1934, 1, 2; "Mr. Henderson's 'Tip,' " July 24, 1934, 16; Henderson quoted in Russell Owen, "Ten Baffling Questions NRA Must Answer," October 7, 1934, 21, all in *NYT*. Roosevelt quoted in Bernstein, *Turbulent Years*, 18.

78. Leuchtenberg, *Franklin D. Roosevelt*, 53, 117.

79. "Wallace to Urge Monopoly Curbs," *NYT*, January 9, 1935, 2.

80. Milwaukee agent quoted in "Price-Fixing Foes and Friends Heard," January 10, 1935, 3; CAB quoted in "Codes Hurt Public, NRA Board Is Told," January 7, 1935, 25; consumer councils quoted in "Consumer Groups Score Price Fixing," January 11, 1935, 16; Douglas quoted in "Consumers Held Chief NRA Victims," June 27, 1934, 21, all in *NYT*.

81. "Wallace Discusses Prices," August 11, 1934, 24; "Rise in Food Prices Seen," August 12, 1934, 2; "AAA Maps Right on Food Gougers," August 13, 1934, 1, 3; "Living Costs May Rise 7% in Winter, Says Wallace," August 14, 1934, 1, 3, 16; "Relief Units Plan Wider Food Buying," August 15, 1934, 15; "Roosevelt Takes Charge of Drought Aid, Warning Food and Grain Gougers," August 16, 1934, 12; "President Drops Tariffs on Feed," August 21, 1934, 1, 3; "Warns of False Price Rumors," August 21, 1934, 3; " 'Profiteering,' " August 22, 1934, 16, all in *NYT*; Howe quoted in "AAA Opens Fight on Profiteering," *Epic (Los Angeles) News*, September 24, 1934, in AAA Papers, Records of the Consumers' Counsel, Iris Walker Office Files, Box 5, Photostat File.

82. "Rising Food Costs as Viewed by AAA," May 12, 1935, IV, 10; Protesters quoted in "Price Drive Shuts Many Meat Shops," May 27, 1935, 3; "Boycott of High-Priced Meat Spread by Militant Housewives," May 28, 1935, 27; Housewives quoted in "Meat Prices Fight Will Go to Mayor," May 30, 1935, 19; "Six Are Arrested in Meat Boycott," May 31, 1935, 17; "Meat Prices Still High," June 3, 1935, 19; "Mayor's Aid Asked by Meat Dealers," June 11, 1935, 22; "Dealers Find Mayor Lax in Meat Strike," June 14 1935, 17; "100 Picket Meat Plants," June 15, 1935, 4, all in *NYT*; Annelise Orleck, *Common Sense and a Little Fire: Women and Working-Class Politics in the United States, 1900–1965* (Chapel Hill: University of North Carolina Press, 1995), 234–41; Elizabeth Faue, *Community of Suffering and Struggle: Women, Men, and the Labor Movement in Minneapolis, 1915–1945* (Chapel Hill: University of North Carolina Press, 1991), 113; Darlene Clark Hine, "The Housewives' League of Detroit: Black Women and Economic Nationalism," in *Visible Women: New Essays on American Activism*, ed. Nancy A. Hewitt and Suzanne Lebsock (Urbana: University of Illinois Press, 1993), 223–41.

83. "Buyers Trampled By Meat Strikers," July 28, 1935, 3; "Women Plan Fight on All High Prices," August 4, 1935, 3; "Consumers Widen Boycott in Detroit," August 11, 1935, IV, 6; "Chicago Housewives Plan Meat Strike," August 19, 1935, 2; "Wallace Warned by Meat Strikers," August 20, 1935, 38; "Food Price Inquiry Put up to Roosevelt," August 24, 1935, 3; "Price Rises Cause Political Reaction," August 25, 1935, IV, 7; "Meat Price Strike Spreads," September 5, 1935, 17; "Roosevelt Orders Food Cost Survey," September 29, 1935, 27, all in *NYT*. "Irate Housewives Demand Wallace Cut Meat Prices," *Washington Evening Star*, August 19, 1935; Detroit Delegation to Washington of the Central Action Committee

against the High Cost of Living, "Statement of the Delegation"; "Women Urge U.S. Probe of Meat Prices," *Washington Times,* August 19, 1935; "Housewives' Army 'Conquers' Capital," *Washington Herald,* August 20, 1935, all in AAA Papers, Records of the Consumers' Counsel, Office File of Donald Montgomery, Entry 7, Box 3, Detroit Delegation Meat Prices Press Clippings Folder.

84. "Pecora Aide Named for Curb on Pools," July 19, 1934, 27; "Wallace Opposes Bread Price Rise," October 17, 1935, 25; "AAA Aide Opposes Bread Price Rise," October 20, 1935, 20; "U.S. Again Probes Bread Cost," November 3, 1935, IV, 12; "Bread Prices Studied in 9 Cities," November 7, 1935, 20; "Buffalo Bread Prices Rise," November 26, 1935, 10, all in *NYT.*

85. Helen Sorenson, *The Consumer Movement: What It Is and What It Means* (New York: Harper, 1941), 120. On New Deal Democratic voters, see Wenger, *New York Jews and the Great Depression,* 103–35; Kristi Andersen, *The Creation of a Democratic Majority, 1928–1936* (Chicago: University of Chicago Press, 1979), 83–126; Gerald H. Gamm, *The Making of New Deal Democrats: Voting Behavior and Realignment in Boston, 1920–1940* (Chicago: University of Chicago Press, 1989).

86. Sorenson, *Consumer Movement,* 82–136, quote on 84; "Women Get Advice on Better Buying," *NYT,* October 1, 1935, 25; Werner Gabler, *Labeling the Consumer Movement* (Washington, DC: American Retail Federation, 1939), 21–33.

87. Glickman, "Strike in the Temple of Consumption."

88. "Dr. Hamilton Heads Consumers' Survey," August 1, 1935, 2; "Consumers' Agency to Get Price Data," August 18, 1935, IV, 7; quotes in "New Agency Acts for Consumers," September 9, 1935, 2; " 'Cabinet' to Direct Consumer Division," October 12, 1935, 6; "Milk Consumers Declared Fooled," October 25, 1935, 4; "Bureaus Help Consumers," November 24, 1935, IV, 11, all in *NYT.* "The Coordination of Consumer Agencies," 5; "Salvaging the Consumer Services," June 5, 1935, both in NRA Papers, Advisory Bodies, CAB, Office Files of Emily Newell Blair, Box 2 (February–November 1935), Consumers' Division, N.E.C. Material Folder.

89. "Spurt in Advertising Predicted by Kobak," *NYT,* June 9, 1935, 12; Blair quoted in "Consumer Change Is Seen," *NYT,* June 13, 1935, 5.

Chapter Four
The New Deal and the Problem of Wages, 1935–1940

1. "Wagner Defends Bill as Fulfillment of 7A," *NYT,* May 26, 1935, IV, 10.

2. Wagner quoted in Christopher Tomlins, *The State and the Unions: Labor Relations, Law, and the Organized Labor Movement in America, 1880–1960* (New York: Cambridge University Press, 1985), 100; AFL, *Rights as Workers* (1933), Saposs Papers, Box 24, Labor and the Government Research Materials; Lewis quoted in Irving Bernstein, *The Turbulent Years: A History of the American Worker, 1933–1941* (Boston: Houghton Mifflin, 1969), 41, 126–71.

3. Phil Levy to Leon Keyserling, Memo, n.d., Keyserling Papers-GTL, Box 1; Leiserson quoted in William Leiserson, notes for testimony before the Senate Committee on Education and Labor on S. 2926, March 16, 1934, Leiserson Papers, Box 49, Speeches and Addresses, 1931–1934 Folder; James Gross,

The Making of the National Labor Relations Board: A Study in Economics, Politics, and the Law (Albany: State University of New York Press, 1974), 17.

4. Typescript, n.d., Leiserson Papers, Box 49, Speeches and Addresses, 1931–1934 Folder; Wagner quoted in Leon Keyserling, "The Wagner Act: Its Origin and Current Significance," *George Washington Law Review* 29 (1960): 217.

5. Bernstein, *Turbulent Years*, 217–315; Elizabeth Faue, *Community of Suffering and Struggle: Women, Men, and the Labor Movement in Minneapolis, 1915–1945* (Chapel Hill: University of North Carolina Press, 1991), 72–83; Janet Irons, *Testing the New Deal: The General Textile Strike of 1934 in the American South* (Urbana: University of Illinois Press, 2000).

6. " 'Terror' Charged by Auto Workers," December 16, 1934, 5; Foreman quoted in "NRA Paints Unrest in Auto Industry as a 'Dark Picture,' " February 8, 1935, 1, 6, both in *NYT*; "Labor Notes," *Nation*, March 6, 1935, 280.

7. "NRA Research Body Cites Profits Rise," February 26, 1935, 10; Henderson quoted in "Declares Profits Gain over Wages," June 27, 1935, 2; "Profits and Wages," October 7, 1935, 14, all in *NYT*; "Truthless Statistics Dishonestly Interpreted," *BW*, March 23, 1935, 36.

8. "Roosevelt Backs NRA Labor Clause," *NYT*, September 8, 1934, 1, 2; Peter Irons, *The New Deal Lawyers* (Princeton, NJ: Princeton University Press, 1982), 226–30; Bernstein, *Turbulent Years*, 323.

9. Milton Handler to Robert Wagner, May 29, 1934, Box 1, Folder 9; Address by Milton Handler, General Counsel of the NLB before Legal Division of the NRA, Box 1, Folder 10; Keyserling quoted in Memo, "Miss Perkins Suggested Changes," Box 1, Folder 9; and Keyserling Memo, "Response to Draft of Labor Bill by Donald Richberg," May 1935, Box 1, Folder 5, all in Keyserling Papers-GTL. See also Kenneth Casebeer, "Drafting Wagner's Act: Leon Keyserling and the Pre-committee Drafts of the Labor Disputes Act and the National Labor Relations Act," *Industrial Relations Law Journal* 11 (1989): 73–131.

10. Handler to Wagner, May 29, 1934; Milton Handler to Leon Keyserling, n.d., Keyserling Papers-GTL, Box 1, Folder 10. See also Stanley Vittoz, *New Deal Labor Policy and the American Industrial Economy* (Chapel Hill: University of North Carolina Press, 1987); Tomlins, *The State and the Unions*; and Colin Gordon, *New Deals: Business, Labor, and Politics in America, 1920–1935* (New York: Cambridge University Press, 1994).

11. "Program for a Study of the Role of the Government in Labor Relations," March 13, 1934; Evans Clark to William Leiserson, July 6, 1934, both in Leiserson Papers, Box 40, Twentieth Century Fund (TCF) 1934 Folder. Evans Clark to Edward Filene, July 9, 1934; Press Release, October 15, 1934, both in TCF Papers.

12. Beth Wenger, *New York Jews and the Great Depression: Uncertain Promise* (New Haven, CT: Yale University Press, 1996), 10–32; J. Michael Eisner, *William Morris Leiserson: A Biography* (Madison: University of Wisconsin, 1967), 6–7, 9–13, 26, 30; Gross, *Making of the NLRB*, 175n115; "David Saposs," *NYT*, November 16, 1968, 37.

13. *Property vs. Human Values* and *A University Professor for Councilman in the Fifth Ward*, campaign pamphlets in the 1923 election for Toledo, OH, city councilman, Box 51; Paul Douglas to Leiserson, July 22, 1932, Box 11, in Leiserson

Papers. William Leiserson, *Adjusting Immigrant and Industry* (New York: Harper, 1924); William Leiserson, "Ohio's Answer to Unemployment," *Survey Graphic,* December 1932, 643–50; Eisner, *William Morris Leiserson,* 13–18, 30–43, 50–58.

14. Saposs quoted in David Saposs to Harry Millis, March 23, 1934; Saposs to Evans Clark, March 26, 1934, March 30, 1934, April 6, 1934, in Saposs Papers, Box 3, Correspondence, January–March 1934 Folder; Edward Filene, "Labor Unions: Research Project for the Twentieth Century Fund," January 30, 1934, TCF Papers.

15. William Leiserson, "Labor Under the New Deal," *Railway Clerk,* November 1934, 437–38.

16. Leon Keyserling, "Citizenship Essay," Beaufort, South Carolina, High School, 1923, Keyserling Papers-HSTL, Box 16. On Keyserling, see Transcript of Oral History Interview with Leon Keyserling, May 3–19, 1971, Oral History Collection, HSTL.

17. Paul Douglas to Evans Clark, March 16, 1935, Leiserson Papers, Box 41, TCF 1935, March–December Folder; Bernstein, *Turbulent Years,* 318–30.

18. Minutes, Meeting of the Special Committee on the Role of Government in Labor Relations, February 16, 1935, Leiserson Papers, Box 41, TCF 1935, January–February Folder; TCF Press Release, "Permanent Federal Labor Law Enforced by New United States Labor Commission Urged," March 4, 1935, Leiserson Papers, Box 41, March–December Folder; William Davis to Robert Wagner, March 24, 1935, Leiserson Papers, Box 41, TCF 1935, March–December Folder; TCF, "Special Committee on Government and Labor," March 12, 1935, Keyserling Papers-GTL, Box 1, Folder 11; "Filene Group Gives Labor Law Plan," March 4, 1935, 2; "2,500,000 Workers in Company Unions," April 29, 1935, 4, both in *NYT;* "The Government and America's Labor," *NYT Book Review,* June 23, 1935, 5.

19. "Wagner Defends Bill as Fulfillment of 7A."

20. Leon Keyserling, "Third Draft," n.d., Keyserling Papers-GTL, Box 1, Folder 18; Leon Keyserling to William Leiserson, Leiserson Papers, Box 28.

21. "Speech of Senator Robert Wagner of New York upon Introduction in the Senate of His National Labor Relations Bill," February 21, 1935, Keyserling Papers-GTL, Box 3; *Congressional Record,* 74th. Cong., 1st. sess., May 15, 1935, 79, pt. 7:7848–49.

22. Maurice Leven, Harold Moulton, and Clark Warburton, *America's Capacity to Consume* (Washington, DC: Brookings Institution, 1934), 126–27; J. S. Lawrence, "Poverty and Plenty," *Review of Reviews,* October 1934, 15–17, 45–46.

23. All quoted in Jacob Karro to David Saposs, October 1, 1936, Saposs Papers, Box 3, Correspondence 1936 Folder.

24. Rabbi Sidney Goldstein, in "Joint Statement by the Churches of Christ in America, National Catholic Welfare Conference, and Central Conference of American Rabbis," to Robert Wagner, March 22, 1935, Keyserling Papers-GTL, Box 1, Folder 1; "Strikes Minimized by Miss Perkins," *NYT,* May 21, 1935, 35; Kroger worker quoted in Kenneth Casebeer, "Clashing Views of the Wagner Act: The Files of Leon Keyserling," *Labor's Heritage* 2 (April 1990): 50.

25. Bronx resident quoted in Wenger, *New York Jews,* 98–99; Irons, *New Deal Lawyers,* 98–99.

26. "Wagner Labor Bill Passed by Senate by Vote of 63 to 12," May 17, 1935, 1, 4; "President Orders Speed on NRA and Wagner Bills," May 25, 1935, 1, 2, both in *NYT*; Wagner quoted in "Address by Robert Wagner, of New York, Made over a National Broadcasting Company Network," May 21, 1935, Keyserling Papers-GTL, Box 3; Bernstein, *Turbulent Years*, 340–49.

27. *U.S. Statutes at Large* 49 (1935): 449; "Rights of 7A Restored," June 20, 1935, 1, 2; "Both Houses Clear Wagner Labor Bill," June 28, 1935, 6; "Roosevelt Signs the Wagner Bill as 'Just to Labor,'" July 6, 1935, 1, 2, all in *NYT*; Gross, *Making of the NLRB*, 174–79.

28. Newton Baker to Edward Filene, May 25, 1935; Edward Filene to Evans Clark, May 28, 1935; Edward Filene to Newton Baker, May 29, 1935, all in Filene Papers, Box 35, Folder 2.

29. "Chamber Denounces Plans of New Deal but Advisors of President Uphold Him," *NYT*, May 3, 1935, 1, 4; "Labor Relations Runaround" and "No Obedience!" *BW*, July 6, 1935, 22, 40; "'Rather Go to Jail' Than Accept Wagner Bill, Says U.S. Steel Executive," *NYT*, May 25, 1935, 1; Bernstein, *Turbulent Years*, 334–39.

30. Gordon, *New Deals*, 240–79; Anthony Badger, *The New Deal: The Depression Years, 1933–1940* (New York: Hill and Wang, 1989), 230–32. See also Frances Perkins, "The Social Security Act," *Vital Speeches of the Day*, 1935, 792–94.

31. "Roosevelt Defends AAA before 14,000 in Chicago," "Texts of the President's Speeches before Farmers and Notre Dame Students," and "Roosevelt to the Farmers," *NYT*, December 10, 1935, 1, 12, 24. For the attack on AAA, see Irons, *New Deal Lawyers*, 133–99.

32. Donald Johnson and Kirk Porter, eds., *National Party Platforms: 1840–1972* (Urbana: University of Illinois Press, 1973), 360–63; Franklin D. Roosevelt, *The Public Papers and Addresses of Franklin D. Roosevelt*, vol. 5, ed. Samuel I. Rosenman (New York: Random House, 1938), 568, 572; For soak-the-rich taxation, see Badger, *New Deal*, 94.

33. Johnson and Porter, *National Party Platforms*, 366; "Doubled Living Cost Predicted," November 30, 1935, 17; "Women to 'War' on Costs," October 3, 1935, 19, both in *NYT*.

34. Hoover quoted in Richard Polenberg, ed., *The Era of Franklin D. Roosevelt, 1933–1945: A Brief History with Documents* (Boston: Bedford/St. Martin's Press, 2000), 116–17; "Consumer Called 'Forgotten Man,'" *NYT*, October 7, 1935, 4.

35. Kristi Andersen, *The Creation of a Democratic Majority, 1928–1936* (Chicago: University of Chicago Press, 1979); David Plotke, *Building a Democratic Political Order: Reshaping American Liberalism in the 1930s and 1940s* (New York: Cambridge University Press, 1996); Gregory Field, "'Electricity for All': The Electric Home and Farm Authority and the Politics of Mass Consumption, 1932–1935," *BHR* 64 (spring 1990): 32–60; Jordan Schwarz, *The New Dealers: Power Politics in the Age of Roosevelt* (New York: Knopf, 1993), 195–245.

36. Nelson Lichtenstein, *Walter Reuther: The Most Dangerous Man in Detroit* (New York: Basic Books, 1995), 220–47.

37. Irons, *New Deal Lawyers*, 230–43, 272–89.

38. Henderson quoted in "New Deal Aides Warn on Prices," April 25, 1937, 19; "WPA Economist Predicts Collapse in the Fall If Prices of Commodities

Spurt Again," May 25, 1937, 41, both in *NYT*. See also Alan Brinkley, *The End of Reform: New Deal Liberalism in Recession and War* (New York: Vintage Books, 1995), 23–24.

39. "Wages and Prices," *Monthly Survey of Business of the AFL*, April–May, 1937, 1.

40. Jackson quoted in "High Cost of Living Put on Trial Here," January 12, 1937, 35; "Consumer Bodies Form Federation," May 6, 1937, 46; "Consumer Groups at Critical Stage," May 16, 1937, 57, all in *NYT*.

41. United Conference against the High Cost of Living to "Dear Consumer," September 23, 1937; "Statement by the [UCHCL] against the Increase in Gas Rates," n.d. [1938]; "Gas Facts," n.d., "Statement of the [UCHCL] on the Dies Committee Attacks on the Consumer Groups," n.d., all in O'Connor Papers, Box 130, Folder 21; "Consumers Begin Cheap-Milk Fight," *NYT*, November 23, 1937, 1, 2; Helen Sorenson, *The Consumer Movement: What It Is and What It Means* (New York: Harper and Row, 1941), 10, 102–6, 117–19.

42. Sorenson, *Consumer Movement*, 127–28.

43. *Women Do 85% of the Buying*, LWS pamphlet, c. 1938, LWS Papers, Box 1, Folder 12; Dublin quoted in Landon Storrs, *Civilizing Capitalism: The National Consumers' League, Women's Activism, and Labor Standards in the New Deal Era* (Chapel Hill: University of North Carolina Press, 2000), 97; Lawrence Glickman, "The Strike in the Temple of Consumption: Consumer Activism and Twentieth-Century American Political Culture," *JAH* 88 (June 2001): 99–128. See also Michael Denning, *The Cultural Front: The Laboring of American Culture in the Twentieth Century* (London: Verso, 1996).

44. Minutes of meetings of the LWS of Chicago, September 27, 1938, October 11, 1938, October 13, 1938, November 15, 1938, LWS Papers, Box 1, Folder 8. On O'Connor, see the biographical note in the finding aide for O'Connor's papers.

45. "Sees Buyer Strike as Public Service," September 7, 1937, 30; "Puts Bread Price at a 7-Year High," January 9, 1938, 1, 23, both in *NYT*.

46. "New Competition Faced by Industry," April 1, 1934, II, 15; Nystrom quoted in "Consumer Groups to Grow under NRA," April 4, 1934, 40; Warbasse quoted in "Stores Welcome Price-Rise Halt," April 29, 1934, II, 17, all in *NYT*; Horace Kallen, "Consumers, Organize!" *Christian Century*, June 27, 1934, 858–60; Ronald Tobey, *Technology as Freedom: The New Deal and the Electrical Modernization of the American Home* (Berkeley: University of California Press, 1996); Badger, *New Deal*, 169–86; Ellis W. Hawley, *The New Deal and the Problem of Monopoly: A Study in Economic Ambivalence* (Princeton, NJ: Princeton University Press, 1966), 202; Schwarz, *New Dealers*, 235–45; James Warbasse, "The Cooperatives and the NRA," *Nation*, November 15, 1933, 561–62.

47. "Wages Must Go Up, E. A. Filene Warns," July 15, 1937, 37; "Edward A. Filene, 77, Dies in Paris," September 26, 1937, 9, both in *NYT*. Lincoln Steffens, *The Autobiography of Lincoln Steffens* (New York: Harcourt, Brace, 1931), 603.

48. "Criticizes Lewis Plan," *NYT*, July 6, 1936, 8.

49. "16 Crafts Fight Industrial Union," October 4, 1935, 46; "Labor Still Divided on Form of Unions," October 20, 1935, V, 7; "Fist Fight Puts A. F. of L. in Uproar," October 20, 1935, 22; "Lewis Quits Office in the Federation," November 24, 1935, 1, 12; "Charges Reds Back C.I.O. Movement," September

23, 1936, 4; "A. F. of L. Units Back General Motors," January 9, 1937, 18, all in *NYT*. See also Steve Fraser, *Labor Will Rule: Sidney Hillman and the Rise of American Labor* (New York: Free Press, 1991), 324–52; Tomlins, *The State and the Unions*, 140–47; and Roosevelt quoted in William E. Leuchtenburg, *Franklin D. Roosevelt and the New Deal, 1932–1940* (New York: Harper and Row, 1963), 243.

50. Frederic Lee, "A New Dealer in Agriculture: G. C. Means and the Writing of *Industrial Prices*," *Review of Social Economy* 46 (October 1988): 180–202; Joseph Palamountain, *The Politics of Distribution* (Cambridge, MA: Harvard University Press, 1955); Jonathan Bean, *Beyond the Broker State: Federal Policies toward Small Business, 1936–1961* (Chapel Hill: University of North Carolina Press, 1996), 17–36, 67–88; Nancy Beck Young, *Wright Patman: Populism, Liberalism, and the American Dream* (Dallas: Southern Methodist University Press, 2000), 73–104; Carl Ryant, "The South and the Movement against Chain Stores," *Journal of Southern History* 39 (May 1973): 207–22.

51. Evans Clark, "Corporations Invade Retail Selling," *NYT*, September 7, 1924, VIII, 4; Tom Mahoney, *The Great Merchants: The Stories of Twenty Famous Retail Operations and the People Who Made Them Great* (New York: Harper and Row, 1955), 257–60; William Leach, *Land of Desire: Merchants, Power, and the Rise of a New American Culture* (New York: Pantheon Books, 1993), 272–81; Susan Strasser, *Satisfaction Guaranteed: The Making of the American Mass Market* (New York: Basic Books, 1989), 203–51; Advertisement for Gimbels, *NYT*, February 13, 1938, 42.

52. "Price Swing," *BW*, July 21, 1934, 20; Louisville manager quoted in David A. Horowitz, *Beyond Left and Right: Insurgency and the Establishment* (Urbana: University of Illinois Press, 1997), 116.

53. Edward Filene to Franklin Roosevelt, April 1, 1936, Filene Papers; Miller quoted in Horowitz, *Beyond Left and Right*, 122; Walker quoted in "$3,000,000,000 Rise Is Seen in Steel," *NYT*, May 25, 1937, 41; Palamountain, *Politics of Distribution*, 170.

54. Thomas K. McCraw, "Competition and 'Fair Trade': History and Theory," *Research in Economic History* 16 (1996): 207–9; "Low-Priced Dishwashers Planned," *NYT*, August 12, 1934, II, 15.

55. Ralph Cassidy Jr., "Maintenance of Resale Prices by Manufacturers," *Quarterly Journal of Economics* 53 (May 1939): 454–64; *Labor World* quoted in Horowitz, *Beyond Left and Right*, 123; Ryant, "South against Chain Stores," 216, 218–19. On sales taxes, see Mark Leff, *The Limits of Symbolic Reform: The New Deal and Taxation, 1933–1939* (New York: Cambridge University Press, 1984).

56. Howard quoted in Ryant, "South against Chain Stores," 217; Caroline F. Ware and Gardiner C. Means, *The Modern Economy in Action* (New York: Harcourt, Brace, 1936), 36–43, 53–55, 136–37, 152–61, 231; "Sees Price System Shift," *NYT*, July 16, 1936, 25; Raymond Moley, "The War against Efficiency," *Newsweek*, September 5, 1938, 40.

57. "U.S. Bureau Sought by Consumer Units," February 20, 1938, 48; Consumers National Federation quoted in "Consumer Group to See Roosevelt," February 24, 1938, 8, both in *NYT*; Robert Lynd, "Democracy's Third Estate: The Consumer," *Political Science Quarterly* 51 (December 1936): 504, 515; Robert Lynd, "The People as Consumers," in *Recent Social Trends in the United States* (New York: McGraw-Hill, 1933), 911.

58. Quoted in Theodore Rosenof, *Dogma, Depression, and the New Deal: The Debate of Political Leaders over Economic Recovery* (Port Washington, NY: Kennikat Press, 1975), 50–51, 100.

59. "Blames Big Firms for Trade Slump," November 30, 1937, 42; "Today on the Radio," January 1, 1938, 24; Ickes, Jackson, and Henderson quoted in "Message Interests," January 2, 1938, 1, 2, all in *NYT*.

60. Henderson quoted in "Blames Big Firms for Trade Slump," "Economists Trace Slump to Prices," *NYT*, March 5, 1938, 25; S. T. Williamson, "Who's Who and Why among the Present New Dealers," *NYT Book Review*, April 9, 1939, 2; Katie Louchheim, ed., *The Making of the New Deal: The Insiders Speak* (Cambridge, MA: Harvard University Press, 1983), 105–10, 115, 209; Joseph Lash, *Dealers and Dreamers: A New Look at the New Deal* (New York: Doubleday, 1988), 241.

61. Arthur Krock, "Policy Conflict Pushed by Divided Democrats," *NYT*, January 9, 1938, 69; Jules Backman, "The Causes of Price Inflexibility," *Quarterly Journal of Economics* 54 (May 1940): 474–89; Rufus Tucker, "The Reasons for Price Rigidity," *AER* 28 (March 1938): 41–54.

62. Robert Skidelsky, *John Maynard Keynes, The Economist as Savior, 1920–1937* (New York: Penguin Press, 1992), 405–571; Brinkley, *End of Reform*, 65–105; Alan Sweezy, "The Keynesian Revolution and Its Pioneers: Keynesians and Government Policy, 1930–1939," *AER* 62 (May 1972): 116–24.

63. Means quoted in National Resources Committee, Industrial Section, *The Structure of the American Economy, Part I: Basic Characteristics* (Washington, DC: GPO, 1939), 21; Theodore Rosenof, *Economics in the Long Run: New Deal Theorists and Their Legacies, 1933–1993* (Chapel Hill: University of North Carolina Press, 1997), 49–85.

64. "Roosevelt Hears Advisers on Ways to Spur Business," November 9, 1937, 1, 2; Arthur Krock, "Experts Now Drafting Remedy for Recession," April 3, 1938, 65; Felix Belair Jr., "Roosevelt Maps Anti-trust Action," April 3, 1938, 29, all in *NYT*; Lash, *Dealers and Dreamers*, 317–33.

65. "The Text of President Roosevelt's Recovery Program Message to Congress," *NYT*, April 15, 1938, 12. See also Hawley, *New Deal and the Problem of Monopoly*, 406–10; Brinkley, *End of Reform*, 97–101.

66. "Roosevelt Asks Inquiry on Monopoly" and "The Text of President Roosevelt's Message to Congress on Monopoly," April 30, 1938, 1–2; Borah quoted in "Committee Plans Monopoly Inquiry," July 2, 1938, 3, all in *NYT*; Hopkins quoted in Hawley, *New Deal and the Problem of Monopoly*, 409.

67. One important exception to this is Alan Brinkley, who sees the TNEC as the harbinger for a Keynesian commitment to stabilizing consumer demand through government spending. *End of Reform*, 123–36.

68. "Monopoly Inquiry Sifts Price Bases," August 1, 1938, 2; Henderson quoted in "Recession Prophet Now Sees Upturn," July 17, 1938, 8, both in *NYT*.

69. Thurman Arnold, "An Inquiry into the Monopoly Issue," *NYTM*, August 21, 1938, 2, 15; Arnold quoted in Thurman Arnold, "What Is Monopoly?" *Vital Speeches of the Day*, July 1938, 570. Hawley, *New Deal and the Problem of Monopoly*, 416, 427–38, 456–71, "pork chops" quote on 427; Charles Geisst, *Monopolies in America: Empire Builders and Their Enemies from Jay Gould to Bill Gates* (Oxford: Oxford University Press, 2000), 155–66; Wilson Miscamble, "Thurman Arnold

Goes to Washington: A Look at Antitrust Policy in the Later New Deal," *BHR* 56 (spring 1982): 1–15.

70. Storrs, *Civilizing Capitalism*, 177–205, Dublin quoted on 188; Henderson quoted in "Seek Import Bill in Wage-Hour Curb," July 4, 1937, 16; "Calls Wages Bill Vital to Recovery," July 20, 1937, 13, both in *NYT*; Fraser, *Labor Will Rule*, 391–412; Benjamin Kline Hunnicutt, *Work without End: Abandoning Shorter Hours for the Right to Work* (Philadelphia: Temple University Press, 1988), 239–49.

71. Charles Jackson, *Food and Drug Legislation in the New Deal* (Princeton, NJ: Princeton University Press, 1970).

72. "Taxpayers Revolt," November 10, 1938, 1, 15; "Revolt of Electorate Ends One-Party Rule," November 13, 1938, 73, both in *NYT*. On the 1938 election, see Badger, *New Deal*, 262–69; James T. Patterson, *Congressional Conservatism and the New Deal: The Growth of the Conservative Coalition in Congress, 1933–1939* (Lexington: University of Kentucky Press, 1967), 211–87; and Clyde Weed, *The Nemesis of Reform: The Republican Party during the New Deal* (New York: Columbia University Press, 1994), 169–203.

73. Senate TNEC, *Final Report of the Executive Secretary*, 77th Cong., 1st sess., March 15, 1941; "Leon Henderson Mentioned as Successor of Douglas as Chairman of the SEC," March 30, 1939, 35; "A Sketch of the Expected New Chairman," March 31, 1939, 20; "Henderson Picked for Place on SEC," April 25, 1939, 31, all in *NYT*.

74. Mission statement quoted in Sorenson, *Consumer Movement*, 121; Alice Belester testimony, TNEC, *Investigation of Concentration of Economic Power, Part 8: Problems of the Consumer*, Hearings, 76th Cong., 1st sess., May 10–12, 1939, 3285–3309.

75. "Monopoly Inquiry Enters New Field," May 7, 1939, VI, 5; Belester quoted in "Consumers' Viewpoint Is Presented by Housewives in Monopoly Inquiry," May 11, 1939, 4; Ayres quoted in "Committee Upholds Advertising Role," May 12, 1939, 4; "Hopkins Projects a Buyers' Service," May 13, 1939, 6, all in *NYT*; Montgomery quoted in TNEC, *Investigation of Concentration of Economic Power, Part 8*, 3283–87, 3376–96; Kirstein quoted in Werner Gabler, *Labeling the Consumer Movement* (Washington, DC: American Retail Federation, 1939), 3.

76. "The Consumer Movement," *BW*, April 22, 1939, 52; Sorenson, *Consumer Movement*, 56–81.

77. "Dies Investigator Says Reds Utilize Consumer Groups," December 11, 1939, 1, 14; "Voorhis Attacks Dies, Matthews," December 12, 1939, 22; "President Cryptic in Discussing Dies," December 13, 1939, 19; "Warning Sounded on 'Witch-Hunting,' " December 14, 1939, 18; " 'Un-American' Consumers," December 17, 1939, 72; Consumers National Federation quoted in "Red Charges Denied by Consumer Group," December 13, 1939, 19, all in *NYT*.

78. "Accuses Industry of War on Unions," January 5, 1938, 14; "Score Employers as Causing Unrest," January 6, 1938, 8; "Links Union Gains to the Labor Act," June 11, 1939, 23; "A.F.L. Group Plans C.I.O. Ouster Move," September 27, 1937, 1, 2; "Communists Rule the C.I.O.," August 14, 1938, 1, 31; "NLRB Aide Urged Force, Dies Says," November 21, 1938, 2, all in *NYT*.

79. "Says NLRB Aides Assisted in Strike," December 15, 1939, 1, 20; "Inquiry into the NLRB," December 17, 1939, 72, both in *NYT*. See also the

correspondence in Kirstein Papers, Box 39, Berkshire Knitting Mills Folder: Edwin Smith to Louis Kirstein, November 13, 1936; Phillip Reilly to Louis Kirstein, December 15, 1939; Memo, December 15, 1939; Edwin Smith to Louis Kirstein, January 6, 1940; Louis Kirstein to Edwin Smith, January 8, 1940; and James Gross, *The Reshaping of the National Labor Relations Board: National Labor Policy in Transition, 1937–1947* (Albany: State University of New York Press, 1981), 168–71. On Leiserson, see Tomlins, *The State and the Unions*, 196–224.

80. "Join 20th Century Fund Board," *NYT*, June 29, 1937, 23; Storrs, *Civilizing Capitalism*, 243; Lichtenstein, *Walter Reuther*, 223, 493n7.

81. Consumers National Federation quoted in "Consumers to Seek Federal Price Unit," October 22, 1939, 62; Ayres quoted in "Wider Listing of Costs Asked to Aid Buyers," November 12, 1939, 60, both in *NYT*.

82. "Profiteer Inquiry Asked by President," *NYT*, October 1, 1939, 1.

83. "Fairless Admits 'Extra' Price Talks," November 8, 1939, 26; "New Deal Seeks Steel Price Source," November 12, 1939, 52; "Prices to Engage Monopoly Inquiry," December 3, 1939, 18; "National Economy Surveyed by TNEC," January 2, 1940, 36, all in *NYT*.

84. Ware quoted in TNEC, *Investigation of Concentration of Economic Power, Part 30: Technology and Concentration of Economic Power*, Hearings, 76th Cong., 3d sess., April 8–26, 1940, 17214; Sorenson, *Consumer Movement*, 86–87, 102.

85. TNEC, *Investigation of Concentration of Economic Power, Part 30*, 17205; Robert Lynd, foreword to Persia Campbell, *Consumer Representation in the New Deal* (New York: Columbia University Press, 1940), 10, 13; Lynd, "Democracy's Third Estate."

Chapter Five
The Consumer Goes to War, 1940–1946

1. The most comprehensive history of the Office of Price Administration (OPA) is the 18-volume government-commissioned study written under the direction of Harvey C. Mansfield, Price Executive, Durable Goods, Price Branch, Office of Price Administration. For a thorough overview, see Harvey C. Mansfield, *A Short History of OPA*, vol. 15 in *Historical Reports on War Administration: Office of Price Administration* (Washington, DC: GPO, 1947). See also Meg Jacobs, " 'How About Some Meat?': The Office of Price Administration, Consumption Politics, and State Building from the Bottom Up, 1941–1946," *JAH* 84 (December 1997): 910–41; Ira Katznelson and Bruce Pietrykowski, "Rebuilding the American State: Evidence from the 1940s," *Studies in American Political Development* 5 (fall 1991): 301–39, esp. 322–25; Andrew H. Bartels, "The Office of Price Administration and the Legacy of the New Deal, 1939–1946," *Public Historian* 5 (summer 1983): 5–29; and Barton J. Bernstein, "The Truman Administration and the Politics of Inflation" (Ph.D. diss., Harvard University, 1963). For general descriptions of rationing and price control during the war, see Richard R. Lingeman, *Don't You Know There's a War On? The American Home Front, 1941–1945* (New York: Putnam, 1970), 234–70; John Morton Blum, *V Was for Victory: Politics and American Culture during World War II* (New York: Harcourt,

Brace, 1976), 90–116; and Barbara McKlean Ward, ed., *Produce and Conserve, Share and Play Square: The Grocer and the Consumer on the Homefront during World War II* (Hanover, NH: University Press of New England, 1994).

2. Caroline F. Ware, *The Consumer Goes to War: A Guide to Victory on the Home Front* (New York: Funk and Wagnalls, 1942), 78.

3. Bruce Catton, *The War Lords of Washington* (New York: Harcourt, Brace, 1948); Blum, *V Was for Victory*, 117–46; David M. Kennedy, *Freedom from Fear: The American People in Depression and War, 1929–1945* (New York: Oxford University Press, 1999), 456–59, 478, 783. On contracts, see Paul A. Koistinen, "The Hammer and the Sword: Labor, the Military, and Industrial Mobilization, 1920–1945" (Ph.D. diss., University of California-Berkeley, 1964), 620, 664.

4. Somervell quoted in Richard Polenberg, *War and Society: The United States, 1941–1945* (Philadelphia: Lippincott, 1972), 220; *Fortune* poll cited in William L. O'Neill, *A Democracy at War: America's Fight at Home and Abroad in World War II* (New York: Free Press, 1993). Nelson Lichtenstein describes labor relations as a Faustian bargain in *Walter Reuther: The Most Dangerous Man in Detroit* (New York: Basic Books, 1995), 175–93. See also Steve Fraser, *Labor Will Rule: Sidney Hillman and the Rise of American Labor* (New York: Free Press, 1991), 441–94; Christopher L. Tomlins, *The State and the Unions: Labor Relations, Law, and the Organized Labor Movement in America, 1880–1960* (New York: Cambridge University Press, 1985), 247–81; and Nelson Lichtenstein, *Labor's War at Home: The CIO and World War II* (New York: Cambridge University Press, 1982).

5. Franklin D. Roosevelt, Fireside Chat on National Defense, May 26, 1940, in *The Public Papers and Addresses of Franklin D. Roosevelt,* 1940 vol., ed. Samuel I. Rosenman (New York: Random House, 1941), 238.

6. Samuel Lubell, "The Daring Young Man on the Flying Pri-cees," *SEP*, September 13, 1941, 84.

7. Kennedy, *Freedom from Fear*, 627; "Dollar Pinching Is in Style as War Touches Average Family," *Life*, November 1941, 102–4.

8. Elliott quoted in National Defense Advisory Commission (NDAC), Office of Production Management, Press Release, January 22, 1941, Ware Papers, Box 42; Lichtenstein, *Walter Reuther*, 165, 169; Lichtenstein, *Labor's War at Home*, 39–41.

9. Kennedy, *Freedom from Fear*, 469–70; Robert A. Divine, *The Reluctant Belligerent: American Entry into World War II*, 2d ed. (New York: Knopf, 1979), 108–9; Amy Bentley, *Eating for Victory: Food Rationing and the Politics of Domesticity* (Urbana: University of Illinois Press, 1998).

10. Lubell, "Daring Young Man," 84; Roosevelt quoted in Office of Price Administration and Civilian Supply (OPACS), Press Release, April 12, 1941, Box 42; Henderson quoted in OPACS, Press Release, June 26, 1941, Box 43, both in Ware Papers; OPACS, Minutes of Staff Meetings, May–July 1941, Henderson Papers, Box 34; Leon Henderson, Address to the National Association of Manufacturers, December 3, 1941, Gilbert Papers, Box 12.

11. Lubell, "Daring Young Man," 13, 82.

12. Henderson quoted in Mansfield, *Short History of OPA*, 35; Karl Niebyl, "Summary of Official Activities, Economics Section, Consumer Division," November 7, 1940, Ware Papers, Box 30.

13. Harriet Elliott to Leon Henderson, n.d. (1941), Ware Papers, Box 27; "Price Rises Seen Over Cut in Goods," *NYT*, July 21, 1941, 17; Lichtenstein, *Labor's War at Home*, 44–47; Gardiner Means to Harold Smith, May 21, 1941, Ware Papers, Box 29.

14. Elliott quoted in Transcript of Harriet Elliott interview on NBC Radio Network, "Women in the National Defense Program," August 28, 1940, Box 27; NDAC, Press Release 66, August 8, 1940, Box 42; Harriet Elliott to J. P. Harris, "Weekly Operations Progress Report," September 10, 17, and 24, 1940, Box 27; NDAC, Consumer Division, "A Guide to the Use of *Consumer Prices*," November 15, 1940, Box 36, all in Ware Papers.

15. Ware quoted in Caroline Ware to Harriet Elliott, "Consumer Movement," June 25, 1940, Box 27; Summary of Discussion at Conference of National Civic Organizations, Office of the Consumer Adviser, NDAC, August 2, 1940, Box 30; Harriet Elliott to Helen Hall, July 5, 1941, Box 28; NDAC, Consumer Division, "Coordination of Consumer Programs," Bulletin No. 2, October 14, 1940, Box 36, all in Ware Papers.

16. Caroline Ware to Harriet Elliott, December 10, 1940; Caroline Ware to Harriet Elliott, "Conferences with Various Groups," July 8, 1940; Ware quoted in Caroline Ware to Harriet Elliott, "Principles Governing our Program," July 8, 1940; Caroline Ware to Harriet Elliott, "Consumers Reports and Advisory Services to Consumers," July 8, 1940; Minnie Fisher Cunningham to Harriet Elliott, "Mobilization of Lay Groups to Participate Constructively in Defense Program," July 9, 1940; Caroline Ware memo, "Contacts with the Public," n.d., in Box 27; OPA, Consumer Division, "Highlights of the Consumer Program," January 1, 1942, Box 37, all in Ware Papers; Ware, *Consumer Goes to War*, 204–5; Judith N. McArthur and Harold L. Smith, *Minnie Fisher Cunningham: A Suffragist's Life in Politics* (Oxford: Oxford University Press, 2003).

17. Harriet Elliott, "Plan for Social Defense through Women's Community Defense Service," November 25, 1940, Box 27; OPA, Consumer Division, "National Defense Consumer Information Centers," Bulletin No. 14, September 1941, Box 36, both in Ware Papers; Leon Henderson, Press Conference, April 12, 1941, Henderson Papers, Box 28; OPA, Consumer Division, "Maintenance of Fair Rents during the Emergency," Bulletin No. 7, January 7, 1941, and "Suggested Emergency Fair Rent Legislation," Bulletin No. 10, both in Ware Papers, Box 28; Marshall B. Clinard, *The Black Market: A Study of White Collar Crime* (New York: Rinehart, 1952), 188.

18. League of Women Shoppers (LWS), *Newsletter*, February 1941; LWS, Minutes of National Board Meeting, January 17, 1942; LWS, *Bulletin*, Columbus, OH, January 1942, all in LWS Papers, Box 1, Folder 11; OPA, Consumer Division, "Highlights of Consumer Activities," Field Staff Bulletin No. 12, December 10, 1941, Box 37; Material to Be Used for Exhibit, C.I.O. Convention," November 8, 1941, Box 28; "Proceedings of the First Annual Conference of the Congress of Women's Auxiliaries of the CIO," Detroit, MI, November 17–21, 1941, Box 32, all in Ware Papers.

19. OPA, Consumer Division, "Activities Suggested to or Requested of Field Staff," Field Staff Bulletin No. 12, December 10, 1941, Box 37; Frances Williams to Caroline Ware, February 14, 1941, Box 29; Frances Williams to Caroline

Ware, February 18, 1941, Box 29; Frances Williams to Loda Mae Davis, May 6, 1941, Box 29, all in Ware Papers.

20. OPACS, Consumer Division, "Preliminary Budget Justification," n.d. [April 1941], Ware Papers, Box 28; Ware, *Consumer Goes to War*, 223.

21. Louis Kirstein to Franklin D. Roosevelt, September 4, 1940, Kirstein Papers, Box 30; Fred Lazarus Jr., "The Retailer in National Defense," address before the Conference of National Trade Organizations, called by Consumer Advisor, NDAC, August 29, 1940; NDAC, Press Release 85, August 30, 1940, both in Ware Papers, Box 30.

22. Bureau of the Census, *Statistical Abstract of the United States, 1944–1945* (Washington, DC: GPO, 1945), 416; Franklin D. Roosevelt, Message to Congress, July 30, 1941, in *Public Papers and Addresses of Franklin D. Roosevelt,* 1941 vol., ed. Samuel I. Rosenman (New York: Random House, 1950), 285; OPACS, "Character of Government Control of Prices During the World War," August 1, 1941; OPACS, "The Universal Impact of Inflation: What It Means to Various Groups," August 8, 1941, both in Henderson Papers, Box 28.

23. Roland Young, *Congressional Politics in the Second World War* (New York: Columbia University Press, 1956), 90–95; John Mark Hansen, *Gaining Access: Congress and the Farm Lobby, 1919–1981* (Chicago: University of Chicago Press, 1991), 78–97; Chester Bowles, *Promises to Keep: My Years in Public Life, 1941–1969* (New York: Harper and Row, 1971), 32–36.

24. Senate Committee on Banking and Currency, *Emergency Price Control Act of 1942,* 77th Cong., 2d sess., 1942, S. Rept. 931, 3; *Emergency Price Control Act of 1942,* 77th Cong., 2d sess., H.R. 5990; FDR quoted in LWS pamphlet, *Women Do 85% of the Shopping,* 1942, LWS Papers, Box 1, Folder 12; Nora Baldwin, "Henderson Calls Price Bill Weak," *NYT,* January 25, 1942, 33; John Kenneth Galbraith, *A Life in Our Times: Memoirs* (Boston: Houghton Mifflin, 1981), 106–75.

25. Galbraith, *Life,* 1–70, 128–36, 163–66; OPA Staff to Leon Henderson, "Retail Price Control," February 16, 1942, Henderson Papers, Box 30; General Max quoted in Mansfield, *Short History of OPA,* 43.

26. Franklin D. Roosevelt, Fireside Chat, April 28, 1942, in *The Public Papers and Addresses of Franklin D. Roosevelt,* 1940 vol. (New York: Random House, 1950), 227–38.

27. Mansfield, *Short History of OPA,* 29–33, 65–70.

28. Leon Henderson, Press Release PM 2924, n.d., Henderson Papers, Box 26; Lubell, "Daring Young Man," 86.

29. A. C. Hoffman to J. K. Galbraith, June 17, 1942; J. K. Galbraith to Leon Henderson, June 18, 1942; Franklin D. Roosevelt to Claude Wickard, June 19, 1942, all in Henderson Papers, Box 26; Mansfield, *Short History of OPA,* 51; Roosevelt quoted in *Congressional Record,* 77th Cong., 2d sess., September 7, 1942, 88, pt. 5:7043–44.

30. OPA, Press Release, October 22, 1942; J. K. Galbraith to Leon Henderson, June 18, 1942; Leon Henderson to James F. Byrnes, October 20, 1942, all in Henderson Papers, Box 26.

31. Overall, inflation continued at an average rate of 0.5 percent a month. Mansfield, *Short History of OPA,* 51. Richard Gilbert, "Retail Price Plan,"

December 5, 1942, Henderson Papers, Box 29; Peter G. Franck and Milton Quint, eds., *Problems in Price Control: Pricing Techniques*, vol. 8 in *Historical Reports on War Administration: Office of Price Administration* (Washington, DC: GPO, 1947), 67–72.

32. Fred Lazarus Jr. to Louis Kirstein, June 22, 1942; Filene's Memo to Division Managers and Buyers, "Methods of Posting Ceiling Prices," May 13, 1942; Filene's "Ceiling Prices for Toilet Goods," May 18, 1942; Advertisement for Filene's, *BG*, April 30, 1942, all in Kirstein Papers, Box 40.

33. Leon Henderson to Franklin Roosevelt, April 13, 1942; "Memorandum for the President Urging an Anti-inflation Program," April 17, 1942, both in Henderson Papers, Box 26; Melvyn Dubofsky, *The State and Labor in Modern America* (Chapel Hill: University of North Carolina, 1985), 182–91; Kennedy, *Freedom from Fear*, 640–43.

34. Vorse and United Steel Workers district official quoted in Lichtenstein, *Labor's War at Home*, 114–16.

35. William Green, Memorandum, July 31, 1942, FDR Papers-OF, Box 4920; *Women Do 85% of the Buying*, n.d.; League of Women Shoppers, Minneapolis, MN, *Newsletter*, May 1942; League of Women Shoppers, Columbus, OH, *Newsletter*, February 1943, all in LWS Papers, Box 1, Folder 11.

36. Johnson quoted in William Stafford to Leon Henderson, June 24, 1942, Henderson Papers, Box 27. For lack of funds for enforcement, see Clinard, *Black Market*, 62–68, 98–99.

37. Stephen E. Ambrose, *Nixon, Vol. 1: The Education of a Politician, 1913–1962* (New York: Simon and Schuster, 1987), 101–4. See also Milton Viorst, "Nixon of the O.P.A.," *NYTM*, October 3, 1971, 70–76.

38. Richard Gilbert to J. K. Galbraith, "General Rationing," March 7, 1942, Gilbert Papers, Box 12; OPA, "Report on Rationing," November 25, 1942; Kiplinger Washington Agency, "Kiplinger Agricultural Letter," December 5, 1942, both in Henderson Papers, Box 29; Hansen, *Gaining Access*, 95; John W. Jeffries, *Wartime America: The World War II Home Front* (Chicago: Ivan R. Dee, 1996), 152–56; Blum, *V Was for Victory*, 221–34; Young, *Congressional Politics*, 22–24.

39. Mansfield, *Short History of OPA*, 55; Thomas Emerson to Chester Bowles, "Report on Enforcement," August 9, 1943, Clinard Papers, Box 39.

40. Dick Deverall to Philleo Nash, January 20, 1943; Philleo Nash to A. H. Feller, January 27, 28, February 5, 1943; Bridges quoted in Dick Deverall to Philleo Nash, February 17, 1943; Philleo Nash to A. H. Feller, February 26, 1943, all in Deverall Papers, Notebooks, OPA, vol. 2.

41. CIO *Labor Herald* quoted in Philleo Nash to A. H. Feller, January 27, 28, February 5, 11, 1943, ibid.; Kennedy, *Freedom from Fear*, 638–44; Lichtenstein, *Walter Reuther*, 203–25.

42. UAW quoted in Richard Deverall to Clarence Glick, "Labor Unions and the O.P.A.," May 20, 1943, Deverall Papers, Notebooks, OPA, vol. 2.; AFL quoted in "Living Costs in Cities Rise 21% in Two Years," May 20, 1943, 14; Advertisement by UAW-CIO, "Yes, We Have No Potatoes," May 20, 1943, 15; "Low-Paid Workers are Unable to Keep Pace with Rising Prices, Welfare Agencies Report," May 20, 1943, 24, all in *NYT*.

43. Brown quoted in OPA, Press Release, May 28, 1943, Henderson Papers, Box 27; Advertisement by UAW-CIO, "A Congress of the People by the People

for ?" *NYT*, June 3, 1943, 15; Richard Deverall to Clarence Glick, June 3, 1943, Deverall Papers, Notebooks, OPA, vol. 2. For the fight over subsidies, see Young, *Congressional Politics*, 109–22.

44. OPA quoted in Prentiss M. Brown (OPA administrator), transcript of address delivered over the Mutual Network, April 30, 1943, Gilbert Papers, Box 13; Mansfield, *Short History of OPA*, 55–59, 225–26; Bartholomew H. Sparrow, *From the Outside In: World War II and the American State* (Princeton, NJ: Princeton University Press, 1996), 97–125; Young, *Congressional Politics*, 130–43; Hugh Rockoff, *Drastic Measures: A History of Wage and Price Controls in the United States* (New York: Cambridge University Press, 1984), 85–126.

45. House Committee on Banking and Currency, *Extension of Emergency Price Control Act, Vol. 1: Hearings*, 78th Cong., 2d sess., April 12–May 5, 1944, 19–20, 39; Delman's Shoes advertisement, "Footwear That Requires No Ration Coupons," *NYT*, January 25, 1944, 16; Louis Kirstein telephone conversation with Mr. Reisman, August 5, 1941, Kirstein Papers, Box 67; "Leftovers Can Be Tasty!" and "No Meat, But Enough Protein," *Good Housekeeping*, January 1944. Throughout the war, the *NYT* printed daily menus in its "News of Food" column that included ration information. For wartime cookbooks, see Doris Weatherford, *American Women and World War II* (New York: Facts on File, 1990), 206. Galbraith interview in Studs Terkel, *"The Good War": An Oral History of World War II* (New York: New Press, 1984), 323. Blum, *V Was for Victory*, 91, 98.

46. "Bowles Stresses Need for Gardens," April 9, 1944, 22; "Roosevelt Extols Victory Gardeners," January 23, 1945, 16; "Presses Drive for Fats," January 25, 1944, 16; Procter & Gamble Advertisement, February 28, 1944, 34; "Save Waste Paper for War!" January 12, 1944, 25, all in *NYT*.

47. Advertisement for FADA Radio and Electric Company, "Let's Bust 'Em Wide Open," *NYT*, February 5, 1944, 8. On the bond campaign, see Blum, *V Was for Victory*, 16–21; Lawrence Samuel, *Pledging Allegiance: American Identity and the Bond Drive of World War II* (Washington, DC: Smithsonian Institution Press, 1997); and Mark H. Leff, "The Politics of Sacrifice on the American Home Front in World War II," *JAH* 77 (March 1991): 1296–1318.

48. Anne Maxwell, "Rationing Has Its Points," *Woman's Home Companion*, August 1943, 8–9; Office of Economic Stabilization, Press Release, February 7, 1943, FDR Papers-OF, Box 4920.

49. "Text of the President's Annual State of the Union Address," *NYT*, January 12, 1944, 12; Bartels, "Office of Price Administration and the Legacy of the New Deal," 19.

50. "Congress and the Cost of Living," *NR*, August 2, 1943, 167–68; Young, *Congressional Politics*, 24–26; Imogene Putnam, *Volunteers in OPA*, vol. 14 in *Historical Reports on War Administration: Office of Price Administration*, (Washington, DC: GPO, 1947), 69, 162; William Jerome Wilson and Mabel Randolph, eds., *OPA Bibliography, 1940–1947*, in *Historical Reports on War Administration: Office of Price Administration, vol. 3 of Miscellaneous Publications*, (Washington, DC: GPO, 1947), 265; Mansfield, *Short History of OPA*, 297–318. For Bowles's claim, see House Committee on Banking and Currency, *Extension of Emergency Price Control Act, Vol. 1*, 39.

51. D'Ann Campbell, *Women at War with America: Private Lives in a Patriotic Era* (Cambridge, MA: Harvard University Press, 1984), 224; OPA, "Campaign

Outline for Home Front Pledge Campaign," June 30, 1943; OPA, "The Home-front Pledge Campaign Book," 1943, both in Box 1, Folder 12; Calla Van Syckle, OPA, to National League of Women Shoppers, July 10, 1943, Box 1, Folder 9, all in LWS Papers; Putnam, *Volunteers in OPA*, 65, 88–89. For a general sampling of OPA's publications aimed at the consumer, see Wilson and Randolph, *OPA Bibliography, 1940–1947*, 207–70.

52. Mansfield, *Short History of OPA*, 244; Chester Bowles testimony, Senate Committee on Banking and Currency, *Extension of Emergency Price Control Act of 1942: Hearings*, 78th Cong., 2d sess., March 15–April 28, 1944, 30; OPA quoted in OPA, "Manual of Price Panel Operation," March 20, 1944, Ware Papers, Box 33.

53. Putnam, *Volunteers in OPA*, 51–52. See also Campbell, *Women at War with America*, 63–100.

54. Jessica Mitford, *A Fine Old Conflict* (New York: Knopf, 1977), 23–61. This San Francisco OPA office was notoriously radical. For a description of its union and Communist Party involvement, see Carl Bernstein, *Loyalties: A Son's Memoirs* (New York: Simon and Schuster, 1989), 68–82.

55. Clair Wilcox, "In Defense of Price Control," *NYTM*, October 10, 1943, 12; Bowles, *Promises to Keep*, 44; Bowles quoted in "Bowles to OPA," *Newsweek*, August 9, 1943, 46–47; "OPA's New Deal," *BW*, August 28, 1943, 16–17; Selden Rodman, "Chester Bowles," *Harper's*, April 1946, 300–308.

56. Bowles quoted in Putnam, *Volunteers in OPA*, 47. In addition to Ware, the other members of the Consumer Advisory Committee included Helen Hall of the National Federation of Settlement Houses, Eleanor Fowler of the CIO Women's Auxiliary, Maie Fox Lowe of the American Federation of Labor Auxiliaries, Ella Baker of the National Association for the Advancement of Colored People, Grace Hamilton of the Atlanta Urban League, Katharine Armatage of the League of Women Shoppers, Esther Cole Franklin of the American Association of University Women, Harriet Howe of the American Home Economics Association, Florence Wyckoff of the National Consumers' League, Belle Mazur of the League of Women Voters, Ruth Lamb Atkinson of the National Congress of Parents and Teachers, Hazel Kyrk of the University of Chicago, Colston Warne of the Consumers Union, and Katharine Van Slyck of the American Association of Social Workers. Robert Lynd also briefly served. OPA, Press Release, December 1, 1943, Box 35; Caroline Ware to Chester Bowles, January 27, 1944, Box 34; Minutes of OPA Consumer Committee, March 14 and 15, 1944, Box 31; OPA, "The OPA Consumer Advisory Committee," December 1944, Box 32, all in Ware Papers.

57. Mansfield, *Short History of OPA*, 248. See also "OPA Checks Up," *BW*, March 18, 1944, 17–19. For OPA appeals to black consumers, see Wilson and Randolph, *OPA Bibliography, 1940–1947*, 213; Putnam, *Volunteers in OPA*, 68. See also Frances Williams, "Minority Groups and OPA," *Public Administration Review* 7 (spring 1947): 123–38.

58. Clinard, *Black Market*, 98–107; Putnam, *Volunteers in OPA*, 165.

59. "OPA Seeks Women as Price Wardens," February 24, 1944, 20; "OPA Starts Test of Price Control," April 11, 1944, 22, both in *NYT*; Putnam, *Volunteers in OPA*, 62; Chester Bowles, "You Can Make or Break the Black Market," *Woman's Home Companion*, December 1943, 4, 118.

60. PTAs quoted in OPA, Atlanta Region, "PTAs of the South Unite in Plan to Hold Prices," *We the People of the United States*, March 1944; "Organizations throughout the South Pool Their Strength in Wartime Effort to Hold Prices and Prevent Inflation," both in Ware Papers, Box 33; "Ceiling Charts Get 'Feminine Touch,'" *NYT*, February 12, 1944, 17.

61. Bowles quoted in Putnam, *Volunteers in OPA*, 90; Caroline F. Ware, "The Long Shadow of Mr. Bowles," *Survey Graphic* 35 (April 1946), 139; Chester Bowles, "OPA Volunteers: Big Democracy in Action," *Public Administration Review* 5 (spring 1945): 350–59; Bowles, *Promises to Keep*, 61–74; Ware, *Consumer Goes to War*, 198, 195.

62. O. Ruehe to the Editor, "OPA's Plan Held Unworthy," *NYT*, February 11, 1944, 12; "Kitchen Gestapo," *BW*, September 4, 1943, 75–76; Putnam, *Volunteers in OPA*, 103, 145.

63. Cohn quoted in "Opposes Price Law to Control Profit," February 9, 1944, 23; Bowles quoted in "Bowles Says OPA Bars Price 'Chaos,'" April 13, 1944, 36; "Price Law Changes Undergo Revision," April 14, 1944, 12, all in *NYT*; Minutes of OPA Consumer Advisory Committee, March 14, 1944, Ware Papers, Box 31; Esther Cole Franklin, Francis McPeek, Millard Rice, Katharine Armatage, Leslie Perry, Elizabeth Magee, Jeanetta Welch, James Patton, Margaret Cross, Elizabeth Christman, and Omar Ketchum to Chester Bowles, March 10, 1944, Ware Papers, Box 24.

64. Donald Montgomery, "Congress Considers 48 Proposals Aimed at Weakening OPA," *United Auto Worker*, April 1, 1944; OPA Labor Policy Committee, "Report on Extension of Price Control Legislation," March 15, 1944; Philip Murray to Presidents of International and National Unions, March 27, 1944, all in UAW-Montgomery Papers, Box 9; Stein testimony, House Committee on Banking and Currency, *Extension of Emergency Price Control Act, Vol. 1*, 991–1005. For Annie Stein's political affiliations, see Bernstein, *Loyalties*, 93–94, 175, 208–12. On OPA support for "test purchases," see Consumer Advisory Committee to Chester Bowles, March 16, 1944, Ware Papers, Box 34.

65. Campbell, *Women at War with America*, 177; Wycoff testimony, House Committee on Banking and Currency, *Extension of Emergency Price Control Act, Vol. 2: Hearings*, 78th Cong., 2d sess., May 8–19, 1944, 1701; "Women Criticize WPB," *NYT*, March 20, 1945, 16.

66. "Urge OPA to Widen Price Ceiling Scope," *NYT*, March 19, 1944, 34; Somers testimony, House Committee on Banking and Currency, *Extension of Emergency Price Control Act, Vol. 2*, 1676; Katharine Armatage and Katherine Van Slyck to H. Burke Fry, March 20, 1944, Ware Papers, Box 35. See also Colston Warne, "Pulling the OPA's Teeth," *Current History* 6 (May 1944): 410–16.

67. Murray quoted in Thomas A. Stapleford, " 'The Most Important Single Statistic': The Consumer Price Index and American Political Economy, 1880–1955" (Ph.D. diss., Harvard University, 2003), 441–42; George Meany and R. J. Thomas, *Cost of Living: Recommended Report for the Presidential Committee on the Cost of Living* (Washington, DC: Congress of Industrial Organizations, 1944).

68. Donald Montgomery to Walter Reuther, May 1, 1944, UAW-Montgomery Papers, Box 9. According to the Clearing House, the most reliable members of Congress on consumer issues included Robert Wagner, Harry Truman, Allen

Ellender, Joseph Guffey, Jerry Voorhis, Mike Mansfield, Mary T. Norton, Emanuel Celler, Estes Kefauver, Lyndon Johnson, and Henry M. Jackson. In general, cotton, dairy, and other farm bloc representatives joined Republicans in voting against OPA measures while northern Democrats, especially those from industrial states, supported price controls. Consumer Clearing House, "A Voting Record on Consumer Issues of the 78th Congress, 1943–1944," October 14, 1944, Ware Papers, Box 35; "Consumers Stress Control of Prices," *NYT*, May 15, 1944, 16.

69. Belle Hoffman to Jessie O'Connor, October 27, 1943, LWS Papers, Box 1, Folder 9; Johnson testimony, House Committee on Banking and Currency, *Extension of Emergency Price Control Act, Vol. 2*, 1661.

70. Chester Bowles to Regional OPA Administrators, June 10, 1944, Ware Papers, Box 33; Chester Bowles to Jessie Lloyd O'Connor, August 4, 1944, LWS Papers, Box 1, Folder 9; "OPA Names Woman Aide," *NYT*, August 6, 1944, 39; George H. Gallup, *The Gallup Poll: Public Opinion, 1935–1971, Vol. I* (New York: Random House, 1972), polls of September 15, 1942, 347–48; August 31, 1945, 522–23; October 24, 1945, 535; March 4, 1946, 561; and May 24, 1946, 579.

71. "Smith Denies Attempt to Kill Price Control in Probe of OPA," *Washington Post*, June 8, 1944, 4; LWS, Minutes of the Seventh Annual Membership Meeting, May 9 and 10, 1944, LWS Papers, Box 1, Folder 3; Nathan Robertson, "Sen. Taft Admits Openly He Favors Higher Prices," *PM*, April 27, 1944, 6; Young, *Congressional Politics*, 107–8; James Gross, *The Reshaping of the National Labor Relations Board: National Labor Policy in Transition, 1937–1947* (Albany: State University of New York Press, 1981), 200–225.

72. Putnam, *Volunteers in OPA*, 110–15.

73. Consumer Advisory Committee to Chester Bowles, April 10 and July 5, 1944, Box 34; OPA, Press Release, August 3, 1944, Box 35; Consumer Advisory Committee to Chester Bowles, "Reinstitution of Consumer Price Lists," memorandum, January 24, 1945, Box 32, all in Ware Papers.

74. Bowles, *Promises to Keep*, 91; Wilfred Carsel, *Wartime Apparel Problem*, vol. 3 in *Historical Reports on War Administration: Office of Price Administration* (Washington, DC: GPO, 1947); Murchison testimony, House Committee on Banking and Currency, *Extension of Emergency Price Control Act, Vol. 1*, 1083–1106. On the textile industry, see Stanley Vittoz, *New Deal Labor Policy and the American Industrial Economy* (Chapel Hill: University of North Carolina Press, 1987), 119–34.

75. Montgomery testimony, House Committee on Banking and Currency, *Extension of Emergency Price Control Act, Vol. 1*, 965–66; "Price Relief Asked on Work Clothing," April 1, 1944, 19; "Consumer Leaders Hail Fabric Order," November 25, 1944, 16, both in *NYT*. See also Mansfield, *Short History of OPA*, 68–80; Paul O'Leary, "Wartime Rationing and Governmental Organization," *American Political Science Review* 39 (December 1945): 1089–1106; Barton J. Bernstein, "The Removal of War Production Board Controls in Business, 1944–1946," *BHR* 39 (summer 1965): 243–60.

76. "Consumers Thank President," April 15, 1944, 8; "Bowles to Tighten Control of Prices," January 4, 1945, 24, both in *NYT*; Taft testimony, Senate Committee on Banking and Currency, *Inflation Control Program of OPA: Hearings*, 79th Cong., 1st sess., October 23–25, 1945, 30–32; Trade associations quoted in " 'Profit-Squeeze' by OPA Condemned," *NYT*, February 2, 1945, 24.

77. Putnam, *Volunteers in OPA*, 140; Harvey Levenstein, *Paradox of Plenty: A Social History of Eating in Modern America* (New York: Oxford University Press, 1993), 87, 97; Campbell, *Women at War with America*, 251.

78. Lewis Corey, *Meat and Man: A Study of Monopoly, Unionism, and Food Policy* (New York: Viking Press, 1950), 7–9, 179–84; Anonymous, "Confessions of a Black-Market Butcher," *SEP*, August 24, 1946, 17, 101–3. Deconcentration of the meat industry occurred as a result of technological improvements in motor-car refrigeration that allowed for packing at the source. With low entry costs, independents could take advantage of these nonmetropolitan, nonunion job markets and produce at lower costs. They were also helped by the rise of independent wholesalers and retail chains. Richard Arnould, "Changing Patterns of Concentration in American Meat Packing, 1880–1963," *BHR* 45 (spring 1971): 18–34; Jimmy Skaggs, *Prime Cut: Livestock Raising and Meatpacking in the United States, 1607–1983* (College Station: Texas A & M University Press, 1986), 130–69.

79. "Hungry Meat Eaters Lick Chops over Suspension of Rationing," *Newsweek*, May 15, 1944, 29–30; Consumer Advisory Committee to Chester Bowles, July 18, 1944, September 20, 1944, Ware Papers, Box 34; "OPA, WFA Blamed in Meat Shortage," January 14, 1945, 33; "Big Meat Supply Is 'Underground,'" February 1, 1945, 21; "'Famine' in Meat Is Reported Near," March 19, 1945, 13; Packers quoted in "The Nation's Food," April 1, 1945, B2; Bushfield quoted in "Senator 'Out for Meat,'" April 13, 1945, 30, all in *NYT*; Ralph Robey, "Beefsteaks and Bureaucrats," *Newsweek*, April 9, 1945, 73.

80. Food wholesalers quoted in Clinard, *Black Market*, 149; "Rep. Hartley Fears Tremendous Black Market in Textiles," *Herald-News (NJ)*, June 23, 1945, in Clinard Papers, Box 39; Blum, *V Was for Victory*, 299–300; Jeffries, *Wartime America*, 159–69.

81. "Text of Inflation Report to Roosevelt," April 8, 1945, 34; "Hahn Forecasts Strong Protests against OPA Cost-Absorption Plan," July 29, 1945, S5, both in *NYT*; William H. Davis, Chester Bowles, Marvin Jones, and George W. Taylor to Franklin D. Roosevelt, April 7, 1945, Ware Papers, Box 31.

82. Donald Montgomery, "The Product Standard in OPA Price Ceilings," January 16, 1945; Montgomery quoted in Donald Montgomery to Philip Murray, February 16, 1945; Donald Montgomery "Renewal of Price Control Legislation," February 22, 1945; Donald Montgomery, "Stabilization–1945," March 6, 1945; Donald Montgomery, "Wages, Production and Conversion after V-E Day," n.d. [1945], all in UAW-Montgomery Papers, Box 10; Murray testimony, Senate Committee on Banking and Currency, *Extending the Emergency Price Control and Stabilization Acts of 1942, as Amended: Hearings*, 79th Cong., 1st sess., February 27–March 22, 1945, 303; Aide to Montgomery quoted in Ted Silvey to Donald Montgomery, March 6, 1945, UAW-Montgomery Papers, Box 9.

83. Women's and labor groups quoted in "22 Groups Support Extension of OPA," May 28, 1945, 21; "Oppose OPA Amendments," March 21, 1945, 10; League of Women Shoppers quoted in "Consumers Fight Price Ceiling Rises," May 3, 1945, 20; "Bids Women Voters Back Price Curbs," May 11, 1945, 16; New York City women quoted in "Queens Women Fight Food Black Market," April 13, 1945, 14, all in *NYT*; Atkinson testimony, Senate Committee on Banking and Currency, *Extending the Emergency Price Control and Stabilization Acts of 1942, as*

Amended, 269–72; House Committee on Banking and Currency, *1945 Stabilization Extension Act (Revised): Hearings,* 79th Cong., 1st sess., June 4–14, 1945, 113–15.

84. Fowler and Gelles testimony, House Committee on Banking and Currency, *1945 Stabilization Extension Act (Revised),* 157, 162; Hall testimony, Senate Committee on Banking and Currency, *Extending the Emergency Price Control and Stabilization Acts of 1942, as Amended,* 321.

85. Bureau of the Budget, "Some Reconversion Problems: Attitudes and Expectations on Prices, Price Control, Supply, Etc.," September 17, 1945, Ware Papers, Box 31; Department of Information, OPA, "Opinion Briefs, no. 9," July 7, 1945, UAW-Montgomery Papers, Box 9.

86. Clinard, *Black Market,* 88, 106.

87. Budge Van Lee (Fort Worth, TX) to Chester Bowles, November 7, 1945; Mrs. Bessie Beckett (CA) to Bowles, December 6, 1945; Ruth Beers (Arlington, MA) to Bowles, n.d.; Sidney Boyton (Elyria, OH) to Bowles, November 19, 1945; Elizabeth Riley (Madison, WI) to Bowles, January 2, 1946, all in OPA Papers, Executive Offices, Office of the Administrator, Chester Bowles, Administrative Correspondence, Letters Addressed to the Administrator from the General Public, Box 4. In March 1946, 80% thought OPA was doing a fairly good to excellent job and 73% thought OPA should be continued: March 4, 1946, poll in Gallup, *Gallup Poll,* vol. 1, p. 561. In May, polls showed 75% support for another year of price controls for food, 78% for rent control, 70% for clothing ceilings, and 66% for price controls on automobiles, radios, and other manufactured goods: May 24, 1946, poll, ibid., 579. "How About Price Control?" *Fortune,* April 1946, 8, 14.

Chapter Six
Pocketbook Politics in an Age of Inflation, 1946–1960

1. NAM quoted in "Would You Like some Butter or a Roast of Beef," in "NAM Newspaper Advertising, 1946–1947, A Review," NAM Pamphlets. Sloan quoted in Nelson Lichtenstein, "Taft-Hartley: A Slave Labor Law?" *Catholic University Law Review* 47 (spring 1998): 771.

2. Chester Bowles, Address to the National Association of Manufacturers, December 7, 1945, Henderson Papers, Box 30; Bowles statement, Senate Special Committee to Study and Survey Problems of American Small Business Enterprises, *Problems of American Small Business, Part 76: Hearings on the Impact of Price Controls and Stabilization Policies on Small Business,* 79th Cong., 1st sess., December 4, 1945, 8856.

3. House Committee on Banking and Currency, *1946 Extension of the Emergency Price Control and Stabilization Acts of 1942, as Amended, Vol. 1: Hearings,* 79th Cong., 2d sess., February 18–March 19, 1946, 655–62; Lew Hahn, "Why You Can't Buy a Shirt," *SEP,* March 30, 1946, 20; Wherry quoted in Lawrence Sullivan, "The High Price of Price Control," *NB,* March 1946, 98.

4. "Baruch Submits Post-war Report," February 17, 1944, 15; "Wallace Sees Rise in Post-war Living," February 7, 1944, 15; "Wallace Proposes New Jobs

Agency," February 12, 1944, 8, all in *NYT*. On postwar forecasting, see Everett E. Hagen, "The Reconversion Period: Reflections of a Forecaster," *Review of Economic Statistics* 29 (May 1947): 95–101; and W. S. Woytinsky, "What Was Wrong in Forecasts of Postwar Depression?" *Journal of Political Economy* 55 (April 1947): 142–51. On reconversion policy, see Craufurd D. Goodwin and R. Stanley Herren, "The Truman Administration: Problems and Policies Unfold," in *Exhortation and Controls: The Search for a Wage-Price Policy, 1945–1971*, ed. Craufurd D. Goodwin (Washington, DC: Brookings Institution, 1975), 11–15; Barton J. Bernstein, "The Truman Administration and the Politics of Inflation" (Ph.D. diss., Harvard University, 1963), 198–219; and Allen J. Matusow, *Farm Policies and Politics in the Truman Years* (Cambridge, MA: Harvard University Press, 1967), 1–52.

5. George Soule, "Wages, Prices, and Employment," *NR*, November 5, 1945, 592–94; Goodwin and Herren, "Truman Administration," 12–13; Barton J. Bernstein, "The Truman Administration and Its Reconversion Wage Policy," *Labor History* 6 (fall 1965): 214–31.

6. Walter Reuther, "GM v. the Rest of Us," *NR*, January 14, 1946, 41–42; Nelson Lichtenstein, *Walter Reuther: The Most Dangerous Man in Detroit* (New York: Basic Books, 1995), 228–35. See also Barton J. Bernstein, "Walter Reuther and the General Motors Strike of 1945–1946," *Michigan History* 49 (September 1965): 260–77.

7. Walter Reuther to President Truman, February 21, 1946, Truman Papers-OF, Box 1010; George H. Gallup, *The Gallup Poll: Public Opinion, 1935–1971* (New York: Random House, 1972), vol. 1, pp. 535, 551; Hugh Rockoff, *Drastic Measures: A History of Wage and Price Controls in America* (New York: Cambridge University Press, 1984), 101–2; Romney quoted in Lichtenstein, *Walter Reuther*, 230.

8. "The Mayor Joins the Fight against Inflation," March 7, 1946, 30; "Mayor Heads Unit Fighting for OPA," April 25, 1946, 31; "Labor and Women Back OPA Control," April 30, 1946, 24, all in *NYT*; Melvyn Dubofsky, *The State and Labor in Modern America* (Chapel Hill: University of North Carolina Press, 1994), 193–94.

9. John Snyder to Senator Wagner, April 15, 1946, Truman Papers-OF, Box 1010; Truman quoted in Barton J. Bernstein, "The Truman Administration and the Steel Strike of 1946," *JAH* 52 (March 1966): 801; Addison Cutler and Robert Benes, *Studies in Industrial Control*, vol. 6 in *Historical Reports on War Administration: Office of Price Administration*, (Washington, DC: GPO, 1947), 60–78.

10. "Farm Bloc on the March," *BW*, March 2, 1946, 15–16; Truman quoted in Harvey C. Mansfield, *A Short History in OPA*, vol. 15 in *Historical Reports on War Administration: Office of Price Administration* (Washington, DC: GPO, 1947), 99, 100–101; Matusow, *Farm Policies and Politics*, 52–62.

11. Labor quoted in Bernstein, "Truman Administration and the Politics of Inflation," 245–46; Anne Stein, "Post-war Consumer Boycotts," *Radical America* 9 (July 1975): 156–61; "Unorganized Consumers Hold Key to Buyers' Strikes," *BW*, July 20, 1946, 16.

12. Anderson quoted in "Anderson Warns Farmers on Meat," *NYT*, September 25, 1946, 16; Bernstein, "Truman Administration and the Politics of Inflation," 324–27; Matusow, *Farm Policies and Politics*, 59.

13. "Steakleggers," *Time*, October 21, 1946, 42; "Country Is Near 'Famine' in Meat, Centers Report," September 24, 1946, 1, 8; "Horse Meat Consumption by New Yorkers Is Rising," September 25, 1946, 1, 17; "Rodeo Opens as Spectators Pine for Steaks," September 26, 1946, 27; "Horse Meat Mart Here Soon Is Likely," September 26, 1946, 31; "Near-by Hospitals Down to Minimum of Meat Supplies," September 29, 1946, 1, 4; "10,000 Women in Lines at 3 Meat Stores; Police Reserves Called to Prevent Crush," October 5, 1946, 9; "Burglar in Butcher Shop Finds Cupboard All Bare," October 10, 1946, 34; "Queens Restaurateur, Worried over Meat, Dives off Brooklyn Bridge and Survives," October 10, 1946, 35, all in *NYT*; A. J. Liebling, "The Wayward Press: The Great Gouamba," *New Yorker*, December 7, 1946, 88–97.

14. "Would You Like Some Butter," NAM Pamphlets; Lewis Fox (Beverly Hills, CA) to Harry S. Truman, September 21, 1946, OPA Papers, Executive Offices, Administrative Correspondence, Box 17, Meat Shortage Complaint File (hereafter cited as Meat Complaint File).

15. Eleanor Born (New York, NY) to Paul Porter, September 26, 1946, OPA Papers, Meat Complaint File; R. H. Guy (Waterville, ME) to Chester Bowles, May 7, 1946, OPA Papers, Executive Offices, Administrative Correspondence, Box 17, Disapproval of OPA File. Though the letter equating OPA to Prohibition was written in May, the anti-OPA letters, including references to Prohibition, exploded in the fall. For overall declining levels of support, see Gallup, *Gallup Poll*, vol. 1, May 24, 1946, poll, 579; October 5, 1946, poll, 602.

16. Ethel Hoffner (Hartford, CT) to Chester Bowles; M. Howart (Brooklyn, NY) to Paul Porter, May 2, 1946, OPA Papers, Executive Offices, Administrative Correspondence, Box 17, Disapproval of OPA File.

17. See, for example, "The Politics of Meat," *Time*, October 7, 1946, 21; "Meat: Political Slaughter," *Newsweek*, October 7, 1946, 29–30; "No Meat, No Votes?" *Newsweek*, October 14, 1946, 33–34; "Sabotage by the Meatmen," *NR*, October 21, 1946, 504.

18. Louise Pierson to Paul Porter (New York, NY), n.d.; Marguerite Pendergast (New York, NY) to President Truman, September 20, 1946; Altha Johnson (Santa Ana, CA) to Paul Porter, September 28, 1946; Josephine Clarke (Los Angeles, CA) to Paul Porter, September 30, 1946; Mary Holmes (Cleveland, OH) to Paul Porter, September 26, 1946; Charlotte Wheeler (Oyster Bay, NY) to Paul Porter, September 27, 1946; Agnes Shitoukan (Washington, DC) to Paul Porter, September 25, 1946, all in OPA Papers, Meat Complaint File.

19. "President: Election Eve Price Retreat," *Newsweek*, October 21, 1946, 31–34; "Key Issues in 1946 Election: Price Control at Top of List," *USNWR*, October 25, 1946, 24–25; Truman quoted in Harvey Levenstein, *Paradox of Plenty: A Social History of Eating in Modern America* (New York: Oxford University Press, 1993), 99.

20. Irwin F. Gellman, *The Contender: Richard Nixon; The Congress Years, 1946–1952* (New York: Free Press, 1999), 49, 25–88. On meat prices, see Lewis Corey, *Meat and Man: A Study of Monopoly, Unionism, and Food Policy* (New York: Viking Press, 1950), 184.

21. "Why We Won—Why We Lost: Candidates Analyze the Election," November 15, 1946, 26–29; "The New Cycle in Politics: Break in Democratic

Coalition," November 15, 1946, 13–14; "Congress's Shift to Home Affairs," November 22, 1946, 22–23; "Crisis for the Democrats: Loss of Power in Key Cities," November 29, 1946, 22–23, all in *USNWR*; "Election Results throughout Nation and Make-up of New Senate and House of Representatives," *NYT*, November 7, 1946, 16. The most thorough treatment on the 1946 election is James R. Boylan, *The New Deal Coalition and the Election of 1946* (New York: Garland, 1981). For the low turnout of voters, see Lichtenstein, *Walter Reuther*, 257. For the farm vote, see Matusow, *Farm Policies and Politics*, 62–64.

22. Advertisements in "NAM Newspaper Advertising, 1946–1947: A Review," NAM Pamphlets; "New Labor Laws Vital, Mosher Says," February 19, 1947, 50; "Costs Must Be Cut, Says NAM Leader," June 17, 1947, 43, both in *NYT*.

23. Wilson quoted in "The Right to Strike?" *Harper's*, December 1946; "Inflation: Whither the Wage-Price Spiral?" *Newsweek*, August 19, 1946, 66; Case testimony, House Committee on Education and Labor, *Amendments to the National Labor Relations Act, Vol. 1: Hearings*, 80th Cong., 1st sess., February 5–7, 1947, 124.

24. "Twelve Times No: The Welder, the Painter, the Press Operator . . . Auto Workers Prefer Cheaper Bread and Meat to Higher Pay," *Newsweek*, February 3, 1947, 22–23; Baruch quoted in Mansfield, *A Short History of OPA*, 27.

25. "Stabilizing Duties Shifted to OWMR," *NYT*, July 26, 1946, 9; Senator James Murray to President Truman, July 9, July 18, July 24, 1946; Senator Wagner to President Truman, July 9, 1946, all in Truman Papers-OF, Box 1567; Philip Murray to President Truman, July 9, 1946, in Keyserling Papers-HSTL, Box 17. The classic work on the Employment Act is Stephen Kemp Bailey, *Congress Makes a Law: The Story behind the Employment Act of 1946* (New York: Columbia University Press, 1950). Keynesians pushed to make government spending automatic when the economy slowed. But Keyserling as well as the congressional sponsors rejected the act as simply a spending bill.

26. Robert Wason (president of NAM) to President Truman, March 9, 1946, Truman Papers-OF, Box 1567; Edwin Nourse to President Truman, July 29, 1946; Edwin Nourse to Walter Salant, Leon Keyserling, and John D. Clark, November 14, 1946; Leon Keyserling to Edwin Nourse, August 23, 1946; all in Keyserling Papers-HSTL, Box 5; Nourse statement, August 9, 1946, Truman Papers-OF, Box 1564. For divisions between Nourse and Keyserling, see also Michael A. Bernstein, *A Perilous Progress: Economists and Public Purpose in Twentieth-Century America* (Princeton, NJ: Princeton University Press, 2001), 108–14.

27. Biographies of Staff Members, Keyserling Papers-HSTL, Box 8. See also Edward S. Flash, *Economic Advice and Presidential Leadership: The Council of Economic Advisers* (New York: Columbia University Press, 1965), 29–33.

28. Keyserling to CEA and Staff, "Business Economists' Response to the First Report," March 25, 1947, Keyserling Papers-HSTL, Box 5; Goodwin and Herren, "Truman Administration," 21–23; Alan Gruchy, *Contemporary Economic Thought: The Contributions of Neo-institutional Economics*, (Clifton, NJ: Augustus M. Kelley, 1972); Robert M. Collins, "The Emergence of Economic Growthsmanship in the United States: Federal Policy and Economic Knowledge in the Truman Years," in *The State and Economic Knowledge: The American and British Experience*, ed. Mary O. Furner and Barry Supple (New York: Cambridge University Press, 1990), 165–66.

29. Ralph Robey, *The Facts versus the Nathan Report* (New York: National Association of Manufacturers, December 1946), 18, NAM Pamphlets; Wilson quoted in "Will Industry Generally Be Able to Absorb Wage Increases Now Being Made without Raising Prices?" *USNWR,* May 9, 1947, 36.

30. "New Group Plans Battle on Prices," January 18, 1947, 12; "Public Declared for Lower Prices," January 24, 1947, 30, both in *NYT.*

31. "Lower Prices Held Aim of Retailers," April 9, 1947, 21; "Basic, Wider Cuts in Prices Sought to Fight Inflation," April 18, 1947, 1; " 'Newburyport Plan' Gains New Backers in New England and Elsewhere," April 24, 1947, 1, 18, all in *NYT;* "Truman's Buttonholing Tactic," *BW,* April 26, 1947, 15–16; "Bargain Sale Catches On," *BW,* May 3, 1947, 17–18; "U.S. Tackles the Price Problem," *Life,* May 5, 1947, 27–29; "Prices: The Spiral Goes Round and Round," *Newsweek,* May 5, 1947, 25–26; "Nothing Doing, Mr. President," *Newsweek,* June 2, 1947, 19.

32. Howell John Harris, *The Right to Manage: Industrial Policies of Business in the 1940s* (Madison: University of Wisconsin Press, 1982); David Plotke, *Building a Democratic Political Order: Reshaping American Liberalism in the 1930s and 1940s* (New York: Cambridge University Press, 1996).

33. Harriman quoted in George Lipsitz, *Rainbow at Midnight: Labor and Culture in the 1940s* (Urbana: University of Illinois Press, 1994), 169–70; "The Stop-Lewis Bill," *NR,* June 23, 1947, 5–7; "Blame It on John," *NR,* July 21, 1947, 9–10; Kennedy testimony, House Committee on Education and Labor, *Amendments to the National Labor Relations Act, Vol. 3: Hearings,* 80th Cong., 1st sess., February 20–28, 1947, 1080; House report quoted in Lichtenstein, "Taft-Hartley," 767–78.

34. "Taft Says Truman Is Man to Blame for Higher Prices," *NYT,* June 7, 1947, 1, 2; Mosher testimony, House Committee on Education and Labor, *Amendments to the National Labor Relations Act, Vol. 4: Hearings,* 80th Cong., 1st sess., March 1, 3–7, 1947, 2685; "Landon Gives Anti-inflation Plan," *NYT,* April 23, 1947, 1; "Will Industry Generally Be Able to Absorb Wage Increases Now Being Made without Raising Prices?" *USNWR,* May 9, 1947, 36–37.

35. "Mayor, at AFL Rally, Warns Bill Will Stamp out Freedom," June 5, 1947, 1, 3; Murray quoted in A. H. Raskin, "60,000 CIO Unionists March to Garden for Veto Rally," June 11, 1947, 1, 3, both in *NYT;* Meany quoted in Lichtenstein, "Taft-Hartley," 766.

36. Keyserling to Clark Clifford, June 3, 1947, August 20, 1947, Box 8; CEA to Truman, June 16, 1947, Box 6, both in Keyserling Papers-HSTL.

37. Alonzo L. Hamby, *Beyond the New Deal: Harry S. Truman and American Liberalism* (New York: Columbia University Press, 1973), 182–94.

38. Ibid., 311–15; Matusow, *Farm Policies and Politics,* 191–221.

39. "ADA Board Urges Special Session to Control Prices, Aid Europe," *ADA World,* September 23, 1947; "Blueprint: The ADA's Plan to Beat the Bust," *NR,* May 26, 1947, 7–8; Chester Bowles, "Challenge to the Business Man," *NYTM,* October 5, 1947, 10, 52–54; "National 'Buyers' Strike' Slated over Meat," July 12, 1947, 16; "Food, Clothing, Housing to Be Examined for Plots to Raise Costs," August 13, 1947, 1; "Industry to Blame, Says Paul Porter," September 14, 1947, 5; "Protest Planned in City to Impress U.S. Price Hearing," September 22, 1947, 1; "Consumers Lay Plans," May 15, 1948, 30, all in *NYT;* Galbraith testimony,

Senate Committee on Banking and Currency, *Meat Control: Hearings*, 80th Cong., 2d sess., January 29–February 3, 1948, 35.

40. "Truman Calls Special Session November 17 on High Prices and Relief in Europe," October 24, 1947, 1–2; "Truman Demands Price and Pay Controls," November 18, 1947, 1, 2; "Truman Controls Plan Is 'Totalitarianism' Step, Senator Declares," November 18, 1947, 1, all in *NYT*.

41. Samuel Lubell, *The Future of American Politics* (New York: Harper and Row, 1965 [1951]), 10; Julie C. Algase (chairman, League of Women Shoppers) to President Truman, October 2, 1947; President Truman to Julie C. Algase, October 4, 1947, both in Truman Papers-OF, Box 327; Melvyn P. Leffler, *A Preponderance of Power: National Security, the Truman Administration, and the Cold War* (Stanford, CA: Stanford University Press, 1992), 141–81; Ellen Schrecker, *Many Are the Crimes: McCarthyism in America* (Boston: Little, Brown, and Company, 1998), 189–290.

42. "Truman Demands Congress Continue Session and Pass Price Control," June 15, 1948, 1, 3; "Boycott Widened on Prices of Meat," August 6, 1948, 20, both in *NYT*; "Behind the Inertia on Inflation," *Newsweek*, August 16, 1948, 61; "Mrs. Douglas to Show Congress Economics of Market Basket," *Washington News*, April 28, 1948; D'Amelio quoted in "A New Spurt in the Spiral," *Newsweek*, July 26, 1948, 62.

43. Transcript, India Edwards Oral History Interview, January 16, 1969, HSTL, 19–22; "Housewives for Truman, 1948," Edwards Papers, Box 3; India Edwards, *Pulling No Punches: Memoirs of a Woman in Politics* (New York: Putnam, 1977), 7–11, 102–3, 110–19; Kathleen Hall Jamieson, *Packaging the Presidency: A History and Criticism of Presidential Campaign Advertising* (New York: Oxford University Press, 1996), 34; Sean Savage, *Truman and the Democratic Party* (Lexington: University Press of Kentucky, 1997), 83–84.

44. Truman in Pennsylvania quoted in Hamby, *Beyond the New Deal*, 251; "Steel Is Accused of Inflation Acts," July 29, 1948, 18; Truman in Kentucky quoted in "Truman Denounces NAM as Destroyer of Price Controls," October 1, 1948, 1, 20, both in *NYT*; "Why Truman's 'Fight on Inflation' Is a Phony," *SEP*, August 14, 1948, 118; *Viewpoints: Regarding Politics and Inflation* (Washington, DC: Republican National Committee, 1948), in RNC Pamphlets.

45. "Our Laboristic President," *Fortune*, December 1948, 84; Lichtenstein, *Walter Reuther*, 304–6; Hamby, *Beyond the New Deal*, 267–74.

46. "Truman Asks Increased Taxes, Debt Cut, Taft Labor Act Repeal, Authority to Build Steel Mills," January 6, 1949, 1; "Truman Asks Million Jobs, Extension of Rent Curbs, More Buying Power for '49," January 8, 1949, 1, both in *NYT*; "The Fair Deal Begins: The President Charts the Course," *NR*, January 17, 1949, 3–4.

47. Draft of Interagency Working Group, "A Bill . . . Cited as Economic Stability Act of 1949," January 15, 1949, Truman Papers-OF, Box 1076; CEA to President Truman, "Legislation to Effectuate Stabilization Policies," January 14, 1949, Box 5; Leon Keyserling to Senator O'Mahoney, February 5, 1949, Box 8, both in Keyserling Papers-HSTL; *Iron Age* quoted in Paul Tiffany, *The Decline of American Steel: How Management, Labor, and Government Went Wrong* (New York: Oxford University Press, 1988), 60, passim; "Truman Bill Asks Curbs on Inflation, Power to Produce," *NYT*, February 16, 1949, 1; "Don't Cut Production—Build

Purchasing Power," *CIO Economic Outlook*, April 1949; "Reuther Explains the 'Reuther Plan,' " *NYTM*, March 20, 1949, 17, 62–63.

48. Taft quoted in "Industry Attacks Truman's Program to Impose Controls," February 17, 1949, 1, 12; Editorial Board quoted in "All-Out Controls," February 17, 1949, 22, both in *NYT*. The business press was quick to exploit and expose CEA differences: "Economists in Politics," *BW*, March 26, 1949.

49. "When Governments 'Plan,' " May 28, 1949, 14; "Full Employment Goal of ADA Plan," July 20, 1949, 20; Edward Collins, "Senator Byrd and the CEA," August 1, 1949, all in *NYT*; Gerhard Colm to Leon Keyserling, "Review of Economic Programs," April 11, 1949, Keyserling Papers-HSTL, Box 7; President Truman to Senator O'Mahoney, June 23, 1949, Truman Papers-OF, Box 1565. On the 1949 recession, see A. E. Holmans, *United States Fiscal Policy, 1945–1959: Its Contribution to Economic Stability* (Oxford: Oxford University Press, 1961), 102–31; Flash, *Economic Advice*, 18–61; and William Wagnon Jr., "The Politics of Growth: The 1949 Recession and the Truman Administration" (Ph.D. diss., University of Missouri, 1970).

50. Byrd quoted in "Pump-Priming Move Started to Meet Economic Declines," July 15, 1949, 1, 14; American Bar Association quoted in "Judges on Stand under Bar Inquiry," September 8, 1949, 21; Moulton quoted in "New Threat Seen to Free Economy," November 11, 1949, 39, all in *NYT*; Tiffany, *Decline of American Steel*, 83–102.

51. "Dr. Nourse Resigns as Truman Adviser," *NYT*, October 18, 1949, 1, 31; "Dr. Nourse and the C.E.A.," *NYT*, October 19, 1949, 28; Philip Murray to President Truman, October 20, 1949; Walter Reuther to President Truman, October 21, 1949, both in Keyserling Papers-HSTL, Box 6; Second Annual Report of the President's Council of Economic Advisers, January 1, 1948, Keyserling Papers-HSTL, Reports File; "An Appraisal of Official Economic Reports," Meeting of the Conference Board Economic Forum, *Studies in Business Economics* (January 1948): 10; Philip Murray, "The Gap between Prices and Wages," *Atlantic*, July 1948, 25–30.

52. "President Reassures Nation, National Output above 300 Billions Forecast on Advisers' Data," *NYT*, July 12, 1949, 1, 15; Leon Keyserling to Clark Clifford, September 16, 1949; Leon Keyserling to Clark Clifford, Charles Murphy, and David Lloyd, "Memorandum Relating to $4000 Minimum Standard of Living," both in Keyserling Papers-HSTL, Box 8.

53. Leffler, *Preponderance of Power*, 355–60, 373; Lester Brune, "Guns and Butter: The Pre-Korean War Dispute over Budget Allocations: Nourse's Conservative Keynesianism Loses Favor against Keyserling's Economic Expansion Plan," *American Journal of Economics and Sociology* 48 (July 1989): 357–71.

54. "More Textiles Move South," *BW*, August 16, 1947, 17–18; "Flight South?" *Commonweal*, October 8, 1948, 608–9; "What's Behind the Nashua Mill Shutdown?" *BW*, October 23, 1948, 44–56; "White House Picks 11 Areas for Federal-Spending Help," *NYT*, August 10, 1949, 1, 16; Chester Bowles (governor, CT) to John Steelman, July 20, 1949; Secretary of Commerce Charles Sawyer to John Steelman, "Report on Visit to New England," July 30, 1949, both in Truman Papers-OF, Box 3. See also R. Alton Lee, "Federal Assistance to Depressed Areas in the Postwar Recessions," *Western Economic Journal* 2 (fall 1963): 1–23; and Sar A. Levitan, *Federal Aid to Depressed Areas: An Evaluation of the Area Redevelopment*

Administration (Baltimore: Johns Hopkins Press, 1964). On regional decline see, John T. Cumbler, "From Bolts of Cotton to Hamburgers: The Deindustrialization of New England," in *The Changing Landscape of Labor: American Workers and Workplaces,* ed. Michael Jacobson-Hardy (Amherst: University of Massachusetts Press, 1996), 1–16; William Hartford, "Unions, Labor Markets, and Deindustrialization: The Holyoke Textile Industry," in *Labor in Massachusetts: Selected Essays,* ed. Kenneth Fones-Wolf and Martin Kaufman (Westfield, MA: Institute for Massachusetts Studies, 1990); and Barry Bluestone and Bennett Harrison, *The Deindustrialization of America: Plant Closings, Community Abandonment, and the Dismantling of Basic Industry* (New York: Basic Books, 1982).

55. Bell quoted in Lichtenstein, *Walter Reuther,* 280–81; Mike Davis, *Prisoners of the American Dream: Politics and Economy in the History of the U.S. Working Class* (London: Verso, 1986), 82–101; David L. Stebenne, *Arthur J. Goldberg: New Deal Liberal* (Oxford: Oxford University Press, 1996), 68–77.

56. Lubell, *Future of American Politics,* 75, 218–19.

57. Peter F. Drucker, "Why Don't We Stop This Inflation," *SEP,* May 5, 1951, 34; Stebenne, *Arthur J. Goldberg,* 75; Wagnon, "Politics of Growth," Chap. 8.

58. Caroline Ware to Charles Wilson (defense mobilization director), "Consumer Participation in Defense Mobilization Agencies," March 29, 1951; Walter Reuther to James Loeb (executive secretary, ADA), April 27, 1951; "Anti-inflation Conference—1951," program listing; Seymour Harris, "Statement on Behalf of the Americans for Democratic Action," May 1951; John Gunther to "Dear Friend," May 31, 1951, all in ADA Papers, Box 1, Legislative Files, Anti-inflation Conference Folder; James Carey, "The Racketeers of Inflation," *Vital Speeches,* July 1, 1951, 552–54; "Price Control—A Key to Mobilization," *CIO Economic Outlook,* April 1951, 25–31.

59. Matusow, *Farm Policies and Politics,* 225; Mildred Reynolds (Raleigh, NC), to the Editor, "The Way We Live Now," *NR* June 18, 1951, 2–3; Mrs. Green quoted in Harry S. Truman, "Economic Controls," *Vital Speeches,* July 1, 1951, 550.

60. Rockoff, *Drastic Measures,* 177–84, Ackley quoted on 182; Charles Wilson, "Inflation Dangers," *Vital Speeches,* August 1, 1951, 610–12; Housewives quoted in "Food: Prices at Peak," *Newsweek,* July 9, 1951, 72. Beef prices had increased by 50 percent since January 1950. See also Paul G. Pierpaoli Jr., *Truman and Korea: The Political Culture of the Early Cold War* (Columbia: University of Missouri Press, 1999), 82–118.

61. Herbert Stein, *The Fiscal Revolution in America* (Washington, DC: AEI Press, 1990), 241–92; Robert M. Collins, *The Business Response to Keynes, 1929–1964* (New York: Columbia University Press, 1981), 142–72.

62. Sumner Slichter, "How Bad Is Inflation?" *Harper's,* August 1952, 53–57; "Sumner Slichter Bets Americans Will Choose Inflation," *BW,* October 25, 1952, 100–102. For the idea of a trade-off between low levels of unemployment and inflation, see A. W. Phillips, "The Relation between Unemployment and the Rate of Change of Money Wage Rates in the United Kingdom, 1861–1957," *Economica* 25 (November 1958): 283–99.

63. See the following polls in Gallup, *Gallup Poll,* vol. 1: September 22, 1950, 939; October 31, 1951, 1018; September 2, 1953, 1166–67; January 5, 1955, 1300; July 2, 1955, 1344–45; October 27, 1956, 1451; June 14, 1957, 1493;

September 15, 1957, 1514–15; November 6, 1957, 1523; February 2, 1958, 1539; March 23, 1958, 1545; February 27, 1959, 1595; May 27, 1959, 1610; October 16, 1959, 1632. E. A. Goldenweiser, "Must We Pay More for Everything?" *Harper's*, April 1951, 97–104.

64. David Potter, *People of Plenty: Economic Abundance and the American Character* (Chicago: University of Chicago Press, 1954), 84; "Inflation: The Permanent Dilemma," *BW*, May 24, 1952, 32–33; "The Discontented: Real Target of the Political Campaigners," *BW*, October 13, 1956, 26–27; James T. Patterson, *Grand Expectations: The United States, 1945–1974* (New York: Oxford University Press, 1996), 311–48.

65. William H. Whyte Jr., "The Cadillac Phenomenon," *Fortune*, February 1955, 108–9; William H. Whyte, "Budgetism: Opiate of the Middle Class," *Fortune*, May 1956, 156; Vance Packard, *American Social Classes in the 1950s: Selections from Vance Packard's* The Status Seekers, ed. Daniel Horowitz (Boston: St. Martin's Press, 1995), 33; Daniel Horowitz, *Vance Packard and American Social Criticism* (Chapel Hill: University of North Carolina Press, 1994), 133; Richard H. Pells, *The Liberal Mind in a Conservative Age: American Intellectuals in the 1940s and 1950s* (New York: Harper and Row, 1985), 333–34.

66. Editors of *Fortune* magazine, in collaboration with Russell Davenport, *U.S.A.: The Permanent Revolution* (New York: Prentice-Hall, 1951), 91; Judith Stein, *Running Steel, Running America: Race, Economic Policy and the Decline of Liberalism* (Chapel Hill: University of North Carolina Press, 1998), 8–9.

67. *Fortune* editors, *U.S.A.: The Permanent Revolution*, 90; Nelson Lichtenstein, *State of the Union: A Century of American Labor* (Princeton, NJ: Princeton University Press, 2002), 98–140.

68. "Who Gets Hurt by 53-Cent Dollar," *USNWR*, September 28, 1951, 11–13; "Inflation Woes," *Commonweal*, September 28, 1951, 588; Henry Pringle, "Middle-Class Squeeze," *NB*, November 1951, 42–43, 60–61. Charles S. Maier, "The Politics of Inflation in the Twentieth Century," in *The Political Economy of Inflation*, ed. Fred Hirsch and John H. Goldthorpe (Cambridge, MA: Harvard University Press, 1978), 37–72.

69. Hansen quoted in Walter Morton, "Keynesianism and Inflation," *Journal of Political Economy* 59 (June 1951): 264, 260; Henry Hazlitt, "We Have Asked for Inflation," *Newsweek*, May 7, 1951, 72.

70. Harold Hinton, "McCarthy Accuses Keyserlings Again," *NYT*, April 22, 1952, 14. For shifting agendas of women's groups, see Mary Jean Houde, *Reaching Out: A Story of the General Federation of Women's Clubs* (Chicago: Mobium Press, 1989), 269–311, and Elaine Tyler May, *Homeward Bound: American Families in the Cold War Era* (New York: Basic Books, 1988).

71. "Another Round," *Commonweal*, August 15, 1952, 451–52; "Are You Better Off Than before Korea?" *USNWR*, August 22, 1952, 11–13.

72. Donald Johnson and Kirk Porter, eds., *National Party Platforms: 1840–1972* (Urbana: University of Illinois Press, 1973), 501; Gary Reichard, *The Reaffirmation of Republicanism: Eisenhower and the Eighty-third Congress* (Knoxville: University of Tennessee Press, 1975), 13, 16–17, 24.

73. Patterson, *Grand Expectations*, 258–59, 348. Television ads quoted in Edwin Diamond and Stephen Bates, *The Spot: The Rise of Political Advertising on*

Television (Cambridge, MA: MIT Press, 1992), 38, 41, 56–57; Jamieson, *Packaging the Presidency*, 39–89; and Paul F. Boller Jr., *Presidential Campaigns* (New York: Oxford University Press, 1996), 282. John Sloan, *Eisenhower and the Management of Prosperity* (Lawrence: University Press of Kansas, 1991), 14.

74. "Wage-Price Inflation Ahead?" *USNWR*, May 11, 1956, 25–28; Sloan, *Eisenhower*, 108, 134; H. Scott Gordon, "The Eisenhower Administration: The Doctrine of Shared Responsibility," in *Exhortation and Controls*, ed. Goodwin, 95–134.

75. Bureau of the Census, *Historical Statistics of the United States: Colonial Times to 1970* (Washington, DC: GPO, 1976), Series E 135–66, p. 210; George Humphrey, "True Prosperity in America," *Vital Speeches*, January 1, 1957, 186; Hauge quoted in Sloan, *Eisenhower*, 115–16.

76. "Steel—Why the Inflation Threat," *Newsweek*, June 4, 1956, 72; "Inflation Race—Who's Ahead, Who's Behind," August 3, 1956, 95–97; "It Now Costs More than Ever to Live," August 31, 1956, 44–45; "Who's Making the Big Money," August 31, 1956, 111–12, all in *USNWR*.

77. Henry Hazlitt, "Built-in Inflation," *Newsweek*, May 28, 1956, 86, quoting U.S. Steel Corp., *Annual Report* (1956); Roger Blough, Annual Address to U.S. Steel Stockholders, May 7, 1956, excerpted in "A Picture of the Wage-Price Spiral at Work," *USNWR*, May 18, 1956, 64–66.

78. *Purchasing Power: Facts versus Fallacies* (New York: National Association of Manufacturers, April 1956); *A New Force for Inflation* (New York: National Association of Manufacturers, May 1956), both in NAM Pamphlets. For the right-to-work campaign, see Elizabeth A. Fones-Wolf, *Selling Free Enterprise: The Business Assault on Labor and Liberalism, 1945–1960* (Urbana: University of Illinois Press, 1994), 94–96, 261–74.

79. Goldstein quoted in Rick Perlstein, *Before the Storm: Barry Goldwater and the Unmaking of the American Consensus* (New York: Hill and Wang, 2001), 37; John Kenneth Galbraith, "Are Living Costs Out of Control?" *Atlantic*, February 1957, 37–41; Stein, *Running Steel*, 17, 22–25.

80. Estes Kefauver, *In a Few Hands: Monopoly Power in America* (New York: Pantheon, 1965), 3; Stein, *Running Steel*, 18–22; Charles Geisst, *Monopolies in America: Empire Builders and Their Enemies from Jay Gould to Bill Gates* (Oxford: Oxford University Press, 2000), 212–16.

81. Reuther quoted in "Senate Inquiry Set on Price Increases," June 30, 1957, 68, and A. H. Raskin, "A.F.L.-C.I.O. Maps Higher-Pay Drive," February 9, 1958, 1, both in *NYT*. see also "Reuther Puts Plan up to Eisenhower," August 20, 1957, 17; "Reuther Plan Studied," August 22, 1957, 14; "G.M. Turns down Reuther's Plan to Cut Car Prices," August 23, 1957, 1; "Chrysler President's Reply to Reuther," August 24, 1957, 16; "Ford Turns Down Reuther's Offer," August 25, 1957, 1; "Reuther Urges U.S. Adjudge Price Rises," January 29, 1958, 1; A. H. Raskin, "Reuther No. 1 Target of G.O.P. Campaigners," October 19, 1958, E7, all in *NYT*. Goldwater quoted in Lichtenstein, "Taft-Hartley," 788–89.

82. "Reuther Assails Pricing of Autos," April 6, 1958, 71; A. H. Raskin, "Slump Is Cutting Income of Unions," May 9, 1958, 1; "Steelworkers Backed; Reuther Pledges the 'Full Support' of Union Group," July 12, 1959, 47, all in *NYT*; Thomas J. Sugrue, *The Origins of the Urban Crisis: Race and Inequality in*

Postwar Detroit (Princeton, NJ: Princeton University Press, 1996), 143, passim; Lichtenstein, *Walter Reuther*, 346–69.

83. Jack Metzgar, *Striking Steel: Solidarity Remembered* (Philadelphia: Temple University Press, 2000); Sloan, *Eisenhower*, 124–30; Stein, *Running Steel*, 20.

84. Gallup, *Gallup Poll*, vol. 1: polls on January 8, 1960, 1700; April 29, 1962, 1764.

85. Lucy Black Creighton, *Pretenders to the Throne: The Consumer Movement in the United States* (Lexington, MA: Lexington Books, 1976), 31–43; Packard quoted in Horowitz, *Vance Packard*, 106.

86. Creighton, *Pretenders to the Throne*, 52–68; David Vogel, *Fluctuating Fortunes: The Political Power of Business in America* (New York: Basic Books, 1989), 37–112.

87. Daniel J. Boorstin, *The Image; or, What Happened to the American Dream* (New York: Atheneum, 1961), 3; Galbraith quoted in Pells, *Liberal Mind*, 169, 165–261; Daniel Horowitz, *The Anxieties of Affluence: Critiques of American Consumer Culture, 1939–1979* (Amherst: University of Massachusetts Press, 2004).

Epilogue
Back to Bargain Hunting

1. David L. Stebenne, *Arthur J. Goldberg: New Deal Liberal* (Oxford: Oxford University Press, 1996), 279–315, Kennedy quoted on 495n65; William J. Barber, "The Kennedy Years: Purposeful Pedagogy," in *Exhortation and Controls: The Search for a Wage-Price Policy, 1945–1971*, ed. Craufurd D. Goodwin (Washington, DC: Brookings Institution, 1975), 135–92; Judith Stein, *Running Steel, Running America: Race, Economic Policy and the Decline of Liberalism* (Chapel Hill: University of North Carolina Press, 1998), 7–36; Allen J. Matusow, *The Unraveling of America: A History of Liberalism in the 1960s* (New York: Harper and Row, 1984), 39–53, Yale University speech quoted on 48; Julian E. Zelizer, *Taxing America: Wilbur D. Mills, Congress, and the State, 1945–1975* (New York: Cambridge University Press, 1998), 179–211.

2. Hugh Rockoff, *Drastic Measures: A History of Wage and Price Controls in the United States* (New York: Cambridge University Press, 1984), 200–233; Allen J. Matusow, *Nixon's Economy: Booms, Busts, Dollars, and Votes* (Lawrence: University Press of Kansas, 1998); Neil de Marchi, "The First Nixon Administration: Prelude to Controls," in *Exhortation and Controls*, ed. Goodwin, 295–352.

3. Sam Walton with John Huey, *Sam Walton, Made in America: My Story* (New York: Doubleday, 1992), 9.

4. Bob Ortega, *In Sam We Trust: The Untold Story of Sam Walton and How Wal-Mart Is Devouring America* (New York: Times Business, 1998), 202–8, 284–303, 318–45; Dana Frank, *Buy American: The Untold Story of Economic Nationalism* (Boston: Beacon Press, 1999), 187–213, 249.

Index

Page references in italics refer to illustrations.

POLITICS AND SOCIETY IN TWENTIETH-CENTURY AMERICA

Cities of Knowledge: Cold War Science and the Search for the Next Silicon Valley
by Margaret Pugh O'Mara

Labor Rights Are Civil Rights: Mexican American Workers in Twentieth-Century America
by Zaragosa Vargas

Pocketbook Politics: Economic Citizenship in Twentieth-Century America
by Meg Jacobs